Cultural Geography

Cultural Geography

A Critical Introduction

Don Mitchell
Syracuse University

Blackwell
Publishing

BLACKWELL PUBLISHING
350 Main Street, Malden, MA 02148-5020, USA
9600 Garsington Road, Oxford OX4 2DQ, UK
550 Swanston Street, Carlton, Victoria 3053, Australia

First published 2000

11   2008

Library of Congress Cataloging-in-Publication Data

Mitchell, Don.
  Cultural geography : a critical introduction / Don Mitchell.
      p.cm
  Includes bibliographical references and index.
ISBN 978-155786-891-6 (hardback); ISBN 978-155786-892-3 (paperback)
  1. Human geography. 2. Culture I. Title
  GF41. M55 2000
  306—dc21   99–049423

A catalogue record for this title is available from the British Library.

Set in 10 on 12 pt Times New Roman
by Kolam Information Services Pvt Ltd, Pondicherry, India
Printed and bound in Singapore
by Markono Print Media Pte Ltd

The publisher's policy is to use permanent paper from mills that operate a sustainable forestry
policy, and which has been manufactured from pulp processed using acid-free and elementary
chlorine-free practices. Furthermore, the publisher ensures that the text paper and cover board
used have met acceptable environmental accreditation standards.

For further information on
Blackwell Publishing, visit our website:
www.blackwellpublishing.com

Contents

List of Figures

Acknowledgments

In 1995, John Davey (then at Blackwell Publishers) suggested I write a "critical introduction" to cultural geography appropriate for beginning graduate or advanced undergraduate students that could then "filter down through the curriculum." I didn't imagine how hard that task would turn out to be. But I thank John anyway, and before anyone else, because the ensuing five years have forced me to seriously and deeply engage a literature – that of cultural geography – for which I have always felt a deep ambivalence. In the process, I have learned that it is possible, and even at times enjoyable, to construct and develop a coherent and, I think, politically progressive, theory (or set of theories) of cultural geography. I have learned that there is a great political potential, thus far unrealized and usually not even properly approached, in the "cultural turn" in geography. Among the most important reasons for thanking John for setting me this task was that it forced me to figure out how to write about difficult theoretical and political positions in a manner that is (I hope!) accessible and engaging.

If John Davey commissioned the book, Jill Landeryou (also now no longer at Blackwell) saw it to completion, providing encouragement when needed along with helpful advice. She has been wonderfully lenient as deadlines have passed, word counts have ballooned, and illustrations have multiplied. I very much appreciate also the help of Joanna Pyke, who has helped me through the intricacies of the production process. Valery Rose's careful reading and copy-editing have unearthed and corrected numerous errors, large and small, and made the book more readable.

Jim Duncan and Ulf Strohmeyer read my original proposal and provided early encouragement and numerous helpful suggestions about content, approach, and topics to be covered. I hope they see their influence in what follows, even if I often honored their suggestions in the breach. Stuart Aitken and David Ley read the complete manuscript. They provided not only a great deal of encouragement (I couldn't ask for nicer critics), but did me the favor of enumerating my dozens of sins of commission and omission. I have heeded their advice on many matters, but just as often I insisted on seeing as a virtue what they took to be a sin. Given that, I can't even ask their forgiveness; I can only express my gratitude. Brigit Baur read almost the whole manuscript (and would have read the whole thing if I had found a way to get it done when I promised) and likewise provided many helpful ideas, large and small. I look forward to returning the favor.

I relied heavily on the research assistance and continual good advice of Bruce D'Arcus. He read many early drafts, providing innumerable helpful comments and suggestions, helped track down weird references and background information on the numerous examples I used, and pointed me towards things I needed to be reading, whether I knew it or not. Early on, Jocasta Champion, just finishing an undergraduate and beginning a graduate degree in geology at the University of Colorado, read several chapters and helped me make my writing appropriate to students like her. Students in a senior-level class on American suburbia at the University of Colorado helped me understand the suburban landscape; I am convinced they taught me far more than I taught them. And students in a first-year "World Cultures" class at Syracuse University have put up with successive drafts of the chapter on sex and sexuality. I thank them for making me clarify some of my arguments.

Betsy Hearn and Brendan McTear, students at Syracuse University, did fantastic work in tracking down illustration ideas. Thelma Gilbert found many of the actual pictures and did the hard work of clearing copyright. I have also benefited from the slide collections of Susan Millar, Bruce D'Arcus, Caroline Nagel, Tim Oakes, and Christoph Schuster (who also helped me understand German citizenship debates). Mike Kirchoff drew the maps and diagrams at short notice. More importantly, he knew just the right questions to ask me to assure that the figures show what I want them to. Bob and Ann Millar helped me locate material and photographs in Scotland; I appreciate their detective work and couldn't have made some of my arguments without it.

I am continually indebted to Lynn Staeheli, whose friendly skepticism makes her not only the best kind of skeptic, but more importantly the best kind of friend. That she shows such glee when she unleashes Topher and Danny on me will be forgiven. Other friends influential in this book (whether they know it or not) include Scott Kirsch, Tim Oakes, Richa Nagar, and Brian Page, all of whom have helped shape the arguments that follow.

My most important words of acknowledgment must go to Susan Millar. She has not just helped with this book (which she has, over and over, with encouragement, ideas, criticisms, leads, arguments), she has had to live with it, even in those years when we lived across the country from each other. She has known when the writing has not been going well (and has let me know she has known!) and when it has (and reminded me that there are things of greater importance). For both, thank you.

D. M.

A Critical Introduction

A president of the food conglomerate Nabisco once looked forward to the day when we all lived in "a world of homogeneous consumption" where everyone eats the same foods – presumably processed by Nabisco itself (quoted in Norberg-Hodge 1996: 20). Not to worry, globalization theorist Roland Robertson responds. Globalization, he avers, leads to increased cultural differentiation, not homogenization. His proof? McDonald's caters its menus to the tastes and desires of local cultures. After all, Robertson astutely notes, one can get wine and beer at McDonald's in Europe, teriyaki burgers in Japan, and rice in China. It's not just all Big Macs, all the world over. And if that's not proof enough that globalization maintains rather than undermines cultural difference, then Robertson is also happy to point to tourism, which, as he says, demands global differences, otherwise why would tourists bother to travel?[1] Robertson's remarks could simply be dismissed as silly – or as a confirmation rather than denial of the Nabisco president's dream of a globally homogeneous culture – except that in their very ridiculousness they point to key questions behind (or which ought to be behind) the contemporary study of cultural geography: What constitutes significant cultural difference? What are the sources and processes of cultural differentiation? How are these sources and processes of cultural differentiation linked to developments in political economy (from the local to the global scale)? How is cultural change – the dialectic between sameness and difference – negotiated, contested, or struggled over? Who has the power to produce "culture" – the power to say that being able to eat rice at McDonald's is a significant achievement in the preservation of cultural diversity?

These are the questions that animate this book. In the chapters that follow, the goal is to explore the struggles that make "culture," to show how they get worked out in particular spaces and places – in particular landscapes – and to show how struggles over "culture" are a key determinant, day in and day out, in the ways that we live our lives – and in what therefore constitutes *significant* cultural difference. I take as a starting point the fact that we live in a world defined by continuous culture wars. These are wars over the shape of everyday life, over the production and maintenance of social meanings, and, most importantly, over the distribution of power, justice, and social and economic advantage. Such issues have only recently become an integral part of cultural geographic research. Indeed, as recently as a decade ago, radical

---

1   These comments were made as part of Roland Robertson's lecture, "The Limits and Opportunities for Opposition to Globalization," Syracuse University, February 19, 1999. But see Robertson (1992).

social geographers made something of a career for themselves by bemoaning the sorry state of cultural geography, pointing to how, with its endless studies of housetypes, field patterns, log-cabin construction methods, and place-imagery in music lyrics, it was antiquarian, particularistic, and socially irrelevant.

Even as late as 1989, new models of cultural geography (models patterned on the pioneering cultural theory work of the British cultural studies movement, the cultural materialism of British Marxist Raymond Williams, intriguing developments in "post-structural" theory associated with a host of French philosophers and social theorists, and to some extent feminism) were few enough, and new enough, that British cultural geographer Peter Jackson could confidently outline a new "agenda for cultural geography" that was compact, limited in scope, and politically focused. Jackson (1989: 171) argued that such an agenda (an agenda that remains an important touchstone for the book that follows) should be focused on "the relationship between culture and society, emphasizing the political dimensions of this relationship implicit in the idea of cultural politics." Indeed, Jackson's book *Maps of Meaning* lays out a quite comprehensive survey of cultural geography as it relates to Cultural Studies in fewer than 200 pages.

Such a comprehensive survey would be impossible now. The intervening years have seen an amazing proliferation of cultural work – and not only in the discipline of geography either. Indeed, there has been a sharp, and widely remarked, "cultural turn" within the social sciences as a whole. This cultural turn has been coupled with a similarly sharp "spatial turn," not only in the social sciences, but in the humanities too. Cultural geography has thus been thrust into the limelight. If a decade ago Jackson could present an agenda *for* cultural geography, then in some senses it could now be said that cultural geography *is* the agenda, but it is an agenda without any clear focus. Cultural geography – like cultural studies more generally – has rushed off in a million new directions, focusing new theoretical energy on traditional concerns like foodways, folk cultures and the cultural landscape, and developing new research foci on everything from psychotherapy, to critical race studies, to the cultural politics and cultural geography of sexuality and gender. Much of this work is celebratory of "difference" and "resistance," some of it (along with Roland Robertson) collaborationist with the forces of economic globalization, some of it consisting of incisive interventions in the structure of social life, but all of it has a new-found interest in "culture." To borrow the title of a recent collection of work by young British scholars, cultural geography is now simply "all over the place" (Shurmer-Smith 1996).

A *Critical* Introduction

There is no way, therefore, that I can survey, much less analyze, the breadth and depth of cultural geography in this book. The field is too unwieldy, too chaotic, too diffuse. I can, however, offer a *critical* introduction to the geographic study of culture. By "critical" I mean two things. In the first place, this book takes a position, a stance. It seeks, by both drawing on and critiquing current cultural geographic research, to present the *best* way to understand cultural production and cultural change. That is, I try to make a coherent argument about how cultural geography *should* be studied, and I make no bones in the book about my own position on matters. In other words, I have written this book as an argument about cultural geography, seeking to show how it can make critically important interventions into cultural–political struggles. To do so, I have been selective in what I present (it would have been impossible to be otherwise), but my selection itself is based on a particular intellectual–political position. That position can be described as materialist and Marxist. The important point, however, is that my primary goal has been to show how "culture" is never any *thing*, but is rather a struggled-over set of social relations, relations shot through with structures of power, structures of dominance and subordination. Such a position (like any intellectual position) comes with its own set of blinkers; my goal has been always and everywhere to make those blinkers as *invisible* to the reader as possible. As I say, I am making an argument about cultural geography (and about cultural struggle and change); and it is an argument I want to win.[2] Like Peter Jackson, I have an agenda for cultural geography.

That leads to the second sense in which this book is a *critical* introduction. I expect the reader to be every bit as critical of me, and the arguments I make, as I am of the material I analyze. Learning, like political change, proceeds through struggle. Only by engaging with ideas, debates, and intellectual and political positions, does knowledge advance. Only by struggling over *why* arguments are made, and theories are developed as they are, can one come to understand one's own position on matters of crucial political and intellectual importance.

Strategies and silences

Given that, let me say something about the strategies I employ in this book – since these strategies have inevitably involved omitting sustained analysis of some fairly important areas of cultural geographic theorizing. That is, let me make at least partially visible some of the biases I try to render invisible in pages that follow, if for no other reason than to convince the reader to focus on the arguments I do make rather than the ones I do not.

Cultural Geography: A Critical Introduction is a text constructed from others' texts. I rely on the work of countless geographers, sociologists, art historians, cultural theorists, journalists, anthropologists, political scientists (etc., etc.), to help me make the arguments I set forth. I use other people's words; I develop and criticize their theories; I expand upon their points. To make the arguments I make, I *rely* on other people's arguments. But if I rely on texts, this is not a book *about* texts. My goal is not (only) cultural theory construction; nor is it (only) to critically deconstruct others' ideas, to engage in a hermeneutic exercise designed to explicate the meaning of important (or not so important) theorists. Rather my goal is to use others' texts to shed light on social, political, economic, and cultural processes and struggles. My

2   I realize that such a remark is problematic at a time when more and more scholars are seeking more cooperative modes of knowing; it will certainly strike some as masculinist. But it is my strongly held belief that argumentation is both salutary, and, if conducted honestly, no bar to either intellectual or political cooperation. The opposite of argument and disagreement is a stifling conformity.

goal is to explain the world rather than to explain *theories* about the world. That is, I examine ideas and theories, political interventions and journalistic accounts, not for their own sake, but to understand just what is happening "on the ground" in numerous settings, from the immigrant enclaves of eastern German cities to the malls of North America. I may have opened this book by relating the comments of a rather prominent cultural theorist, but I care far less about those comments than the actual processes they reflect (and reflect upon): in this case the expansion of a certain form of corporate, franchise capitalism that is making over everyday life in almost all corners of the globe, and which is leading to a certain *kind* of diversity within a certain *kind* of homogeneity.

So my first strategy is to always make sure the book remains more about cultural geographical processes, struggles, and changes, than cultural geographic theory for theory's sake. To that end, as often as possible I argue from example. My examples are largely (though not entirely) drawn from that realm of social experience that has come to be called the "culture wars." Culture wars are those battles over the meaning and structure of the social relationships (for example, between men and women, gays and the heterosexist world, capital and labor), the institutions (the media and other culture industries, global economic governing bodies, oppositional social movements), and the spaces (particular landscapes, the controlled spaces of the mall or television studio) that govern our lives. I have focused on particular instances, both historical and contemporary, of cultural struggle, to show how these structure – and are structured by – the geographies in which we live. Related to this, my major theoretical position in this book is that no decent cultural analysis (geographic or otherwise) can draw on culture *itself* as a source of explanation; rather culture is always something to be *explained* as it is socially produced through myriad struggles over and in spaces, scales, and landscapes. Culture wars allow us to see "culture" "in the making"; they allow us to see how "culture" is always and everywhere inextricably related to social, political, and economic forces and practices.

My second strategy is to continually balance depth of analysis and breadth of coverage. As I have indicated, the study of cultural geography has mushroomed in the last decade, and I have had to be judicious in what I write about here. In large part the decision about what sorts of cultural geographic theory I explore is determined by the particular social struggles I examined. But it is also a function of what I find to be the most compelling, and politically efficacious, areas of analysis. Readers already steeped in the history of geographic theory in the past decade or so will thus no doubt wonder about some curious silences on my part.

I engage in no direct and sustained analysis of post-structuralist theory, for example. In large part, this is because I have found much of the endless explication of post-structuralism in geography to be of little use in understanding cultural–political change. Too often such work remains trapped in a rarefied, closed, and often quite unintelligible world defined only by the texts the theorist has chosen to read and explicate; the actual social practices of the world are but receding memories in too much self-consciously "post-structuralist" work. To put that another way, given that my goal has been to explore material cultural production and change, the debates about what post-structuralism is or might be, how it differs from the bad old structuralism, and how its mode of theorizing is necessarily radical and liberating, are simply diversionary. I have drawn on post-structuralist ideas when they have been helpful for explanation; I have not, in this book, sought to outline what the post-structuralist moment in academia might be all about.[3] My firm belief is that geography needs to recommit itself to the analysis of and intervention in social and political struggles, and use theory to that end; much post-structuralist debate, to my reading, leads in just the opposite direction – towards political quiescence and academic over-intellectualizing.

Nor will readers find much direct engagement with postmodernism. My reasons are similar to those for post-structuralism (especially as it relates to political intervention). As with post-structuralism, I have drawn on postmodernist theorizing when it has been useful for understanding and explaining political–cultural transformation and struggle. That said, there have been a number of good works designed to understand how postmodern theorizing, cultural productions, and urban forms are linked (but not reducible) to transformations in political-economic and social structure. I draw on these works in two main areas. First when I seek to establish a theory of the "political economy of culture" (chapter 3) and then again when I examine the nature of cultural politics (chapter 6).

Still another silence concerns postcolonial theory. There is much in postcolonial theory that is directly relevant to the points I want to make about structures of domination and subordination throughout the book, and about the changing nature of global domination too. My reason for not directly addressing this work is related to a third strategy I adopted. I realized early on that despite a real personal desire to learn more about developing parts of the world, and despite the fact that cultural geography (especially new cultural geography) has been overweeningly Eurocentric, I was simply incompetent to write about most of the developing world. My own research is almost exclusively American-based; my own teaching focuses (with some small exceptions) on the social and cultural geography of the developed world. I feel wholly inadequate to the task of writing a cultural geography text focused outside "the North." So what follows is largely (though not entirely) limited to examples and struggles from North America and Europe. That said, it is certainly the case that postcolonial theory has much to offer for understanding development and change in the core, and I have occasionally drawn on it in what follows for just that reason.

A related silence concerns a fourth strategy that guided the writing of this book. Contemporary cultural geography has at least some of its roots planted in the rich research traditions inaugurated by Carl Sauer at the University of California, Berkeley (see chapter 1). Sauer's legacy itself, however, is bifurcated. His methodological pronouncements in the 1920s and 1940s helped create an important focus on the cultural landscape. In American cultural geography this led to a field of research focused on exploring the way that the landscape served as a "cultural spoor." That is, the landscape was read and deciphered for the evidence it gave up concerning the nature – and direction of movement – of the culture(s) that occupied it. But much of Sauer's own empirical work, and some of the methodological positions he outlined in the 1950s and 1960s also helped establish geographers as important investigators of cultural ecology. Following Sauer, there has been an important exploration of how peoples – especially traditional societies – lived *in*, *on*, and as *part of* the world. There

---

3 Readers interested in post-structuralist approaches to cultural geography will find a good example of the possibilities and limitations of the approach in Shurmer-Smith and Hannam (1994).

are important links between the two sides of the cultural geography tradition Sauer established, and there is a whole history of debate about which side is Sauer's "true" legacy (see Price and Lewis 1993a, 1993b; Cosgrove 1993a; Duncan 1993a; Jackson 1993a), but again in part because of my own competencies and interests, but also because of the sheer vastness of the cultural (and political) ecology literature, I restrict my analysis of cultural geography in this book to that part of the field most closely aligned with the general field of cultural studies, rather than cultural ecology. It would take a very different kind of book than the one I have written to adequately analyze the traffic between cultural ecology and the sorts of cultural processes outlined here. That's a book, in fact, that very much needs to be written.

My fifth strategy, and one related to my silence about cultural ecology, has been to always search for the politics of "culture." This has entailed repeatedly asking: *who* produces culture – and to what end? Given that, readers will be surprised to find no sustained analysis of the primary "culture industries," such as television, film, the music industry, and the news media. "Culture industries" do, however, figure *sub rosa* throughout the book as a *foundation* upon which and through which culture is produced. They are part of what I call (following Sharon Zukin) the "critical infrastructure" of cultural production. My focus has instead been on the culture industry's products and how those products are assimilated into everyday life or contested through both disorganized and organized social practices. My argument is that it is in the interaction – the struggle – between the production of "culture" and its use that "culture" is produced, not as a thing, but as a relationship.[4] So when I ask *who* produced culture, I always turn to the study of *relationships*; when I ask *why* it is produced, I turn to questions of power.

Together, these strategies and silences give *Cultural Geography* its focus. That focus is on cultural struggle, on the imposition of social control through "cultural means," and on the construction of and resistance to the cultural spaces that define social life in different settings. So what, then, can be found in *Cultural Geography*?

A Guide to What Follows

First of all, the reader will find a *political* (or better a *political-economic*) theory of culture, a theory which is, I think, particularly well suited to explaining cultural struggle. In a recent essay, Clive Barnett (1998: 634) has suggested that it simply does not do to construct culture "as a model of politics by other means," suggesting instead that "the analysis of culture might be better pursued by foregrounding of the social structuration and differential distribution of capacities to produce meanings." While I support the general thrust of Barnett's essay, which is to question the rather chaotic and "catholic . . . theoretical treatment of culture" by contemporary human geographers (and to turn attention to the study of meaning-producing institutions), it is hard to see how foregrounding the study of the processes by which the capacity to produce meaning is distributed can be anything *but* political.

---

4   That said, and as will be clear, I do not adopt a simple model of consumer sovereignty. Rather, I show throughout that the power to define, to produce, and to structure social life is a big power indeed.

Part I of *Cultural Geography*, "The Politics of Culture," thus establishes the grounds for a politics and political economy of culture. Chapter 1 begins with an analysis of three culture wars, having to do with the representation of history, the rise of racist nationalism, and the politics of art in an age of deindustrialization. These wars allow us to ask just what culture might be and to explore how it has historically been treated in cultural geography. The chapter concludes by showing that traditional notions of culture in cultural geography were, by the 1960s and 1970s, simply inadequate to the task of explaining either local or more global cultural transformations.

Chapter 2 thus turns to contemporary theories of culture in cultural geography and traces their roots through the rise of cultural studies in Britain in the post-World War II era. The relationship between cultural geography and cultural studies is traced, and new approaches to culture are shown to be much better at explaining contemporary (and past) cultural movements and developments than traditional geographic theories. But I also argue new theories are still hampered by a sense that culture can be identified as a "thing," as something that exists and has, of its own accord, a real political and social efficacy. Chapter 3 thus seeks to establish firmer social, political, and economic grounds for understanding just what culture *is* (and particularly for what it is *not*). In this chapter I establish what a "political economy of culture" might be and show how it is helpful in exploring and explaining cultural change. Among other things, this chapter broaches the question of what constitutes effective resistance to the power of cultural production, providing the grounds upon which a richer analysis of the cultural politics of resistance will be established later in the book.

First, however, in Part II, "The Political Landscape," we turn to a consideration of the most traditional of cultural geography's research foci, the landscape. Arguing from three primary examples (two of which will be familiar to seasoned readers), chapter 4 scrutinizes the social production of landscape so as to see just how landscape is both a "work" and "does work" in society. That work is the work of structuring social relations between people, and it is closely bound up in the way that landscape – or more accurately, the "landscape way of seeing" – is ideological. Meaning is naturalized in the landscape, and only through concerted contestation are those sedimented meanings prized open.

Chapter 5 broadens the discussion of landscape to examine how the "work" that landscape does figures into systems of social reproduction. By examining the various metaphors that govern our understanding of landscape (such as seeing the landscape as a text or a stage) and linking them to important axes of cultural differentiation (such as gender), this chapter explores how landscape functions both as a source of meaning and as a form of social regulation. Moving from gendered landscapes to the peculiarly sign-laden (but almost meaningless) landscape of the mall, the chapter shows how and to what ends space is structured by particular social and cultural practices.

The examination of how space is shaped and is shaped by cultural struggle is broadened and deepened in Part III, "Cultural Politics." Chapter 6 opens the section with an examination of the dialectic between resistance and control – and of the role of political action in mediating these. Tacking between popular culture events (the advent of the Sex Pistols and the miniaturization of music, to name two) and moments of keen political upheaval (the Tiananmen Square occupation and the Paris rebellion of 1968), I show the strategies and tactics of resistance and spectacle to be fully bound up with each other. Each works to define the "situation" of the world (as the activists in Paris '68 used to say), and it is towards the continual transformation of those situations that cultural political struggle must be geared.

The next four chapters are designed to explore different aspects of that transformative cultural struggle. Chapter 7 focuses on sex and sexuality, showing how new spaces for the performance of identity are wrested from the normative sexual ordering of the world. Beginning with George Chauncy's ground-breaking discussion of the making of a "gay world" in pre-World War II New York, and expanding out to a consideration of the relationship between sexuality and capitalism, the making of contemporary gay spaces, and the new forms of politics associated with AIDS, the chapter links the struggle over sexual worlds (and sex more generally) to the social structuring of space.

This discussion of how identity is a function of space (and vice versa) is further developed in chapter 8, which takes as its focus the geography of gender and the politics of feminism. Here, following the lead of both feminist scholars and feminist activists, the social construction and maintenance of the boundary between public and private space, as it relates to the normative policing of gender roles, is shown to be a keen point of political contention. But that struggle over space has led to a reconsideration of just what space *is*, and how best to theorize it. And an examination of that issue entails questioning just what *gender* is, and so I examine how gender itself is "performed" in certain kinds of spaces. Finally, the chapter returns to the questions raised in Part II about landscape and meaning. Contrasting two strikingly different feminist approaches to the question of gender and visuality, the chapter concludes by showing that the culture wars over gender, *because* they are so much wars over space, are some of the most contentious of the day.

Chapter 9 turns to "race." Examining the arguments against the idea that there is any biological basis to race, the discussion here focuses on how "race" is made real nonetheless "on the ground." A main focus of analysis in the chapter is the high-selling racist "analysis" of the relationship between intelligence and "race," *The Bell Curve*. This book is a focus of attention because it relies on a peculiar, and particularly ugly, geographical vision to make its claims: namely, that in a "just world" everyone "naturally" "has their place," both socially and geographically. The degree to which rac*ism* is a geographical project is nowhere better shown than in the geographical theories underlying *The Bell Curve*. But words alone do not make a racist geography, and so the chapter next looks at how space itself is reconfigured so as to reproduce not just race but racial domination. Looking at the "perfect system of control" that apartheid was meant to be in South Africa, liberatory notions that space is a foundation for the *performance* of identity (as discussed in chapter 7) are radically turned on their heads. Space is also the die that casts identity in stone.

To the degree that space makes race, it raises questions not just of identity but of *identification*. Chapter 10 thus examines the question of how identity is related to space by turning to the politics – and political economy – of national identity. The idea and materiality of nations and nationalism are explored, using contemporary Germany as a case study. The chapter raises the question of why nationalism has increased at a time which many cultural, economic, and political theorists identify as one of "deterritorialization." The question of just what "deterritorialization" – and "deterritorialized identities" – might be is explored and the only answer that can be given is the same one that is reached throughout the book: it all depends on who you are, how you are situated in relationship to power, and whether you control, or are controlled by, the forces of cultural change.

The production of cultural spaces, I argue throughout this book, is always the production of what Doreen Massey has identified as *power geometries*: the shape and structure of the space in which our lives are given meaning. Power geometries are powerful forces, forces that are themselves continually transformed through unrelenting struggle, whether that struggle is open rebellion against the "situations" that govern our movements and give form to our thoughts, or the more mundane, everyday accommodation to ongoing cultural, political, and economic change. But to say that raises an important question: how can culturally *just* "situations" be created, institutionalized, and maintained in the first place? By way of a conclusion to *Cultural Geography: A Critical Introduction*, I broach that question, but by no means fully answer it, for the answer, I hope this book shows (if it shows nothing else), cannot be determined abstractly, only in the resolution of the ongoing culture wars of the times.

Cultural Geography/Cultural Justice

Cultural Geography: A Critical Introduction is therefore designed as an intervention in those culture wars. Yet I have no illusions about the effects that a single book might have. At best I hope students and other scholars will take the arguments I make in this book seriously enough that they will begin to wonder what constitutes, and how best to work towards, the production of cultural *justice*. Whether the analysis of cultural geography I make here is correct or not, I want it to have the effect of spurring action, the action of further study and analysis, certainly, but also the action of political intervention. So heed the words of Scoop Nisker, the news announcer for KSAN radio in San Francisco (back when KSAN was the voice of alternative culture). He used to end his broadcasts by exhorting his audience: "If you don't like the news, go out and make some of your own." I say the same thing. If you don't like the geographies I describe in the pages that follow, go make your own. For if you don't, Nabisco and McDonald's – and countless others – will make them for you.

Part I

The Politics of Culture

Culture Wars: Culture is Politics by Another Name

Culture Wars

The new Convention Center in downtown Denver, Colorado, like many similar urban revitalization projects, was built by wiping out an existing neighborhood – some of the last low-income housing in the downtown area. Completed in 1990 and costing $126 million, the city and the State of Colorado hope that the million-square-foot Convention Center will help Denver remain competitive in a growing convention economy.[1] Of that $126 million, $200,000 went to University of Colorado artist Barbara Jo Revelle to create a two-block-long mosaic called "Colorado Panorama: A People's History" (figure 1.1). There are 168 faces in the mosaic, ranging from traditional "heroes" of Western history like Kit Carson to coal miner organizer Mother Jones and Denver Black Panther founder Lauren Watson. Many of the others are ordinary people, notable perhaps only in the communities in which they lived: farmers, local activists, miners, and so forth.

From the beginning the mosaic was controversial. City officials asked Revelle to remove several of the faces she proposed: among them an AIDS activist, a Chicano

---

1 Already by 1995, however, managers of the Center were complaining that it was not large enough to bring in the most prestigious and profitable conventions and had begun making noises about a need for a bond issue to support expansion; see *Westword*, September 5–11, 1996.

Figure 1.1 Part of the "Men's Wall" of Barbara Revelle's controversial mosaic "Colorado Panorama: A People's History" on the wall of the Denver Convention Center. The 600-foot long mosaic consists of thousands of gray-toned industrial tiles (and some color ones) arranged to represent the faces and activities of people important to Colorado – whether politicians and explorers or farmers, children, and activists. The mural is located in an out-of-the-way delivery and pick-up site, but was controversial from the beginning. By including contentious figures – Black Panther and labor activists, ordinary women and men, and those like Kit Carson who participated in the genocide of Native Americans – Revelle sees her mosaic as "an attempt to represent history, not to whitewash it." Image used by permission of the artist; photograph by D. Mitchell.

civil rights activist, and Lauren Watson. Revelle refused. "I see history as concurrent stories. It's not a 'pioneer heroics' kind of thing. These people were not necessarily role models or heroes. But they do reference different chapters in Colorado history" (quoted in Shanti Jefferson 1996: 12). After threatening to quit the project altogether, Revelle was given permission to include all the faces she had planned. But she was not given permission to complete the project. She had allotted $9,000 of the commission to produce a key to the faces – actually a computer touch screen that would allow visitors to call up the biographies of those enshrined – which would explain each person's place in Colorado's history and culture. The city used the money for other purposes.

The key to the mural is now finally being made. But Revelle has been excluded from the team creating it. It has instead been entrusted to historian Tom Noel (also of the University of Colorado), who is most notable for his boosterish histories of the city and state. The computer touch screen idea has been dropped. The new version of the key will limit each biographical entry to one or two lines. The key will be housed in glass cases near the mural. Revelle is worried about what the key will do to her art: "They [the city] wanted a non-controversial, nice, generic history, that didn't challenge anyone or focus on any bad history. But all good art is controversial" (quoted in Shanti Jefferson 1996: 12).

This may seem like a pretty minor skirmish in what perennial United States presidential candidate Patrick Buchanan memorably termed the "Culture Wars" – those battles, rooted in ideology, religion, class difference, the social construction of racial, ethnic and gender difference, and so on that mark contemporary society. The battlefronts in the culture wars are many and varied. In the United States they have included everything from long-running battles over abortion and the use of drugs, to curriculum in schools, to what is broadcast on TV. Globally, they can be seen in the reassertion of fundamentalist religious beliefs in all religions, battles against the "Americanization" of the media, reassertions of national identity, pride, and prejudice, and attacks on immigrants, foreigners, and minority ethnic populations. What makes these *culture* wars is that they center as much on questions of identity (personal, ethnic, and national), social values, and control over meaning, as they do on the more "traditional" battlegrounds of territory, economy, and military might. But as we will see throughout this book, such a distinction between cultural wars and other manifestations of power (and resistance to it) is hardly sustainable.

The Colorado mural is instructive, though, because the terms of the debate over it are indicative of the sorts of social, political, and economic tensions that mark contemporary society – and the culture wars that are so much a part of its landscape. The controversy around Revelle's mural asks us to consider how different ideals, different "cultures" are represented and contested. Like other wars, wars over culture are territorial, they literally *take place*, whether that place is on the wall of a convention center, on the city streets outside, or in the print and electronic media. Culture wars are about defining what is legitimate in a society, who is an "insider" and who is an "outsider." They are about determining the social boundaries that govern our lives. These arguments get repeatedly played out in numerous arenas, as with, for example, debates over what constitutes "the canon" in Anglo-American literature, in which "multiculturalists" argue for inclusion of more women, and more people of color,[2] or as in the rather ugly fights over how history should be taught in American schools (as happened when the UCLA National Center for History in the Schools released the national "history standards" which sought to indicate the sorts of historical study students at various grade-levels should engage in).[3] Such debates, which often seem quite far removed from geography, seek to set the boundaries that define high and low culture, the legitimate from the illegitimate. They work to create the contours that define what counts as "proper" knowledge, "proper" behavior, or "proper" relations between groups. Here, then, we are unavoidably mired in geography – and, I will show in the course of this book, not only of the metaphorical sort indicated by the use of "boundaries" and "contours" above. Rather arguments over "culture" are arguments over real spaces, over landscapes, over the social relations

---

2   An excellent evaluation of these debates can be found in Bérubé (1994); for an approach less sympathetic to identity politics than Bérubé's, see Gitlin (1995).

3   The debate was ugly. Pundits working in conservative think tanks such as the Heritage Foundation and the American Enterprise Institute busily counted up names in the document, finding, for instance, that whereas "Harriet Tubman, an African American who helped rescued slaves by way of the underground railroad, is mentioned six times[,] [t]wo white males who were contemporaries of Tubman, Ulysses S. Grant and Robert E. Lee, get one and zero mentions respectively" (Cheney 1994). While this seemed to prove to conservatives (and many "liberals" in Congress) that the Standards completely rewrote American history after a false, "politically correct" image, it seemed to escape their attention that the Standards were not a textbook, and not designed as a direct document to be read and studied by students, but a set of guidelines for approaching history in a more inclusive, more truthful, and more relevant way (see Nash and Crabtree 1994; Gluck 1994). Be that as it may, the United States Senate voted unanimously to condemn the Standards document, even though most of the Senators had neither seen nor read it. The debate, quite clearly, was less about the teaching of American history, and far more about how American nationalism was to be defined (*New York Times* 1994). For a detailed discussion of a similar debate at a more local level, see Gitlin (1995), 7–36.

that define the places in which we and others live.

If a controversy over a piece of art in Denver seems minor, or if debates over who should be considered a great writer, or which Americans should be learned about in history classes seem too academic, consider the importance of "culture wars" in relationship to the resurgence of right-wing nationalism in France. Revelle's mural asks us to think seriously about who is part of Colorado – quite literally. It asks us, by displaying history *right there*, on that wall for residents and visitors alike to confront, who counts as a Coloradan. In that sense, it is a clearly territorial statement. For Revelle, it is about marking Colorado as an inclusive territory. For city officials, that sense of inclusiveness is threatening. The issue in France is much the same. The rise of a xenophobic nationalism in the 1990s is probably the single most important political fact in France; and it is no less important for the developing (if haltingly) unification of Europe in the European Union.[4] Jean-Marie Le Pen and his National Front party have made racism an acceptable topic of political discussion and outlook for the first time in postwar France. The Rightist government (ousted in 1997) and the administration of Gaullist President Jacques Chirac, found itself continually acquiescing to the demands of the National Front, especially in terms of "tightening" immigration laws. In France, now, children born in France of immigrant parents are not automatically eligible for citizenship (they must apply for it at age 16); it is harder for immigrants from Africa (including especially the former French colonies there) to obtain visas for work and visiting; and French citizens are required to "report" neighbors and family members whose visas may have expired. Despite the growing respectability and acceptance of right-wing racism in France, a 1972 law (expanded in 1990) makes it a civil crime to incite ethnic or racial hatred; that is, the French state has made it its business to regulate conflict between ethnic groups, and is on record as supporting a more inclusive French polity than that proposed by Le Pen. The arguments in the 1990s have been precisely over just how inclusive that polity should or should not be. This is a culture war of *deadly* seriousness (see Singer 1996; Mairowitz 1997).[5]

If the rise of racist nationalism marks a contour of the culture wars in France (to say nothing of Germany, the republics of the former Yugoslavia, or Britain), then in many other parts of the world (the USA quite clearly included), the rise of religious fundamentalism indicates another. Whether in Turkey, Afghanistan, Saudi Arabia, suburban California, Israel, or India, fundamentalist versions of Christian, Muslim, Jewish, and Hindu beliefs have all found new vigor – and political power – in the past

---

4   The resurgence of the Socialist Party in the 1997 elections can be understood as both a reaction to Le Pen, and his racist, anti-immigrant organizing, *and* a reaction to the forces of globalization (and the sense of displacement that comes with them) that have allowed Le Pen to be so successful. Like Patrick Buchanan in the 1996 American presidential election, who tapped a populist nerve of discontent over globalization that was rooted in both cultural and economic uncertainty, Le Pen has galvanized right-wing populism and turned it into a potent political force.
5   It is also a deadly issue in Germany where anti-Turkish militancy has led to arson, Turk-bashing, and organized murder on an unprecedented scale. It should be noted that, in both France and Germany, the reassertion of violent racism has been met by forceful counter-demonstrations (for example in Strasbourg in 1997 during the convention of the Nationalist Party, tens of thousands of French workers and students took to the streets to protest the Party's presence; racist violence in Germany in 1992–3 had led to massive marches against xenophobic violence). But it has just as often been met by rather weak response from heads of state, especially Germany's ex-Chancellor Helmut Kohl (Kinzer 1994).

two decades. If the predictions of global futurists from the 1950s and 1960s were to be believed, the overriding fact of the late twentieth century was going to be the steady increase of secularism, as religious mysticism gave way before the steady corrosive power of science (and capitalism). The world was modernizing, and thus the need for religion was steadily decreasing. But instead of the clinical secularism prophesied, religions have been *gaining* adherents, and fundamentalist sects have been gaining them fastest of all. Many of these sects have at their heart a cultural agenda, one through which they seek to transform the mores of society such that people behave as they interpret people *should* behave before God. Hence in Colorado, Oregon, Maine, and countless cities and towns around the USA, voters, well-organized through church congregations and religious television and radio broadcasts, pass laws making it impossible for gay men and women to be protected by law from discrimination. Throughout the United States fundamentalist majorities have been elected to school boards where they have mandated such things as the teaching of creationism as a theory every bit as legitimate as evolutionary biology, and that homosexuality is an "immoral lifestyle." In Afghanistan, the new Taliban regime requires women to be fully covered when in public, to quit school and work, and to lead a nearly fully sequestered life. Even necessary medical services are denied women. In Israel, laws are proposed – and widely supported – that make conversions to Judaism legitimate only if performed by the Orthodox Rabbinate. Under those laws conversions by rabbis from other sects would not be recognized by the state (Fein 1997). Among other things, these battles are transforming, in different ways in different places, but always through that medium we most usually call "culture," the very meaning of citizenship in the modern world. Where once the notion of liberal individualism (allied as it was with the growth of capitalism) seemed ascendant, now there seems to be a much stronger sense of the importance – and power – of moral, cultural communities (which has done little to slow the advance of capitalism, showing instead how easily discourses of individual rights can be divorced from it).

Now take one final "culture war" example, one perhaps closer in spirit to the story about the mural in Denver, and one seemingly less earth-shattering and death-dealing than the examples of racist nationalism and religious fundamentalism. When Glasgow, Scotland, was named the "European City of Culture" in 1990, reactions there and around Europe ranged from incredulity (after all Glasgow was a declining, gritty, industrial city, not a center of culture!), to pride (finally Glasgow was being recognized for what it was: a place of culture), to outrage (just *whose* culture was being feted, anyway?). This last was mostly expressed by cultural and labor activists who saw the various plans for the Year of Culture as part of a concerted effort to erase the militant workers' history of the city – and to continue, as Seán Damer (1990: 18, emphasis in original) put it, to insure that the yuppies of the city "are able to enjoy their enhanced lifestyle *at the expense of* the unemployed and low-paid workers living in the aptly-named peripheral [housing] estates. The latter are an embarrassment in Thatcher's Britain." The Year of Culture designation, after all, was a means both to illustrate and to reinforce Glasgow's transformation to a "postindustrial" economy, to precisely the model of development Thatcher's government was promoting throughout Great Britain (Boyle and Hughes 1991).

To market the city's European City of Culture designation, the Labour city government employed Thatcher's house PR firm, Saatchi and Saatchi, which quickly concocted the slogan "There's a lot Glasgowing on in 1990," a slogan that indicates just how much the hard, violent image of a grim, mean Red Clydeside had been transformed in the 1980s.[6] As Damer documents, as late as 1983, the image of Glasgow in the national media "was of a filthy, slum-ridden, poverty-stricken, gang-infested city whose population consisted of undersized, incomprehensible, drunken, foul-mouthed, sectarian lumpenproletarians who were prone to hit each other with broken bottles and razors without warning" (Damer 1990: 1; see also Spring 1990). By 1988, however, that image had been largely reversed. Now "Glasgow's Miles Better" than other de-industrialized cities (as one heavily promoted slogan of the 1980s put it), boasting a rousingly successful international Garden Festival, new museums and theaters, revitalized and lively pedestrian shopping streets (one now with a Warner Brothers' Studio store replete with cartoon-infested marquee hanging garishly over the street), a new Royal Concert Hall, up-scale malls like Princes Square and St. Enoch Centre, a surprising assortment of Victorian housing and office buildings saved from the wrecker's ball, and a string of parks and open spaces that must be the envy of all other heavily industrialized cities. There are even a few shipbuilding cranes still standing,[7] adding interest and a certain sense of immense history to the skyline. Glasgow is a far more interesting and intriguing city than Edinburgh (even if it still is overshadowed by that city in the tourist trade). What is there not to like in this transformation?

One answer to that question, Damer avers, can be found in comparing the images of the city produced by photographers Oscar Marzaroli and Colin Baxter in the 1950s–1960s, and the 1980s, respectively (figures 1.2 and 1.3). In the earlier photos, the images are of "ordinary Glasgow people doing ordinary Glasgow things" : football fans, winos, women shopping, street demonstrations. In the latter, the pictures are almost exclusively of buildings, often taken from the air, and softened by a light, hazy sun. The transition, one could say, is from a city of public spaces, a city of people at home in the city, not wealthy, but not abject either, to a city as *landscape*, a place devoid of residents, a landscape in which people are only visitors and welcome mostly as consumers (especially of imagery). The city-as-landscape does not encourage the formation of community or of urbanism as a way of life; rather it encourages the maintenance of surfaces, the promotion of order at the expense of lived social relations, and the ability to look past distress, destruction, and marginalization to see only the good life (for some) and to turn a blind eye towards what that life is constructed out of (see chapter 5).

Such a transformation is not all for the worst. "It is wonderful to see Woodlands, Govanhill and Partick as restored residential and shopping areas," Damer (1990: 10) writes. "Glaswegians are entitled to garden festivals, riverside walkways, more and better galleries, good restaurants, decent comfortable pubs, civilised drinking hours,

6   Glasgow, together with the neighboring towns astride the Clyde River, was perhaps the most politically radical region in Britain in the first decades of the twentieth century. Sustained agitation around issues of housing, working conditions, and basic rights such as free speech, led to remarkable public and electoral success for Scottish socialists and communists. This working-class political power, in all its complexity (see Damer 1990, chapter 4), is called up in a longstanding nickname for the Glasgow region: the Red Clydeside.
7   One of which was festooned in 1989 with a full-size straw model of a locomotive by artist George Wylie in a surprisingly effective and popular parody of and lament for Glasgow's past as an industrial might powered by ship and locomotive building.

Figure 1.2 "Football, Forth and Clyde Canal, Near Pinkston, 1962," by Oscar Marzaroli. Marzaroli's photographs focus on aspects of everyday life in Glasgow, showing the city to be constructed out of well-used, often public, spaces. While Marzaroli was adept at urban landscape photography, the cumulative weight of his photographs is to show the city as a lived place, one that was home to people of many classes. © Anne Marzaroli.

Figure 1.3 "The River Clyde and Glasgow City Centre," by Colin Baxter. Baxter specializes in photographs from the air. His lush, color pictures are almost completely devoid of people and depict the city as a *landscape* in a manner that accords well with its new-found status as a city of culture and upscale consumption. Used by permission.

good entertainment, a wide range of shops, food and goods, and, in general, a clean, attractive and safe city" (Damer 1990: 12).[8] But, as he also notes, it is essential that we also understand for whom "Glasgow's Miles Better," and at what cost this new landscape has been constructed. The high-rise council-flat estates are as drug- and crime-ridden as ever, and unemployment exceeds 60 percent in some of them; their residents are fully isolated both from the rejuvenated center-city and from the surrounding, beautiful countryside by inadequate public transportation. But perhaps such isolation is not entirely unintentional: how else could Glasgow be sold to the incoming middle classes as a place of leisure, beauty, and culture, without simultaneously making the Glasgow these visitors and residents *see* palpably *not* a city in which some 45 percent of the population lives in areas of "multiple deprivation."

Nor should they be too often reminded of Glasgow's industrialized, radicalized, working-class past. And it is here that much of the political organizing at the time of the Year of Culture centered. For the artists and activists organized as "Workers City," the City of Culture designation, and the rise of a New Glasgow, was to be fought on the grounds that "it is difficult seeing the 'culture' tag as being anything other than a sham accolade to help grease the wheels of capitalist enterprise and smooth the path for politicians" (McLay 1988: 3, in Kelman 1992). The erasure of "the glory and heroism of those who resolutely engaged reaction and put Glasgow in the vanguard of revolution" during the famous Red Clydeside of the 1920s, made possible by "the camouflage business" of culture-mongering and shopping district regeneration, was a sin against history – a sin against the noble, if now often degraded, lives of the city's workers (McLay 1988). At its most forceful, the Workers City critique was unsparing:

> For although modes of repression and control in State bureaucracies may have changed, relying today as much on advertising conmanship as on police coercion, and although the new capitalist-controlled computer technologies exploit and impoverish and degrade us in ways hardly imaginable even fifty years ago, yet it is repression for all that, it is still exploitation, it is still impoverishment, and it is still degradation.   (McLay 1988)

Workers City purported to speak, in this language, for "the Real Glasgow," suggesting that *that* Glasgow had little but disdain for the Year of Culture. James Kelman (1992: 1–2) was clear in whom Workers City saw their constituency to be:

> The name "Workers City" carries obvious connotations but it was chosen to directly challenge "Merchant City" [both a nickname for Glasgow and the name of a significant redevelopment project in the city center], highlighting the grossness of the fallacy that Glasgow somehow exists because of the tireless efforts of a tiny patriotic coalition of fearless 18th century entrepreneurs and far-sighted politicians. . . . The personal wealth of those earlier individuals . . . [was] founded on slavery, but the city of Glasgow wasn't, and

---

8   Even so, such a city comes with other costs. The shopping precincts of downtown, for example, are now intensely surveyed by an around-the-clock closed-circuit television (CCTV) system. See Fyfe and Bannister (1996).

its present-day citizens have to survive in spite of its current crop [of entrepreneurs and politicians].

Others dismissed Workers City and its pretensions to speak for a movement of working-class citizens. "Instead, the active process of hegemony and the activities of the popular press have had the effect that amongst the general population of the city only a very limited opposition movement has arisen," according to cultural critic Ian Spring (1990: 123). Yet whether Spring undermines or in fact confirms precisely Workers City's claims about the importance of "conmanship," the important point is that over something seemingly so benign as declaring a city a center of culture in Europe a lively and important debate developed, a war of words over culture, its importance, and its meanings to the different – and differently situated – people of Glasgow and Scotland. Like the mural in Denver, the debates over the City of Culture and the transformation of the Glasgow landscape raise questions about who culture is for, who belongs in and to the space of a city, and who is to be represented in those spaces. These, then, are the same questions, if differently inflected, as those raised in the dozens of culture wars, little and big, raging over and in contemporary nationalist movements.

So, in all these examples and the infinite others that could just as easily be given, just what is going on? There are numerous ways we could explain these "culture wars." In this book I will take one particular – and I think particularly compelling – way to explain not just the contemporary, but also numerous past culture wars. To foreshadow the argument I will make throughout *Cultural Geography: A Critical Introduction*: it is my sense that it is no accident that the culture wars being fought *now*, over the end of the twentieth and beginning of the twenty-first century have a particular shape and style to them: they are battles over cultural identities – and the power to shape, determine, and, literally, *emplace* those identities. My most important point is that any culture war – now or in the past – is both a reflection of, and an ongoing contribution to, the geographies we build in the world. Each successive battle transforms the geography in which it takes place and therefore creates new contexts – new geographical *situations* – within which the next round of struggle occurs. But these geographies are not only – and never can be only – "cultural." Instead, they are part of a recursive set of relationships between what we call "culture" and the changing political and economic fortunes of different places and different peoples. Hence, as the political economy "globalizes" (a process at least as old as capitalism itself), as it constantly revolutionizes the very basis of its own existence, it tends to undermine whatever sureties about identity have built up over the long haul of time. Moments of intense political and economic restructuring (the long crisis of capitalism from the 1870s until the beginning of the 1900s, the Depression and War decades of the 1930s and 1940s, and the globalization wave that began with the crisis of 1973 and has only gained momentum in the past two decades) are also moments of intense cultural restructuring. To understand culture, I will argue throughout this book, we must look at battles over it. To understand the battles, though, look at the material conditions for those battles – the changes in political economy, the changes in technology, the changes, literally, in the historical *shape* of the world. By examining the geography of culture, then, we can get a better handle on how it is that our social worlds are constructed and contested, how we do and do not live together, and how, historically, these constructions and contestations have created the *material contexts* within which new struggles for cultural determinacy, for cultural autonomy, for cultural control, and for cultural rights take place. It is therefore essential, I think, to try to understand the construction of culture historically – or better, historical-geographically – for it is only by understanding how these battles over culture have been determined over time by the material geographical conditions within which they occur, that we can begin to understand the contemporary shape of the cultural world.

That is the purpose of this book: to *explain* the social and cultural worlds in which we live.[9] But to do so there is one thing we cannot do. As odd as it may seem, we cannot use "culture" itself as a means of explanation. Instead, it is "culture" that, in every case, needs explaining. Otherwise we would, in essence, end up explaining culture with culture; we would end up saying no more than "this culture behaves like this because that's its culture" (as when we say, "Balkan peoples fight each other because that is their culture – and it has always been like that"). Such a conclusion is less than useless. It tells us absolutely nothing. There is a second reason we cannot use "culture" to explain the world: as we will see in the next two chapters, "culture" has no ontological basis.[10] To put that in plain English, if still counter-intuitively, when we use the word "culture," we are really not referring to anything at all. Instead, we are drawing on what could be called an empty abstraction – an abstraction that has no referent in the material world. People do not "have" culture. Nor do "cultures" simply and autonomously exist, as something real, solid, and permanent. Instead, there is only a very powerful *ideology* of culture, an ideology that asserts people do this or do that because of "culture"; or, at the very least, asserts that "culture" exists as a realm, level, or medium of social interaction. As the very words "medium," "realm," and "level" indicate, such assertions very quickly take us into the realm of mysticism (see chapter 3).

If we want to understand the culture wars, then, we have to do two things. First we need to understand what "culture" is and what it isn't. Then we need to look at how what gets called culture is itself socially constructed through all manner of contests and cooperations over the materials – places, jobs, pictures, foods, art, histories, ethnicities, sexualities, etc. – that make up our lives. What we will see is that while "culture" can't explain, while *there's no such thing as culture* (Mitchell 1995b), our fights over culture are deadly important. And they're inescapably geographic too. They shape the spaces we live in just as the spaces we live in shape them. Culture wars are wars like any other.

---

9   I understand cultural *explanation* to be an essential part of cultural geography. Many in the discipline would disagree and claim the best we can do is cultural *interpretation*. My hope is that the readers of this book will take these debates about interpretation and explanation as seriously as we take the culture wars going on around us – for they are part of them.

10   "Ontology" refers to theories or statements about what the world *really* is, or must be like. An ontological statement is one that claims a foundation in that which actually exists in the world. A companion to "ontology" is "epistemology" which refers more to a *system of knowledge*. Hence, a philosophy or theory operates both at the ontological level (it suggests what the world is really like), and at the epistemic level (it posits a systematic means for knowing that world, even if that system itself may be non-foundational).

What is "Culture"?

How is it possible to claim both that culture does not exist and that it is one of the most important forces in our lives? Part of the answer stems from the nature of the term itself. "Culture" is an incredibly complex word. Most of us use the term without thinking much about it. We speak frequently about English culture, or Chinese culture, or Hispanic culture. Or when we don't understand something, like the civil wars in the former Yugoslavia, we often say, "Well, that's just their culture. They've been fighting each other for centuries." But then we also refer to art, to symphonies, to plays as "culture" – or perhaps "high culture." And as soon as we do that, we want to also talk about "popular culture," whether that is defined by television, rock stars, or comic books. If there is pop culture, then there also seems to be something called "counter-culture," "indigenous culture," "youth culture," "black culture," "gay culture," "working-class culture," "Western culture," "corporate culture," a "culture of poverty," and "folk culture." And between all of these there seems to be a complex and quite exciting "cultural politics" that more and more defines the way our lives are structured.[11]

So *now* what is culture? On the one hand the word seems to signify a "total way of life" of a people, encompassing language, dress, food habits, music, housing styles, religion, family structures and, most importantly, *values*. On the other hand the term "culture" seems to indicate certain things: works of art, musical productions, the stuff that gets put in museums and concert halls – or in its popular version the things shown on TV and in cinemas, that occur in clubs and stadiums, that appear advertised and displayed in glossy magazines and cheaply produced 'zines. Culture seems to be both a nebulous "structure of feeling" (Williams 1973) that defines the life of people (or perhaps is constructed out of the lives of peoples) *and* a set of productions (like art) that reflect upon, speak to, or attempt to mold that "structure of feeling" through various strategies of representation.

To complicate matters, there is yet another way to think about culture. Much theoretical work in geography, anthropology, history, sociology, and so forth, has distinguished between several "realms" of social life: the economic, the political, the social, and the cultural, for example. Economy, of course, is how people get their living. Politics is how they array power, how winners and losers in a society are determined. Society is the relationships between people and institutions that both derive from and help reproduce political, economic, and cultural forms. It is also the sum total of those forms (as when we say "Australian society"). And culture is . . . well, culture is a lot of things, perhaps what is left over after economics, politics, and society are subtracted. At least that has been one way of thinking of it. But it should be quite obvious that none of these realms is really independent of the others; indeed it seems that each is necessary to define the others. How, for example, can we

---

11   Perhaps the primary advocate of the study of cultural politics in geography is Peter Jackson. A good and accessible summary of his ideas is *Maps of Meaning: An Introduction to Cultural Geography* (1989). Jackson's research on the cultural politics of race and racism, sexuality, street life and consumption is voluminous. Particularly good examples include Jackson 1987a, 1988, 1991a, 1991b, 1992a, 1992b, 1993b, 1994.

understand the economic functioning of a society without a simultaneous understanding of how power is arrayed in that society (which is why scholars often speak
of "political economy")? How can we talk of social relations and institutions without
recourse to a theory of "culture" that allows us to understand how people *represent*
those relationships to themselves and each other (and, again, without simultaneously
understanding political and economic structures)? In this sense, culture is part of a
fully recursive set of relationships that determine how we lead our lives. One way of
understanding culture in this manner is to see politics, economics, and to a large
degree society, as concerned with the *material* relations of society, and culture with
the *symbolic* (though, for geographers, the symbolic can often be read in the material
artifacts people make and leave as markers of their "way of life").[12] The reason for
defining culture this way (as the symbolic, or as that which is not economy, society,
and politics) is that it allows one to see how the different realms interact with each
other, how they structure each other to produce the totality of a society – or should I
say of a *culture* since as we have already seen "culture" indicates the total way of life
of a people?

Finally, and importantly, there is one more quite simple way to think about culture.
Culture is simply that which is not nature.[13]

"Culture" is thus something of a muddle. Among all the ways of understanding
culture, there are perhaps six that are particularly important. First, culture is the
opposite of nature. It is what makes humans human. Second, "culture" is the actual,
perhaps unexamined, patterns and differentiations of a people (as in "Aboriginal
culture" or "German culture" – culture is a way of life). Third, it is the processes by
which these patterns developed (think of it as "culture" making "culture"). Fourth,
the term indicates a set of markers that set one people off from another and which
indicate to us our membership in a group (I am American; I am part of the American
culture). Fifth, culture is the way that all these patterns, processes, and markers are
represented (that is, cultural activity, whether high, low, pop, or folk, that produces
meaning). Finally, the idea of culture often indicates a hierarchical ordering of all
these processes, activities, ways of life, and cultural production (as when people
compare cultures or cultural activities against each other; think, for example, about
the debates in Western nations concerning the supposed inherent inferiority of
Muslim or other ways of life, or think of the debates over the "canon"
discussed above).[14] Proponents of the growing field of "cultural studies" have put it
this way:

> culture is understood both as a way of life – encompassing ideas, attitudes, lan-
> guages, practices, institutions, and structures of power – and a whole range of cultural
> practices: artistic forms, texts, canons, architecture, mass-produced commodities, and so
> forth.   (Nelson et al. 1992: 5)

12   This distinction is highly problematic, and understanding how it is and is not valuable is one of the
major purposes of this book – and of cultural geography. The best discussion to date of these relationships
is Jackson (1989).
13   Of course that explains nothing since perhaps the only word in English more complicated than
"culture" is "nature." See Williams (1976).
14   This schematic rendering of culture is a variation on one I created in Mitchell (1995b), see especially
pp. 104–5.

"Culture" seems to mean everything. Or maybe it is so broad a term it means nothing – or at least not anything analytically useful.

How did we get to such a state of affairs – a state of affairs in which one of the most important terms in our everyday and academic lexicon is so hopelessly confused? The English social critic Raymond Williams (1976: 87–93) traced the lineage of "culture" several years ago.[15] Like so many words, he showed, its meaning has changed often in the course of its development, taking on greater and greater complexity as it has been adopted for use in novel settings. And as with any good word, it will continue to evolve, charging off in new directions when we least expect it. But this is no innocent process. Rather, the development of the word itself is fraught with all manner of power relations, as people have struggled to harness it to their own ends. And, as will become clear throughout this book, I am no exception in the desire to use the idea of culture in specific – and politically charged – ways.

The word culture, Williams explained, derived from the Latin *cultura* indicating "cultivation or tending." As the word developed in French and passed into English by the early fifteenth century, "culture" was used to describe "the tending of natural growth." Over time, the metaphor of tending was extended from plants and animals to the tending of human development, particularly of the human mind. For the most part, even as late as the early nineteenth century, this sense of tending to growth was quite specifically directed at individuals. It was something that one *did*. But so, too, did a second, more general, sense of "tending" begin to develop. Importantly, early uses of this more general sense seemed to indicate differences in class or standing. "Culture" was becoming a term to differentiate the good from the bad, the *cultivated* from the unruly. Jane Austen could thus write of those who possessed "every advantage of discipline and culture" (quoted in Williams 1976: 88). Already by the early nineteenth century a sense of hierarchy, deriving from this notion of tending and cultivation, was integral to the meanings of the term. In Germany and France during the eighteenth century, variations of "culture" were closely associated with "civilization," reinforcing the class aspect of the meanings of "culture".

In the last quarter of the eighteenth century, however, the German philosopher Johann von Herder criticized the common assumption that all this tending and cultivating had led to European society as the pinnacle of all human self-development (see Livingstone 1992: 122–4; Mathewson 1996). He complained specifically of European expansion across the globe, and argued that the "very thought of a superior European culture is a blatant insult to the majesty of nature" (quoted in Williams 1976: 89). Therefore, Herder argued, it was important to speak not of culture in the singular, but rather of cultures in the plural – not only of specific national cultures, but also of different cultures within nations. Here we get to the development of the idea that different cultures, distinguished by class or ethnicity, can exist co-extensively with each other. This sense of plural cultures – and of perhaps oppositional or archaic cultures within the European sphere – was developed by the Romantic movement in such a way as to create a different sense of the term "culture." In this Romantic sense, "civilization" was seen as material and "culture" as spiritual or symbolic.

---

15   Raymond Williams is one of the most influential thinkers in contemporary cultural studies and he has had a big impact on cultural geography in the last two decades too. We will explore his ideas more fully in chapter 2.

By the mid-nineteenth century most of the modern usages of culture (as outlined above) seemed to be in place. The years since have largely seen an *extension* of those uses (the development of the idea of popular culture, for example) rather than a redefinition of them. Williams (1976: 91) concludes his etymological exercise by pointing out that it is precisely the complexity of the term culture that is important. "The complex of senses" that comprise "culture" "indicates a complex argument about the relations between general human development and a particular way of life, and between both and the works and practices of art and intelligence."

Culture in Cultural Geography

Culture has come down to us as a very complex word indeed, highly suggestive in its meanings, and rich in its possibilities. By contrast, its history in cultural geography – at least until quite recently – has been rather more restricted.

Before we get the story of "culture" within cultural geography, let me explain my reasons for telling it. Understanding *how* a key idea in geography is used depends on understanding *why* it has been used in certain ways. So it is essential that we situate the history of "culture" in cultural geography within a social context – a context composed of changes both within the discipline and in the "outside" world. Many find such exercises in the "history of geography" to be either boring or pointless. My own sense, however, is that in order for us to understand why we think the way we do *now* (as geographers) it is essential to understand the historical and social foundations of our thought. Doing geography is no simple exercise in just explaining the truth. Instead, it is an exercise in bringing to bear a set of tools, notions, political commitments, and ways of thinking that themselves have been conditioned – either positively or negatively – by those people and issues that have come before us. While I think cultural geographers should try to explain the worlds they are part of, I also know that explanation is itself always partial and in part a *reaction* to how others have tried to explain the world. Therefore, the context of explanation is essential.

Cultural geography has its roots in a theoretical and political world quite different than what one might expect: not in a world concerned with cultural difference for its own sake, or in one concerned even to delineate the geographies of that difference. Rather, it is not too much of a parody to suggest that cultural geography developed within and as part of a set of "culture wars" just as important for their time as contemporary wars are for ours. As in contemporary culture wars, intellectuals, political operatives, empire builders, and many simply ordinary people were keen to understand why, as they saw it, "Western civilization" was so "superior" to all other cultures or civilizations, so exclusively ordained for greatness at the scale of the world. This was part of the project of empire building. In Britain, particularly, but later in Germany and America, the nineteenth century was one of intensive imperialism.[16] Geographers in these countries saw their work (in a discipline that was just beginning

16   I do not mean to exclude other empires – the fading Spanish and Portuguese, or the resurgent Italian, for example – but the clearest roots of contemporary Anglo-American-Austral cultural geography are in Britain and Germany, with the United States (and to a lesser extent Canada) taking the lead in the first half of the twentieth century.

to define itself) as integral to the project of Empire. This work took two contradictory strains, which themselves eventually came to butt heads in the theories of American geographer Carl Sauer (1889–1975), in whom many historians of geography see the clearest exposition of twentieth-century cultural geography. These two strains are, first, the environmental determinism that sought to link human social behavior to determinants in the physical environment (most prominently climate), and second, folk studies that sought to explain the cultural roots of contemporary European civilization in the ordinary peoples of Europe.[17] We will look at each of these strains in turn. Then we will examine how Carl Sauer, as he took up a position in the geography department at the University of California, Berkeley, in the 1920s, established a particularly American version of cultural geography by explicitly rejecting much of the first and more fully developing the second.

Environmental determinism

Geography has long been caught up in the work of nation and empire building.[18] At the turn of the twentieth century, British geographers, for example, were quite forthright in their expectations for the discipline as a servant to the state: geography was, according to one, "absolutely essential for our well-being, and even for the continuance of the nation as a Power among the states of the world" (Mill 1901: 423, quoted in Livingstone 1992: 216). One way that geographers asserted their importance was by developing a robust language of what David Livingstone (1992: 188) and others have identified as "neo-Lamarckism." Neo-Lamarckism was a sophisticated argument that developed Lamarck's idea that an organism could pass acquired characteristics to its offspring. Along with this, neo-Lamarckians were convinced that "the directive force[s] of organic variation" were "will, habit, or environment" (Livingstone 1992: 188). That is, willful change on the part of an individual, or habits acquired in a particular environment could and would be passed to future generations. They would become, we would now say, part of their genetic make-up. The key point for neo-Lamarckians, especially as they sought to translate this evolutionary history into geographical explanations of cultural difference, was that the "use or disuse of organs was … crucial, contingent as they were on those altered habits, induced by environmental change, that produced different behavior patterns" (Livingstone 1992: 188). As a neo-Lamarckian enterprise, then, environmental determinism argued that the causal mechanisms for cultural behavior were to be found in the environment. Certain environmental conditions created certain habits; and, crucially, these habits were then transmitted *naturally* to successive generations. Environmental determinism, a species of neo-Lamarckiasm, thus held

---

17   It should be noted that this second strain carried with it the seeds of a cultural relativism that is reflected in some of the definitions outlined above; this relativism, developed most fully in anthropology, but apparent clearly in the work of Sauer and his students, has in the last few decades re-entered cultural geography through the influence of cultural studies and postmodernism.

18   The relationship between geography and empire has begun to receive a great deal of attention from historians of geography. In fact, it is within the work on geography and empire, that the methodological and theoretical prescripts for telling socially contextualized histories of the discipline are best developed. Good examples of this work include Godlewska and Smith (1994); Bell et al. (1995).

that the environment – nature – *caused* cultural difference by providing varying conditions under which cultures "grew" and were transmitted from generation to generation.

Environmental determinism's career in geography is fascinating. Though there are other antecedents, the most influential early statements of a theory of environmental determinism come from the German geopolitical theorist, Friedrich Ratzel, who, writing in the last decades of the nineteenth century (in his influential two-volume *Anthropogeographie*), collapsed society into nature through the concept of the organic state and *Lebensraum* (literally: living space). While not so clearly articulating the sense of environmental determination as environmental *control* of human society, Ratzel (responding to both the formation of the German state and its imperialist adventures overseas) argued that the state was essentially a living thing, which, like other organic things needed to grow in order to live.[19] The state was thus, to a large degree, a *natural* link between people and environment, the spatial expression of what became known in Nazi Germany as "blood and soil" – the spiritual, but also organic ties between people and place.[20] Ratzel argued the link between environment and people was not a simple one of determinism (though he did frequently argue in that direction), but nonetheless, he was clear that the social or cultural development of the state (which, remember, was itself organic) was directly related to the state's ability to grow. This sense of *Lebensraum*, coupled with his more ethnographic *Anthropogeographie* together created what Livingstone (1992: 201) has called "a naturalistic theodicy that justified the imperial order in the language of scientific geography."

Thus as Richard Peet (1985) has argued, such neo-Lamarckian environmental determinism – and the broader discourse of "Social Darwinism" – was not simply an exercise in scientific theorizing, or at least scientific theorizing insulated from broader social currents. Instead, environmental determinism was a "legitimation theory" – that is, a theory that served to legitimate the social, political, and economic ambitions of certain social formations. In Peet's (1985: 310) telling, "environmental determinism . . . was geography's contribution to Social Darwinist ideology, providing a naturalistic explanation of which societies were fittest in the imperial struggle for world domination." Environmental determinism, by creating a theory of *natural* superiority, justified European political and economic expansion – if not to those who stood in Europe's way and became grist for its expansionist political-economic mill, then to those "back home" from whom consent for genocidal imperial adventures needed continually to be secured.[21] This is a point we will return to momentar-

---

19   Ratzel's influence in geopolitics and political geography is fascinating, but a discussion along those lines is not the goal here (see Bassin 1987a). Instead, the idea is to outline Ratzel's influence on environmental determinism and hence, indirectly, on cultural geography.

20   Schama (1995) chapter 2, traces some of the ways in which the "blood and soil" link was archeologically and anthropologically made in German history as part of the project of building the imperial German state. Mark Bassin (1987b) argues that Ratzel's work was *appropriated* by Nazis but that in many regards it worked against official Nazi ideology especially since it sought causation in the environment rather than in genetics. Livingstone (1992) confirms this judgment, further arguing that Ratzel believed in the fundamental biological unity of humans. For Ratzel it was the environment that made them different.

21   Kahn (1995) notes reasonably that arguments positing Social Darwinism as legitimation *to* those being colonized do not make sense, the colonized are not so easily fooled. Rather, legitimacy theories work to convince those in power that what they are doing is right, just, and natural.

ily. First it is important to continue tracing environmental determinism's history within geography.

As in Germany, the roots of environmental determinism in the United States are deep, expressed clearly in the work of Nathaniel Southgate Shaler, the Harvard geologist, for example, or in the work of his colleague, the geographer William Morris Davis.[22] It is also clearly evident in the "frontier thesis" of Frederick Jackson Turner (1920). But perhaps the clearest exponent of environmental determinism at the turn of the century was the geographer Ellen Churchill Semple, who popularized and reformulated Ratzel's ideas, giving them a decidedly stronger determinist bent. Semple's purpose was precisely to make geography *scientific* – that is, to show that the study of humans, and especially human groups, could be done scientifically. In her highly influential 1911 book, *Influences of Geographic Environment on the Basis of Ratzel's System of Anthropo-geography*, Semple restated the longstanding "nature–nurture" controversy – the question to what degree one's environment shapes one's being – and elevated it to the level of culture (see also Semple 1903). "In every problem of history," Semple (1911: 2) argued,

> there are two main factors, variously stated as heredity and environment, man and his geographic conditions, the internal forces of race and the external forces of habit. Now the geographic element in the long history of human development has been operating strongly and operating persistently. Herein lies its importance. It is a stable force. It never sleeps. This natural environment, this physical basis of history, is for all intents and purposes immutable in comparison with the other factor in the problem – shifting, plastic, progressive, retrogressive man.

While there was still some room for human initiative, Semple (1911: 1) argued most cogently that "Man is a product of the earth's surface.... [Nature] has entered into his bone and tissue, into his mind and soul." In Peet's (1985: 321) estimation, while popularizing geography as *the* science of human differentiation and culture, Semple managed to attribute "the dominance of some peoples over others...to a supra-human force – the will of Nature as expressed in varying environmental capacities, racial abilities, and mentalities." With these moves, American geography made its bid to be treated as an important – perhaps essential – *science*. Environmental determinism in its American variant thus represented "the scramble for intellectual turf in what would become the social sciences" (N. Smith 1989: 93).

This scramble was ultimately unsuccessful, and by the 1920s, environmental determinism had pretty much collapsed under both the weight of its own contradictions (it was no good at explaining precisely what it sought to explain: human variation across space) and its growing irrelevancy as legitimation theory. By the turn of the century, the period of active European colonial expansion was drawing to a close. As commentators from all manner of political perspectives – from the imperialist geographer Halford Mackinder and the progressive historian Frederick Jackson Turner on through to Marxists such as Lenin and Rosa Luxemburg – liked to note, by the *fin de siècle* the space of the globe was increasingly closed. European (or other) political

---

22 Davis is most famous for inserting evolutionary or organicist notions into the study of geomorphology, but he was equally active in promoting neo-Lamarckian notions of inorganic control over life (including human life) as the proper realm of geographic study; Livingstone (1992), 202–4.

and economic expansion, therefore, could no longer be absolute, lapping up ever more land and peoples, but now had to be relative, constantly refiguring the relations of power in already controlled lands. To the degree that Peet is correct that the *raison d'étre* of environmental determinism was to legitimate European domination in absolute space, then it was less than useful for understanding the reconfiguration of the relative space that marked the new "postcolonial" period.[23] For that, geographers began looking to other theoretical precedents. One response was to redefine geography as the "science of regions," which Richard Hartshorne accomplished most successfully in his magisterial *The Nature of Geography* in 1939.[24] Another, led by Carl Sauer, was to turn to theories of culture as a means of explaining difference. Curiously enough, many of the culture theories American geographers turned to had their roots in the same German intellectual milieu as environmental determinism.

Carl Sauer and cultural theory

Carl Sauer's influence on the development of cultural geography in the United States is hard to exaggerate. For those styled as "new cultural geographers" (see chapter 2), Sauer is best known for his highly influential 1925 essay "The Morphology of Land-scape," but his impact on the discipline is far broader than just that essay (and the numerous debates it has incited and continues to incite). Sauer grew up in the German Methodist farming community of Warrenton, Missouri, eventually attending Central Wesleyan College in that town. After receiving his degree in 1908, Sauer entered Northwestern University to pursue graduate work in petrology. After a year he transferred to the geography program at the University of Chicago. Despite this time in the city, Sauer never lost his love for small places and his "preference for the simpler economies" or rural and archaic cultures (Leighly 1976). After several years teaching at the University of Michigan, Sauer moved to the University of California at Berkeley in 1923. In part as a reaction to the rapid development of California, and in part as a result of his own curiosity for things now shrouded in the mists of time, Sauer increasingly grew to see modern industrial society as wasteful and impoverishing – unsustainable, we would now say. Over the course of his career, therefore, Sauer concerned himself especially with the destruction humans had caused to the landscape, whether in the "cut-over" lands of northern Michigan or the broader trends of global ecological destruction he outlined in his landmark essay, "The Agency of Man on Earth" (Sauer 1956). Indeed, as Sauer grew increasingly

23   In this instance I am using the term "postcolonial" merely to mark the fact that the period of actual European colonial *expansion* was coming to a close: there were few places left to colonize. This usage is not meant to imply either that colonial domination was coming to an end or that Europe somehow ceased to expand its *influence*.

24   Hartshorne was clearly reacting to the disciplinary "identity crisis" that cast a shadow over geography after the decline of environmental determinism as an organizing force. His goal was to show that environmental determinism was an aberration and to establish the systematic study of "areal differentiation" as the chief organizing force in geography. Hartshorne did not see the study of cultural difference as a firm ground for geography and hence argued strongly against the theories and objects of study promoted by Carl Sauer (to whom we turn in the next section).

pessimistic about the future of modern civilization, he turned his attention more and more towards the historical and anthropological roots of human cultures, seeking to understand the "paleogeography of man," through studies of agricultural origins, transformations of ancient family structure, and speculations on the early hearths of human development (see Leighly 1976). As important as Sauer's own research was (and this cannot be doubted), his lasting impact on American cultural geography was also felt through the work of his numerous students. Over the course of his career, Sauer supervised more than 40 PhD dissertations in geography. The authors of many of these became prominent cultural geographers in their own right, both reinforcing and advancing the various agendas for the discipline Sauer established. As Marvin Mikesell remarks (1987: 145), it is too limiting to force Sauer's legacy and influence into the confining boundaries of "cultural geography." "Was the enterprise founded and led by Sauer for more than thirty years a school of cultural geography, as is often supposed," Mikesell asks, "or one of biogeography, historical geography, Latin-American geography, or indeed a geography that defies definition?"

Whatever the best description of Sauer's work, as cultural geography reinvented itself in the last two decades of the twentieth century, with British geographers taking a particular lead (see chapter 2), Sauer's legacy has been an important touchstone of reaction. The traditions of cultural geography Sauer initiated have proved exceptionally durable, and new developments in cultural geography continually have had to come to terms with them. In Sauer's work we can trace many of the prominent themes that dominated cultural geography in the twentieth century: a concern with the material landscape; an interest in cultural ecology and the often deleterious effects of humans on the environment; a desire to trace the origins and diffusion of revolutionary cultural practices such as plant and animal domestication and the use of fire. We can also see in Sauer and the work of those in the traditions he instigated an anti-urban, anti-modern bias with which cultural geography is still trying to come to terms (Entrikin 1984).[25] But Sauer's ideas were not born in isolation, emerging Athena-like out of the head of a god. Rather, they were (and are) a part of important intellectual and political contexts, contexts that shaped, if not determined, the development of cultural geography as a coherent field of inquiry.

When Carl Sauer published his methodological broadside, "The Morphology of Landscape" in 1925 – a work that sought to place culture right at the center of geography's project – he did so in large part as a reaction to what he saw as the errors of environmental determinism. He was concerned to correct the course of academic geography at a time when it was struggling to find firm intellectual grounding in the wake of environmental determinism's failure. Sauer's main purpose was to show that environmental determinism had pretty much got it backwards. It wasn't nature that caused culture, but rather culture, working with and on nature, created the contexts of life. Sauer was especially concerned with *material* aspects of culture, particularly the landscape, which he saw as manifestations of culture's traffic with nature. The evidence of this cultural variation, to Sauer, was most clearly right there in the landscape: the landscape was a manifestation of the culture that made it. Reading a landscape, therefore, provided the geographer with a window on particular cultures themselves. Sauer's ideas along these lines were enormously influential,

25   But for an account by a literary critic who declares Sauer thoroughly modern, see Wyatt (1986).

launching a longstanding and still quite vibrant tradition of landscape studies in cultural geography. We will look at this tradition of landscape studies much more fully in chapters 4 and 5, and we will see there and in a number of other places (including later in this chapter) that Sauer's notions launched a quite problematic understanding of what culture *is*. But to understand why it is problematic, we need first to look at the roots of his cultural theory.

As I said above, Sauer drew on much of the same German intellectual tradition as did the environmental determinists. Not much enamored with the Ratzel translated in Semple's environmental determinism, Sauer nonetheless found much to admire in the more ethnological studies Ratzel published in his second volume of *Anthropogeographie*, entitled *The History of Mankind* (1896; see Mathewson 1996: 104). But perhaps more influential, if only indirectly or by "affinity," was the work of Herder, himself a student of the philosopher Immanuel Kant (see Speth 1987). Writing in the last part of the eighteenth-century, Herder's main project was to develop what could be called an "expressivist" critique of the sort of instrumentalism[26] associated with the Enlightenment. That is, Herder sought to contest understandings of the world that highlighted "utilitarian ethics, atomistic politics of social engineering, and ultimately a mechanistic science" of humans (Taylor 1975: 539, quoted in Kahn 1995: 24). Rather than instrumentality and individualism, expressivism is concerned with the search for meanings, and for understanding how individuals are bounded within cultures, within times, and within places. Expressivism thus brought to the fore numerous notions associated with Romanticism, but it also stressed two key ideas: "first, what we might call the meaning of human cultural life and, second, the diversity of human groups..." (Kahn 1995: 28). Hence Herder added the crucial "s" to the end of "culture," providing a clear foundation for cultural relativism.

As Livingstone (1992: 123) argues, however, Herder's recognition of cultural plurality and relativism sprang largely from "his concern to vindicate the legitimacy of his own cultural traditions" – that is, to find support, in the cultural traditions of the "folk" of Germany, a sense of the German cultural self that was even then being expressed in the creation of Germany as a state. Herder's project, according to the historian Simon Schama, was most clearly designed to "root German culture...in its native soil" by arguing "for a culture organically rooted in the topography, customs, and communities of the local native tradition." The authentic roots of any nation "had to be sought in the unapologetically vernacular arts: folklore, ballads, fairy tales, and popular poetry" (Schama 1995: 102–3).[27]

Yet rooting German distinctiveness in an organic relation with the soil *required* Herder to turn to cultural relativism and to search for cultural diversity. For if what

---

26 "Instrumentalism" refers to the desire to establish full technical control over the environment – both "natural" and "cultural." Some see instrumentalism as the defining impulse of modernism. Perhaps more accurately, such instrumentalism should be seen as a species of "heroic" modernism, in which the technical feats of humankind are sufficient justification in and of themselves for their pursuit. For one example of heroic modernism at work – and how it was countered by an equally modernist, but quite different philosophy of science, in a struggle over large-scale environmental transformation – see Kirsch and Mitchell (1998).

27 Gerhard Sandner (1994) has shown that German cultural geographers (like their counterparts elsewhere) were deeply concerned with indigenous pasts as a means of supporting and aiding the German nation- and empire-building projects.

made Germany distinct was both the uniqueness of place and the long cultural history that developed within that place, then so too must other cultures be a product of their relationship with place. Unlike environmentalists, though, Herder traced this distinctiveness not to some environmental factor *itself* but rather to the long history of local interaction *with* environment and *within* locally rooted societies. Hence, for Herder, throughout the world the "understanding of culture was thus to be achieved not by natural laws, or classificatory devices, but by *Einfühlen* (empathy) and therefore with the qualities of the artist rather than the logician or the scientist. Imagination, reconstructive imagination – not analysis – was the key to grasping the life-world of an entire society" (Livingstone 1992: 123).

We see here, then, the roots of what we now would call "multiculturalism." As Livingstone (1992: 124) concludes,

> a profound respect for community, for difference, for locale thus characterized what might be called the Herdian vision, with the result that, as Isaiah Berlin puts it, "all regionalists, all defenders of the local against the universal, all champions of deeply rooted forms of life... owe something, whether they know it or not, to the doctrines which Herder... introduced into European thought."[28]

If that serves as a good description of contemporary multiculturalism, it is also a fair picture of exactly the sorts of concerns that animated Carl Sauer throughout his long career as America's pre-eminent cultural geographer.[29] There is little evidence that Sauer drew directly on Herder for his understandings of cultural particularism, the need for culture history (as both method and object of study), or to understand cultural development and advancement as a process rooted in the autonomous self-development of a people; but there is plenty of evidence that the expressivist tradition instigated by Herder was deeply influential – just as it remains influential in contemporary multiculturalism (see Mathewson 1996: 100; Speth 1987; Sauer 1941).

While Sauer borrowed the idea of a culture area – that is, a region specific to a particular culture – from Ratzel, he also argued that "I don't think one can have a community [that] is a real social organism without cultural particularism" (quoted in Leighly 1978: 121). And at the risk of oversimplification, it is just this sense of cultural particularism that many of those opposed to multiculturalism in the contemporary culture wars find particularly galling. Where Herder found such particularism necessary to support the construction of a firmly grounded German nation,

---

28   Livingstone is also at pains to point out that Herder's vision was quite teleological, that despite his interest in the particular and the variable, he saw history as having direction, as leading toward a particular end. Unlike contemporary postmodernism and multiculturalism, there is little in Herder's ontology that precludes the modern notion of history with an end.

29   And this may begin to explain why there was something of a renaissance of interest in his work *outside* geography during the 1970s and 1980s when several of his works were republished (together with a collection of his essays) by the Turtle Island Foundation, an environmental organization in the San Francisco Bay Area. See Sauer (1975 [1939]; 1976 [1968]; 1980 [1971]; and 1981). Sauer was clearly concerned to explore the link between environmental knowledge and transformation by indigenous peoples, continuing precisely the sort of "expressivist" critique of instrumentalism that Kahn attributes to Herder. The lasting memorial to this critique was the 1955 Princeton conference on "Man's Role in Changing the Face of the Earth," that Sauer was so central in organizing and guiding. The proceedings of this remarkable conference are in Thomas (1956).

and where he saw it as a *universal* means for understanding cultural difference around the globe, contemporary critics of multiculturalism fear that such particularism threatens to swamp the universalist, rationalist ambitions of "Western Culture" as the true beacon of enlightenment in the world. And *that* is a notion Carl Sauer specifically hoped to deny, seeing in rational "Western Culture" instead the seeds of environmental disaster continually sowed by believers in instrumental, technical, rationality (see especially Sauer 1956). A focus on grounded cultural particularity, for Sauer, insured the maintenance of a bulwark against modern, Western hubris.

Yet in Sauer's work the contours of this "culture," this "cultural particularism," this "stay against [the] confusion" of modernity, are hard to ascertain (Wyatt 1986: 209). The ethnographic, "multicultural" sensibility is clear enough in both his methodological statements and in his empirical research, as is his concern to vanquish ethnocentrism from geography by replacing it with a developed empathy for the peoples and places of the world. Far less clear is what, for Sauer, actually constitutes "culture" beyond some vague sense of historically, geographically derived "difference." Culture seems to him a "whole" – simply an unproblematic "way of life" of a people.[30] Or perhaps, in a formula we will examine in more detail in a moment, culture is something larger and greater than the people who compose it. It is, in this sense, "superorganic," as it both is larger than life and has a life of its own. And as "superorganic," it is determining in the lives of the people who are part of it.[31] It is "culture" rather than "nature" that determines social life, for Sauer, but the exact nature of that culture remains a mystery (and, as it turns out, quite an important mystery for the development of cultural geography as a subdiscipline right up to the present time). To understand why "culture" remained so undertheorized in geography – especially since a theory of culture would seem so essential to Sauer's anti-ethnocentric project – we need to turn for a moment to more direct influences on Sauer's thinking than that provided by Herder.

If the non-ethnocentric "Herdian vision" flourished most fully and was most influential in the consolidating fields of anthropology and geography in the time between the world wars (as Joel Kahn [1995] among others argues), if, that is, that was the *Zeitgeist* within which Sauer was working as he formulated his geography-cum-culture history, then it is also the case that the more direct influences on Sauer's developing ideas about the relationship between culture and landscape were themselves part of this same *Zeitgeist*. Chief among these influences was the work of the "founding figure of American anthropology," Franz Boas (Mathewson 1996: 104). Boas had cut his teeth in the 1890s by vigorously "attacking the theories of leading 'social Darwinists'" (Kahn 1995: 117),[32] just as Sauer sought similarly to undermine

---

30 For a brief discussion of Sauer's changing ideas about the meaning of "culture" see Leighly (1976), 339–40.

31 The degree to which Sauer espoused a superorganic notion of culture is contested by cultural geographers and historians of geography. This is an important debate (especially since the contours of it say a lot about contemporary culture wars) and we will explore it fully below. Whether Sauer was a dyed-in-the-wool superorganicist or not, it is incontrovertible that one of his most influential students, Wilbur Zelinsky, was. See especially Zelinsky (1973); see also Duncan (1980).

32 By the mid-1920s, precisely the time Sauer was formulating his culture-history, anti-ethnocentric approach to human geography, Boas was making his anti-racist cultural theories public, publishing in such outlets as the left-leaning weekly *The Nation* and in the popularizing *Current History*.

Social Darwinism through his own methodological pronouncements three decades later. In addition to thoroughly eschewing the racist implications of determinism, Boas sought to explore the *particular* ways in which the natural and social environment both conditioned and was conditioned by cultural interaction in a bounded society. More explicitly Boas argued that to understand other cultures, the scholar had to take care to eliminate her or his *own* cultural values: "...it seems to me necessary to eliminate the peculiar combination of the development of cultural forms and the intrusion of the idea of our estimate of their value, which has nothing to do with these forms," Boas wrote to the arch-environmental determinist Ellsworth Huntington (quoted in Livingstone 1992: 226).[33] Boas thus imbibed what Livingstone (1992: 294) calls a "mild cultural relativism that insisted that cultures could only be understood in their own terms and therefore that ranking on a hierarchical scale was impossible."

Two of Boas's most prominent students were Alfred Kroeber (1876–1960) and Robert Lowie (1883–1957), both of whom, as members of the anthropology faculty at the University of California, seem to have had a direct influence on Carl Sauer's thinking about cultural particularism and relativism.[34] Kroeber's affinity to Sauer is perhaps clearest in the former's interest in the development and distribution of "culture areas," which he defined as geographical regions sharing particular distributions of culture traits (cf. Kroeber 1904). But it is also clear in his desire to understand culture holistically; that is, like Sauer, Kroeber was keen to explore the ways that particular associations of culture traits not only mapped what was distinctive about a particular people, but also how those traits interacted to map a total way of life, whether of a tribe of California Indians, or the first peoples to domesticate plants. Kroeber (1936: 1) put it this way: "The concept of a culture area is a means to an end. The end may be the understanding of culture processes as such, or of the historic events of cultures." A few years later, Sauer (1952: 1) echoed these words precisely: a geographer "is interested in discovering related and different patterns of living as they are found over the world – culture areas. These patterns have interest and meaning as we learn how they came into being. The geographer, therefore, properly is engaged in charting the distributions over the earth of the arts and artifacts of man, to learn whence they came and how they spread, what their contexts are in cultural and physical environments."

Robert Lowie (1947: 434) focused much of his work on understanding the importance of diffusion to cultural development and change, arguing that while diffusion "creat[ed] nothing" itself, it "nevertheless makes all other agencies taper almost into

33 Clearly this is a sentiment that would appall the current crop of cultural conservatives who strive so diligently to always array other cultural values against their own (presumably superior) values.
34 There are those in geography, concerned to protect Sauer's reputation as a solitary and fully original genius (as if there could be such a thing), who seek to deny the influence of anthropologists such as Kroeber (see Kenzer 1987). Yet Sauer (1925) made direct reference to Kroeber in his important "Morphology of Landscape," precisely to demolish environmental determinism and elevate the importance of cultural particularism. In his obituary of Sauer, John Leighly (1976: 338–40), who moved to Berkeley from Michigan to continue studying with him, makes it clear that Sauer "quickly established cordial relations with [Kroeber and Lowie], especially with Kroeber." For a hint at the range of interaction between Sauer and Kroeber, see the correspondence excerpted as part of Macpherson (1987); see also Livingstone (1992), 296–7, note 135.

nothingness beside it in its effect on the total growth of human civilization." But beyond this Sauer's affinity for Lowie probably resided in their shared skepticism about the nature of "progress." Sauer saw little in modern industrial society of long-term worth, even arguing a few years after World War II that "our whole western civilization in its modern form . . . is a violation of natural order which will bring about its collapse" (quoted in Martin 1987: xv). For Sauer, the evolution of modern society had ripped civilization from its roots in the natural world. Similarly, Lowie argued that cultural evolution was not necessarily "progressive." As one biographer summarizes, Lowie argued that "particular races, languages, or cultures may either level off, retrogress or become extinct. . . . Lowie also denied the inevitability of moral progress" (Driver 1972: 482). Cultural particularity, Boas's incipient multicultural-ism, thus served to stave off hubris, and to return anthropologists and geographers alike to the study of differences, rather than hierarchies.

If cultural anthropology provided a touchstone for Sauer's ideas of cultural parti-cularity, it was a more directly geographical tradition that allowed him to show that the relationship between culture and environment was far more complex than envir-onmental determinism had ever allowed. Sauer coupled his readings in American anthropology with German theories of *Landschaft* (variously translated as landscape or landscape science) associated with Passarge, "chorology" (the science of regions) associated with Richthoften, and studies of how natural landscapes are transformed into cultural ones, associated with Hettner, to "conceive of geography as cultural history in its regional articulation" (Livingstone 1992: 297). This was a thoroughly original program for American geography, and in it geographers have rightly seen the birth of a particular *kind* of cultural geography. It is a geography that was historical, that took cultural relativism as its starting point, and that was interested most particularly in the ways that human cultures transformed the natural world to create cultural landscapes or cultural regions (see especially Sauer 1941, 1974).

The morphology of landscape

This, then, was the context within which Sauer's remarkable essay "The Morphology of Landscape" was written – and to which, over time, it contributed. The essay itself is a dense, scholarly definition of what geography could and should be. Dismissing the ruins of American environmental determinism as "divine law transposed into natural law" and a "rigorous dogma of materialistic cosmology," and declaring that "causal geography had its day," Sauer drew the attention of American geographers instead to a European renaissance of what he called "our permanent task" – "the classical tradition of geography as chorological relation" (Sauer 1925, in Leighly 1963: 320). His goal was to re-establish geography as a respectable science – a task all the more important because no other discipline had claimed for itself the "section of reality" that comprised geography. That "section of reality" – one that he asserted was "naively given" by the very nature of the world – was the "landscape" (1963: 316–17). Sauer therefore argued that "the task of geography" was to establish "a critical system which embraces the phenomenology of landscape in order to grasp in all of its meaning and color the varied terrestrial scene" (1963:

320).[35] Sauer used the term "landscape" to "denote the unit concept of geography, to characterize the peculiarly geographic association of facts," and suggested that "equivalent terms" for landscape might be " 'area' and 'region.' " Sauer's use of the term "characterize" should not be misinterpreted. Unlike many at the time (and especially later), Sauer did not argue that the goal of geography should be merely to *describe* "geographical associations of facts," as important as that job clearly was. Rather, in "The Morphology of Landscape," Sauer developed a sophisticated methodology to also characterize how those associations of facts came to be.

The first step of the methodology was, indeed, areal description. Sauer was at pains to make clear that such description was meant to be *generic*; that is, "the geographic landscape is a generalization derived from the observation of individual scenes" (1963: 322). The means to this end, for Sauer, was to develop a "predetermined descriptive system." The first step in this system was to make an elementary distinction between the natural and cultural landscape. The natural landscape existed as fully natural only "before the introduction of man's activities" in a particular area, yet it was still useful for studies of the contemporary scene to make this distinction because then different *processes* – natural and cultural – could be abstracted out to see both how they worked independently and how they worked in tandem. Any natural scene, Sauer averred, begins as a set of factors: "geognostic" (the underlying geology), climatic, vegetational, and so on. Over time these factors interact with each other to create the specific landscape forms (climate, geomorphic features, soil, specific associations of vegetation, etc.) that comprise the morphology – the shape and structure – of the natural landscape itself (1963: 333–41).

Such description of natural landscapes (including the description of the processes at work over time that give shape and structure to them) was, according to Sauer, merely preliminary: the real task for geographers was to see how this natural landscape was both the stage for, and the prime ingredient in, human geographic activity. "The natural landscape is being subject to transformation at the hands of man, the last and for us [geographers] the most important morphological factor. By his culture he makes use of the natural forms, in many cases alters them, in some destroys them" (1963: 341). Sauer is clear on the importance of the "agency of man on earth" (as he put it in a later landmark essay). "The cultural landscape is fashioned from a natural landscape by a culture group," Sauer writes. "Culture is the agent, the natural area is the medium, the cultural landscape the result. . . . The natural landscape is of course of fundamental importance, for it supplies the materials out of which the cultural landscape is formed. The shaping force, however, lies in the culture itself" (1963: 343) (figure 1.4). With this statement – quite bold for its time in American geography – Sauer forcefully reverses environmental determinism: the forms of the cultural landscape – that which a culture group fashions out of and imposes upon the natural landscape – "are derived from the mind of man, not imposed by nature, and hence are cultural expressions" (1963: 343). The cultural landscape is therefore an *effect* and

35 "Phenomenology" has two primary meanings. In the sense in which Sauer uses it here, it means the science of phenomena – that which can be perceived as objects, occurrences, or facts. The second meaning refers to the philosophical movement of phenomenology, which focuses on detailed descriptions of conscious experience. This movement was influential in the development of humanistic cultural geography in the late 1970s and early 1980s.

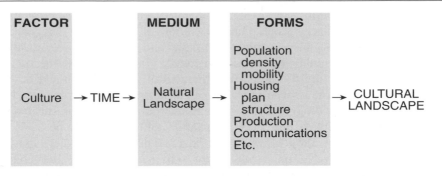

Figure 1.4 Carl Sauer's schematic representation of the morphology of landscape. Note that in contrast to environmental determinism, "culture" becomes the primary agent of change, and the results of that change – the "cultural landscape" – is what is to be explained.

culture (working in, with, and against nature) is a – if not *the* – cause of what we see in any scene upon which we look. From a base in description, in other words, Sauer developed a powerful methodology for understanding the *processes* through which landscapes developed.

Over time, the cultural landscape becomes incredibly complex: with each "introduction of a different – that is alien – culture" in an area, a "rejuvenation of the cultural landscape sets in, or a new landscape is superimposed on remnants of an older one" (1963: 343). The accreted layers of the cultural landscape could therefore be peeled back by an attentive geographer to determine exactly "cultural history in its regional articulation." Specifically, Sauer and his numerous students (and countless others influenced by his ideas) developed the methodology laid down in "The Morphology of Landscape" to show how cultural development and transformation (including conquest of indigenous peoples by imperial powers) constantly created and recreated the places and landscapes in which people lived. This was (and remains) an immensely exciting project, and for Sauer it was one of increasing urgency as the twentieth century wore on and the degree to which the ability of humans to transform the earth – with bulldozers, chainsaws, bombs, and nascent biotechnology – seemed to steadily increase.

Sauer's own political commitments, however, were not necessarily adopted by all who followed in his footsteps. If Sauer's "Morphology" directed geographers to a more subtle notion of causality than that espoused by environmental determinism – a notion that sought to understand how people lived *in* place and thus shaped it, rather than vice versa – and if it also directed attention to the agency of human cultures, it also reasserted a renewed importance for descriptive studies. After all, one of the purposes of studying the landscape was to determine just what the evidence of "culture" was. Sauer himself suggested that geographers needed to concern themselves with the description of the cultural forms that comprised the landscape. "There is a strictly geographic way of thinking of culture," Sauer argued; "namely, as the impress of the works of man upon the area." Hence, particular attention was to be paid to such material artifacts – the evidence of the impress of the works of man – as building materials and types, forms of production and communication, and the arrangement of the population (dispersed, concentrated, etc.). The fifty years after

"Morphology" was published, therefore, saw a torrent of studies of just these things by cultural geographers – the origin and diffusion of house and barn types or vernacular production systems, and the study of the layers upon layers of material artifacts in particular places, for example – studies that often did little to address the degree or nature of human environmental transformation. Indeed, such studies increasingly became divorced from the cultural ecology that Sauer himself more and more turned towards in the later years of his life. Cultural ecology, in fact, flourished as a largely separate field from what came to be known, in the post-World War II years as American cultural geography. Sauer therefore needs to be recognized as important founder of not one, but two geographical subdisciplines: cultural ecology and cultural geography. That is why it is hard to overestimate Sauer's influence on geography. Statements such as this one, therefore, are hardly rare: "At his death [in 1975] the American people as a whole lost one of the most articulate scholars this century has yet to produce" (Callahan 1981: xv).

Superorganicism and Its Discontents

Yet, for all that is valuable (and there is a lot) in Sauerian cultural geography,[36] in hindsight there seems to be something missing. Sauer's interests were diverse, and they were guided by a keen sense of the importance of cultural values in shaping the face of the earth (for better or for worse). But, as we have seen, Sauer was largely concerned with *effects*, with the *shape* rather than the *shaping* of the earth. That is, he (and even more so many of his students) saw geography's concern not to be with "the inner workings of culture" (as two of Sauer's students famously put it [Wagner and Mikesell 1962]), but with the *outcome* of culture as it worked on the world. The "permanent task" of geographers, after all, was developing a "phenomenology" of landscape, with the way that "culture" went to work on nature so as to produce a cultural landscape, rather than with theorizing culture itself. Hence "culture" was radically undertheorized in Sauer's own work (and that of many of his students and acolytes); it was the taken-for-granted of human life. For Sauer, "culture" probably accorded with the anthropological sense of a "total way of life," but none of the sorts of nuanced understanding of the role of conflict in this "way of life" apparent in the works of, for example, Raymond Williams (see chapter 2), is apparent in Sauer's work – or for that matter in American cultural geography as a whole at least until the late 1970s (see Williams 1958, 1961, 1982).

Wilbur Zelinsky and superorganicism

This is not to say that theories of culture were entirely ignored by American cultural geographers. Indeed one of Sauer's own students, Wilbur Zelinsky, took great pains

---

36 The development of contemporary cultural geography has been most directly influenced by the cultural geographic tradition Sauer established; cultural ecology has been less important (though by no means absent) as an influence in "new cultural geography." For that reason I concentrate more on cultural geography than cultural ecology in this and the next chapter.

to theorize culture as "superorganic" in his influential *Cultural Geography of the United States* (1973). And, as one survey of the discipline has commented, most American cultural geographers implicitly deployed similar assumptions of superorganicism in their work and seemed quite content to do so (Rowntree et al. 1989). "Superorganicism" refers to the belief in a force larger than and relatively independent of the lives of humans themselves. "Superorganic culture" therefore refers to the ontological assumption that culture is a real force that exists "above" and independent of human will or intention. "Obviously, a culture cannot exist without bodies and minds to flesh it out," Zelinsky (1973: 40–1, original emphasis) wrote; "but culture is also something both of *and beyond* the participating members. Its totality is palpably greater than the sum of its parts, for it is superorganic and supraindividual in nature, an entity with a structure, set of processes, and momentum of its own, though clearly not untouched by historical events and socio-economic conditions."

He did not shy away from the implications of theorizing culture as superorganic, arguing at one point (1973: 70–1) that

> the power wielded over the minds of its participants by a cultural system is hard to exaggerate. No denial of free will is implied, nor is the scope for individual achievement or resourcefulness belittled. It is simply that we are all players in a great profusion of games and that in each cultural arena the entire team, knowingly or not, follows the local set of rules, at most bending them slightly. Only a half-wit or a fool would openly flout them. But as in chess, the possibilities for creativity and modulation are virtually infinite.

Writing in the early 1970s, Zelinsky was reflecting the progressive, liberal hopes of his generation of American scholars.[37] So by conceptualizing culture thus, Zelinsky (1973: 38) was able to proclaim, as regards the United States, that:

1   useful nonstereotypic statements can be made about the cultural idiosyncrasies (that is, national character) of an ethnic group taken as a whole;
2   the population of the United States does indeed form a single large, discrete ethnic group;
3   statements about the character of the larger community cannot be, indeed should not be, transferred to individuals because of sharp discontinuities of scale.

But consider the context within which this statement was published. The year 1973 saw the full flowering of the Watergate scandal, which threatened the political unity of the country. The previous years had seen growing, and increasingly violent, dissent over the USA war against Vietnam, culminating in the National Guard murder of

---

37   Zelinsky is a remarkable person. He was the first member of the Union of Socialist Geographers to be elected president of the Association of American Geographers, the major organization of academic geographers in the US. He used his presidential address (published in 1975) to attack "scientism" in geography, thereby prying open the door for the full entrance of humanistic modes of knowing. Yet the opening pages of *Cultural Geography*, published almost concurrently, are a stirring call for a more scientific approach to culture. An ardent assimilationist, in academia and in the United States, Zelinsky was an early advocate for greater inclusion of women in the discipline; yet he has shown himself reluctant to accept the changes in research focus women have brought with them (see Zelinsky 1987). In some senses, this latter position is not contradictory. Assimilationism, after all, implies assimilation *to* a larger, hegemonic whole, and thereby little disruption to "business as usual."

four students at Kent State University in 1971. In Berkeley (where Zelinsky did his PhD in the early 1950s), a militant "Third World" student strike had kept National Guard soldiers on campus throughout the 1968–9 school year, and it, coupled with thel bloody confrontation over People's Park in May, 1969, had propelled Ronald Reagan (then governor of California) to national political prominence. Concurrently, in a number of cities around the USA, militant Black Panther organizations had been set up to make good on Malcolm X's promise that African American equality would be achieved "by any means necessary." And throughout the summers of 1967 and 1968, city after city witnessed severe rioting in African American ghettos as blacks saw gains made during a decade of civil rights protest increasingly threatened by a militant white backlash. In California, and throughout the Southwest, Chicano activists were creating their own militant movements to throw off more than a century of oppression at the hands of a political-economic system dominated by Anglo-Americans. During the same period, the women's movement reinvigorated itself, militantly developing a new brand of feminism that explicitly sought to challenge the patriarchal structure of contemporary society. These years too saw the development of the American Indian Movement and the confrontations it engendered on Alcatraz Island in San Francisco Bay and at Pine Ridge and Wounded Knee, South Dakota (figure 1.5). And they saw the rise of a quite distinctive Asian American civil rights movement. Couple all that with a rapid increase in the numbers

Figure 1.5 Wilbur Zelinsky was celebrating the unity of American culture in his book *The Cultural Geography of the United States*, right at a moment of peak political and cultural dissent. From the Civil Rights Movement and urban riots of the 1960s to the anti-war, women's, and American Indian movements of the early 1970s, the United States was marked by violent struggle over·questions of social inclusion, citizenship, and justice. Here, American Indian activists affiliated with the American Indian Movement stand guard at the Sacred Heart Catholic Church after occupying the reservation town of Wounded Knee, South Dakota, in March 1973. Photograph courtesy of UPI/Corbis; used by permission.

of foreign nationals immigrating to the United States, the wars of independence heating up throughout Africa and Asia, continued USA adventurism in the countries of Latin America, and the beginnings of the end of the USA global economic and political dominance that had marked the postwar years, and a simple sense of American insular unity seemed a particularly perverse notion to more and more people.

So in this regard, Zelinsky's *Cultural Geography of the United States* is a clear intervention into the "culture wars" (and the Cold War!) of his time – unabashedly reasserting the essential *unity* and exceptional *peculiarity* of the United States, seeking to show that commonalities between the peoples of the country were greater than the differences prominent at the moment, and that despite the globalization of politics and economics, the United States remained culturally unique (even as it exported its own cultural products and imported many others). But there is a difference between Zelinsky's intervention and the sorts of cultural wars that mark the current scene: Zelinsky's was a self-consciously *liberal* plea, that sought to find room for all under the common tent of America. His last lines in the book make this abundantly clear:

> We live in a period of rapid structural change in terms of ongoing cultural processes in the United States and of penetrating the most fundamental questions concerning human thought and behavior, as they are constrained within the cultural matrix. We can also anticipate a period of almost revolutionary insights that will vastly enrich our understanding of what we have been, who we are now, the most likely forms for future cultural dealings among people, places, and things, and even how they can be manipulated so as to give ourselves a fighting chance for survival and salvation. (Zelinsky 1973: 140)

Most simply, Zelinsky (1973: 70) asserts that in "its ultimate, most essential sense, culture is an image of the world, of oneself and one's community"; and *Zelinsky*'s image is that of an essential unity that is more important than all the factious differences that might separate us. He stakes a lot on this claim, for it is precisely this essential unity that will lead to salvation and survival.

The mechanisms that make culture "work" are quite complex for Zelinsky, since it is a "thing" greater than the sum of its parts. It will not do, Zelinsky warns, to either read up from individual to culture, nor to read down from culture to individual. Individual behavior cannot predict cultural structure any more than cultural processes can predict individual behavior. Culture is thus theorized *first* as "an assemblage of learned behavior"; *second* (and more importantly) as a "structured, traditional set of patterns for behavior, a code or template for ideas and acts"; and *third* (and most importantly) as a "totality" that "appears to be a superorganic entity living and changing according to a still obscure set of internal laws" (Zelinsky 1973: 71–2). The focus of cultural geography, then, should be on the study of how culture *itself* works itself out across space and in place.[38] Subcultures can be recognized in the

---

38   For Zelinsky (1973: 71–2), this sense of culture was entirely idealist: "The nation-state idea is perhaps the neatest illustration of the transpersonal character of cultural systems.... Whatever the genesis of the idea [in the case of the USA], it was certainly not the conscious fabrication of any identifiable cabal of nation-builders, but rather a spontaneous surge of feeling that quickly acquired a force and momentum of its own....Individuals who entertain the nation-state idea are born and die, and some may even have

landscape (or in other artifacts of culture), but we need to understand, according to Zelinsky, how they are related to the autonomous (but still changeable) *whole* of American culture. And it is precisely in this effort that geographers can make an important contribution. Zelinsky's project, then, turns out to be a cultural geography determined to support and maintain cultural unity in the face of the factiousness that defines the modern world (for in that unity lies our salvation). In this regard, Zelinsky's geographical theory of culture, seeking to posit the essential unity of humans that remains despite and because of all the cultural differences that mark them, is firmly in the Boasian camp. As with Boas, the definition of culture Zelinsky develops is as much a reflection of his political goals and ambitions as it is a faithful description of reality. And that term "faithful" is apt, for reading Zelinsky more than 25 years after his book was published, the cultural theory reads, especially in the light of his own contemporary history and all that has happened since, like an incredible (and in many ways admirable) act of faith. But it is also obvious that such a grand, assimilationist theory provided very few tools for understanding the volatile world within which Zelinsky was writing. In this regard it seems to depart in some ways from the Boasian ideal of cultural relativism, and accord much more strongly with the sort of relativism Herder advocated as a program of nation building.

Think back to the controversy of Barbara Revelle's mural with which I opened this chapter. Many of those whom Revelle pictured in her celebration of what *she* understood American culture to be were precisely those who were willing to go against the grain of the dominant and domineering trends of their times, seeking exactly to "flout the rules of the game." Zelinsky, seemingly, would declare such efforts to be the efforts of "half-wits" and "fools." [39] Zelinsky's equation of "culture" with the level of the nation is telling in this regard. If "useful, non-stereotypic statements" can be made about "national character" in the way that Zelinsky suggests, then French nationalist attempts to rid France of Algerians or Moroccans are seemingly excused: how can they possibly be part of the culture of France, without surrendering all that is part of their *own* (separate) traditions?

The critique of superorganicism and the birth of "new cultural geography"

Given these concerns, it is not surprising, then, that not all cultural geographers were ready to follow Zelinsky's faith, instead finding in his theories of culture all manner of

doubts or reservations; but the idea marches on, quite clearly beyond the control of anyone...." "Idealism" refers to the theoretical approach to human affairs that claims that *ideas* (rather than practices, historical events, etc.) are the driving force of society. Guelke (1974) has defined idealism in geography as the effort "to understand the development of the earth's cultural landscape by uncovering the thought that lies behind cultural landscapes." This definition is obviously consonant with Zelinsky's project. The issue of idealism, and its counterpart "materialism," has become central to debates in geography over the importance and usefulness of the idea of culture, as we will see in the next two chapters.

39   To be fair, Zelinsky has been staunch in his support of the rights of minority groups in the United States, arguing they are essential to the mosaic that makes up the culture. The sorts of issues, I am raising, I think, Zelinsky would relegate to the level of politics, not culture. But that is precisely the problem: culture and politics simply cannot be divorced, and efforts to do so merely play into the hands of those who would use "culture" to exclude rather than include.

problematic statements about both what culture was and how it worked in the social world. In fact, the explicit and implicit adoption of superorganicism by those working in the Sauerian tradition served as a key target for those who wanted to invent a more nuanced, more sociological sense of culture to help them understand the conflictual world of which they were part. At the very least, and most importantly, they wanted a theory of culture that incorporated theories of *power*, for without these, they felt there would be little means for understanding how cultural geographies were *really* made in the everyday struggles of life. Chief among the critics of cultural geography's superorganicism was James Duncan, who in 1980 published a striking attack on superorganicism in cultural geography.[40] Duncan's point was relatively simple: cultural geographers implicitly and explicitly had adopted superorganic notions of culture; superorganicism wrongly *reified* culture as a thing rather than a process;[41] and such reification made it impossible to understand the sociological and psychological components of culture. In short, Duncan (1980: 194–6) argued that superorganicism erased the role of individuals in society, reducing them to mere automatons acting out the dictates of a mysterious, independent larger-than-life force called culture. Moreover, superorganic culture implied that people were "conditioned" into certain habitual responses, and thus acted like Pavlov's dogs, largely devoid of control over their own behaviors.

Duncan (1980: 197) argued that the "term culture could be saved if it were not treated as an explanatory variable in itself but used to signify contexts for action or sets of arrangements between people at various levels of aggregation." Or more simply, "That which has been termed 'culture' can be reduced to the interaction between people." He was proposing, then, a more sociological definition for culture that would take as its focus the "many problematic social, political, and economic relationships" that govern our lives (Duncan 1980: 198). If this seems to leave no room for "culture" as a level of analysis somehow different from "society," "politics," or the "economy," that was part of the point: Duncan was concerned to collapse those distinctions so as to better understand how culture was constructed and how it worked in society. But such a sense of collapse is only sustainable if we ignore the sorts of theoretical developments around "culture" that were happening elsewhere – in British cultural studies, most particularly, beginning as early as the 1950s and making their way into geography at just about the same time Duncan was writing his broadside against American superorganicism. We turn to these developments in chapter 2.

Conclusion: The Irrelevancy of Cultural Geography

If Duncan's attack on cultural geography made one direct hit at the intellectual core of the subdiscipline, showing that its central (if often unacknowledged) theoretical

---

40   Duncan (1980) generated a great deal of controversy. Two responses (Richardson 1981; Symanski 1981) were quickly published in the *Annals*, and in the years since defenders of traditional American cultural geography have vacillated between denying they implicitly adopt superorganicism and admitting that they do, but seeing nothing wrong with it (see Rowntree et al. 1989; Price and Lewis 1993).

41   To "reify" means to take a mental construct and imbue it with an "independent existence and causal efficacy"; Duncan (1980), 181; citing Berger and Pullberg (1964–5).

base was deeply flawed, then a second hit came from a cohort of young geographers, many of them British, interested in questions of culture. To them, much of American cultural geography was simply irrelevant, focusing on the evidence of cultural transformation of the landscape, and therefore (as they saw it) on such esoterica as barn types in Pennsylvania, the diffusion of housetypes across the continent, and the intricate evolution and distribution of particular types of blowguns among native populations of South America. All of these seemed to a new generation of geographers as little more than examples of how monolithic, unexamined cultures flowed across the landscape. As Peter Jackson (1989: 19) put it, American cultural geography's reliance on superorganicism – or more accurately, its unwillingness to think hard about the "inner workings of culture" – led to "an almost obsessional interest in the physical or material elements of culture rather than its more obviously social dimensions. This focus on culture-as-artifact has led to voluminous literature on the geographical distribution of particular culture traits from log buildings to graveyards, barn styles to gasoline stations." Moreover, Sauer's interest in cultural origins coupled with distrust of technological modernism, had led several generations of American cultural geographers to focus nearly exclusively on the rural, the archaic, the "primitive," and the local, at the expense of large-scale processes, urban areas and events, and the forces of modern life. As American (and British) cities burned in the wake of race riots, the collapse of the manufacturing economy, and fiscal crisis upon fiscal crisis, American cultural geographers were content to fiddle with the geography of fenceposts and log cabins – or so the critique launched by the "new cultural geography" at the end of the 1970s claimed.

Throughout the discipline of geography from the mid-1960s on, calls for greater "relevancy" were increasingly common. Geographers dissatisfied with the prevailing regionalism of the pre- and post-World War II years experimented first with a version of scientism that came to be known as the "quantitative revolution," in which the laws governing geographical behavior were supposedly to be divined. But as the unrest of the 1960s progressed, more and more geographers turned from that model too, seeing it as hopelessly technocratic at best, and asking precisely the wrong questions at worst. David Harvey, the codifier of much of the "quantitative revolution" in his impressive *Explanation in Geography* in 1969, had by 1973 begun exploring the importance of Marxist approaches for understanding the geographies of inequality and social justice (Harvey 1969, 1973; for an excellent account, see Peet 1998). In the wake of a renewed public interest in environmental and ecological problems, questions of nature were put back on the geographical agenda (in an often quite radical way) (Smith 1990; see also Olwig 1996a). And still other geographers, reacting in part to the level of abstraction that drove the law-finding quantitative revolution and what they saw as a too strong focus on the social structures of society in Marxism, experimented with various philosophies of humanism to get a handle on the ways in which individuals lived in the world (for reviews see Bunske 1996; Peet 1998; good examples of humanistic geography are Ley and Samuels 1978; Buttimer 1993).

The 1970s and 1980s were times of exceptional ferment in geography, reflecting the sorts of social unrest and experimentation that marked the end of the long postwar economic boom and the period of quiescence (or stalemate) that seemed to define the middle years of the Cold War. It is not surprising, then, that cultural geography would be (to some rather rudely) yanked out of its backwater, and placed front and center in theoretical developments in geography. Superorganicism would not do. Nor could cultural geography remain overwhelmingly focused on the rural, the archaic, and the esoteric. What geographers like Duncan and Jackson were demanding was just the sort of political "relevance" that was sweeping other aspects of geography. And there was a very simple reason for their demand – they knew that culture was just too important a concept to leave languishing, precisely *because*, they argued, culture *is* politics. The culture wars then heating up throughout the world, whether the seemingly insignificant – like a fight over who makes a key for a public mural – or the profound – such as what the status of minority groups should be within newly independent states and as part of a global diaspora that seemed to be unsettling the very idea of the nation-state (see chapter 10) – were simply too important to be ignored in favor of what many young geographers regarded as cloistered academic trivia. Cultural geography as it entered the 1980s was ill-equipped to deal with the controversies stirred up by events as varied as a dispute over how Colorado history should be represented, the rise of a new racism in France, or the erasure of working-class lives and history from a city trying to reinvent itself in the image of "culture." It also seemingly had nothing to say about the rise of a new wave of feminism, the continued globalization of capital, the increased importance of the politics of sexuality, or even, more broadly, about the way politics itself was becoming ever more "cultural." In short, the world changed in the 1960s and 1970s. And cultural geography needed to change with it. It is to these changes that we now turn.

2

Cultural Studies and the New Cultural Geography

The Relevancy of Cultural Geography

The global transformation that has become so obvious since the late 1960s was not sudden, but was the result of many converging forces: structural economic change at global and local scales; struggles for independence in the colonial world with the resultant decline of old empires; the Cold War struggle for a new kind of political and economic imperialism; the subsequent erosion of American hegemonic power, perhaps best illustrated by the American defeat in Vietnam; the rise of OPEC as an economic and political force on the world stage; the upsurge of activist, often identity-based politics in the core countries (feminism, gay rights, civil rights, etc.); new patterns of international and regional migration that saw increasing numbers of postcolonial peoples moving to core metropolises such as London, Paris, and New York; the globalization of media and commodities; the budding realization of the ecological costs of business-as-usual in both developed and developing countries; and, with these, a growing sense on the part of many, particularly in the developed world, that old ways of building and understanding worlds – the sleek visions of modern rationalism evidenced in international architecture (figure 2.1), scientific reasoning, and the celebration of the technological sublime – were simply inappropriate for the world as it now operated.

Consider, for example, the differences in sensibility implied on the one hand by Donald Fagen's nostalgic (and slightly ironic) remembrance of being a teenager

Figure 2.1 Internationalist, modernist architecture represents a sleek vision of a future organized around principles of efficiency, universal reason, and the power of technology. Architecture such as this – in this case in San Diego, California – represents for some an outmoded cultural vision, one that says more about technocratic domination than about the possibilities of a limitless future. Photograph by Susan Millar, used by permission.

looking into the future at the end of the 1950s in his 1981 song "IGY," and on the other by the Sex Pistols' 1977 anthem to youth disenfranchisement in their punk classic "God Save the Queen." Fagen, in the voice of a male American teen, sings of a bright, boundless future:

> Standing tough under the stars and stripes
> We can tell
> This dream's in sight
> You've got to admit it
> . . .
> The future looks bright
> On that train all graphite and glitter
> Undersea by rail

Ninety minutes from New York to Paris
Well by seventy-six we'll be A.O.K.
...

Here at home we'll play in the city
Powered by the sun
Perfect weather for a streamlined world
There'll be spandex jackets one for everyone
...

A just machine to make big decisions
Programmed by fellows with compassion and vision
We'll be clean when their work is done
We'll be eternally free yes and eternally young.   (Fagen 1981)

Such a vision of a gleaming future – the scientific, technological modernism of the early Cold War at its most appealing – had all but vanished by "seventy-six." Things were not at all A.O.K.

Better than any other band of the time, the Sex Pistols captured both the disillusionment of young Brits and Americans *and* the cynical commercial culture beginning to blossom (see chapters 3 and 6 below). The Sex Pistols' vision of the future could not have been more different from Donald Fagen's reconstruction of the 1950s:

God save the Queen
The fascist regime,
They made you a moron
A potential H-bomb.

God save the Queen
She ain't no human being.
There is no future
In England's dreaming

Don't be told what you want
Don't be told what you need.
There's no future
There's no future
There's no future for you
...

Oh God save history
God save your mad parade
Oh Lord God have mercy
All crimes are paid.

When there's no future
How can there be sin
We're the flowers
In the dustbin
We're the poison
In your human machine

We're the future
Your future.   (Sex Pistols 1977)[1]

How can one begin to understand the massive changes – in society, in the economy, in the vision of what the world is like – encapsulated by these two songs? How did we get from the dream of supersonic train rides, space colonies, and spandex jackets for everyone to a world of "no future" in which people's best hope is to be the "poison in your human machine"?

In a style perhaps less compelling than either Donald Fagen or Johnny Rotten, David Harvey (1989a: vii) has famously argued the case this way: "There has been a sea-change in cultural as well as in political-economic practices since around 1972. This sea-change is bound up with the emergence of new dominant ways in which we experience space and time." Harvey claimed that this cultural sea-change was inextricably connected to (if not entirely determined by) structural changes in the global economic system, and in this he is correct. But even so, cultural change seems to be a phenomenon experienced in and of itself; the unsettling of the world through political-economic change is often experienced as an unsettling of cultural verities. It is experienced as a war not just on capitalist *value*, but on social and cultural *values*. This is not new. One hundred and fifty years ago Karl Marx and Friedrich Engels (1998 [1848]: 38) succinctly summarized in the *Communist Manifesto* what we now call time-space compression:

> Constant revolutionizing of production, uninterrupted disturbances of all social conditions, everlasting uncertainty and agitation distinguish the bourgeois epoch from all earlier ones. All fixed, fast-frozen relations with their train of ancient and venerable prejudices and opinions, are swept away, all new-formed ones become antiquated before they can ossify. All that is solid melts into air, all that is holy is profaned. . . .

The sea-changes of the last part of the twentieth century are but a more recent manifestation of the revolutionizing imperative of capitalism which Marx and Engels so well described. The changes that rock the world through the "constant revolutionizing of production [and] uninterrupted disturbances of all social conditions" clearly get worked out, as Marx and Engels's language makes clear, in both constant political struggle,[2] and in the culture wars of which the political and religious Right is so fond.

---

1   "God Save the Queen" caused a panic in Britain: "Patriotic workers refused to handle [it] . . .; A & M, the band's second label, destroyed what few copies were produced. Finally released on Virgin, the Sex Pistols' third label, 'God Save the Queen,' was erased from the BBC charts and topped the hit parade as a blank, thus creating the bizarre situation in which the nation's most popular record was turned into contraband" (Marcus 1989: 10). As will be discussed more fully in chapter 6, the Sex Pistols were very much a product of the "culture industries" – as much as they stirred those industries up. The line between resistance and commodification is a very fuzzy one.

2   These changes can still be felt, for example, in the on-going realignment of political parties in Great Britain and the USA, in the dismantling of the welfare state and in structural adjustments all around the world, in the collapse of remaining political empires (such as the Soviet Union) and the consequent changes in military and economic policy, in the rise of militant property-rights activists and racist nationalists, and, of course, in the continued destruction of decent work and education possibilities for hundreds of millions of people around the globe as capital becomes ever more adept at playing one non-regulatory low-wage state off against another, in search of a stay against inevitably falling rates of profit.

In such a world, cultural geography seemed to have little relevancy so long as it remained focused on uncovering presumably timeless and unchangeable customs of seemingly isolated cultures, on three or four presumably eternal cultural constants of some nationality or ethnicity, on distribution of material cultural artifacts, or on ways in which "culture" effaces difference (as with Zelinsky's analysis of "the" culture of the United States).[3] Superorganic views of culture, or even just a poorly theorized cultural geography intent on describing the uniqueness of peoples and places, is clearly inadequate to describing new (or even old) "experience[s] of space and time."[4]

In the United States, with the weight of the Sauerian tradition still hanging heavy, a clear break with the longstanding traditions (and irrelevancy) of cultural geography was quite slow in coming. As noted at the end of chapter 1, even as late as 1989, "mainstream cultural geography seem[ed] satisfied with the superorganic" (Rowntree et al. 1989: 212). That was not the case in Britain, where a new generation of geographers, many of them trained not in the traditions of cultural geography, but rather in social geography, began to look explicitly at cultural issues. And they looked not to hidebound notions of culture handed down by generations of American cultural geographers and anthropologists, but rather to the emerging field of "cultural studies," an explicitly "multicultural," clearly political enterprise bent on theorizing the ways in which "culture" is "a domain in which economic and political contradictions are contested and resolved" (Jackson 1989: 1). These British geographers saw culture as a *form* of politics, but also as something apart from politics. It was to them a "map of meaning" for understanding how social relations are "structured and shaped ... [and] also the way those shapes are experienced, understood and interpreted" (Clarke et al. 1976: 11, quoted in Jackson 1989: 2). In short, by drawing on contemporary developments in social and cultural theories, British cultural geographers were concerned to explore a central, and exceedingly *relevant*, part of social life: the structure of experience in a changing world.

---

3   This is not to say geographers should abandon all study of "tradition" or localized cultural habits. Indeed, struggles over what constitutes the "tradition" of a place or people is integral to the ongoing culture wars. As Raymond Williams (1977: 116, emphasis added) makes clear:

> the hegemonic sense of tradition is always most active: a *deliberately* selective and connecting process which offers a historical and cultural ratification of a contemporary order. It is a very powerful process, since it is tied to many practical continuities – families, places, institutions, a language – which are indeed directly experienced. It is also, at any time, a vulnerable process, since it has in practice to discard whole areas of significance, or reinterpret or dilute them, or convert them into forms which support or at least do not contradict the really important elements of the current hegemony.

In other words, a hegemonic attempt to define *the* tradition is always open to dispute by counter-hegemonic forces.

4   A long-term interest in cultural geography has been the study of the "sense of place." The goal of many of the studies is to determine the presumably timeless "essence" of some place as it is understood and developed by its inhabitants. Doreen Massey (1994) has recently creatively rehabilitated this area of study by theorizing a specifically "global sense of place" that is always defined relationally to the development and transformation of other places and peoples around the globe. Crucially, Massey understands "global sense of place" to be something that is constructed through a multitude of social, political, and economic processes working at multiple scales, from the global to the most local (see also chapter 10, below).

For Peter Jackson (1989: 2), perhaps the chief spokesperson for these early developments in the "new cultural geography," cultural geography needed to particularly focus not on "culture itself" but on "cultural politics." He further argued that this focus on cultural politics was itself a product of "its immediate political context":

> What is there about the current politics of fiscal retrenchment, privatization, and economic recession in Thatcher's Britain or Bush's America that might be relevant to a revival of interest in cultural studies? Why have such phrases as "enterprise culture," "Victorian values," and "moral majority" gained such sudden salience? Is the age of the yuppie and corporate culture, of urban heritage and rural nostalgia, of football hooliganism a response to national economic decline? Or does it not also represent the growing confidence of the "consumption classes" and the increasing alienation of the impoverished and despairing "underclass," each with its own distinctive geography?   (Jackson 1989: 5)

To find answers to questions such as these, Jackson and other "new cultural geographers" turned away from developments in American cultural geography and looked to both home-grown British and international variants of "cultural studies" – an amalgam of studies that each in its own way sought to come to grips with the transformation of experience that marked the contemporary world. But they sought also to explicitly "spatialize" these studies, by showing how space and place are central to the "maps of meaning" that constitute cultural experience. To understand the development of "new cultural geography," it is therefore important to look first at the roots and influential developments within cultural studies itself.

Cultural Studies

If American cultural geography finds its roots in a reaction to environmental determinism and the nationalist cultural relativism of late nineteenth-century German scholars, then the British variant of new cultural geography looks to a scholarly tradition that, while it too is often anti-ethnocentric even as it celebrates the rootedness of particular "folk cultures" in the soil of Britain, has a quite different history. But like Sauer's response to environmental determinism, or Herder's or Boas's celebration of cultural relativism, British Cultural Studies are rooted in the "culture wars" of their time.

The roots of cultural studies

The immediate post-World War II period in Britain was one of drastic economic, political, and social change, a period of relative upheaval in the rather rigid British class system that was signaled as early as 1945 when Winston Churchill's conservative wartime coalition government was thrown out of office in favor of a Labour government promising the nationalization of basic industries and services and the (at least partial) democratization of the education system. This was a time, too, of active decolonization, of the often forced dissolution of the British Empire. Beginning with India, the most important of Britain's colonies, and rapidly spreading to Palestine, Egypt, sub-Saharan Africa and various outposts in the Mediterranean and Caribbean seas, Britain was forced to give up colonial control, either because of sustained struggles for independence, or because of the sheer cost of maintaining an empire. The dissolution of the empire hardly meant Britain's isolation from the peoples it had conquered. Rather, increasing numbers of Indians, Pakistanis, Barbadians, Jamaicans, Malays, and Kenyans migrated to the old imperial core cities – London, Liverpool, Manchester, Birmingham, Glasgow – in search of education and work, forcing Britain into a stark recognition of the "multicultural" nature of its former imperial ambitions.

Together with returning British veterans of World War II – those conscripted and volunteer members of what the historian E.P. Thompson (1980: 131, quoted in Inglis 1995: 87) described as an "ingenious civilian army, increasingly hostile to the conventional military virtues which became . . . an anti-fascist and consciously anti-imperialist army" – these "new" Britons forced changes in the structure and purpose of both the education system and leftish cultural politics (and, as we will see with Raymond Williams, these two spheres should not be held artificially apart).

Raymond Williams   One of the key figures in the development of cultural studies is Raymond Williams, whose excavation of the concept of culture we examined in chapter 1. Williams's biography is indicative of the portentous changes outlined above, and it is often invoked as a means of explaining why cultural studies developed as it did.[5] After being raised in a working-class household on the Welsh borders, attending Cambridge on scholarship, and serving in the army during World War II, Williams took a job teaching in the adult education program coordinated through Oxford University in the late 1950s and early 1960s. There he found a community of students and scholars in many ways similar to himself: working-class people trying to negotiate the chasm between their everyday lives and experiences, and the "official" culture celebrated in academia. More than anything, Williams wanted to show how his and his compatriots' lives were a valid part, indeed a central part, of life in Britain – as important as, and probably more important than, either the lives of the landed aristocracy with their manor-house life, regattas, and cosmopolitanism, or the urban and suburban bourgeoisie with their gardens, magazines, and commuter husbands. In many regards, reading Williams reminds one of reading Sauer (see especially Sauer 1976). There is the same concern with the ordinary and the everyday, and, particularly, with the shape of the land that forms through and within localized cultures:

---

5   Williams himself frequently used autobiography as a tool for exploring cultural change. His 1958 essay "Culture is Ordinary" (Williams 1993) is a masterful blending of autobiography and cultural critique, that goes far in explaining how Williams's own biography led to his concern to take ordinary, working-class history seriously. For a full, if misguided and horribly written, biography of Williams, see Inglis (1995).

> Culture is ordinary: that is where we must start. To grow up in that country [the Black Mountains of Wales] was to see the shape of a culture, and its modes of change. I could stand on the mountains and look north to the farms and the cathedral, or south to the smoke and flare of the blast furnace making a second sunset. To grow up in that family was to see the shaping of minds: the learning of new skills, the shifting of relationships, the emergence of different language and ideas. My grandfather, a big and hard labourer, wept while he spoke, finely and excitedly, at the parish meeting, of being turned out of his cottage. My father, not long before he died, spoke quietly and happily of when he had started a trade-union branch and a Labour Party group in the village, and, without bitterness, of the "kept men" of the new politics. I speak a different idiom, but I think these same things.   (Williams 1993: 6)

But there are great differences between Williams's sensibility and Sauer's. In the first place, Williams starts not from homogeneity, even within small geographic areas, but rather with difference – most particularly the class difference that is the fundamental structuring reality of ordinary life not just in Britain, but in all the modern world. This sense of class is there in Williams's invocation of trade unions and Labour politics, in his remembrance of his grandfather being evicted. And as Williams (1993: 6) goes on to say, "Every human society has its own shape, its own purpose, its own meanings. Every human society expresses these, in institutions, and in arts and learning." If that is the case, Williams avers, then it is not just the institutions of "high culture" – or even just the dominant institutions of a time and place – that need to be explored to understand the culture of a place. Rather it is the alternative, or even simply the more ordinary institutions of everyday life that also are central to culture. Without a clear class analysis that shows how these various institutions come together, how they are important for *different* kinds of learning and art, Williams argued, then it is impossible to understand how any society has its "own shape" or its "modes of change."

  This, then, is a second way in which Williams's sensibility differs from Sauer's. Williams is explicitly concerned with elucidating the mechanisms by which culture changes. Where Sauer was interested in the slow, long-term massive change that accompanied the invasion of a place by a new group, Williams wanted to show the political and economic form that change took – on the relatively fine timescale of ordinary life – without thereby reducing all cultural change to political economy. And he wanted to show how these small, ordinary processes and changes added up, in the long haul, to a "long revolution" in the conduct of human affairs (cf. Williams 1961). For this, Williams knew that cultural analysts had to grapple with the workings of the economy – something Sauer and his students continually shied away from – and, from that economy, they had to understand the recursive development of a particularly modern "way of life." To do this, Williams elaborated a transformed version of Marxist historical materialism into what has come to be called "cultural materialism." "Materialism" is often summed up in Marx's famous dictum, that "it is not the consciousness of men that determines their being, but their social existence that determines their consciousness" (Marx 1970a: 21; see also 1970b: 47). As Peter Jackson (1989: 33) explains, "the common emphasis in all materialist analyses is their refusal to treat the realm of ideas, attitudes, perceptions and values as independent of the forces and relations of production. Instead, culture is seen as a reflection

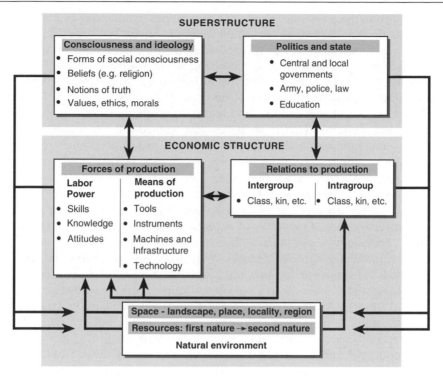

Figure 2.2 A sophisticated base-superstructure model. The social relations of existence (economics in the broadest sense of the term) "give rise" to a superstructure of norms, beliefs, laws, and political institutions that justify and reproduce those social relations. In its crudest forms the economic base is seen to directly "determine" the cultural superstructure. More sophisticated analyses seek to explore the social relations within and between the base and superstructure and see the direction of causality moving in both directions (as indicated by the arrows in this diagram). Adapted from Peet (1998).

of the material conditions of existence. A materialist approach, by definition, concentrates on the material conditions of society."[6] For some Marxists that came to mean that the social world could be reduced to a "superstructure" which was *determined* by the "base" of the political economy (see Williams 1977: 75–141; 1980: 31–49). That is to say, the workings of the economy – and perhaps struggles over it – produced a certain social structure, a certain culture, a certain consciousness (figure 2.2).

Such an extreme economic determinism was in fact quite rare in Marxist analysis. But nonetheless, it was the case that the "cultural" side of things was undertheorized

---

6   In fact, Raymond Williams's cultural materialism (1977, 96–7) denies that culture is a "reflection" of material conditions, except in a very limited and specialized sense. Indeed, he argues quite forcefully that to see culture as a "reflection" is not "materialist enough," because such a notion "suppress[es] the actual work on material" implicit in any cultural production. Moreover, it seems to abstract "culture" out of the "material conditions of existence" and hold it out as a "realm apart." As I will argue in chapter 3, such an error is endemic in cultural geography. Williams argues instead that materialist approaches to culture need to see "culture" as a *mediation* which is always and everywhere an active and integral part of the social condition of existence.

in relationship to the economic aspects of modern life.[7] Convinced that a materialist analysis was the only reasonable way to understand society, Williams sought to show not how the economy determined culture, but rather how there were "multiple forces of determination, structured in particular historical situations" (Jackson 1989: 35–46; Williams 1977: 88). In tandem with the historian E.P. Thompson (1963, 1975), Williams showed how "culture" was always and irrevocably "political" – a site of continual struggle and negotiation – and that it was fully imbricated in the workings of the political economy. That is, struggles that seemed fully "cultural" were often essential for determining the shape of the economy, just as economic struggle often shaped culture (as the passage from Williams above shows so clearly).[8] To put that in the terms of the Marxist theory they were both critiquing and developing, such a notion of mutual determination implies that it makes little sense to understand "base" and "superstructure" as *separate* spheres of life. Everyday life was *always* an indissoluble product of the forces of *both* the "base" of economy and the "super-structure" of ideology, social practice, state institutions, and so on.

Therefore, more than Sauer or Zelinsky, Williams was at pains to show the specific ways in which individuals and institutions interacted, the ways that particular, highly specific "ways of life" were constructed out of rather general processes of economic and cultural struggle. As Fred Inglis (1993: 53) has put it, Williams had a keen ability to "grasp the multiple connections between imagination and power." This, then, is a third difference between Sauer's and Williams's sensibilities. If Sauer's own bio-graphy encouraged him to distrust the modern and to shy away from theories of power, then Williams's biography encouraged just the opposite. The workings of power in everyday life were inescapable in his upbringing as the son of a railway signalman and unionist, and as a scholarship student at Cambridge at the outbreak of World War II (see Williams 1973; Inglis 1995; *The Times* 1988; Thompson 1988). And an exploration of the effects of powerful systems – of economy, governance, and thought – on the valuable culture of ordinary people remained an unwavering theme of Williams's right through his career – in adult education, to be sure, but also after being appointed to the faculty and eventually an endowed professorship at Cam-bridge.[9]

"Power" is a key idea that Williams (among others) brought into studies of culture by the early 1960s – an idea that is striking by its absence in earlier cultural studies, no matter how sensitive those studies may have been to ethnocentrism and the import-ance of cultural relativism. The relationship between "imagination and power" is "usually presented as the opposition between oppressive power and the liberated imagination: politics versus letters. . . . But of course Williams repudiates the 'versus' " (Inglis 1993: 53). That is to say, one of Williams's key projects was to show how power made literature (or other cultural forms) – sheer acts of will and imagination –

---

7   That said, there is a long tradition of Marxist cultural theory, beginning with Marx's *German Ideology* (and, in fact, a good deal of *Capital* itself) and continuing through Georg Lukács, Walter Benjamin, Antonio Gramsci, the Frankfurt School, and on into the field of cultural studies itself. Many of these developments in Marxist cultural theory will be picked up in the pages that follow.

8   A good introduction to the work of Williams as it relates to the study of landscape is Daniels (1989).

9   Edward Said's remembrance of Williams in *The Nation*, March 5, 1988, explores the importance of notions of power to Williams's work.

possible.[10] Hence, as much as Williams trusted his own autobiography as a touchstone for elucidating "culture" as it worked in Britain, he did not easily subscribe to a cult of individualism. Rather his whole point – like Marx's before him – was to see how individuals were always situated within the total context of society, and *therefore* able to act and reflect.[11]

Raymond Williams's contribution to the development of cultural studies (and hence to some contemporary forms of cultural geography) was to begin to show how power worked in and through culture, how individuals and institutions were both makers and products of total "ways of life," which themselves were intimately bound up with the material workings of a political economy, and how, in the end, because of all that, culture was the most ordinary thing in the world. If culture was in any way "the best that was thought and known," as Matthew Arnold famously defined it, then Williams showed how, contrary to Arnold (and Williams's own teacher F.R. Leavis), the "best" was the property of ordinary people, it was a product of their everyday lives.

In this, however, Williams, like many of the New Left, expressed a deep ambivalence toward popular or "mass" cultural forms – pop music, movies, romance novels, and later TV. On the one hand, aspects of these cultural forms were clearly expressions of popular tastes and inventiveness. And the new technologies of popular culture, film, television, recordings, were themselves of great potential value for those who wished to explore ordinary lives. On the other hand, the obvious commodification of these cultural forms, their clear complicity in the maintenance of capitalism (after all, mass cultural forms circulated precisely by making money, first and foremost), and their singular ability to push out more local, less "mass" cultural forms, made artifacts of mass culture objects of ready suspicion. Here Williams echoed his teacher Leavis, whose suspicions about popular culture were anything but ambivalent. Leavis used his own deep reading of literary works to promote a right-wing critique of capitalist culture that saw the corrosive effect of the commodity as an enemy of "culture," and not as an aspect of it – an attack on popular culture most advanced (if given a quite different inflection) in the immediate postwar period by another of Leavis's students, Richard Hoggart.

Richard Hoggart　Richard Hoggart was as ambivalent towards the mass culture so prevalent in the immediate postwar years as was Williams. For like Williams, Hoggart was concerned to show how culture – and particularly cultural practices – were inextricably part of a "whole way of life," and in that, the role of mass culture was problematic at best. "For him culture was an important category because it helps us understand that one life-practice (like reading) cannot be torn out of a large network constituted by many other life-practices – working, sexual orientation, family, say"

10　In this there is some affinity between Williams and Michel Foucault, who argued for a "positive" rather than "negative" understanding of power: power was not so much the ability to oppress action as the ability to make action happen in certain forms (and not others).

11　Williams (1976: 161) notes that "individual originally meant indivisible," and that "the development of the modern meaning from the original meaning is a record in language of extraordinary social and political history." In short, the modern notion of the "individual" as separate from and opposed to "society" developed with the decline of old feudal bonds and the development of new modes of philosophical and especially economic thinking beginning in the late seventeenth century.

(During 1993b: 1). But Hoggart understood that cultural texts and practices were not just books and reading (or art and gazing on pictures, serious music and listening done in a concert hall), but the whole panoply of activities we have come to call "pop" or "mass" culture. Like the canonical texts of "high" culture, these "texts" of everyday life could be read to understand how they fit into and reproduced that "large network of life-practices."

Hoggart's most famous book, and the one that is often evoked as a founding text of cultural studies, is *The Uses of Literacy* (1957). Simon During (1993b: 3) calls this book "schizophrenic" because "[i]ts first half contains a heartfelt evocation of traditional industrial working-class communities, relatively untouched by commercial culture and educational institutions, while its second half mounts a practical-critical attack on modern mass culture." The tension, then, is one between the celebration and perhaps the preservation of what Hoggart saw as a more "authentic" working-class culture, and the sorts of mass cultural forms that animated the very people Hoggart wanted to celebrate. But as Inglis (1993: 50) argues, even with this ambiguity one can find in the pages of Hoggart's book "a main source from which the best and most celebratory studies of later pop music will come. *The Uses of Literacy* made the decisive break with the canonical study of culture, made it on behalf of a new constituency of young men and women in the academy, and gave back to that generation the strong and excellent values of its formative experience of culture."

The point is that, at its roots, cultural studies has a deep tension between valuing the traditional and "folk" practices of working people (and of indigenous cultures at home and abroad), and a fascination – sometimes quite critical, other times not – with popular and mass culture. Simon During (1993b: 3–4) traces this tension in cultural studies to shifts in the nature of the working class itself. The postwar boom led, in Britain, to a short period of nearly full employment, and this, coupled with a massive investment in state-supported housing, the expansion of large-scale "Fordist" manufacturing at the expense of smaller firms, the growth in consumption (particularly of consumer goods such as radios, appliances, and later TVs), in turn fueled the dissolution of the sort of communal working-class culture Hoggart sought to celebrate in *The Uses of Literacy*.

> As the old working-class communal life fragmented, the cultural studies which followed Hoggart's *The Uses of Literacy* developed in two main ways. The old notion of culture as a whole way of life became increasingly difficult to sustain: attention moved from locally produced and often long-standing cultural forms (pub life, group singing, pigeon-fancying, attitudes to "our mum", dances, holidays at camps and close-by seaside resorts, etc.) to culture as organized from afar – both by the state through its educational system, and by what Theodor Adorno and Max Horkheimer . . . called the "culture industry," that is, highly developed music, film, and broadcasting businesses.   (During 1993b: 4)

Importantly, this move was accompanied by a clear sense in which "culture" could not be separated from politics. Indeed, it was precisely the point of many practitioners of cultural studies in its early years that "cultural politics" themselves were now at least as defining of contemporary life as the class politics that seemed to drive the prewar years.

This is not to say that cultural politics completely replaced class politics, but rather that class politics were more and more subsumed *within* cultural politics. For analysts such as Hoggart and Williams, "cultural forms of all kinds are [understood as] the result of specific processes of production" (Jackson 1989: 36). To the degree that this is so, cultural analysis must focus on the *relations* – or politics – of production: the role of advertisement designers, or record producers, for example, or even of those people, like waiters in restaurants, who help us to *know* our culture (Zukin 1995; see also chapter 3, below).

All this, however, leaves the idea of culture back in the midst of the muddle from which cultural studies continually seeks to rescue it. Is culture the same as practice? As artifact? As produced thing? Or is it more? Is it a way of knowing and under-standing? A way of making sense of the world? And if it is the latter, *how* do we come to know? What are the processes by which meaning is made available? These questions animated the Birmingham Centre for Contemporary Cultural Studies that Richard Hoggart founded in 1964, and which flourished under the direction of Stuart Hall in the 1970s.

Stuart Hall   Like Algerians in France, Hispanics in the United States, Hong Kong Chinese in Canada, or Japanese in Australia, Caribbean (or other postcolonial) people in Britain have made it impossible to speak easily of a homogeneous "British-ness."[12] Even the class-divided sense of English culture developed by the likes of Williams, Thompson, or Hoggart seemed to fragment even further as more and more people from India, Pakistan, Barbados, Jamaica, Kenya, or Nigeria moved to the metropolitan core of the former British Empire in the years after World War II. In actuality, it was not so much that culture fragmented – as it is impossible in any event to speak of a unitary culture – but rather that the obvious differences between the peoples calling Britain (or America, or France) home made such heterogeneity highly visible. Culture not only had to be understood; it was actively fought over in the changing residential and shopping districts of the city (see S. Smith 1989; Smith and Mercer 1987).

In many ways, Stuart Hall is representative of these transformations of the ethnic geographies of global society – the "fixed, fast-frozen relations" that *seemed* to define life – that came with the breakdown of the colonial system beginning around World War I (and that continues through the present).[13] The new political and structural realities of the modern and postmodern eras, Hall insisted, required people to develop new "maps of meaning." These maps were inextricably connected to one's "position" in society. In essence, they depended in many ways on one's own biography – though that biography, in turn, was itself dependent upon the social, political, and economic structure of the world into which one was born and lived. Born and raised in Jamaica, the child of parents who "were locked into this terrible reverence for the mother

12   Not that the immigration of people of color into Britain was necessary to indicate just how hetero-geneous Britain was. The very term "Britishness" is problematic, as it already effaces deep and deeply held divisions between English, Welsh, Scots, Irish, and other peoples thrown together in the "United King-dom."

13   An excellent discussion of these transformations, especially as they relate to such "high culture" forms as the novels of Jane Austen and the operas of Verdi, is Said (1993).

country [Britain] and the United States," Hall (who himself had strong sympathies with the Jamaican independence movement) came to Oxford as a Rhodes Scholar in 1951 (Hall quoted in Sanders 1994: 17; see also Chen 1996). While Hall discovered he was one of a fairly significant community of outsiders at Oxford – working-class scholarship students, others from the far reaches of the British Empire – even the importance of that community to his own intellectual formation and personal life did little to allay his sense that he was never fully at home in Oxford. The overwhelming, and stifling, "Englishness" of the place left an indelible mark on Hall and his thinking. Not desiring to return to Jamaica, however, Hall made his way as a member of a "hybrid" world, not quite English, not quite Jamaican. "I know both places intimately, but I am not wholly of either place" (quoted in Chen 1996: 490).

That sense of outsideness has lent Hall's work extraordinary force as a critique of British political economy and society.[14] Given his prominence (along with Williams, E.P. Thompson, and Richard Hoggart, Hall was instrumental in establishing the British New Left; he was also the first editor of the important *New Left Review*), it has also lent cultural Marxism a particular and important inflection, namely a focus on questions of identity and identification and on cultural hegemony (cf. Hall 1996). Hall traces the origins of the New Left – and hence the particular development of British cultural Marxism – to "the moment of the two imperialisms: The Anglo-French invasion of Suez and the invasion of Hungary by Soviet tanks, within a month of each other in late summer 1956..." (quoted in *New Statesman and Society* 1996: 25). At that moment, Hall (1992: 279) writes, "I came into Marxism backwards: against the Soviet tanks in Budapest, as it were." By this he means that he, like others, was forced to rethink the Marxist project; and Hall, in many ways, found its legacy inadequate for understanding the present historical moment. "I've always been dissatisfied with Marx's handling of the relationship between culture and economy, culture and politics" (quoted in Sanders 1994: 18). The formation of the New Left, and its interest in precisely that relationship between culture, politics, and economy (which is there in Williams, in Thompson, and in Hoggart, as it is in Hall), has been profoundly important both for developments in the intellectual history of the postwar period, and for the remaking of society itself during that period. The theoretical work of the New Left, adopted by many in social movements as diverse as the student radicalism of the 1960s and the anti-nuclear campaign of the 1980s, has had a particularly important – if often unacknowledged and always contested – influence on the development of cultural, geopolitical, and economic policy.

But, no matter how important Hall's own biography may be, he would be the first to argue that such cultural change – and especially the experience of cultural change – cannot be *reduced* to biography or to some individual or even group identity. Instead, Hall was at pains to show how such identities as his own were themselves a product of, and contested through, relations of power. For this he turned to the theories of the Italian communist and political theorist Antonio Gramsci – particularly focusing on Gramsci's concept of *cultural hegemony*.

---

14 It has also led to some discomfort; the role of a black intellectual in white society is nothing if not problematic: "I'm expected to speak for the entire black race on all questions theoretical, critical, etc. and sometimes for British politics, as well as for Cutural Studies. That is what is known as the black man's burden..." (Hall 1992: 277).

Antonio Gramsci and cultural hegemony Gramsci is most famous for the writing he did in prison during Mussolini's reign in fascist Italy. Collected together in the *Prison Notebooks* (Gramsci 1971) and elsewhere, Gramsci's writing is sweeping in scope (examining everything from the growth and function of the state under capitalism to the role of education in cementing the social integration of society), often quite abstruse (especially if you are not intimately familiar with the political machinations of Italy between the wars and the changing role of the Communist Party in that politics), sometimes so coded as to seem inexplicable (since he was writing in such a manner as to elude prison censors), and highly fragmentary. Even so, there are several overriding themes that concerned Gramsci during his years in prison, the most prominent of which – excluding perhaps a general concern with theorizing the State – was his desire to explicate a theory of cultural hegemony.[15] Fred Inglis (1993: 76), in his typically avuncular way, has put the question of hegemony thus: "What on earth is it, in schools or on the telly, which makes rational people accept unemployment, killing queues in hospitals, ludicrous waste on needless weaponry, and all the other awful details of life under modern capitalism? Is the chance of sunny holidays, sexy videos and a modest pay rise per year enough of an answer? This is the problem of hegemony." Put another way, the problem of cultural hegemony is one of determining how and why subordinate people seem to consent to their own domination, why they seem to so frequently go against what "objectively" looks to be in their own best interest. Or more precisely, the question of hegemony is: When and under what conditions do people consent to rule by a dominant group (or set of institutions), and when do they resist that domination? In short, then, Gramsci wanted to theorize the relationship between "consent" and "coercion" in the world, and since these relations were so frequently "cultural" (rather than simply economic or military), the idea of cultural hegemony allowed for such a theorization. And it allowed for it in quite subtle ways.

In studies of geopolitics, "hegemony" often simply means "power" – the power to decide how the world should be arrayed, and how it should work as a geopolitical system. A "hegemon" is the ruling power of an era, as was Britain during the nineteenth century, or, perhaps, the United States after World War II. In these studies of geopolitics, it is clear that the hegemon never rules without resistance – either from others desiring the throne (like the USSR), or subordinate states and colonies seeking to challenge the power of the hegemon on their own soil (as with the frequent uprisings against British power in India). Gramsci adopted this idea of power and resistance and transported it to the cultural realm as a means of explaining the "social integration" of class-riven societies. Frequently, ruling groups – dominant classes – simply resort to violence (or the threat of violence) to maintain their control. But just as frequently, such control is won instead through the seemingly "'spontaneous' consent given by the great masses of the population to the general direction imposed on social life by the dominant fundamental group" (Gramsci 1971: 12). That is, dominant groups work to *make* consent to the prevailing order seem *natural*. In this sense, the theory of cultural hegemony is also a theory of *ideology* (a point to which

15 A good discussion of Gramsci's life, focusing on his intellectual and political development, is Hoare and Nowell-Smith (1971).

we will return in a moment) that seeks to understand how ideologies are made, and how they attain an aura of "naturalness" that almost makes it impossible to think some thoughts.

Yet people do, sometimes, think those thoughts, and, by acting on them they opt to directly oppose the established order. The problem then for the ruling class is to bring those resisters back into line, either by transforming its own ideology and practices to accommodate – at least partially – the demands of the resisters, or through the use of force (which is often a very expensive undertaking, both economically, and in terms of the legitimacy of the ruling group). To move off this abstract level, Gramsci argued that some kinds of issues were more important to the ruling class of a society than others. He "had in mind the values, norms, perceptions, beliefs, sentiments, and prejudices that support and define the existing distribution of goods, the institutions that decide how this distribution occurs, and the permissible range of disagreement about those processes" (Lears 1985: 569). In other words, cultural hegemony establishes the parameters within which debate and struggle over the shape of society – as defined by who gets what – may occur. It sets the terms of debate.

But for Gramsci, cultural hegemony was above all a *relationship* between powerful and less powerful groups in society, a relationship itself established through a dialectic between the manufacturing of consent and the occasional resort to coercion by dominant groups, and the continual resistance (real and potential) of subordinate groups. Hegemony is thus "live" in that it is ever-changing, ever-shifting in its contours. "From this perspective," Jackson Lears (1985: 569) summarizes, "the maintenance of hegemony does not require active commitment by subordinates to the legitimacy of elite rule. Less powerful people may be thoroughly disaffected. At times they may openly revolt through strikes, factory takeovers, mass movements, and perhaps the creation of a counterhegemony. But normally most people find it difficult, if not impossible, to translate the outlook implicit in their experience [i.e. their sense that the prevailing social structure is unjust] into a conception of the world that will directly challenge the hegemonic culture."

Nonetheless, in all kinds of ways, and every day, people *do* challenge – or perhaps modify – *their* relations to the prevailing order, working the material of society into the means for a better life for themselves, perhaps, or into a means for expressing their own *place* in the world (through, for example, creative approaches to mass consumerism, developments of alternative style, or in the economic realm, through loafing, petty stealing, or other means of redressing economic imbalance). In this sense, the hegemony of an era, supported and defined in part by ruling ideologies, is *never* stable. Subordinate groups continually "see through" the ideologies that support hegemony – sometimes clearly, sometimes with great difficulty. Ideology itself works through "euphemizing" the social relations it is meant to explain. As James Scott (1985: 204) has put it:

> Here we are concerned with appearances, with the mask that exercise of economic or political power typically wears. Things in this domain are rarely as they seem; we should expect disguises, whether they are self conscious nor not. . . . The executive who fires some of his work force is likely to say that he "had to let them go." This description of his action not only implies that he had no choice in the matter, but that those "let go" were done a favor.

The executive "euphemizes" his action, deflecting attention away from the economic system that requires increased profit at the expense of workers, and claims it was a "natural" thing, something over which he, and his company, had no control. Moreover, the firings were in reality in the workers' best interests. Yet as Scott (1985: 205) goes on to remark, "Those who are beneficiaries of this magnanimous act are likely to take a different view; their metaphors are usually more colorful: 'I got the sack'; 'I was axed.'" The workers thus "penetrate" the ideology of their corporate bosses, exposing it for what it is: a willful act in the *employers'* own interest. The use of euphemism thus seeks "to mask the naked reality of power relations"; but the act of penetration continually seeks to strip off the masks to expose what is beneath (Mitchell 1993: 114).

The point is that cultural hegemony is both consented to *and* contested – sometimes effectively, sometimes not. So it must always be actively *maintained*. It must be invested in by the ruling group in order to assure that it does not collapse by repeated penetration by subordinate groups. Hence, hegemony is a dynamic relationship between domination and subordination requiring continual ideological work. In this sense, the sorts of ideologies that prop up hegemony should not be understood as some sort of simple "false consciousness" on the part of dominated (or even dominant) people, as certain theories of ideology suggest. Ideology should not be seen as "simply a set of wrong ideas, but [as] a set of ideas rooted in practical experience, albeit the practical experience of a given social class which sees reality from its own perspective, and therefore only in part. Although in this way a partial reflection of reality, the class attempts to *universalize* its own perception of the world" (Smith 1990: 15). For Peter Jackson (1989: 52), ideology should be understood as any statement or belief that "fails to make clear the interests it represents," and thus suggests that it is important to understand that subordinate groups produce ideology too. The important issue is to understand the relationships between dominant and subordinate ideologies, so as to see how each penetrates the other.

The Centre for Contemporary Cultural Studies   Understanding the struggle inherent in hegemony – exploring the various means by which hegemony is produced and contested and by which ideology becomes "common sense" – became the central concern of the Centre for Contemporary Cultural Studies and Birmingham University during the 1960s and 1970s. The problematic established by the Centre was one of determining, after the "disruptions" of the Depression and World War II, precisely the nature of the current social hegemony that defined British society. As Stuart Hall (1979: 16) put it in an introduction to a collection of essays written at the Centre in the 1970s, "The 'settlement'" of political and labor disruption caused by the war and depression, and "defined by the revival of capitalist production, the founding of the welfare state and the 'Cold War,'" seemed "to bring economic, political and cultural forces into new kinds of relation, into a new equilibrium." In short, the Centre set as its central question: "what type of social formation was now in the making?" The Centre adopted a working definition of culture derived from the seminal work of Raymond Williams and E.P. Thompson, a definition that stressed "above all, ... the necessary struggle, tension and conflict between cultures and their links to class cultures, class formations and class struggles – the struggles between 'ways of life' rather than the evolution of '*a* way of life'" (Hall 1979: 20). And it used that definition to focus work on *both* the expression of dominant culture (through, for example, studies of the popular press) *and* studies of youth and other subcultures, the study of deviance and ethnographic studies of schooling and work.[16]

By the 1980s, the Centre had augmented its definition of culture by drawing on what Hall calls a "complex Marxism" (which sought to thoroughly rework the base-superstructure model of social determination), and turned its attention to the means by which "Thatcherism" arose as a defining totality of cultural, political, and economic life. The question was one of how Thatcherism organized popular consent for its policies and practices. Beginning with the collective book *Policing the Crises*, and following with a series of essays on the cultural-political nature of what Hall famously described as the "authoritarian populism" of the times (essays that examined everything from the dirty work of party politics, to the politics of race, to the role of the media in constructing its own audiences), the Centre's work deconstructed contemporary Britain – as defined through both its "official" and its "popular" culture – with a forcefulness and vigor found in few other areas of academia (Hall et al. 1978; Hall and Jacques 1983; Hall 1988; Centre for Contemporary Cultural Studies 1982; Gilroy 1987).[17] But it was around this time also that the Centre's "business as usual" was "interrupted" (as Hall [1992] puts it) by feminism.

Hall (1992: 282) suggests that the impact of feminism on the Centre's work – and on cultural studies more generally – was little short of revolutionary: "It has forced a major rethink in every substantive area of work." At the Centre, Hall (1992: 282) has recalled, it was as if feminism "broke in; interrupted, made an unseemly noise, seized the time, crapped on the table of cultural studies." The impact of feminism, and feminists, was just that unsettling to business-as-usual, and to the men that ran that business. The first important intervention by feminists at the Centre was the volume *Women Take Issue* (Women's Studies Group 1978), which documents the difficult and "painful" (Hall 1979: 39) transformation of the Centre's work as it engaged with feminists and feminism in the 1970s. One of the first issues raised – and still a key issue in cultural studies and cultural geography (see chapter 8, below) – was the theorization of the role of *reproduction*[18] as integral to the material social structure of society. In turn, re-emphasizing reproduction – and assuring it received the theoretical attention it deserved – also implied retheorizing *production* itself as not just capitalist, but patriarchal too. "A theory of culture which cannot account for patriarchal structures of dominance and oppression is, in the wake of feminism, a non-starter" (Hall 1979: 39). In other words, gender and sexuality (chapters 7 and 8) had to be understood as central to the workings and functioning of power itself. Or to put that in the terms established at the outset of this section, feminism truly brought with it the necessity for rethinking the base-superstructure problematic. No longer was it possible to study

16   The most famous of these are probably Willis (1977) and Hall and Jefferson (1976).
17   Hall left the Centre in 1979 but his influence on its work is still clearly evident during the 1980s. Likewise, the questions and problematics developed at the Centre remained driving forces in Hall's own work.
18   "Reproduction," or more formally *social* reproduction can be defined as the everyday perpetuation of the social institutions and relations that make possible the material conditions of life. The important point is that social reproduction is never guaranteed, but is also a moment of potential struggle and transformation.

the presumptive base – the workings of the economy – without also and at the same time studying what had been seen as epiphenomenal to that base (relations of family, ideologies of gender, social structures of sexuality, etc.).

Additionally, because questions of sexuality and gender could not be divorced from either the "personal" or the "political" – because they were always admixtures of both – feminism in cultural studies marked, for the Centre, "the 're-opening' of the closed frontier between social theory and the theory of the unconscious," and therefore marked an important engagement with psychoanalysis (Hall 1992: 282). For Hall (both at the Centre and after he left it in 1979 to become professor of sociology at the Open University) these engagements – with feminism, with "complex Marxism," and with the general problem represented by the fact that "culture is neither the process of the unconscious writ large nor . . . the unconscious simply the internalization of cultural processes . . ." (1992: 291) – meant concerted inquiry into "the dangerous area of the subjective and the subject" (1992: 282). Coupled with on-going research on "race" (see chapter 9, below), ethnicity, and the transformations wrought by the global diaspora of "Third World" peoples (see chapter 10), the focus on feminism has also led to fruitful studies of cultural and social identity – its formation, its contestation, its political importance.[19]

In sum, then, as it moved through studies of counter-hegemonic cultural forms and practices, into research on the political, social, and economic bases of Thatcherism, and on to (continued) theorizations of "the subject" and subjectivity, the Centre for Contemporary Cultural Studies has both responded to (and to some degree helped shape) the political exigencies of the moment. And it has also thereby been instrumental in establishing a good portion of the agenda of cultural studies as a whole. Its impact, in other words, has been enormous, helping to spark an "explosion of interest in cultural studies" (Nelson et al. 1992: 1). Like Richard Hoggart and Raymond Williams, Stuart Hall and the Centre for Contemporary Cultural Studies (both during and after Hall's tenure as director) form important roots for cultural studies as a whole – and through it, for "new cultural geography" as well.

The field of cultural studies

If these are the social, biographical, and theoretical roots that established cultural studies as a realm of inquiry in the second half of the twentieth century, they are roots that have borne a cornucopia of fruits – fruits that are themselves hard to define and classify. As it has been transplanted into new soil (North America, the former colonies of the British Empire, the "Third World"), as new "gardeners" have come to tend those fields (women, postcolonial, subaltern peoples), and as new rootstalk has been grafted on to the old stock (feminism, postmodernism, post-structuralism), cultural studies has proliferated and evolved. It is a field virtually impossible to summarize.

---

19 For examples of the sorts of developments made by Hall and his colleagues on questions of subjectivity and identity, see Hall and du Gay (1996).

The key starting point for cultural studies, however, is easily described. As John Fiske notes, "culture" as it is understood in cultural studies "is neither aesthetic nor humanist in emphasis, but political" (Fiske 1992, quoted in Storey 1996: 160). Cultural studies, in the eyes of its practitioners, is "committed to the study of the entire range of society's arts, beliefs, institutions, and communicative practices" (Nelson et al. 1992: 4). The range of research rallying under the banner of cultural studies is therefore breathtaking. It includes everything from concerted efforts at culture theory development (as we have seen with Williams and Hall, and as we will continue to see throughout the rest of the book), to empirical studies of people's television-viewing habits; from examinations of the political power of sexual "deviance" to decodings of symbolic codes of pornography; from studies of national identity formation to the politics of shopping; from sports to rock music; from jazz to public art; from street carnival to AIDS; from the cultural construction of scientific knowledge to the theory of language; from race to gender to sexuality to ethnicity; from style to ideology; from resistance to subjectivity; from history to geography; from sociology to psychology; and from political economy to "Rambo and the Popular Pleasures of Pain" (as one 1992 essay is subtitled).

Certainly influenced by the agenda set by the Centre for Contemporary Cultural Studies, practitioners in the burgeoning field of cultural studies also drew, in the 1980s and 1990s, explicitly on the influential work of French structuralists and post-structuralists such as Jacques Lacan, Julia Kristeva, Louis Althusser, Michel Foucault, Jean-François Lyotard, Roland Barthes, Pierre Bourdieu, Luce Irigaray, Gilles Deleuze, and Felix Guattari. Perhaps the most important point taken from the work of the French theorists was that "theory" itself was political, and incapable of "stand[ing] outside the field it claimed to tell the truth about as if it were a 'meta-discourse'" (During 1993b: 15). Cultural theory, therefore, in many ways turned in on itself in an endless swirl of hermetic self-reference, as theorists sought to unravel the politics not of the world outside of theory, but of theory itself (since, so the argument goes, it is not even *possible* to know the world without theory). There is an important political move here: as culture was seen more and more to be political to its core, theories about culture became relatively depoliticized – that is, if we take for the moment a definition of politics that sees it as the attempt to act on and change the world. The preferred mode of analysis for cultural studies was to understand cultural movements and practices – along with whole fields of "otherness" – as relatively autonomous, as valuable in their own right, and not necessarily as always and everywhere even potentially "oppositional." "This new mode of cultural studies no longer concentrated on reading culture as primarily directed against the state," as had been the case with Williams, Hall, and other founding New Leftists. Rather, it worked to "affirm 'other' ways of life on their own terms.... This moment in cultural studies pictured society as much more decentred" than the Birmingham Centre, and developed what Simon During (1993b: 15–16) calls "a looser, more pluralistic and postmodern, conceptual model than those which insist that capitalism and the free market produce interests *structurally* unequal and in conflict with each other." Unlike the social democratic thought that drove much of the early work in cultural studies (and which was absolutely the cornerstone of Williams's theories of culture), "the new cultural studies no longer aimed at a radical transformation of the whole system of social fields" (During 1993b: 16).

In other words, at exactly the moment that capitalism, in response to its crises of the 1970s was engaged in a radical *global* restructuring, cultural studies – or at least significant parts of it – both globalized itself *and* turned away from seeking to understand the *totality* of social life. Now it was precisely the *local* (both in terms of geographical scale and in terms of social sweep) that garnered the most interest. This has meant – for better *and* for worse – a shift from the study of social life in its totality, to the study of social life in all its plurality. The shift is not complete, however, and in reality, cultural studies, like new cultural geography, works productively through the *tensions* implicit in understanding "culture" as *both* part of an integrated whole *and* a set of often radically disarticulated practices. This book too is a product of exactly that tension (though it'll become quite clear in the next section and in chapter 3, if it isn't clear enough already, just which side of the tension in cultural theory I favor).

The New Cultural Geography

Whatever the validity of my analysis of the field, what is important at this point is that all this work in cultural studies – emphasizing culture, society, power, domination, resistance, style, consumption, and ideology – developing in the 1970s and really taking off in the 1980s, was immensely exciting to a new cohort of British geographers concerned to understand the *geography* of cultural processes in a new way. As early as 1980, Peter Jackson could enter a "plea for cultural geography" that, drawing on developments in the humanistic geography of the 1970s, proposed a *rapprochement* with British social geography, so as to better understand the geography of culture and society as they worked together to shape the experience of everyday life.[20] Three years later Denis Cosgrove (1983), whose work we will examine more closely in chapter 4, suggested the time was ripe for developing a "radical cultural geography," centered exactly on issues of power, dominance, and the control of space and culture by elite groups. For both of them, as for others engaged in developing a "new cultural geography," the goal was to create a "thoroughly politicized concept of culture" so as to turn "attention to areas of social life that have rarely been treated by geographers" (Jackson 1989: 45), such as ideologies of race, the role of language and discourse in producing cultural spaces, the development and maintenance of subcultures, issues of gender, sexuality, and identity, and the way in which landscapes and places are more than just congeries of material artifacts or empty containers awaiting social action.

The 1980s were heady times for geographers – just as they were for workers in cultural studies. There was much that needed geographers' attention. The economic transformations of the 1970s were still ricocheting across the economic and political landscape: the decade began with the rise of Thatcher in Britain and Reagan in America and closed with the destruction of the Soviet Empire in Eastern Europe (marked by movements as seemingly cultural as they were political; the Velvet

---

20   Jackson makes his "plea" in the absence of any reference to the Birmingham Centre for Contemporary Cultural Studies. By the end of the 1980s, however, the Centre's work had become quite central to Jackson's.

Revolution in Prague was spearheaded by a playwright, after all), and the protests at Tiananmen Square. Through all this change, "cultural" issues remained at the forefront. The religious right in America surged toward power on the coattails of Reagan's election; white nationalism blossomed in Britain, France, and Germany; economic change – including the globalization of "culture industries" – was startlingly rapid; and disparities in wealth between the richest and the poorest within developed nations and between developed nations and the rest of the world increased steadily, as wealth was massively transferred from the poor to the rich. Yet even as this transfer of wealth continued apace, it was frequently euphemized under a language of natural rights and cultural justice. The free-market wisdom of Thatcher and Reagan preached that wealth was simply a function of talent, that those who were poor were poor by dint of their own, often cultural, failings. For geographers, these changes – in ideology and in social structure – implied a need to focus on the role of space and place in adjudicating cultural power. For human geographers more generally, they have led to what is now widely accepted as a "cultural turn" in the discipline as a whole (see Gregory 1994).

Postmodernism and the cultural turn

As importantly, it implied to geographers a need to come to terms with the nature of "postmodernity," which, it seemed, was inherently spatial.[21] Postmodernism is an exceptionally slippery idea. Usually it is contrasted with modernism, particularly the "high modernism" that seems to have marked the twentieth century. If modernism was defined by a faith in rationality, in progress, in the sort of high-minded seriousness that marked international-style architecture and the music of Berg, Schoenberg, or Stravinsky, then,

> the typical postmodernist artifact is playful, self-ironizing and even schizoid; and . . . it reacts to the austere autonomy of high modernism by impudently embracing the language of commerce and commodity. Its stance towards cultural tradition is one of irreverent pastiche, and its contrived depthlessness undermines all metaphysical solemnities, sometimes by brutal aesthetics of squalor and shock. (Eagleton 1987, quoted in Harvey 1989a: 7–8l; see figure 2.3)

Put another way, postmodernism stresses heterogeneity, whereas modernism is accused of seeking homogeneity; postmodernism looks to multiple, competing discourses, whereas modernism seems to always want a single "metanarrative" capable of explaining everything; postmodernism is infatuated with the indeterminacy of language, knowledge, and social practices and the elusive search for "meaning," while modernism stands mired in the overweening and impossible desire for self-contained explanation, for rational action in the face of perfectly knowable processes and actions. Or at least that is how the opposition between modernism and

---

21 An early popularizer of postmodern theory in geography was Michael Dear (1986, 1988, 1991). For a critique of how postmodern theories have been adopted by geography, see Strohmeyer and Hannah (1992).

Figure 2.3 Horton Plaza Shopping Center in downtown San Diego. All the ironic and playful attributes of postmodernist architecture are on display here. Compare Horton Plaza with the modernist sensibilities on display down the road in figure 2.1. Instead of a sleek, efficient, rational future, on display here is an attractive (though fully commodified) past linked to architectural quotation from around the Mediterranean world. Photograph by Susan Millar; used by permission.

postmodernism is usually structured by those wishing to promote the postmodern cause.[22]

The degree to which such caricatures of modernism and postmodernism are accurate, and indeed, the degree to which it can be said we are now living in postmodern times, is highly debatable (see Benko and Strohmeyer 1997). Indeed, some see the "postmodern turn" in social sciences and humanities – with its multifaceted concern with (and some would say uncritical wonder at) all matters cultural, and its retreat from studies of economic systems and processes of exploitation, coming as it did just as the political and economic right gained ascendency – as marking a rather complete surrender to the forces of reaction.[23] No matter how wonderful various forms of

22 For a wonderful exploration of how quintessentially postmodern sensibilities have long been an important strain of modernism itself, see Berman (1982).
23 In the USA, this critique has resolved itself into a rather acrimonious debate on the left about the value of "identity politics" for progressive politics in general. For key interventions, see Gitlin (1995); Tomasky (1996); Kelley (1998). In geography debate has most recently revolved around the importance and place of "class" in geographical analysis: see Smith (1999).

cultural resistance may be, the argument goes, a rapacious economy is still ruining the lives of most people in the world. To turn from "metanarratives" that can explain this processes is political suicide.[24] The "cultural turn" in the social sciences, which it can be argued is roughly equivalent with the postmodern turn, represents in this rendering a squandering of intellectual resources. It, like cultural studies as a whole, also represents a retreat from the sorts of concerns that animated Williams's cultural materialism, which explicitly sought, after all, to theorize the indissolubility of "culture," "politics," "economy," and so on.

Whether that critique of postmodernism (which is related to the one of cultural studies) is just or not, what is clear is that the language of postmodernism represented a sharp break from past languages of social theory, especially in the emphasis it put on *space*. So added to the postmodern and cultural "turns" of the 1980s, was a spatial turn. All of a sudden the language of space and place was everywhere. And geographers, used to being on the margins of academic discourse, sat up and took notice. Michel Foucault (1986: 22), perhaps the pre-eminent social philosopher of the age, put the matter this way:

> The great obsession of the nineteenth century was, as we know, history: with its themes of development and suspension, of crisis and cycle, themes of the ever-accumulating past, with its great preponderance of dead men and the menacing glaciation of the world.... The present epoch will perhaps be above all the epoch of space. We are in the epoch of simultaneity: we are in the epoch of juxtaposition, the epoch of the side-by-side, of the dispersed. We are at a moment, I believe, when our experience of the world is less that of a long life developing through time, than that of a network that connects points and intersects with its own skein.

For Edward Soja (1989), such a recognition by the likes of Foucault implied an important "reassertion of space in social theory" – a reassertion in large part made possible by the postmodern turn in social theory, and made necessary by the postmodernization of the economy and society. For British cultural geographers, these transformations in social thought and in society itself demanded a better theory of culture than that provided by the American cultural geography criticized by James Duncan (see chapter 1 above). Particularly, it demanded close attention to the sorts of developments in cultural studies we have just outlined.

The scope of new cultural geography

If, in 1980, Peter Jackson could enter a plea for cultural geography, suggesting it was about time to redefine the field, and if by 1989, he could still offer a coherent *agenda* for a new cultural geography – that is, if by the end of the 1980s, the field was still largely waiting to be defined – that was no longer the case at the end of the 1990s. There has been an amazing blossoming of work that could be classed under the banner "new

---

24 The most sustained and influential critique along these lines is Harvey (1989a). A metatheory of postmodern geographies was developed by Soja in *Postmodern Geographies* (1989), but he has moved towards a more clearly postmodern postmodernism in the ensuing years; see Soja (1996).

cultural geography." Indeed there has been so much work that scholars assigned the task of summarizing the yearly developments for the "Progress Reports" annually published in *Progress in Human Geography* have taken to throwing up their hands in defeat: the field is now just too unwieldy to encapsulate neatly in a short essay – or even, for that matter, a long book (Matless 1995). Nonetheless, some of the important contours and developments can be briefly outlined here. It is the task of the remainder of this book, however, to more fully and critically (though by no means completely) engage with the ferment of activity that has marked new cultural geography. The important point to note is that, as Linda McDowell (1994: 155) puts it, "what is published and taught under the rubric of 'cultural geography' changes in response to the political and economic climate of the times and the structures of disciplinary power."

Perhaps the area of cultural geography to gain the earliest sustained criticism and reconstruction by new cultural geography was the traditional field of landscape geography (chapters 4 and 5, below). New cultural geographers addressed the landscape issue on four fronts. First, they sought to connect the very idea of landscape to its historical development as part of the capitalist and Enlightenment transformation of Europe in the early modern period.[25] That is to say, the goal of many studies has been to show how the land was made over in the image of "landscape" – a particular, and particularly ideological "way of seeing" the land and people's relationship to that land. Second, other geographers reinvigorated the notion of "reading" the landscape (an idea implicit in Sauer's "Morphology of Landscape" and perhaps best developed during the 1970s by Peirce Lewis), to problematize the whole notion of exactly what constitutes the "text" to be read – and precisely how it is possible, in any event, to read it. That is, work began to focus more clearly on the interpretation of the *symbolic* aspects of landscapes (Lewis 1979; Daniels and Cosgrove 1988; Duncan 1990; Duncan and Duncan 1988). Third, where much traditional cultural geography had examined rural and past landscapes, some new work interested in landscape and culture focused on urban and contemporary scenes (Domosh 1996b; King 1996; Knox 1993b). Finally, a sustained feminist critique of landscape studies – and of the very idea of landscape – has been launched (see Rose 1993: chapter 5). With the exception of the feminist intervention, none of these areas of development is completely new in cultural geography. As early as the 1950s cultural geographers had begun to interrogate the landscape idea;[26] and studies of symbolic landscapes were certainly not absent from the literature either – after all, what was the study of typical housetypes of a region if not a study of the symbolic forms by which people lived? (for a review, see Holdsworth 1993). Neither were urban studies completely absent in older work (see, for example, Lewis 1976).[27] What changed was the sensibility and the political interests researchers brought to these topics in the 1980s and 1990s. Studies of landscape were infused with strong evaluations of the politics of

25 Particularly influential has been the work of Denis Cosgrove (1984; see chapter 4 below). But see also Olwig (1984, 1993, 1996b).
26 Perhaps the most noted essays along these lines were by the architectural critic-cum-geographer J.B. Jackson, who used his magazine *Landscape* to interrogate everything from the very idea of landscape to the subconscious ways in which Americans constructed their cityscapes.
27 There is also a long tradition, particularly in Britain, of studies of changes in urban morphology. An excellent example is Whitehand (1992).

class, gender, race, ethnicity, and eventually sexuality. Social contestation, rather than the invisible working of culture, was put at the forefront of landscape analysis (Mitchell 1996a).

As studies of the social differentiation of space have gained prominence in landscape geography, so too has the study of the necessary spatiality of identity itself become an issue of deep concern within cultural geography. On the one hand, this concern with identity – and with cultural politics more broadly – has been evident in the growing study of forms of cultural resistance (chapter 6, below). The question for such work has been one of precisely how it is that, given the overweening power of the economy, various states, militaries, and even the confederated media and culture industries, to shape our lives and our *selves* for us, ordinary people can continue to make their own histories and geographies anyway. Concerned with questions of cultural and geographical transgression, "resistance studies" seek to explore the contours of cultural control and contestation (Cresswell 1996; Pile and Keith 1997; Sibley 1995). Resistance is the very stuff of cultural politics.

On the other hand, the concern within cultural geography for understanding spatial differentiation and the construction of identity has also led to an explosion of research on the cultural-geographic politics of sexuality (chapter 7, below), gender (chapter 8), race (chapter 9), and national identity (chapter 10). David Matless (1995: 397) describes such work as studies of "performative moral geography," and that notion of performativity is helpful in reminding us that identity is always a (spatial) social practice – not just a set of ideas or ideologies floating somehow above and beyond the actions of people. Much of this research manifests itself as studies of the local conditions that underwrite the performance of identity (see Bell and Valentine 1995b; Duncan 1996a; Jackson 1991b; Keith and Pile 1993). But as geographers have explored the truism that identity is as often as not constructed through consumption (chapter 3; see also Brewer and Porter 1993; Ewan 1988; Sack 1988, 1992), the larger-scale processes necessary for identities to form have also come under increasing scrutiny. In a world knitted together by global production and consumption, according to McDowell (1994: 159), "identity is not place specific; the locality in a strictly geographical sense plays no part in [some people's] sense of self. Style is cosmopolitan, not local . . ." (see also Price 1996). Or, perhaps more accurately, for *most* people it is *both* cosmopolitan and local.

So too are racism, homophobia, and the oppressions of gender and class. For that reason – and because of the growing recognition that culture *is* politics – there has been a growing body of literature in cultural geography and cultural studies that examines the geography of cultural citizenship, exploring how new forms of identity transform or contest developed political, economic, and social boundaries (chapter 10, below; see Matless 1996 for a summary). In addition to identity formed through gender, sexuality, race, and class, questions of *national* identity formation (and the production of national cultures) are of immediate importance in the wake of the collapse of the Cold War and the unsettling of the relatively static nation-state system that governed the world in the post-World War II era (cf. Daniels 1993; Hooson 1994). Examinations of national identity seek to understand the changing geographies of political belonging and political efficacy – and they often find that such changing geographies both underpin and are underpinned by changing productions of "culture." Driving much of this work on identity is a search for the conditions that thwart or make possible what Andrew Ross (1998) has helpfully called "cultural justice."

"Culture" is spatial

As should be clear from the foregoing, cultural geography in the 1990s, to understate the case, exploded. The proliferation of new topics, new theoretical developments, and new research agendas has been such that adequately summarizing the work is impossible. Two points should be noted, however. The first is that the "cultural turn" is not limited to the subfield of cultural geography. Rather, in all manner of human geographies – from economic to political, from urban to regional, from feminist to Marxist – "culture" has become a primary focal point of study. Indeed, even as early as 1991, some were worrying that "the cultural" was becoming hegemonic in geography at the expense of important research into political and economic developments (Thrift 1991; Sayer 1994). Whatever the validity of the complaint, it is clear that there has been a remarkable convergence on "cultural" questions throughout the field of human geography. The second point is that if during the 1980s, one could "describe UK cultural geography in three words: Cosgrove, Daniels, and Jackson," that is certainly no longer the case (Duncan 1993b: 372). While the early development of Anglophone cultural geography may have largely been an American enterprise, British geographers, many trained in social rather than cultural geography, have taken the lead in the last decade in transforming the discipline – and they have done so in a multiplicity of voices. Inevitably, there has been discord, as new voices (feminist, post-structuralist, etc.) have entered the chorus – sometimes quite forcefully, other times rather surreptitiously. So to speak of cultural geography in the singular is probably misleading (Duncan 1994).

Yet if there is any consensus in all this new work in cultural geography, it is simply that, no matter how it is approached, "culture" *is* spatial. If, as Raymond Williams argues, culture is ordinary, it is so because it insinuates itself into our daily worlds as part of the spaces and spatial practices that define our lives. Older cultural theory in many ways stressed *time*, suggesting that cultural traditions were handed down from generation to generation. New cultural theory, as it is developing in geography, cultural studies, and many allied disciplines, stresses *space*, understanding culture to be constituted through space and *as* a space. To the degree that that is the case, spatial *metaphors* have become indispensable for understanding the constitutions of culture. Culture is understood to be a realm, medium, level, or zone, for example. In a typical passage, Denis Cosgrove and Peter Jackson (1987: 99) argue that culture should be understood as "the medium through which people transform the mundane phenomena of the material world into a world of significant symbols to which they give meaning and attach value"; and hence, culture "is the very medium through which change is experienced, contested and constituted" (Cosgrove and Jackson 1987: 95). Or as Jackson (1989: 2) later put it, culture is "the level at which social groups develop distinct patterns of life," and hence "are *maps of meaning* through which the world is made intelligible." Culture is in this sense a "sphere" of human life as important as, but somehow separate from, other "spheres" like politics, the economy, or society. In the next chapter we will critically examine such spatial metaphors, for though they can be exceptionally fruitful for understanding cultural contest and change, they also bring with them severe limitations, not least in that they reiterate rather than challenge a "base-superstructure" model of society.

In addition, these spatial metaphors rather ironically tend to echo exactly the superorganic notion new cultural geographers criticize Zelinsky for: there seems to be in this reformulation of "culture" an overriding sense that culture is every*thing* – or any*thing* – and that it exists as a "realm apart."[28] Culture consists in practices, but it is also a "system of signification." Culture is a way people make sense of the world (the stories they tell themselves about themselves, in Clifford Geertz's formulation), but it is also a system of power and domination. Culture is a means of differentiating the world, but it is also global and hegemonic. Culture is open and fluid, a "text," as James Duncan (1990) puts it, always open to multiple readings and interpretations, but it is something with causative power (as when "culture increasingly fashion[s] strategies of resistance" [Keith and Cross 1993: 27]) and hence must be unitary and solid enough to be efficacious. Culture is a level, or sphere, or domain, or idiom; but it is also a whole way of life. Culture is clearly language – or "text," or "discourse" – but it is also the social, material construction of such things as "race" or "gender." Culture is a point of political contact, it *is* politics; but it is also both ordinary and the best that is thought and known. If culture is all this (and probably a lot more too), no wonder the "critical" and "cultural" turn in geography (as elsewhere) has in many ways been a turn away from *explanation* and towards an exploration of *meaning*. What else is there, critical geography and cultural studies seem to be asking, but a search for meaning in the midst of all this confusion?

Conclusion

One thing is clear, in any event: the new versions of culture take as their touchstone, whether implicitly or explicitly, precisely the sort of cultural relativism that Herder so long ago advocated. The multiculturalism made necessary by this development of cultural theory has blossomed into a full-blown discipline of cultural studies. In turn, geographers have drawn on cultural studies to reinvigorate their own sense of what the geography of culture is and can be. As will be apparent in the remainder of the book, the intellectual traffic between geography and cultural studies now runs down a two-way street, with practitioners in each field drawing on the insights and work of the other. In summary – and to preview one of the main points of this book – it can be argued that the primary goal of cultural studies is precisely the analysis (and perhaps even the celebration) of the diversity of the world. For this, a *geographical* theory of culture – as level, domain, or system – has been essential. Yet in a fitting bit of irony (since new cultural geography cut its teeth by attacking the Sauerian tradition), it turns out that by so strongly identifying with the cultural studies project of multiculturalism – or cultural particularism – and indeed, by becoming essential to it, new

28 By calling culture a "sphere," Jackson and others directly, if unconsciously, echo exactly the language Kroeber (1917: 22–51) used to describe culture as superorganic.

cultural geography finds itself sitting quite firmly in a geographical tradition inaugurated by Carl Sauer himself in the 1920s: the geographical exploration of cultural difference and change.

Which is all well and good until we ask ourselves just what it was that Johnny Rotten and Sid Vicious – or for that matter, Donald Fagen – were singing about anyway.

3

From Values to Value and Back Again: The Political Economy of Culture

Cultural Productions

The Sex Pistols fizzled in 1978. Despite the band's explosive rise, its demise was more whimper than bang. Sid Vicious was on his way to an overdose; the band was fighting with each other rather than with the world into which it had been born. By the time of its last concert (in San Francisco), "punk was no secret society" – indeed, it had by then become "a representation several times removed." As Greil Marcus (1989: 83–4) has put it, speaking not only of the Sex Pistols but of the people who attended the band's concerts, "it was, at this point, an act: a collective attempt to prove that the physical representation of an aesthetic representation could produce reality, or at least real blood." Even so, the hallmark importance of Punk was precisely that it showed that people, acting collectively still *could* produce reality. They could *make* a future in a world in which there *was* no future. Punk asked – demanded – that people act, that they take the representations amid which they lived and make some*thing* out of them.

And yet its moment was short-lived. It was even more short-lived than the moment of cultural rebellion we now conventionally call "the Sixties." Whatever its long-term impact in the realm of politics, popular culture, and social relations, that earlier moment, cultural critic Thomas Frank (1997a: 8) argues, "was triggered at least as much by developments in mass culture . . . as changes in the grass roots . . . ; its greatest moments occurred on television, on the radio, at rock concerts, and in movies." If "the Sixties" was a rebellion or revolution, then it was one that was manufactured in images – images as often as not produced by advertising agencies on Madison Avenue (figure 3.1). "The Sixties," Frank (1997a) suggests, should be told as "the story of hip's mutation from native language of the alienated to that of advertising." By the time Punk and the Sex Pistols came around, in other words, alternative culture producers were making physical representations of aesthetic representations in a world where aesthetic representations – of cool, of hip, of rebellion, and of alienation – were already *produced* for ready consumers by image-makers working for advertising agencies, movie studios, record companies, and, of course, manufacturers of durable goods such as cars, stereos, and jeans. Our very resistance to the *status quo*, to the world "as it is," was conveyed by the commodities we bought, the music we listened to, and the shows we watched.

What is more, as the mainstream of cultural studies argues, what we consume is now itself more and more *only* images. It's not the flavor or thirst-quenching abilities of Coca Cola that matter, it is the image we project while drinking it. The "use-value" of Levis is not that they keep us clothed, but the image they project (of youth, rebellion, and so forth). Everything is thus a text or picture or more generally a "representation," and those texts, images, and representations are all there are (or all

Figure 3.1 Even the staid Dodge was celebrating "rebellion" and non-conformance as early as 1965. As Thomas Frank argues (see text), for all that "the Sixties" was a product of the politics of the street, it was also manufactured in the design studios of Madison Avenue advertising agencies. Photograph courtesy of Daimler–Chrysler Corporation Historical Archives; used by permission.

that matters). We live in a world of "simulacrum."[1] Reality itself is a representation of nothing more than other representations behind which there are never any "real" things.

There is clearly some truth to this position. In the summer of 1996, the Sex Pistols staged a "reunion tour" (without, of course, Sid Vicious, whom Johnny Rotten has anyway derided as "nothing more than a coat hanger filling an empty space on stage" [quoted in MTV 1996]). The purpose of the tour was quite clear: "We have a common cause: It's your money" (Hilburn and Crowe 1996). The goal for the band was precisely to "re-present" itself, playing all its old songs, restaging (and at the same time mocking) its cries of alienation and rebellion. Or as Gregory Klages (n.d.) says, "The Sex Pistols reunion is a money-grabbing parody, and the band never pretends that it is anything else." The point is that if by 1978, the Sex Pistols provided the opportunity for their audience to transform an aesthetic representation into a physical one, as Marcus says, then by 1996, all that was left were *parodies* of the aesthetics of Punk, parodies produced to make money (despite band-members' occasionally serious-sounding pronouncements that they were reuniting because their music had so much integrity). "We're back . . . with a vengeance," Johnny Rotten (now once again using his given name John Lydon) told MTV (1996). But what they were back *as* was simply an image of what they once were, which itself was an image of rebellion and cultural anarchy, dreamed up by a London boutique owner (see chapter 6, below). History repeats itself, but this time as parody, and universal monikers of rebellion like "Punk" are carefully managed, this time to the potential tune of $20 million (plus royalties from a live album).

In the event, the tour by all accounts was a failure. The band performed poorly, and audiences seemed to only go through the motions of what was expected of them: spitting on stage, throwing things, pissing off the band. The Sex Pistols reunited in a world that was no longer of their own making, as it had been to a greater extent in 1976. Punk was just one more in a long list of commodified experiences, ready to be bought off the shelf or from TicketMaster.

There are at least three important questions that arise from this discussion of cultural production, "cool," and Punk reunions in a culturally changed world. First, just what *is* the relationship between "physical representation" – the solidity of things – and "aesthetic representation"? Second, how are these "representations" produced? What are the conditions under which they are made? And third, how do social values (and economic value) attach to these "representations"? If all we have are representations – what many cultural theorists call "signifiers" – then it is important to understand how these signifiers are produced, how they circulate, and how they are consumed. For Thomas Frank, the answer is fairly straightforward: "culture industries" produce and circulate meaning; business culture produces the hegemonic culture (both straight and hip) and we are all caught in its grip. Business itself has effected a "conquest of cool," and made rebellion something to be bought off the shelf, in the form of bomber jackets, jeans, cds, and "alternative" fruit juices. It has become so much a part of business, in fact, that it forms the core of con-

1 Following the French social theorist Jean Baudrillard, "simulacrum" has come to mean a representation – or copy – for which there is no original.

temporary business leadership books and manuals. Social values and economic value, Frank implicitly argues, are indivisible.

Others, however, suggest that consumers of texts, representations, or significations have much more control over the images through which they fashion their lives. No matter what the intent of the culture industries (and all industries, it seems, are culture industries now), consumers take commodities and give them new meaning, use them in unintended ways, make them their own, and fashion them into something new, "alternative," and resistant to the dictates of the economy or "straight" society. If cultural production seeks to control our thoughts and emotions, our daily lives and our acts of rebellion, then cultural consumption turns the tables on the dictates of production and shows that nothing and no one (else) can ever really control the use and meaning of the products through which we define ourselves (see, for example, Fiske 1989).

And yet such liberatory theories of consumption ring hollow. Reflecting on the results of early theorizing about mass culture by such critics as Theodor Adorno and Max Horkheimer (see below), and on more recent work that asserts that all "readings" of mass or popular culture are a form of "resistance," Michael Denning (1996: 64) sums up the problem nicely:

> If audiences are not the passive, manipulated consumers depicted in early critiques of mass culture, neither are they the unruly, resisting readers imagined by more recent celebrants of popular culture. Though it is true that people make all sorts of bizarre and unintended uses of popular texts, and that virtually any cultural commodity can become a private scripture, licensing oppositional and utopian desires, drives and actions, not to mention anti-social and pathological behaviors, these "readings" rarely have much historical significance. Subaltern experience does not necessarily generate social criticism and cultural resistance; the possibility of popular political readings of cultural commodities depends on the cultivation, organization, and mobilization of audiences by oppositional subcultures and social movements.

That is to say, "resistance" can never be individual (see chapter 6); it must be organized into an effective force. But neither can dominant cultural production ever be individual and anarchic: it too must be organized, and it must find a ready audience, an audience ready to define *its* values, in terms of the values promoted by the cultural production. The question then is one of the *conditions* under which "culture" is produced and resistance organized. What was the difference in the production of *audiences* for the Sex Pistols in 1976 and in 1996? What had changed in the conditions of cultural production? Answering such questions is the purpose of this chapter; and it is certainly one of the key purposes of this book, as these questions clearly haunt every chapter. The important point for us, however, is that "conditions" are always *necessarily* geographic: the issue is what the shape of that geography is, what its components are and how it is organized to promote or resist the production of culture.

So there are two main themes at work in this chapter, both of which will be addressed from several different angles. The first is the relationship between economy and values, between cultural production and cultural consumption. How are values produced, circulated, and consumed? How does economic value provide a context within which social and cultural values are promulgated, transformed, or resisted? The second issue is simply the question of how spaces – the geographies of the worlds we live in – are necessary components of cultural production and consumption. To explore these issues, however, it will first be necessary to critically evaluate cultural theory as it has been adopted into and developed as part of "new cultural geography." In this critique, we will see that "new cultural geography" inadvertently repeats rather than overcomes some of the shortcomings of older geographical theories of culture. It therefore becomes necessary to lay out an alternative theoretical framework for understanding the production, circulation, and consumption of "culture." And finally, it is important to show how this alternative theory allows us to see how "audiences" for cultural production and cultural resistance are organized, and how that organization changes as the spatial context within which they exist changes.

"Traditional" Values, Surplus Value, and the Power to Generalize

Before turning to these issues, it is important to lay out and better define some of the key terms I have already been loosely throwing about in this chapter: value, values, cultural production, and cultural consumption. And the best way to do that is to start with an example from the culture wars, an example that shows just how complex the link between economic value and social values, between cultural production and cultural consumption, can be.

It would be foolish to posit a *direct* link between the workings of the economy and local and national culture wars over artistic expression in America. Yet it would be equally foolish to assume that there is no connection whatsoever. In 1996, the Charlotte Repertory Theater staged Tony Kushner's polemical play about the AIDS crisis, *Angels in America*. The Tony Award-winning *Angels* features, in addition to explicit language and rather pointed commentary on the religious and political right's response to gays and AIDS, a very brief nude scene as an AIDS patient undergoes a medical examination. The Christian Coalition and other religious right groups sought to prevent the opening of *Angels* on the grounds that the nude scene violated North Carolina's indecent exposure law. To assure its ability to produce *Angels*, the Charlotte Rep obtained a court order declaring the nude scene protected under the First Amendment's freedom of speech clause. With this protection, *Angels* was performed as scheduled to sell-out audiences (Yeoman 1998).

But when, a few months later, conservatives won a majority on the county Board of Commissioners, one of their first actions was to cut the county subsidy ($2.5 million) not only to the Charlotte Rep, but to all arts programs. Urged on by the Colorado Springs, Colorado-based fundamentalist organization Focus on the Family, the Board sought to uphold "traditional" Southern values – something that funding the arts presumably precluded. "We have a list of standards, things that we don't believe in," one commissioner told an interviewer. "One of those things in the South is that we don't want to promote homosexuals. In Charlotte, North Carolina, the conduct they engage in is illegal, and you cannot expect that government will provide you with special rights for behavior that society has determined is criminal" (Yeoman 1998: 33).[2] The commissioners took their action, however, *despite* united opposition by the Charlotte business community. The special counsel of the Charlotte-based NationsBank (now part of the largest bank in the USA) argued against cutting arts funding both on free speech grounds and because it might harm the business climate of the region. Culture, and an active cultural scene, is now often seen as vital to the *economic* success of a place. And highly publicized culture wars over what can and cannot be artistically done in a place can scare away tourists, potential investors, and the like. Struggles over art, therefore, can translate into the relative success or decline of a regional economy.[3] One ironic result of struggles such as these in countless communities across the USA is that the very *fear* of having funding cut leads many arts groups to engage in acts of self-censorship.[4] The cultural endowment of a place – which many argue is integral to economic development in the postindustrial era – is diminished *a priori*. Arguments about *values*, to put the point another way, are often also arguments about *value* in the economic sense.

With this relationship between values and value in mind, in this chapter I will propose an alternative means for understanding what culture *is* and what culture *does*. The examples of the Sex Pistols, the "conquest of the cool," and political struggles over acceptable cultural expression in different places indicate that the relationship between values and value is complex. What is less obvious in either example is that it is also complexly – and necessarily – geographic. Nevertheless, there is a relatively simple starting point which will allow us to draw out the geographical implications of these stories. For cultural theorist Fred Inglis (1993: 38), culture "simply *is* the system of humanly expressive practices by which values are renewed, created, and contested." And, in turn, "value" is "the name given to those fierce little concentrations of meaning in an action or a state of affairs which fix them as good or important" (1993: 11). The "relatively simple starting point" is therefore one of locating, naming, and describing the *conditions* under which "fierce little concentrations of meaning" are fixed as "good or important"; and that starting point must always be followed by the obvious question: "Good and important *for whom?*" For what is good for one class, group, or individual is not necessarily good for another: those with the power to determine the *situations* within which "good" is defined (see chapter 6) are usually those who get to determine what counts as good – though never without a fight. In other words, the starting point for an analysis of values or "culture" is simply asking the question: How are these values and cultural meanings *created*?

2   In 1986, the USA Supreme Court upheld state sodomy laws that criminalize gay sex, even between consenting adults in the privacy of their own bedrooms. North Carolina has such a law. The language of "special rights" has become a favorite shibboleth of the religious right's campaign against civil rights for gays.
3   A good examination of the connections between the arts and other cultural productions and postindustrial urban development is Zukin (1995); see also Molotch (1996).
4   Several examples are detailed in Yeoman (1998). The Charlotte Repertory Theater has thus far opted against self-censorship (since controversial plays – because of the controversy they generate – often make up at the box office what they might lose from government subsidy), but has instead cut ancillary programs such as a violence prevention program performed at public schools and discounted tickets for seniors and students.

In the contemporary industrial and postindustrial world, what is considered good and important is largely determined through some form of market calculus. As early as 1960, estimated Clark Kerr (1963), the president of the University of California system, the production, distribution, and consumption of knowledge accounted for some 29 percent of the American gross national product, and he predicted that during the second half of the twentieth century as a whole "culture" would supplant industry (particularly the auto industry) as the driving force of the economy (see the comments by Debord 1994: 130–47). Kerr was hardly alone in his predictions (though his comments are particularly interesting because they proved an important point of reaction for student radicals during the 1960s who saw in his vision for the "multiversity" of the future the complete subjugation of knowledge and human will to the capitalist imperative [Mitchell 1992b]). What is interesting is the degree to which such predictions *underestimated* the economic value that would soon be attached to knowledge and cultural production. The production of "fierce concentrations of meaning" would more and more be inserted into the logic of capitalist development, becoming important "sites" for the generation of not just values, but *surplus value*.

The production of surplus value through the production of knowledge and culture is, in many ways, little different in process than the production of surplus value through the production of more tangible commodities. It requires increasingly sophisticated divisions of labor; that is, it requires legions of people to do the *work* of cultural production. As Guy Debord (1994: 130) put it in his classic account of the *Society of the Spectacle*, "culture is the general sphere of knowledge, and of representations of lived experience, within a historical society divided into classes; what this amounts to is the power to generalize, existing *apart*, as an intellectual division of labor and as the intellectual labor of division." A second starting point for understanding the production of culture, therefore, is to focus on *who* possesses this "power to generalize" and *how* they use it to advance the "intellectual labor of division" – the division of one group from another so as to stabilize and name "culture," and so as to say about their own or other's lived experience: "this is true."[5]

The point, then, is that values – meanings, knowledge about good and bad and about truth and falsehood, about moral ways of life – are inexorably, if not completely, imbricated in the production of capitalist value. "Culture" is a process and object of *labor*. But it is a very complex process and object of labor, one that is not only a *result* of the labor process, but an important input to it too. That is because differences – across space, most particularly, but also in gender, race, ethnicity, and sexuality – are essential to the uneven accumulation of capital itself. If the "way of life" in a particular place structurally *demands* the ownership and maintenance of suburban houses and cars, then labor will be, *ceteris paribus*, more expensive than in regions in which foot travel and corrugated tin shacks are still the norm (Harvey 1982; see also Mitchell 1994). "When the conditions of collective human existence are not only bought and sold on a market integrating a complex division of labor but also turned into conditions of capitalist production and accumulation, they are being used as capital," argues John Gulick (1998: 142). "If culture is defined . . . as a set of norms

---

5   Debord (1994: 141) takes this a step further and argues that under conditions of capitalist production of "culture" "individuals do not actually experience events"; they are only spectators who experience representations of events manufactured for them.

that binds members of a collective organization – be it a nation-state, a neighbor-hood, a business firm, or a social class – to treat and be treated by one another in a certain regular way, then it can be demonstrated that culture . . . may be valorized as a capitalist productive force."

The production of "culture" – as systems of meaning, as "ways of life," as artifacts – is integral to all parts of the capitalist system: it is a "field" – like cool, punk, and the arts – ready to be farmed for profit; it is a means for dividing and sorting labor that produces that profit; and it is an endless stream of artifacts – commodities – hopefully to be purchased by those both directly working on the cultural production line, and those toiling in other parts of the global division of labor. This is a way of thinking of "culture" – as a system (and as a product) of production, as a *political economy* – that the dominant metaphors for understanding culture in new cultural geography (such as we studied in the previous chapter) simply do not capture. It is important, there-fore, to take a moment to more closely examine the shortcomings of these metaphors. This examination will be followed by a fuller explication of the theory of cultural production I have just so briefly outlined.

Cultural Chaos: A Critique of New Theories of Culture

For all that is exciting in the new cultural geography and cultural studies (and there is a lot), there are also important problems in the way that culture has been conceptual-ized – not least of which is that this new conceptualization of culture is quite chaotic, and hence, in many ways, meaningless.[6] As we saw in chapter 2, above, to the degree that "culture" is represented as a "sphere" or a "realm," it perpetuates (despite intentions to the contrary) at worst the sort of superorganicism for which anthropo-logists and geographers have rightly been criticized, and at best a quite unsophisti-cated restatement of the "base-superstructure" model – a restatement that takes for granted a rather clean division between the worlds of economy and culture (Williams 1977, 1980). There is clearly an unconscious recognition of such an inadequacy of cultural theory in new cultural geography and Cultural Studies. It expresses itself through the fact that it is strikingly rare, in both cultural geography and cultural studies more generally, for empirical studies to actually operationalize any of the myriad definitions of culture that have been offered in recent years. Instead of a specification and development of "culture," showing how it *works* in society, there has instead been a proliferation of examples that presumably *constitute* culture: every-day life, works of art, political resistance, economic formations, religious beliefs, styles of clothing, eating habits, ideologies, ideas, literature, music, popular media, and so on. Culture seems to be little more than a list of activities that the analyst has deemed "cultural."[7] Now it may very well be that these activities are vitally important to the ways of life of a people, that they have been under-studied owing to the limitations of earlier conceptualizations of culture, or that new emphases in postmodernism and

6 This section draws on and expands the argument in Mitchell (1995b).
7 In this regard, new cultural geography has much in common with the "old" cultural geography it often derides. One of the hallmarks of older traditions in (particularly American) cultural geography has been its unabashed excitement about the endless variety of cultural forms in the world.

cultural studies have made them central objects of academic analysis. But that does not get beyond the problem of "culture" that confronts both cultural geography and cultural studies at a time of rapid global social and economic transformation: What precisely does culture do? How does it work? To suggest that culture is a realm or map of meaning, or that it is a means for making sense of the world, tells us nothing. Even worse, it forgets all about the issues of power that so concerned Gramsci, Hall, Williams, and others. "Culture" has work to do in society – but perhaps not in the way that the rather optimistic accounts of new cultural geography hope.

Simply seeing "culture" as a convenient term for all the myriad processes that cultural geographers might want to study ignores how words like "culture" participate in "an ongoing 'hidden' discourse, underwriting the legitimacy of those who exercise power in society" (Olwig 1993: 307). And this is the key, both to the problems of cultural theory and to the power of the contemporary culture wars: because the term culture has no clear referent, it is available as a handy tool for arraying power, for organizing the sorts of invidious distinctions that instantiate the power of *some* in the world (at the expense of others). The very ambiguity of the term "culture," in other words, is one of the bases for the culture wars – and not just contemporary ones either. When Matthew Arnold, in the 1860s, famously defined culture as "the *best* knowledge and thought of the time," he was making "a direct response to the social crises of those years, and what he saw as opposed to culture was *anarchy*," Raymond Williams (1980: 3) reminds us. "He did not see or present himself as a reactionary, but as a guardian of excellence and of humane values. That, then as now, was the strength of his appeal." Arnold's appeal does indeed remain strong, and is frequently drawn on by conservative cultural critics, precisely because they can argue – often quite convincingly – that they are indeed the guardians of excellence and of human values, an exercise of power if ever there was one. A theory that sees culture simply as diversity in "ways of life" provides little by way of answer to such powerful claims. Indeed, it is reduced to arguing for or against culture on precisely the grounds Arnold established: the grounds of such politically loaded terms as "best" and "excellence." Moreover, such celebratory theories of culture also miss the way that "the *best* knowledge and thought of the time" is determined not abstractly, but by the concerted effort, the unavoidable work, of many people seeking to pin down a "fierce little concentration of meaning" – a value – with which to determine just what is best. The "best" doesn't just exist: it is actively produced in the midst of the whole cacophony of claims for that title. Is it the director of the Charlotte Repertory Theater or the Mecklenburg County Commissioners who know best? And how do they *know* that they know best? The answer lies in the work done by the producers of knowledge laboring on both sides of that particular divide.

But there is a deeper problem with new theories of culture. They have had the unintended effect of further reifying an essentially empty concept. Culture, which signifies nothing, is turned into a stable referent with clear edges, boundaries, and effectiveness. As Duncan long ago pointed out, making such a move is a fallacy of the first order (see chapter 1). What is needed instead is a new conceptualization that understands right from the beginning that there is *no such ontological thing as culture*. At best "culture" is a handy term, but in the end it really *represents no identifiable process*. To put the argument at its most stark: There is no culture in the world, only differing arrays of power that organize society in this way, and not that. Hence, there is only a powerful *idea* of culture, an idea that has developed (as we saw in chapter 1) under specific historical conditions and was later broadened as a means of explaining material differences, social order, and relations of power. But these explanations are not "culture itself," whether we define culture as a superorganic *thing*, or in the new way that stresses its role as a (still superorganic) *medium* or *domain*. What is needed now, therefore, is not further definition of "culture," hoping to fine-tune away all the problems earlier definitions have presented, but rather a frank admission that while culture *itself* does not exist, the *idea* of culture has been developed and deployed in the modern (and postmodern) world as a means of attempting to order, control, and define "others" in the name of power and profit.

The reason "culture" has become such an intense topic of concern among scholars in the past twenty years is precisely because the idea of culture has become one of the most important tools of power at a time of global restructuring. Academics are responding to structural changes in the world around them: "culture" has more and more become a tool of surplus value extraction, as with the "conquest of cool"; it has become a means of wringing profit out of new markets at home and abroad, and a means for channeling dissent in productive directions.[8] Scholars have responded by trying to get a grip on why culture has suddenly seemed to be so important, has suddenly seemed to be saturating everything we do.

Let me see if I can explain this position, first by showing why culture itself does not exist (that is, by making more concrete my criticisms of culture as it has been theorized in new cultural geography), and then by providing an alternative framework for understanding how the idea of culture functions in society. I call this alternative framework a "political economy of culture."

Culture as mirage: the infinite regress of culture

Geographers are not alone in reifying "culture" as an ontological given. Indeed, Donna Haraway (1989: 308–9; see also Strathern 1987), has suggested that "culture" is a quintessentially "modernist" concept that has been "carved out of an unruly world as an object of knowledge like a modernist work of art – a unit perceived to have its own internal, architectural principles of coherence." In this regard, culture is a concept deployed to stop flux in its tracks and to pull out the essences of a situation, creating the contours of a stable "way of life" where before there had been change and contest. The idea of culture demands a mapping of boundaries and edges, the specification of shape and form (as the "carving" metaphor Haraway uses indicates): in order to be analyzable, culture must become a bounded object that ultimately differentiates the world. Wilbur Zelinsky's *Cultural Geography of the United States* (see chapter 1, above) is a perfect exemplification of this process.

But even in newer, more "postmodern" versions of culture, a good deal of the objectification and boundary-making that marked modernist conceptions of culture remains. Subcultures, counter-cultures, resistant cultures (like Punk or the religious right), along with hegemonic cultures (like, now, "cool"), have all been identified and

---

8   As evidenced by the groaning shelves of books on "business culture" and "culture as business" found at any bookstore.

mapped by practitioners of cultural studies (including new cultural geography), even as it is better understood that these cultures cannot stand as completely discrete and autonomous units (as the particularism of Sauer seemed to suggest). Indeed, practitioners of cultural studies and new cultural geography together like to speak, instead, of plural cultures occupying a single location. But the problem of reification is not thereby avoided.

For James Clifford (1988: 11), "intervening in an interconnected world, one is always, to varying degrees, 'inauthentic.' " One is always "caught between cultures," he says. In a globally interconnected world, "difference or distinctiveness can never be located in the continuity of a culture or a tradition," and so difference is constructed in what he calls the "conjunctural" spaces between cultures. "Identity," therefore, "is ... not essential." Yet even so, cultures exist, according to Clifford. To be "caught between cultures" assumes that cultures and their boundaries *can* be mapped. For us to even begin to find those "conjunctural spaces," we have to know where cultures begin and end, and how they overlap. And *someone* – some outsider, like an ethnographer or geographer – must do the mapping. This is a subtle theory. For Clifford, culture *itself* exists, even if it does not directly construct differences between peoples. Differences between people, because they are cultural, can be mapped and identified, they can be ordered and intellectually controlled. The very *idea* of culture provides a means to stop the flux of "conjunction" so as to reveal marked differences between two discrete cultures that come together in a single space.

But the "notion that humankind is divisible into discrete parcels of social relations" is itself "increasingly questioned throughout the social sciences," and so "all of the varied terms used to label the putative constituent units of human kind prove problematic" (Lewis 1991: 605). Such labels – most particularly "culture" – are thus a victim of what could be called "infinite regress." That is, if culture is assigned ontological status – if it is thought to actually exist as something identifiable – then it must be definable in a coherent and inclusive manner. Yet when definitions of culture are attempted, theorists invariably find themselves resorting to other (external) concepts and realms, each of which itself, it turns out, cannot be defined in an internally coherent and inclusive manner, as with terms such as level, domain, medium, signifying system. These bedrock terms, always receding from the grasp of writers who try to pin down their definitions, end up referring to nothing (or everything). They stand as empty (or over-full) abstractions. With each round of definition, the ontological basis of meaning recedes one step further, always just out of grasp. They have roots in no worlds.

Even so, we continue to parcel humanity into discrete, bounded cultures, even if we acknowledge that the boundaries may be porous. We continue to insist that culture exists, even if we can never say what it is. So in this sense – and this is absolutely essential for understanding how "culture" works in the world – culture *does* in fact come into being, possessing the power to determine social relations, meaning, and all the other things practitioners of cultural studies hope it does, but now in a whole new way. When someone (or some social formation) has the *power* to stop the infinite regress of culture, to say "this is what culture *is*"; and to make that meaning stick (by, for example, saying "this is what we will and will not fund"), then "culture" as an incredibly powerful *idea* is made real, as real as any other exercise of power. Aesthetic representations are turned into physical representations. And this is why culture wars are so deathly important.

As an abstraction or covering term, culture is made to function as explanation of difference, whether by geographers and ethnographers, or by cultural critics, marketers, or geopolitical strategists. The empty, meaningless abstraction of "culture" is filled with meaning and made concrete, not in the working of culture itself, but in the process of *defining* culture. Halting the infinite regress of culture in practice is a process of social struggle. Terms such as culture "have a very vague definition because it is only *when* there is a dispute, *as long as it lasts*, and *depending* on the strength exerted by dissenters [to proposed meanings] that words such as 'culture' . . . receive a precise meaning. . . . In other words, no one lives in a 'culture' . . . *before* he or she clashes with others" (Latour 1987: 201). The sociologist of science Bruno Latour explains that the production of knowledge (like knowledge about culture) is a process in which unstable "lists" of activities and process, possessing no real morphological definition, are struggled over by contending parties seeking to define the world in their own terms. When one party proves victorious (for whatever reasons, but always having to do with gathering the power to make its claims stick), the lists become *reified*; they become *reality* (Latour 1987: 201). In this, Latour's explanation has strong parallels with Gramsci's discussion of hegemony. Knowledge is always contested, but it is nonetheless the case that some forms of knowledge become more powerful than others; they become hegemonic. Most importantly, these reified lists take on an appearance of nature, they seem obvious and unchangeable, as when we unthinkingly agree that the wars in central Africa are a product of a millennium of cultural conflict, or that "cool" really is a form of resistance. Seen in this way, the invocation of "culture" becomes a means for representing relations of power. "Culture" is a representation of "others" which solidifies only insofar as it can be given objective reality (by some powerful group) as stasis in social relations. In this sense, it is the idea of culture that is important, not some mythical culture itself.

The idea of culture is not what people are doing; rather, it is the way people make sense of what they have done. It is the way activities are reified *as* culture. The list of processes and activities that practitioners of cultural geography and cultural studies use to exemplify culture are important not because they *are* culture, but because, through struggle over the power to define them, they *are made* to be culture. The problem with much new cultural geography is that it buys into the reification; it assumes that culture does exist, because someone powerful has said it does. Instead, cultural geographers need to begin the task of determining how and why particular processes and activities come to be deemed "culture," and why precisely that is important. In other worlds, cultural geographers should be engaged in the task of determining not what culture is – since it is nothing – but rather how the *idea* of culture works in society. To call culture a level or domain makes little sense. Culture is instead a powerful name – powerful because it obscures what it is meant to identify. If "culture" is politics by another name (as it is), then it is so by dint of its function as *ideology*.

All of this may seem to argue that the "spatial turn" in social theory (see chapter 2, above) has been for naught (at least as far as geographers are concerned), that we, as geographers, won't have that central place at the table of cultural theory that seemed to be promised by the turn to space as a key variable in social change. On the contrary: the recognition that "culture" is "only" an idea, only an ideology, clears an even bigger spot at the table for spatial analysis because, at the level of ontology, ideology is impossible without geography (after all, what are "physical representations" other than things with definable spatial attributes such as shapes, boundaries, and edges). To see why, we need now to turn to an alternative framework for understanding how the idea of culture functions in the world.

An Alternative Framework: The Political Economy of "Culture"

Culture as ideology

To begin, we need to understand that the idea of culture is itself one of the key "players" in local and global systems of social reproduction. The idea of culture is one of the means by which society is integrated, by which the hegemony of one class or faction is advanced (and thus one means through which ongoing *resistance* to that hegemony is structured and understood). If "culture" is a false reification (like "race" – see chapter 9, below), then, to slightly modify the way I phrased it earlier, the key question for cultural geography is: Who reifies? It should be clear that the idea of culture is always an idea that works *for* some set of social actors (even if they are always opposed by other actors). The implementation of the idea of culture is a socially intentional process. The idea of culture is itself ideology: "a system of signification which facilitates the pursuit of particular interests" (Thompson 1984; quoted in Baker 1992: 3).

The definitional relationship between "ideology" and current definitions of "culture" is striking. For historical geographer Alan Baker (1992: 5), ideologies attempt to "sanctify an entire life-world by bringing every part into its compass: hence the emphasis on the sacred and the profane, light and dark, inside and outside, 'us' and 'them'...." Ideologies can thus be described as "complete systems, fulfilling by nature a globalizing function; they also claim to offer an overall representation of society, its past, present and future, are integrated into a complete *Weltanschauung*" (Duby 1985: 151). This, then, is precisely the work that culture does: "The distinction between such practices [of ideology] and their structure or frame" such as is made in culture-as-realm theories "is problematic...because...the apparent existence of such unphysical frameworks or structures is precisely the effect introduced by modern mechanisms of power and it is through this that modern systems of domination are made" (T. Mitchell 1990: 561). To translate: when both powerful social actors and cultural theorists suggest the existence of some metaphysical realm or sphere of unphysical life called culture, they reinforce the ideological work of "culture"; they reinforce the power to define social life as somehow beyond the workings of society itself, and instead locate it in a mythical realm of "meaning" or even "nature." The *metaphor* of culture is precisely what tethers the abstraction of "culture" to the material world.

By locating social interaction in discrete cultures, and by enclosing some activities as "cultural" (and therefore an attribute of a people or a realm within which meaning resides), contentious activities are abstracted into the partial truth contained in the idea of culture: namely that there are true and deep differences between people. An emphasis on the idea of culture, conversely, allows us to see how such partial truths are universalized and globalized – and to what end.

In some rather optimistic versions of postmodern ethnography, the recognition that all truth (like "cultural truths") is partial leads to "a liberation . . . in recognizing that no one can write about others any longer as if they were discrete objects or texts" (Clifford 1986: 25). But a more realistic analysis would place such "partial truths" within the relations of power that produce them. Hence, while postmodern ethnographers and many in cultural studies might not want to universalize those partial truths, while they might want to respect the fluidity of "culture," the whole purpose of the idea of culture is to do just the opposite. There are plenty of people who are quite content to reify, and to speak for "others," since it is clearly in their material interest to do so. Advertisers, politicians, corporate location experts, marketers, pundits, travel promoters, rock stars and all manner of other social agents are all too happy to continue trading in essentialism either in the name of cultural pluralism (which after all is highly marketable) or in the name of outright oppression. The idea of culture is constantly implemented to the profit and power of many different social agents. "Culture" sells, and a reified notion of culture explains everyday society. That is why the very idea of culture must be understood if we want to see how cultural geographies are made. Otherwise, the power that resides in the ability to deploy this idea will remain mysterious, and cultural geography will return to its passion for celebrating difference and uniqueness, without ever understanding how that difference is actively produced – and why.

"Culture" and economy: questions of social reproduction

All this returns us to the huge questions laid out at the beginning of this chapter. How *does* the idea of culture work in society? And for whom does it work? In whose interest is the idea of culture deployed? What relations of power are maintained through the ability of powerful social actors to halt its infinite regress? In short, is there intentionality behind the deployment of the idea of culture?

The answer to the last question is decidedly yes. To understand why, we need to understand that in the contemporary world "culture" is not a realm, but an industry: it is a key component of the production of economic (and other) value. Think of it this way:

> If we view culture as that complex of signs and significations (including language) that mesh into codes of transmission of social values and meanings, then we can at least begin upon the task of unraveling its complexity under present-day conditions by recognizing that money and commodities are themselves the primary bearers of cultural codes. Since money and commodities are entirely bound up with the circulation of capital, it follows that cultural firms are firmly rooted in the daily circulation processes of capital. It is, therefore, with the daily experience of money and the commodity that we should begin, no matter if special commodities or even whole sign systems may be extracted from the common herd and made the basis of "high" culture. . . . (Harvey 1989a: 299)

David Harvey's point in the above quotation is not that "culture" is entirely *reducible* to the circulation of capital or commodities, but rather that it cannot be *separated* from it, precisely because it is through "production" that the idea of culture circulates.

Fifty years ago, cultural theorists Theodor Adorno and Max Horkheimer (1993: 32–3) made exactly the same point. "Marked differentials such as those of A or B films, or of stories in magazines in different price ranges," they wrote in an essay called "The Culture Industry," "depend not so much on subject matter as on classifying, organizing, and labeling consumers. Something is provided for all so that none may escape; the distinction [between groups of people] are emphasized and extended. The public is catered for with a hierarchical range of mass produced products of varying quality. . . . Consumers appear as statistics on research organization charts, and are divided by income groups . . . ; the technique is that used for any type of propaganda." The important economic and political actors of the modern world, to Adorno and Horkheimer, were the "culture industries": those industries in the business of producing the commodities that defined style and status for the individual or group – the industries that produced the commodities that became "the primary bearers of cultural codes." Individual or group expression was only possible by surrendering entirely to the dictates of the industry, buying this product and not that, but buying *in* nonetheless.

We will question at least this aspect of Adorno and Horkheimer's formulation in chapter 6 when we look at the geography of cultural resistance, but for now, there is much that is obviously correct in the argument they make. Most particularly, we can see that "culture" does not attach to individuals or groups as some essential part of their genetic or social make-up. Rather "cultural life" – that which gets called "culture" – is the mediation of production and consumption in everyday life. This process, as we will see in a minute, demands what Harvey (1989a: 346) has described as "sophisticated divisions of labor," with some people assigned specifically to the task of creating "culture." Their job is to develop the idea of culture so as to normalize or smooth over contradictions between systems of production (which are inherently and grossly unfair) and systems of consumption (which rely on the myth that we *all* can have it all). One of the jobs of people working in the culture industries is to name and define resistances and strategies to the workings of the political economy, to *re*define them as "culture" and hence as an expression of "taste" rather than active resistance. Tastes, of course, can be catered to, and in the process new products can be developed and sold and new markets "carved out" and satisfied. "Consumerism," Thomas Frank (1997b: 34) therefore avers, "is no longer about 'conformity' but about 'difference.' "

And so is production: the ability to wring surplus value out of the production process is more and more a function of operationalizing differences (in living standards, ideals, work habits, and the like) among working people around the globe.[9] In this sense, "culture" is an idea through which the various machinations of the political economy are represented *as* culture (and in which uneven development is naturalized). The idea of culture, then, becomes a means for judging other societies, or factions of *this* society, to determine how they "measure up" to the needs of the

9   The business press is the best source for understanding this process. See also Massey (1984); Harvey (1989a).

global economy, and thus to devise strategies for keeping them properly in line, putting them properly to work, or properly catering to their "tastes."[10] "Culture," as both something produced and consumed, then, is a primary ingredient in geographically uneven systems of social reproduction.

In the current world, we define ourselves through consumption, whether that consumption is of "things" (like clothes, cars, or books) or commodified "images" (such as music, TV shows, or that which is "cool"). As each of these examples show, the line between images and things is an arbitrary one. I drew it between things that can be held and things that can only be apprehended, between physical and aesthetic representations. But what are clothes without image? TV shows without television sets? Music without CDs and boomboxes? Is a Maxell audio tape a "thing" or an "image" (figure 3.2)? One of the jobs of the culture industry is precisely to constantly draw and redraw, blur and obfuscate, that line between image and thing, to make something desirable precisely *because* of the image it projects. And to return to a point made in chapter 2 during the discussion of Gramsci's notion of cultural hegemony, the degree to which a society is "integrated" is through our buying into *images* of that society – images defined through what we purchase (political ideas, politically correct running shoes, musical taste, identification with, or disdain for, cultural or ethnographic "others").

Figure 3.2   Image is everything. Maxell has used this advertisement for 20 years now, creating a deep association between the power and quality of the sound of its audio tapes and the image of a certain kind of life. The product being sold does not even appear in the ad. Photo: Advertising Archives.

10   Sometimes such discipline is as plain as the gunships that steam into "Third World" harbors to safeguard the "interests" of advanced capitalist countries. See Enloe (1990). More recently it has been expressed through the discipline of International Monetary Fund and World Bank-imposed "structural adjustments" aimed at undermining the growth of social welfare programs and at forcing integration of less industrialized countries into the global market. See Bello (1994); and Thomas-Emeagwali (1995).

In the localizing strategies of ethnographic research, for example, which is an integral part of the production of "cultural" commodities (such as pottery, clothing design, or tourist destinations), such integration of our *own* society proceeds by reifying the "otherness" of other people, by bringing the "strange" into the parlors of the "ordinary."[11] The medium of such representations of otherness, according to Edward Said (1993), has long been the cash economy. Localization of "subcultures"; exoticization of overseas "others"; social integration across class differences within a society: all of these are historically enmeshed within the expanding and globalizing capitalist political economy. The salient fact of contemporary life, as Harvey (1989a: 344) has written, is the way in which "cultural life" "more and more . . . gets brought within the grasp of the cash nexus and the logic of capital circulation." Harvey (1989a: 344) is quick to point out that such a theorization of culture does not imply that all activity within the system called cultural is "reinforced or discarded according to the *post hoc* rationalizations of profit making"; nonetheless, the logic of capital "has long been implicated in these activities."

Thus, what gets called culture is part and parcel of systems of social reproduction, both at the local level and on a global scale. "Culture" is represented as part of, or as a pristine remainder in, a globally integrated system of social reproduction led (if not dictated) by a set of industries designed to profit from the maintenance of certain *kinds* of difference between and within people. "Ways of life" are represented as part of this global system, yet their relative autonomy is always assumed. That is, the currency of "culture" is precisely its ability to integrate by denying connection, by emphasizing and extending difference (to paraphrase Adorno and Horkheimer). The value of the idea of culture is that it can be used to represent and reify social and geographical difference by obfuscating exactly the thing that *makes* connectedness: the workings of the global political economy. The infinite regress of culture is halted, in many instances, by the process of making money from perceived difference, all the while assuring continued integration into, and participation in, an economically (and politically) dominated world system.[12] Perhaps the clearest example of this is the growing industry of ethnic tourism, which makes money by precisely integrating difference into a global system of cultural and industrial production (see, for example, Van den Berghe 1994) (figure 3.3).

The "critical infrastructure"

The differentiation of commodities, meanings, and ways of life within an overall political economic unity is not a process that just happens. Rather, "culture" – like economic unity – is actively *made*.[13] It is a product of the work of millions of people.

11   This is a paraphrase of a point made by Strathern (1987).
12   This notion of constructed differences within overarching unity is a mainstay of Marxist social theory. Besides being a cornerstone of Marx's *Capital*, it is integral, to select three works that have been particularly influential in geography, in the work of Harvey (1989a), Lefebvre (1991), and Debord (1994).
13   In the case of economics, unified systems of production, exchange, and consumption are currently being constructed on the global scale by bureaucrats in such institutions as the World Trade Organization (whose president likes to declare, "we are writing the constitution of a single global economy") and the Multilateral Agreement on Institutions (MAI) negotiators from the Organization for Economic Coopera-

Sharon Zukin (1991; see also Zukin 1995; Bourdieu 1984) calls these people and the work they do, the "critical infrastructure" of the cultural economy. The job of the critical infrastructure is to implement ideas about culture, and to solidify ways of life in place, by showing us taste and style, by producing the images and things by which we come to know ourselves and our place in the world. The members of the critical infrastructure are the makers of distinctions: art critics, academic social critics, newspaper columnists, and movie and book reviewers, but also advertising copywriters, waiters, package designers, architects, television producers. So too are geographers or anthropologists concerned with describing the various "others" of the world part of the critical infrastructure. Add to them the politicians and developers seeking to make economic or political profit by selling lifestyles, "community," or the "uniqueness" of place, and you have the "sophisticated divisions of labor" necessary for making the "culture" to which Harvey and Debord refer. There are literally armies making it possible for us to define our "us-ness" and to create our differences from "them."[14]

Figure 3.3 Ethnic tourism makes money out of preserving certain kinds of differences and offering them up for the visual – and consuming – pleasure of visitors. Trading posts in Gallup, New Mexico, trade on the image of the Indian as noble savage and as artisan. Photography by Bruce D'Arcus; used by permission.

tion and Development. Among other points, the (now-suspended) draft MAI declares that "lost opportunity to profit from a planned investment" is grounds for compensation by the nation-state in which the investment was planned. See Rauber (1998).

14 Often *literally* armies: in China, the Red Army is now one of the largest industrial concerns and biggest investors in both durable goods and in culture industries such as film and music making. Armies make culture happen in other ways too: think of the USA invasions of Nicaragua (1912–33) and Guatemala (1954) to protect our taste for bananas and other vital interests, or the old Soviet army's occupations of Prague (1968) and Hungary (1956) to put down what were clearly cultural as well as political revolutions.

Workers in the "critical infrastructure" provide the scaffolding upon which "ways of life" are made and made known. By their activities (predominantly) "the works and practices of intellectual and especially artistic activity" are translated into reified culture" (Williams 1976: 90). In this sense, "culture" does not begin as a realm, level, or even "system of signification" towards which people reach to make sense of their material worlds (as new cultural geographers have suggested). Rather, it is a very clear process of demarcation and interpretation; it is a structured system of representation of both people and things. Like the idea of race (see chapter 9, below), the idea of culture is continually invested and reinvested, made real through the *work* of people.

Borrowing the idea of "cultural capital" from the social theorist Pierre Bourdieu, yet transforming it to show that such capital is the product of the labor of workers in the critical infrastructure and not just an inert "thing" possessed in different degrees by people occupying different locations in the social hierarchy,[15] Zukin (1991: 260) writes that "cultural goods and services truly constitute real capital – so long as they are integrated as commodities in the market-based circulation of capital." Her point is that "cultural" commodities, like images, music, sporty cars, or faddish cuisine, exist in and through the more general circulation of capital and commodities that define capitalism. The role of the critical infrastructure is to ensure that these processes and practices *remain* fully incorporated, no matter how people may seek to appropriate them; their job is also to assure that these processes and practices are made *known* as emblems of "culture," and thus properly distinctive (since it is in that distinctiveness – even if mass-produced – that much of their value lies). Zukin (1991: 111) is thus suggesting what could be called a labor theory of cultural change in which certain workers "provide an aesthetic critique that facilitates upscale consumption" or some other distinctive mode of stylistic consumption.

Of course, this is not a new phenomenon, some postmodern turn of events where capital has suddenly gone cultural (even if there have been drastic changes in the *organization* of capitalist production and consumption). The idea of culture is instead thoroughly implicated in the political economy of global capitalism, and always has been. Even so, the lines between the commodification of things and the commodification of images and representations is constantly reworked, and that implies a need for new ways of understanding the making of "culture" and "cultures" as part of political-economic processes. Where old-style Marxists might have found it useful to distinguish between a "base" of production and a "superstructure" of "culture," such rationale "has by now entirely disappeared," insists Harvey (1989a: 314):

> Cultural production, both high and low, both supportive and critical of capitalist values, has now become so commodified that it is thoroughly implicated in systems of monetary evaluation and circulation. Under such conditions, the varieties of cultural output are no different from the varieties of Benetton's colors or the famous 57 varieties that Heinz long ago pioneered.... Furthermore, all oppositional culture (and there is plenty of it) still has to be expressed in this commodified mode, thus limiting the powers of oppositional movements in important ways.

What sets the present, perhaps postmodern, era apart from past eras is the nature and extent of commodification, not the role that "culture" plays. Harvey's point is instead

---

15   Which is largely how Bourdieu (1984) defines it.

that what gets called culture is by now thoroughly implicated in the continual reproduction of everyday life *because* it is inseparable from the relations of production and consumption though which we *must* define ourselves. Even oppositional movements have no choice but to participate (to a greater or lesser degree, to be sure) in the production and sale of commodities – commodities that do not just *define* the world, but physically and socially give it its *shape* and *structure*. That is why Debord (1994: 126) argued in the 1960s that a real revolution would have to be "that *critique of human geography* whereby individuals and communities . . . construct places and events commensurate with the appropriation, no longer of just their labor, but of their total history." The current "situation," in other words, has to be completely and fully dismantled if "opposition" is to be fully successful (see also Lefebvre 1974).

In just this regard – in the sense that "economics" and "culture" are fully entwined and fully dependent on each other – it has never made any sense to separate "base" from "superstructure" to explain culture, politics, or economics (as "sphere" and "realm" metaphors of culture do): rather that is an ideological move made not just by some Marxist theorists, but even more forcefully by workers in culture industries.[16] Indeed, the idea of culture drives an ideological wedge precisely between the workings of economy and the workings of other aspects of social life. "The *best* knowledge and thought of the time," no less than spiritual qualities, habits and patterns attributed to various "ways of life," can be made to work in systems of domination and social control to the degree that they are seen as free-floating, hovering somewhere above the material social and economic workings of everyday life. If culture is a realm, then it is undeniably a realm of economic production; it is an important site for the production not only of values, but especially of capitalist value.

"Cultural maps," Peter Jackson (1989: 186) has remarked, "are capable of multiple readings" – and these readings are always open to resistance. So they are. Yet it is important to remember that workers in the critical infrastructure labor mightily to ensure that some meanings are closed off and that others are daily available on the racks of Next or The Limited, or on the disks produced by Sony. Culture is thus a system of power fully integrated into the political economy, and the contentious culture wars of the present era must always be read with that in mind. As Jackson (1989: 185) also writes, "meanings must always be related to the material world from which they derive." This is no less true of the meaning of "culture" itself. It derives from the workings of culture-making classes (whether employed by Ted Turner or Focus on the Family) and it is always highly mediated. "Culture" is *organized*. It is not something that directly or organically derives from the tastes, distinctions, or desires of unitary or universal social groups or societies.

Conclusion: Values, Geographies, and Audiences

When the radical Industrial Workers of the World (IWW) wanted to reach and organize an audience for their theories of social revolution in the years before

---

16 Compare Jackson (1991a). If Matthew Arnold and his acolytes on the political right long for an economically unsullied culture they are not alone. As Michael Denning (1996) makes clear, that impulse is also quite strong on the left.

World War I, they went to where the audience was, setting up a soapbox next to or across from the Salvation Army preachers working the parks and street corners of American cities. Both groups – the Salvation Army and the IWW – sought to catch the attention of the masses of poor, "casual" laborers that crowded the skid row sections of American cities. Both sought access to the *means* by which casual laborers got their *meanings* – the word on the street – and to use that means to their own advantage: to preach revolution or salvation. The channels of communication, the processes of meaning and value construction, were the streets and squares of the city themselves. The trick was to *organize* those who loitered or passed through the streets such that they would internalize and act on the values being promoted. Organizing an audience, therefore, was a primary effort of the IWW and the Salvation Army. For the former if not the latter, such organization was a means towards *organized* resistance to the capitalist economy and state that so pauperized transient, migrant, and laid-off workers.

Authorities in American cities took this threat of organization seriously enough that in numerous places – Fresno, San Diego, San Pedro, Denver, Kansas City, Seattle – employers and their allies in the government and police sought to prevent IWW organizers from public street speaking. Employers and city council members knew that control of the streets was an important means for controlling – or promoting – dissent. The IWW fought back (figure 3.4). For them, access to street speaking was one of the few ways that they could reach transient and other "casual" labor. Without the ability to use the streets, an audience – and hence a potentially active body – for resistance would be impossible to organize. The streets were the physical means of production for *meanings*. They were the spaces in which *values* were produced and contested. The result was a series of protracted and often bloody "free speech" fights in which control over the streets was a physical and ideological battleground for the ability to organize, control, and shape the social reproduction of labor.[17]

What are the physical means for meaning and value production now? How has access to audiences changed? Where are the spaces in which an audience may potentially be found and organized, and who controls access to those spaces? How have ideological and physical struggles over the shape of social reproduction been transformed? There are no simple answers to these questions, but there are important trends worth noting. In the first place, spaces of communication and meaning have more and more moved "inside": inside the radio, television, and internet, inside the mall and shopping center, and inside the movie house. These are spaces more readily amenable to monopolized control (over the means of production of meaning) than are the streets. They are also spaces, in modern capitalist society, that are (for the most part) *privately owned*. This is crucial. If the means for organizing an audience, either in favor of or against some set of social meanings, either as a passive audience for mass-produced entertainment, or as an active force for social change, themselves exist primarily for the production of profit, then the *types* of entertainment, possible resistances, and so on, are highly *biased*. The geography of the production of "culture" – and hence the relationship between value and values – is decisive.

---

17 Histories of the IWW Free Speech fights include Foner (1965, 1981); Dubofsky (1988). For a geographical approach, see Mitchell (1996b).

"MOVE ON" FOR SPEAKERS, LATER WILL INCLUDE PICKETS

Figure 3.4 The Industrial Workers of the World used the streets of western American cities to organize an audience for its ideology. Local authorities often violently clamped down on street speaking in a bid to drive the IWW out. Cartoon from *Industrial Worker* (May 9, 1912).

But this is a very different question than asking what culture *is*. Rather, it seeks to see what we *call* culture as always a contested relationship, a relationship in which "context" – geographical, political, economic, social – is everything. That is to say, the question of the relationship between "physical" and "aesthetic" representations can never be decided *a priori*; it can only be unraveled historically and geographically. It is a question that depends entirely on the nature of cultural production (in the broadest sense implied in this chapter) and the nature and organization of "audiences." It is a question that asks us how both domination and resistance are organized over space and time, and how they are often subsumed within and coopted by powerful political-economic forces, how they sometimes break out of that cooptation and change the world. If the Sex Pistols and their audience made a future (out of no future) by throwing into conflict the physical and the aesthetic, then how was the power of their production so thoroughly (if also self-consciously) coopted and tamed only twenty years later? And what prospect is there for another upheaval in popular culture and social life equivalent to the one the Sex Pistols effected? The answer to such questions lies not in "culture" itself, but in the conditions of "culture's" production, as we have seen. The production of new kinds of values can quickly and quite deliberately become a further means for the production of more economic value, more surplus value. They can also quickly and quite deliberately become a locus of organized social resistance.

If that also answers the question of how "representations" (of, for example, what good music is, or, more generally, of what culture "is") are made, then the question of how value attaches to these representations still needs to be addressed. In short, the answer to *that* question is found in the work of the "critical infrastructure" as it goes about its work of dividing and conquering people and places, all for the effect of creating first a profitable labor force, and then organizing an "audience" – a market – for the images and the representations it wants to sell. To understand "culture," the key is not to ask what it is, but to trace its path through "sophisticated divisions of labor" as it is actively *made* (and actively contested).

The value, in other words, of recognizing that culture does not exist *as such* (but that it is an essential ingredient of power and economy nonetheless) is that we can see how the idea of culture works in and through social relations of production and reproduction (including consumption). We can see *who* constitutes the critical infrastructure and how and why they go about their work. We can see who performs the ideological work of reifying culture at any given moment, in any given place, and we can ask who those reifications benefit. We can see how audiences (for products, for resistance) are organized and activated. Looking at these processes is the purpose of the remaining chapters of this book. In a number of different arenas of social life, from landscape to sexuality, from rabid consumption to acts of cultural resistance, from the cultural production of gender to the role of "culture" in defining national citizenship, we will unravel the ongoing making of "culture." In so doing, we will see that geography – spatiality, the production of spaces and places, and the global doings of the economy – is front and center in the processes of cultural production, and hence in systems of social reproduction.

If we wanted to summarize the most important message of all three chapters that make up this first section of *Cultural Geography*, and hence the key point of the book, the best way would probably be to say that the "work of culture" is to advance social reproduction (or societal integration) through the making and marking of differences – differences, as noted above, that do a lot to obfuscate connectedness. But we also need to note that the work of culture is itself a lot of work for those people whose job it is to make such distinctions. If we keep this in mind – that "culture" does work because work makes "culture" – then perhaps we can also gain insight into the nature not only of the cultural geographies that define our lives, but also of the culture wars in which we are presently engulfed. The next two Parts of *Cultural Geography* seek to develop this rather basic point. But, as we will see, there is really little "basic" about that point at all. Its ramifications are countless. To start this exploration, we will now move away from considerations of Johnny Rotten (though he returns in chapter 6), AIDS theater, and the construction and conquest of "cool," and turn instead to a subject that has been more traditionally at the center of cultural geography: the cultural landscape.

Part II

The Political Landscape

4

The Work of Landscape: Producing and Representing the Cultural Scene

Johnstown

For someone unfamiliar with the look and feel of industrial towns, the landscape of Johnstown, Pennsylvania, in the late 1980s was an amazing thing (figure 4.1). There's

Figure 4.1 Johnstown, Pennsylvania (1989). Steel mills still dominated the valleys of the Little Conemaugh and Stony Creek rivers in the 1980s, even as the city itself was suffering from severe economic decline. Photograph by D. Mitchell.

nothing in the California suburban landscape where I grew up (or even the California industrial landscape, for that matter) that is at all comparable. Massive – overwhelming – steel manufacturing plants fill the deep valleys of the Conemaugh and Little Stony Creek rivers. The walls of the valleys are almost sheer cliffs, and the overall effect of the natural landscape is to give the city a compact, tight-knit feel all but absent in the sprawling spaces of the western United States. But the differences between the California suburban and Pennsylvania industrial landscapes are only partially a function of the differences in their natural landscape. Much more of the difference, of course, can be traced to the specific development history (and subsequent decline) of places like Johnstown – a history of development and decline markedly different from the later development of the American West. In the late 1800s, Johnstown was one of the most important steel-producing cities in the country. The leading manufacturer of the steel rails that made possible American settlement in the West, the Cambria Iron and Steel Company (later part of Bethlehem Steel) was also a leader in innovation in the industry, and the mill landscape clearly represents both the power and raw energy of steel-making, and the impressive modernism that marked the high-tech industry of the era. Cambria and its successors and competitors in Johnstown recruited both high- and low-skilled workers from across the USA and Europe. To house them, the steel companies and independent developers built close-packed neighborhoods wherever space in the valley was available. In one small district, Cambria City, there were nearly as many large, stone, architecturally stunning churches (Greek and Russian Orthodox, various ethnic-based Catholic parishes, Presbyterian) as there were bars. On the hill above the Gautier Works, downwind from the belching smokestacks, African Americans were forced to settle after being recruited to Johnstown during a 1919 strike. In the surrounding hills were dozens of small coal "patches" – company (or formerly company) towns built to house miners and their families. In some of the side valleys, there were once hundreds of coking ovens (most of which have since succumbed to the wrecking ball and various attempts at environmental reclamation).

If the evidence of the landscape pointed to a history of frantic development and raucous, sometimes violent, change, Johnstown in the 1980s was a curiously quiet, still, empty-feeling place. A valley that had once been home to 12,000 steelworkers, and in which the roar of open-hearth furnaces and the pall from the smokestacks dominated the senses, by the mid-1980s employed fewer than 2,500. Several of the individual mills had been shuttered and the smokestacks no longer belched much at all. Coking was completely eliminated, and between 1977 and 1983, 40 percent of the area's coal-mining jobs were eliminated. In 1983, Johnstown had one of the highest unemployment rates in the country. When that rate began to decline by the end of the decade, it had as much to do with out-migration as it did with job creation. In the neighborhoods, the real estate market collapsed during the shutdowns, and many workers simply locked up their houses, defaulted on their mortgages, and left town. By 1989, the local newspaper had resorted to printing pictures of the "blight of the week" in hopes of shaming owners and landlords into making cosmetic repairs to houses that no one wanted to buy.[1] Johnstown is not completely devoid of action and

---

1   Some of the material for this section of the chapter comes from Mitchell (1992a). Good accounts of the development and social history of Johnstown are Wallace (1985); Berger (1985); Morawska (1985). The best accounts of the deindustrialization of Johnstown are Metzger (1980, 1985).

Figure 4.2 The Crown America corporate headquarters, Johnstown, Pennsylvania, (1988). The Michael Graves-designed building was constructed with government grants and tax abatements. Keeping Crown America (a designer and builder of malls) located in Johnstown was a key plank in the economic recovery plan of the city after the closing of the steel mills. Photograph by D. Mitchell.

development, however. If the steel mills represent the past in Johnstown, then perhaps the future is represented by the new Michael Graves-designed Crown America corporate headquarters (figure 4.2). Built in 1988 with a combination of state and federal grants, tax abatements, and private money, the Crown America building represents an important victory for the city in its attempts to keep at least some capital investment from fleeing the city for the suburbs, other states, or foreign countries.

Spectacular as it may be, Johnstown's landscape is also quite ordinary. It is little different from countless other deindustrialized towns in the American northeast, from Youngstown, Ohio, to Mohawk, New York, from Manchester, New Hampshire, to Flint, Michigan. In it one can read the history of the industrial development of the United States, and the wrenching decline that followed.[2] But to see landscape in such terms is almost to see it as static: the landscape passively "represents" some history or another. In reality, the landscape itself is an active agent in constituting that history, serving both as a symbol for the needs and desires of the people who live in it (or who

2 At least for a short time: in Youngstown, for example, where as recently as 1980, 24 miles of steel mills stretched along the Mahoning River, now nearly all have been torn down, the very steel of their walls and roofs sold for scrap. In their place now lie 24 miles of highly toxic, nearly useless scrubland. Youngstown's decline – and the often militant worker response that accompanied it – is well told in Maharidge and Williamson (1996) and eloquently evoked in Bruce Springsteen's "Youngstown," on his *Ghost of Tom Joad* album. The history of worker militancy in Youngstown is explored in Buss (1983) and Lynd (1982). The classic account of the deindustrialization of the USA is Bluestone and Harrison (1982).

otherwise have a stake in producing and maintaining it) and as a solid, dead weight channeling change in this way and not that (there are, after all, only a few uses to which a defunct steel mill can be put). "Landscape" is best seen as both *a work* (it is the product of human labor and thus encapsulates the dreams, desires, and all the injustices of the people and social systems that make it) and as something that *does work* (it acts as a social agent in the further development of a place).[3] In that regard too, Johnstown's landscape is just like any other.

In another sense, however, Johnstown's landscape is quite extraordinary. For many who do not live in the region, Johnstown is not remembered as a once-dynamic, innovatory steel-producing center. Instead it is remembered as the site of the spectacular 1889 flash flood that killed more than 2,200 people (of whom 663 bodies were never identified), and left countless thousands of others homeless (figure 4.3). Johnstown had always been prone to flooding, but the extraordinarily wet May in 1889, coupled with criminally negligent "improvements" to a dam on a pleasure lake up river (a lake maintained for the leisure of Pittsburgh's wealthiest industrialists), made disaster inevitable. When the dam at the South Fork Fishing and Hunting Club collapsed just after three in the afternoon on May 31, it sent a wall of water down the valley of the Little Conemaugh River at times exceeding speeds of 40 miles per hour and often, when impeded by stone bridges or other obstructions, reaching heights approaching 100 feet. By the time the flood reached Johnstown itself (some 15 miles from the dam) an hour later, the wave was pushing before it a destructive 35-foot-high wall of trees, lumber, rail cars and engines, animal and human bodies, masonry, and mud. Sweeping through the city, the debris and wave crashed against the hillside opposite where the Little Conemaugh and the Stony Creek combine to form the Conemaugh River. The force of the impact sent a back-wave up the Stony Creek and back across devastated Johnstown. With the full force of the wave thus diffused, a large stone railroad bridge a mile down the Conemaugh river held its

Figure 4.3 Johnstown after the 1889 flood. The scale of devastation was awesome, as was the way it instantly became a sensational worldwide story.

---

3 As a product of human labor, a landscape can be viewed, as Marx put it, as "dead labor" – that is as labor solidified in a particular form. As David Harvey (1982) has shown, the built environment of a place, as dead labor, frequently acts as a fetter on the development and deployment of living labor.

ground and over the next hour an impressive mountain of "boxcars, factory roofs, trees, telegraph poles, hideous masses of barbed wire, hundreds of houses, many squashed beyond recognition, others still astonishingly intact, dead horses and cows, and hundreds of human beings, dead and alive" formed a massive dam (McCullogh 1968: 149). Johnstown was submerged; few houses in the flood plain remained standing and the steel mills were badly damaged. Inevitably, the tangled mass at the stone bridge caught fire, and those people still living and caught in the debris were burned alive.

If the flood itself is remembered for the spectacular devastation it caused (and to some extent for the hubris and negligence of the robber-barons who were too cheap to make proper improvements to the dam on the South Fork Creek), then the aftermath of the flood is remembered for both the sensational reporting that broadcast Johnstown's fate around the world and the rapid mobilization of concern and charity that such sensationalism invoked. The flood was the first major disaster in which Clara Barton's American Red Cross played an important relief role. Barton brought with her an army of fifty doctors and nurses, but they were just a small contingent of the thousands of people who descended on the city to offer their services to the relief effort (many of these were from the ranks of the unemployed and thus were understood, in the language of the day, to be vagabonds and tramps). There were dozens of journalists covering the story too, many from the comfort of hotels hundreds of miles away – which did nothing to lessen their ability to fabricate stories about the lawlessness, vagabondry, and general decline of morals that the flood presumably induced.[4]

Visitors to Johnstown today can see the site of the broken dam (which is a National Historical Park), and then work their way down the path of the flood, through the various villages that were destroyed in 1889, and into the city itself, where an impressive Flood Museum tells the history through artifacts, photographs, oral histories, reconstructions of scenes, and so on. The film made by historian David McCullogh and the Flood Museum from McCullogh's book on the flood (and broadcast as part of McCullogh's *American Experience* television program) is available for viewing. The Flood Museum also dedicates a portion of its space to telling the industrial history of Johnstown, tracing its development from a small farming community, to innovative steel-center, to a landscape of deindustrialization. Outside, visitors can follow a "flood trail" around the city, seeing surviving buildings, imagining the size of the mountain of debris that built up behind the stone bridge, riding an incline plane to the plateau above the city, and visiting the cemetery where the unidentified bodies are buried. In the museum and in the landscape itself, visitors can learn how Johnstown rebuilt after the flood, becoming once again one of the foremost steel-producing cities in the country. Despite the somewhat forlorn aspect the landscape projects now that the mills are quiet, visitors can feel for themselves why Johnstown bills itself as a "city of survivors."

---

4 A shelf of instant books describing both the waters and the lawless immorality flooding Johnstown quickly appeared. See, for example, Connelly and Jenks (1889); Dieck (1889); Ferris (1889); Fox (1889); Johnson (1889); McLaurin (1890) and Walker (1889). These books were part of a genre of sensational, book-length reporting that flourished at the time.

When the steel mills pulled out of Johnstown in the 1980s, many in the city drew on Johnstown's history of survival in the face of disaster (there were two other devastating floods in 1936 and 1977) as a source of strength. Many also saw Johnstown's flood history as precisely the means to assure the city's economic survival in a postindustrial age. The Flood Museum transformed its role into one of "attempting to assist the community in using its historic resources for revitalization and economic development," according to one of its directors. It also transformed its function from a specialized flood museum to a mission of "document[ing] the city" (Richard Burkert, quoted in "The New Johnstown Flood Museum..." 1989: 6). The general goal of economic planners (including the Museum) was to build on tourist interest in the flood by making the whole of the city landscape into a heritage museum that documented not just the flood, but the history of industrial development in the region. The long-term goal of city planners, aided by the National Park Service, representatives from Bethlehem Steel, and various planning consultants, was to use Johnstown's "heritage as a springboard to further develop the city" (Fusco 1988: 3). Johnstown's landscape was well suited to the role of representing the history of steel-making. Unlike much of the Monogahala Valley and cities such as Youngstown, the industrial landscape of Johnstown remained largely intact in the mid-1980s – the mills had not been dismantled for scrap. Indeed, in 1983, at the height of Johnstown's depression, Hollywood came to the city to film *All the Right Moves* precisely because, as one co-producer put it, "we are trying to be realistic. Johnstown has the steel mill and the right look more than anything else. You know you are in a steel town" (*New York Times*, March 21, 1983).

With the aid of the National Park Service's America's Industrial Heritage Project, the city laid ambitious plans for the hundredth anniversary of the flood and beyond. The centennial itself was set as a summer-long series of events including a memorial service for the victims, symphony concerts, parades, and festivals. "Come for the history," the slogan read, "and stay for the fun." The permanent plan for industrial development was ambitious. The planning firm of Lane, French, and Associates created a "Third Century Plan" for the city which it described as a "strategy for the museum and the community to use its historic resources for economic development." Designed to put the history and landscape of Johnstown in the service of economic development, the plan called for three stages and was projected to cost between $57.5 and $70 million. The first stage ($3.5 to $5 million) included the historical preservation of significant buildings and the development of "Discovery Trails" around the city that linked important sites in the flood and industrial history. The second stage called for the creation of a Heritage Park ($12 to $15 million). Several significant buildings were to be renovated and the street that faced the Gautier Works (the site of the oldest mills in Johnstown) was to be reconstructed to look as it did in the mid-nineteenth century. The plan predicted that the Heritage Park would attract up to 200,000 visitors to Johnstown annually. The final stage envisioned the creation of a National Cultural Park ($42 to $50 million), which included the transformation of the sprawling Cambria Works into a retail center, and the linking of all the significant sites by a tramway running on existing company rail tracks. Planners hoped such a Cultural Park would attract a million visitors a year ("The New Johnstown Flood Museum..." 1989).

The Third Century Plan was not without controversy when it was previewed publicly.[5] Among other things, the plans for the Heritage Park presented a particularly sanitized version of the history of ordinary people in the town. While the crassly racist and ethnocentric, sensational reporting of the flood's aftermath (which told of lawless "Huns," hordes of "idle vagabond negroes . . . who will not work," and other tramps scavenging the bodies for gold) is recounted as a colorful incident of the yellow journalism past, little attempt is made to explore and represent the very real geographies of social control implemented in the days and weeks after the flood (Walker 1889). Not all the strategies of social control were strictly necessary for re-establishing housing and sanitation in the wake of an unprecedented disaster; it was also understood by local elites that it was imperative to re-establish the status quo geography of class and ethnicity, the physical landscapes of which had been washed away in the flood (see Mitchell 1989). Nor is there much attempt to explore the racial history and geography of other eras, such as the contentious use of African American strikebreakers in 1919, their attempted "deportation" by the mayor in 1923, and their subsequent ghettoization (which was justified and codified in the public housing and urban redevelopment plans of the 1940s).[6]

Finally, and perhaps most glaringly, the Heritage and Cultural Parks proposed to build on the *industrial* rather than the *labor* history of the city. This is a crucial distinction, because on it rides both the way the history of the city is to be scripted, and the meanings that are to be most strongly attached to the landscape. In the mid-1980s as Bethlehem Steel was shutting down (and knowing full well the devastating multiplier effect that shutdown was going to have), city planners and elected officials determined, no doubt rightly, that the primary objective for the city was to retain existing businesses and attract new economic development to the city. Along with promoting tourism in general, targeted economic activities included the already-mentioned Crown America Corporation (a developer of malls) and various "back office" enterprises, such as sorting and filing operations for insurance companies. As industrial uses were found for some of the mills (such as small, usually non-union, "boutique" mills making small-batch specialty metals), they were to be courted too.

For many of these potential economic activities, including to some degree tourism, officials felt it was essential to present an image of Johnstown as a united community – a community in which class and race interest had always been less important than the common interest of the "community." What was necessary was a consensus history, a sellable history. To be attractive to potential investors, many in Johnstown sought to downplay the contentious labor history that had long marked the place. Johnstown had been a militant center for national steel industry strikes in 1919 and 1937; and as recently as 1981 militant workers at one of the mills (a subsidiary of US Steel) had seen the closure of their plant rather than approve considerable "give backs" (wage and benefit reductions) to the company. But these were traits deemed to

5 My own article critical of these plans (Mitchell 1992a) drew a pained response from the two officials with the Johnstown Area Heritage Association: Miner and Burkert (1992); my response is in Mitchell (1992c).
6 Several chapters in Berger (1985) explore this racist history; on the public housing program and its codification of racist geography, see Mitchell (1993).

be unattractive to potential investors. Instead, a new image of the Johnstown worker was concocted, one that promoted her or his willingness to work hard and to be content with the simplest of things. The head of the Johnstown Chamber of Commerce argued that "Johnstown people are noncomplex people. These people work hard, they stop and have a beer. They watch football games" (*New York Times*, April 21, 1981). Incoming investors would find a ready, willing, and compliant labor force. The history of militant opposition to company practices would be swept under the rug.

And out of the landscape. Culture wars do not take place only in the field of representation. They also clearly rage across (and over) the landscape itself. Culture wars are often about how meaning is made manifest in the very stones, bricks, wood, and asphalt of the places in which we live. There were thus no plans to represent the history of strikes, the geography of violence, or the *politics* of deindustrialization in the Third Century Plan for the makeover of the landscape into a National Cultural Park. By stressing *industrial* history – the history of development, innovation, and the mechanics of making steel – the Johnstown landscape would minimize the contentious past within which such developments and innovations took place. The *work* of the landscape – the role it was assigned by planners – was to represent a heroic history, not a history of conflict. Or to put that differently, the Third Century Plan raised precisely the question facing so many deindustrialized towns and cities around the world that hope to use their landscapes to attract both tourists and investors: Is it possible for a landscape to become both a source of economic development *and* an accurate representation of history? Such a question is fraught with difficulty because it immediately raises others: What is meant by "accurate"? Can "accurate" be divorced from the class, race, or gender interests that are behind those who produce and those who apprehend landscapes?

In Johnstown the answer may never come as funding for the National Cultural Park plan dried up in the early 1990s. Even so, Johnstown has been incorporated into a 500-mile-long Pennsylvania-sponsored "Path of Progress" that winds through the industrial heartland of southwestern Pennsylvania and which attracts more than half a million visitors a year. True to early projections, Johnstown itself draws in almost a quarter million "heritage tourists" each year. Some of those tourists pay $10 for a tour of the old Franklin Works (part of the Bethlehem complex) guided by a laid-off steelworker. The steelworker-guides have been trained by the Open-Hearth Education Project, an organization that promotes, as the *New York Times* (Brant 1996) puts it, an "elegiac, heavily labor-oriented line" – an approach that, despite its apparent success and popularity, the *Times* worries will turn off more tourists than it will attract. Richard Burkert, a veteran of the debates over preservation in Johnstown and the director of the Johnstown Area Heritage Association, hopes, now that the plans for the National Cultural Park have fallen through, that the Open Hearth Project will succeed. "Some people prefer to avert their eyes" from landscapes like Johnstown's "and have their history go away. And it does go away: look at Pittsburgh, where the huge steel mills have been leveled for office parks. Well, it's critical that those mills – the ethic and the spirit residing in them – be remembered someplace" (quoted in Brant 1996). The question, of course, is precisely *whose* and *what* history (whose "ethic and spirit") can and will be preserved in the landscape.

And that is a question that can only be answered by examining just what a landscape is, and just how a landscape goes about doing its "work" in society. What are the functions of landscapes? How do landscapes form? And what do they mean? These are the questions that the history and geography of Johnstown raises as the city develops and declines. And they are the questions that this and the next chapter are dedicated to answering.

If nothing else, the story of Johnstown should indicate that like "culture," "landscape" is a complex and fascinating term (even if its entry into the Anglophone geographical literature was through only its most simple of senses – see chapter 1). Above, I used the term to indicate the broad sweep – or the general look – of Johnstown as a place. I also invoked it to indicate the solid form of the built environment. And, of course, throughout the preceding paragraphs, the sense that the landscape is a form of *representation* (of history or control or economic development and decline) has been clear. Those are only some of the ways that "landscape" is used in scholarship and in everyday speech. In fact, everyday language is evocative of the complexity of the term. "Landscape" means so many things in ordinary parlance: landscape views, natural landscapes, a cultural landscape, the political landscape, the urban landscape, the landscape of your mind, the landscape of your computer screen, landscaping, landscape painting and photography, the economic landscape, and on and on. In ecology, landscape often represents a particular *scale*, in printing and advertising an *orientation*.

The art historian W.J.T. Mitchell (1994: 1) summarizes the complex of meanings that make up the term: "Landscape is a natural scene mediated by culture. It is both represented and presented space, both a signifier and a signified, both a frame and what a frame contains, both a real place and its simulacrum, both a package and a commodity in the package." So landscape is both a place and a "way of seeing," both a sensibility and a lived relation (Berger 1972).[7] We can talk of "landscape tastes" (Lowenthal and Prince 1965) as easily as we can talk of the landscape of the Southern Alps. For some, landscape is a "text," part of the cultural "signifying systems" through which we make sense of our worlds; for others it is a produced space, a form, a socially transformed portion of the earth's surface (Domosh 1996b; Duncan 1990; Meinig 1979). And through all these meanings – indeed integral to each of them – are the relations of life and death, of meaning and forgetting, of violence as well as beauty that always and everywhere structure our lives.

This and the next chapter are dedicated to exploring the complexity – and the importance – of the landscape. We turn first in this chapter to question the relations – and the actual work – that produce landscapes. This question is best answered through example, so we continue to draw on Johnstown while exploring the making of two additional landscapes – Vancouver's Chinatown and Paris's Basilica of the Sacred Heart – to get a sense of the politics of landscape production. If landscapes are produced through specifiable social relations, and hence both the relations of

7   The literature on landscape is huge. Some of the works that have been influential in geography are Barrell (1980); Bender (1993); Bermingham (1987); Cosgrove (1984, 1993b); Cosgrove and Daniels (1988); Daniels (1993); Pugh (1990); Williams (1973); Wilson (1991); Zukin (1991).

production and the resulting product can be studied, then it is also important to remember, as the case of Johnstown shows so well, that landscape is additionally a form of ideology. It is a way of carefully selecting and representing the world so as to give it a particular meaning. Landscape is thus an important ingredient in constructing consent and identity – in organizing a receptive audience – for the projects and desires of powerful social interests.

Chapter 5 picks up this discussion of the dialectic between production of built form and landscape representation by examining how meaning develops and circulates in landscapes. If one of the goals for planners (and for workers) in Johnstown was to *make* the landscape *mean* something, then how did those meanings develop and "stick" (if they did). While many cultural theorists argue that landscapes are blank screens onto which can be projected an infinite array of meaning, I suggest that one of the chief functions of landscape is precisely to *control* meaning and to channel it in particular directions. Yet, that said, it is also certainly the case that landscape meaning is contested every step of the way.

Chapter 5 thus opens with an exploration of the metaphors through which we apprehend and understand landscapes. This examination allows us to see how particular meanings become "concretized" – in the very cement, bricks, and steel of the landscape – and therefore becomes an important agent in the social reproduction of social relations. While chapter 4 is largely concerned with the dialectics of class, race, and nationalism, chapter 5 turns its attention to the relations of gender and how they are euphemized (see chapter 2) and naturalized in the landscape.

Using gender politics as a base, we explore the way that particular aspects of social identity work in and through landscapes. At the same time we look at how particular produced landscapes (suburbia, for example) make ideology concrete and difficult to challenge. The very built form of a place can have the effect of solidifying particular notions about how the world is structured and works. Landscape therefore becomes an essential ingredient for structuring the material social relations that make up the world.

Since landscapes are both systems of meaning and systems of social reproduction, we next turn in chapter 5 to a study of landscapes of consumption – consumption both in the sense it normally takes (the consumption of goods) and in the sense of how people "consume" meanings. As landscapes *par excellence* of consumption, contemporary malls serve as the site for our analysis. But the ethos of the mall (as a particular kind of landscape of consumption) is no longer confined within the mall itself, so we also look at the role of consumption in transforming urban landscapes on a larger scale. The "postmodern city" (as some call it) is these days built more around the economics of consumption than the economics of production (as Johnstown shows), and that has important implications for the production of urban space, for the way it is represented, and for they way we take meaning from it. Taken together, the stories and arguments of both chapters 4 and 5 indicate the degree to which understanding the production and representation of landscapes is essential to understanding the ways in which social reproduction works in any society. Therefore, tying together the themes of both chapters, chapter 5 ends by making explicit the ways in which landscape is an integral aspect of systems of social reproduction (and hence of cultural politics) in contemporary society.

Landscape as Work

Despite the vexing issues that the case of Johnstown raises about how a landscape is formed, how it is controlled and contested, and how it is therefore inescapably ideological, "landscape" still seems such an obvious term. It seems clear that the Lake District, Yellowstone, or the Outback are just simply landscapes (figure 4.4). But according to Kenneth Olwig (1996b), however, the term "landscape" has never been a simple one. If landscape can be understood as a geographical area (as we saw in chapter 1), then it is important to remember that in some parts of northern Europe during the transition from feudalism to capitalism a "landscape" was a particular *kind* of area. "Landscape" was a legal designation that granted to inhabitants greater political rights of self-determination than was available in other regions. In Jutland, "a *landskab* was not just a region, it was a nexus of law and cultural identity" (Olwig 1996b: 633) in which the people "had a greater right to self-determination and to participate in the judicial process and in government" than in surrounding feudal territories (Trap 1864, quoted in Olwig 1996b: 631). This difference in the geography of justice associated with "landscape" in Europe developed because a landscape was understood to be "an area carved out by axe and plough, which belongs to the people who have carved it out. It carries a suggestion of being an area of cultural identity based, however loosely, on tribal and/or blood ties" (Olwig 1993: 311). The implications of this sense of landscape are many. For example, we can immediately

Figure 4.4 Is a landscape ever just "simply" a landscape? The first Superintendent of Yellowstone National Park, Horace Albright, argued that the Yellowstone landscape could not be "complete" until it included these neighboring mountains, now part of Grand Teton National Park. Landscapes are always imbued with social intent. Photograph by Susan Millar; used by permission.

see why "landscape" – as a relation between "a people" and a portion of the natural world to which they are tied by the sweat of their labor – is such a vital force in national identity. As we saw in chapter 1, early ethnographers were often engaged in precisely this goal of delineating the nature of ethnic ties to landscape, in showing how "homelands" were created out of nature, so as to justify nationalist projects.

We can also now understand Carl Sauer's desire to understand landscape as "fashioned from a natural landscape by a culture group" (Sauer 1925: 343).[8] In this sense, landscape is clearly a work, something made, the product of human labor, as Olwig suggests. Through labor we both create and come to know the worlds we make. We transform nature and we transform ourselves. Karl Marx (1987: 173) could have easily been talking about the fashioning of a landscape when he argued (in what is now quite dated language) that:

> [Man] opposes himself to Nature as one of her own forces, setting in motion arms and legs, head and hands, the natural forces of his own body, in order to appropriate Nature's production in a form adapted to his own wants. By thus acting on the external world and changing it, he at the same time changes his own nature.

Sauer never made enough of the self-transformation of society through labor, but the sense of transformation to which Marx refers is there in Sauer's reference in his "Morphology" essay to "culture, itself changing through time," and indeed in much of Sauer's later empirical studies. The important point, and my reason for juxtaposing these two very different thinkers, is simply that just as landscape is a work – a product of the work of people – so too does landscape *do* work: it works on the people that make it. Landscape, in this sense, provides a context, a stage, within and upon which humans continue to work, and it provides the boundaries, quite complexly, within which people remake themselves. For this reason, the social critic and landscape designer Alexander Wilson (1991) refers to landscape as "an activity." He wants us to understand that landscape cannot be static; it is rather an ongoing *relationship* between people and place.

For Sauer, the importance of the landscape – as a product of human labor (or less precisely, of "culture") – was its status as evidence of cultural history. The landscape could be read to determine how it came to be; and as that was accomplished, a researcher could then reconstruct the nature of the culture that made it. To undertake this intellectual work, according to Sauer, a geographer was less interested in *particular* landscapes, than in *generic* landscape forms. Understanding landscape, then, began with that most fundamental of geographical approaches: earth description.[9] In his "Morphology" paper, Sauer (1925: 323–4) gives an example of this type of description:

> The sky is dull, ordinarily partly overcast, the horizon is indistinct and rarely more than a half-dozen miles distant, though seen from a height. The upland is more gently and irregularly rolling and descends to broad, flat basins. There are no long slopes and no

8   As in chapter 1, page numbers refer to the reprinted version of "Morphology" in Leighly (1963).
9   Which, of course, is pretty much the literal translation of "geography."

symmetrical patterns of surface form. Water-courses are short, with clear brownish water, and perennial. The brooks end in irregular borders. Coarse grasses and rushes form marginal strips along water bodies. The upland is covered with heather, furze, and bracken. Clumps of juniper abound, especially on the steeper, drier slopes. Cart traces lie along the longer ridges exposing loose sand in the wheel tracks, and here and there a rusty, cemented base shows beneath the sand. Small flocks of sheep are scattered widely over the land. The almost complete absence of the works of man is notable. There are no fields or other enclosed tracts. The only buildings are sheep sheds, situated usually at a distance of several miles from one another, at convenient intersections of cart traces.

Sauer (1925: 324) goes on to remark that his account of this northern heathland "is not that of an individual scene, but a summation of general characteristics." His method, then, is to draw out the essence of a landscape through generalized description. To do so, the researcher must employ considerable "personal judgment" as to what is significant and for that Sauer has been repeatedly criticized by those who see his methodology as inherently elitist, presented, in the words of Deryck Holdsworth (1990: 193), "as the wise synthesis of a senior scholar who could bring a life's experience to comment on what seemed to be." Sauer has also been criticized simply because his work cannot be "scientific." As he himself argues, "All that can be expected," of researchers "is the reduction of the personal element by agreement on a 'predetermined mode of inquiry,' which shall be logical" (Sauer 1925: 324).

But I think there is another important issue here, one that gets right to the heart of the contradictory nature of the idea of landscape. On the one hand, Sauer is at great pains to stress the role of culture in *making* landscapes. On the other hand, to turn Sauer's phrase back on itself, "the almost complete absence of the works of man is notable." It is not at all clear in Sauer's formulation that landscapes are physically *built* by humans (working individually and socially). They seem rather to just accrete over time. I do not think this is accidental. If landscape is a work of human labor then it is a peculiar work. In many respects it is much like a commodity: it actively hides (or fetishizes) the labor that goes into its making. As Marx famously argued, commodities are objects that have to be made; they are the results of various processes of production. But there is nothing in the form of the commodity that reveals the conditions – the set of social relations – that govern its production. Indeed, all traces of "work" are actively effaced by the seductive charms of the object. The commodity appears fully formed and desirable, not as some product of social struggle over how it should or should not be made.

So too, in some senses, is that the case with landscape. Those who study landscape representations – such as landscape paintings, photographs, and gardens – are repeatedly struck by how effectively they erase or neutralize images of work. More particularly, landscape representations are exceptionally effective in erasing the *social struggle* that defines relations of work. Rather, as in Sauer's description, landscape is made to appear as fully *natural*. This goes not only for such obvious "natural" landscapes as Yellowstone or Victoria Falls, but also for more "cultural" landscapes like villages, towns, and cities like Johnstown. In Sauer's terms such cultural landscapes are simply products of culture. The *struggle* over the labor of making these landscapes is not only immaterial; it is actively minimized – which, of course, was precisely the goal of Johnstown elites during the early and mid-1980s.

If, as Olwig asserts, landscape is a product of work – of the work of the ax and plow – then, conversely, the work that landscape does is to mystify that labor and to make it appear natural rather than social. And the work of those groups opposed to the way the landscape works to naturalize social relations at particular times and places is precisely always to "denaturalize" them – to find ways to unsettle the landscape and to disintegrate it *as* a landscape (Mitchell 1996a: chapter 6). Yet this way of thinking about landscape is almost completely absent in Sauer. For him the landscape expressed not struggle over how the work of making a place livable would proceed; nor did it encapsulate the differential power to *represent* that work of making a living as somehow "natural." Instead, landscape represented a process of cultural *adaptation*: "the feeling of harmony between the human habitation of the land and the landscape into which it so fittingly blends" (Sauer 1925: 343). The key question, however, is to what degree is this "harmony" is illusory. Under capitalism, for example, the products of labor rarely accrue to those who do the work. Rather, workers themselves are quite alienated from the products of their labor, whether that labor creates a specific commodity, or something so generalized as a landscape.

The things that landscape tries to hide, in its insistent fetishization, are the *relationships* that go into its making. These relationships are economic and political to be sure, but they are also clearly products of struggle over issues of race, ethnicity, and gender. The relationships they present to the world through their representations are simply not to be trusted, at least not in their surface appearances. Let me make this clear with two quite different examples.

Vancouver's Chinatown

Kay Anderson calls North American Chinatowns "western landscape types." How can this be? Just take a look at Chinatown (figure 4.5) and its "Chineseness" seems so readily apparent. As Anderson (1991: 3) puts it:

> Popular wisdom has it that the colourful Chinese quarters of Canadian, American, and Australian cities owe their existence to the generations of Chinese immigrants who have made their lives in the cities of the West. The restaurants, pagodas, neon lights, and recessed balconies – the Oriental streetscape – seem to exist through a natural connection between the Chinese and the immigrant experience in the West.

The Chinatown landscape, that is, seems to represent – rather accurately – something only about the immigrant Chinese themselves. The look of the place speaks volumes about the character of the people who inhabit it (see Lewis 1979).

Yet Anderson shows that the making of this landscape – this landscape type – is much more complex than that. Focusing on the Chinatown that developed in Vancouver, British Columbia, Anderson explores the historical record to understand the political, economic, and ideological practices through which Chinatown was and is constructed. Making the obvious seem strange, Anderson remarks that in Vancouver (as indeed anywhere else in the West) "no corresponding term – Anglo town – existed

Figure 4.5 Chinatown, Vancouver. The iconography of North American Chinatowns seem to speak to their "Chineseness." Yet as Kay Anderson has shown, such a reading is far too simple. Photograph by Robin Ward.

in local parlance" (Anderson 1987).[10] Chinese workers and merchants – miners and lumbermen, service workers and store owners – arrived in Vancouver concurrent with Europeans in response to nearby discoveries of gold in 1858. As with their white counterparts, many Chinese stayed on when the mining boom busted, taking jobs in lumber camps, on railroads, in coal mines, or at fish canneries. Chinese workers, however, were typically paid considerably less than were white workers. (Unlike white immigrants, they were also subject to an expensive head tax aimed at discouraging Chinese people from settling in Canada [Anderson 1988: 132].) These Chinese "pioneers," however, did not move into a vacuum. Rather, a whole suite of images – themselves refracted through a highly developed racial discourse (see chapter 9) – about the "nature" of the Chinese circulated among white workers and elites. "Well before any substantial settlement of Chinese was identified as such in Vancouver, a 'place' for them had a distinct reality in local vocabulary and culture," Anderson

10   The existence of myriad "Little Italies," "Poletowns," or other ethnic neighborhoods is no argument against Anderson's point as these were constructed through exactly the sorts of racial and ethnic discourses she explores in the case of Chinatown.

(1988: 135) writes. By 1885 such vocabulary was commonplace. As Canadian Secretary of State Joseph Chapleau intoned, "Had Dante been able to visit Chinatown, San Francisco, he would have added yet darker strokes of horror to his inferno" (quoted in Anderson 1988: 135).

Drawing on received notions about the supposed biological and social superiority of Europeans, whites in Vancouver understood Chinese people to be irredeemably different from themselves. As Chinese workers and merchants began to cluster around Dupont (later Pender) Street at the edge of Bayard Inlet, their presence was met with alarm. White workers thought there was something "natural" in the Chinese ability to subsist on wages so much lower than their own.[11] Elites fretted over possible pollution not just of the physical and moral environment of the Chinatown and nearby districts, but of white racial purity itself. In early 1887, such fears led to an all-out attack on a Chinese settlement in Vancouver in which 300 rioters destroyed residential camps, washhouses and stores, and chased the Chinese residents out of the settlement. The city government turned a blind eye on the rioting, but within a few days the Provincial government was forced to send in a militia to break the "mob rule" that had taken over the city (Anderson 1987: 583). This riot, coupled with the partial protection afforded by the Provincial militia led to a further concentration of Chinese workers and merchants in the Dupont Street area.

Two years before the riot, even before the term "Chinatown" had been applied to any settlement in Vancouver, Secretary of State Chapleau had warned that "their custom of living in quarters of their own – in Chinatowns – is attended with evils, such as the depreciation of property, and owing to their habits of lodging [in] crowded quarters and accumulating filth, is offensive and likely to breed disease" (quoted in Anderson 1987: 585–6). Basing his opinions on a study of San Francisco's Chinatown, Chapleau concluded that the concentrated Chinese presence in Vancouver represented a natural threat to the upright body of citizens in the city. Yet when Chinese tried to move out of "Chinatown," they were met with fierce opposition. Laws were passed requiring that Chinese laundries be located only in the Dupont Street neighborhood; and restrictive covenants on the sale of residences, though not fully legal, were regularly observed.

The city regarded Chinatown through two optics, both of which found support in the landscape itself. On the one hand, the Chinese were naturally unsanitary. The dirt and filth of the district spoke for itself, as did the fact that the city felt compelled to make Chinatown – "along with water, sewage, infectious disease, slaughterhouses, and pig ranches" – an item of special health concern requiring supervision by its own sanitary officer (Anderson 1987: 586–7). This determination was made despite the fact that, as one contemporary observer pointed out (in a statement notable for its uniqueness), "it would be extremely difficult, if not impossible, even in the worst Chinese quarter, to parallel the state of affairs revealed amongst some white men in

---

11   In North America, one of the most influential diatribes against the "yellow peril" was that of the radical reformer Henry George. His argument was that Asians undermined the interests of legitimate, white, working men, and that the migrants to the west coasts of the United States and Canada merely represented the "thin end of the wedge" that culminated in over 500 million people in eastern Asia. On Henry George, see Daniels (1962: 69); on working-class anti-Chinese activism in the USA, see Saxton (1971).

our city not long ago in some of the cabins behind the Imperial Opera House" (quoted in Anderson 1987: 589). While unsanitary conditions were common to many working class districts of the city, it was only in Chinatown that such conditions were linked to some *natural* propensity of the people who lived in the district.

On the other hand, Chinatown was linked in the public imagination to moral depravity. Drawing on a storehouse of images brought back to North America by missionaries posted to China, white Vancouverites (and their government) frequently worried about the influence Chinatown had on the morals of the city as a whole. As Anderson (1987: 589) summarizes these sentiments: "Because the 'Chinese' were inveterate gamblers, 'Chinatown' was lawless; as opium addicted, Chinatown was a pestilential den; as evil and inscrutable, Chinatown was a prostitution base where white women were lured as slaves." It did not matter that representatives from Chinatown itself formally protested the city's pushing white prostitutes into their district from other neighborhoods; nor did it make any difference that the Chinese were at the forefront of calling for greater control of opium *trafficking*, a business largely controlled by whites. Rather, what was important was the *representation* of Chinatown as a natural center for vice, a representation evident right there in the landscape itself (figure 4.6).

As Anderson argues, racial ideology found material referents in the place itself. And the structure of the place (its landscape, in the terms established by Sauer) itself fed into, validated, and transformed the ideology. The physical landscape, then, was a product not of some unique culture, and hence it could hardly be evidence of the qualities of that culture (no matter how often it was put to work as just that kind of evidence). Rather, it was the product of negotiation between those with the "power to define" (Western 1996) Chinatown and those who had to live their lives in it.

The "power to define," which is itself a product of social relations, is always subject to change. In the case of Chinatown, the promotion of it as evil, as a zone *only* of immorality and filth, has given way in the last half century to an image of Chinatown as a place for tourists, a libidinal zone in which non-Chinese people can experience the exoticism of China without actually having to go there. The Orient is brought almost right to our doorstep – and pretty safely too. The image of Chinatown has been transformed from one of pestilence and depravity to one of exotic, fascinating "otherness."

What happened? Several things. During the Depression, as was sometimes the case elsewhere, trade unions began arguing that racial solidarity was essential to class solidarity, that discrimination against Chinese workers served to drive down the wages of white workers as well. The Depression era, in fact, was one of general unrest in North America, and to a greater extent than in the 1880s, the era was one in which new alliances – racial, sexual, political – formed and dissolved, new strategies for living and for community were subject to experiment.[12] This was no fully progressive project that sought to erase the false biological metaphors that governed race construction (see chapter 9), but was rather a process of realization that the exoticism of Chinatown was not so much dangerous as it was an economic opportunity. Older visions of the Orient as an "ancient and venerated civilization" were dredged up and

---

12 For excellent, if quite different, discussions of experimentation in the United States during Prohibition and the Depression, see Denning (1996) and Chauncy (1994).

Figure 4.6 "The Unanswerable Argument," *Saturday Sunset* (August 10, 1907). Landscape here represents all that is immutable about different "cultures" – at least in the minds of those who sought to control and contain the Chinese. Source: Anderson (1991: 87).

put into service as a mode of economic development (Anderson 1988: 140). The Chinese Benevolent Association received permission to build ornate Chinese-style buildings in the heart of Chinatown as part of the 1936 Golden Jubilee celebrations, and Chinese merchants worked hard to realize the sorts of profitable tourist development pioneered in the San Francisco and New York Chinatowns. The creation of a Chinese village for the Jubilee served the "same epistemological separation between 'us' and 'them'" that had always governed Chinese–white relations in Vancouver, but now in a "more benign" mode. In this regard, Vancouver's Chinatown was well on its way to becoming not Europe's immoral opposite, but a profitable (because exotic) "European commodity" (Anderson 1988: 141). Such touristy exoticism did not entirely erase the old images of Chinatown as a den of vice and insalubrity, but rather became "sedimented" within them. The old vision of Chinatown as vice-ridden, now partially sanitized, merely added to the exoticism and sense of adventure white tourists expected to find there. The "store of competing visions" – vice, exoticism, licentiousness, tourist kitsch – that now make the Chinese landscape were all in place (1988: 141).[13]

---

13   There is, of course, a lot more to this story than I have presented here. Anderson's books and articles are both accessible and immensely stimulating. They are also fascinating history. Similarly, Chinatown's history hardly ended in the Depression, ossifying once and for all the meaning of the Chinatown landscape. Rather, both the form of the landscape, and its varied meanings, were and are ever-shifting, ever subject to revision, contest, and negotiation, as Anderson shows so well.

Whether seen as exciting and exotic, or evil and dangerous, it should be clear that the Chinatown landscape represents "an arbitrary classification of space, a regionalization that has belonged to European Society" (Anderson 1987: 583). And as *that*, landscape – in this case the Chinatown landscape – serves as it must: to "reaffirm a...moral order of 'us' and 'them'" (1988: 145). More pointedly, "those with the power of definition can, in a sense, *create* places by arbitrarily regionalizing the external world and attaching to them symbolic significance" (K. Anderson 1991: 249–50, emphasis added; see also chapter 9 below).

Representation, then, is crucial. But what – and whose – representations are ossified in the landscape? In the case of Chinatown, the landscape clearly *incorporates* (not just reflects) the wishes, desires and fears of the surrounding hegemonic white society. But, of course, it does not do so completely. As our discussion of hegemony in chapter 2 indicated, it is inconceivable that a hegemonic order can survive without continual consent and contest by those it seeks to dominate. Hegemony is a two-way street. The Chinatown landscape is a jumbled, compromised thing that results from ongoing struggle. In this regard it is much like Johnstown or any other landscape we might care to examine. The important issue is the relative levels of power of the various competing groups: the degree to which these groups have the power to instantiate their own image of the world on the ground, and in the stones, concrete, bricks, and wood of the landscape. Landscape, and landscape representations, are thus incorporations of power. But sometimes, landscapes are made precisely to intervene in relations of power themselves. They are made to actively *represent* who has power, certainly, but also to *reinforce* that power by creating a constant and unrelenting symbol of it. "[S]uch monuments," according to Janice Monk (1992: 124), "...are intended to commemorate what we value and to instruct us in our heritage through visible expression on the landscape."[14]

Sacré-Coeur

The Basilica of Sacré-Coeur on Montmartre in Paris can be understood in this manner (figure 4.7). As David Harvey's (1979: 363–4)[15] brilliant reconstruction of the historical moment in which the Basilica was built shows, the form, style, and placement of Sacré-Coeur was far from accidental. "Few would argue that the Basilica of Sacré-Coeur is beautiful or elegant," Harvey writes. "But most would concede that it is striking and distinctive, that its direct Byzantine style achieves a kind of haughty grandeur which demands respect from the city at its feet. On sunny days it glistens from afar and even on the gloomiest of days its domes seem to capture the smallest particles of light and radiate them outwards in a white marble glow." Hence, Harvey asserts, the Basilica stands as a symbol of "perpetual remembrance." The question, as with Johnstown and its closed steel mills, is what is to be remembered? What meanings does this monument project, and how does it project them?

14 Monk is referring explicitly to the ways in which gender is powerfully coded in the landscape. We will return to the examination of gender in chapter 5.
15 Page numbers in the text refer to the *Annals* version of the article (1979). The essay has been reprinted in Harvey (1989b).

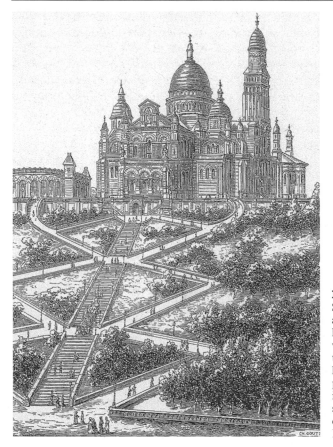

Figure 4.7 The Basilica of Sacré-Coeur. David Harvey's analysis of this monument in the landscape asks whose history – whose memory – is interred at this site. A reconstruction of the history of the Basilica and the political-geographic context within which it was conceived and built shows that that is not at all an easy question. Mary Evans Picture Library.

At one level, the history is plainly there for all to see. A prominent inscription at the Basilica proclaims:

> The year of our Lord 1875, the 16th June, in the reign of His Holiness Pope Pius IX in accomplishment of a vow formulated during the war of 1870–1871 by Alexander Legentil and Hubert Rohault de Fleury ratified by His Grace Mgr. Guibert Archbishop of Paris; in execution of the vote of the National Assembly of the 23rd July 1873 according to the design of the architect Abadie; the first stone of this Basilica erected to the Sacred Heart of Jesus was solemnly put in place by His Eminence Cardinal Guibert. . . .
>
> (quoted pp. 365–6)

But Harvey is convinced – and he is right – that this inscription, and indeed the Basilica itself, hides more history than it reveals. The landscape is a deceptive representation. And conversely, the Basilica represents, plainly in its stones and mortar, a clear intervention in the political and economic history of Paris and France. The landscape couldn't be a clearer representation.

But again, representation of what? For Harvey, the answer lies in the tumultuous class politics of Paris during the nineteenth century. The story, however, begins in the late seventeenth century when Marguerite-Marie Alacoque (later sainted), haunted by visions of the Sacred Heart of Jesus, developed a cult within the Catholic church dedicated to its worship. As the cult spread slowly through France in the following century it found adherents from the monarchy, culminating in the private vows taken by Louis XVI and Marie-Antoinette. As Harvey (pp. 364–5) remarks, such royal adherents are important because they indicate a lasting "association . . . between the cult of the Sacred Heart and the reactionary monarchism of the *Ancien Régime*. This put adherents of the cult in firm opposition to the principles of the French revolution." When the monarchy was restored, the fortunes of the cult advanced, particularly among conservative Catholics.

When Paris was under siege in the last months of the Franco-Prussian war, and with the urban unrest growing during the fall of 1870, Catholic Parisian Alexander Legentil fled the city. From his refuge in the countryside, he vowed in December that "if God saved Paris and France and delivered the sovereign pontiff, he would contribute according to his means to the construction in Paris of a sanctuary dedicated to the Sacred Heart" (quoted p. 366). Attracting other adherents to his cause, Legentil built considerable strength behind the movement to build the sanctuary. But his vision did not go unopposed. As Harvey explains, tensions between the city and the countryside nearly scuttled the proposal as many of the most faithful adherents (and donors) opposed the further centralization of power – symbolic or otherwise – in Paris. Despite this, the backers of the Basilica reaffirmed their determination to build in Paris: "were Paris reduced to cinders," they proclaimed on March 19, 1871, "we would still want to avow our national faults and proclaim the justice of God on its ruins" (quoted p. 367). Only one day earlier, Harvey (p. 367) notes, "Parisians had taken their first irrevocable steps towards establishing self-government under the Commune. The real or imagined sins of the communards were subsequently to shock and outrage bourgeois opinion. And as much of Paris was indeed reduced to cinders in the course of a civil war of incredible ferocity, the notion of a basilica of expiation upon these ashes became more and more appealing."

The history and politics of the Commune are complex and fascinating, but the important issue here is that "rightly or wrongly, the bourgeoisie [of Paris] was greatly alarmed during the 1860s by the emergence of working class organizations and political clubs, by the activities of the Paris branch of the International Working Men's association, by the effervescence of thought within the working class and the spread of anarchist and socialist philosophies" (p. 368). During the siege of Paris, the working classes were essential ingredients in the rather weak attempts by the Government of National Defense to repel the Prussians and break the siege. This alliance seemed to catch the bourgeoisie in a trap between the Prussians and the "red" leadership of the workers. But so too did the workers find their desire for municipal democracy and self-determination betrayed by the national government. Such intrigue led, at the end of October, 1870, to the first insurrectionary movements of what would soon become a civil war. And all this during the continuing Prussian siege of the city: starvation among the mass of the population was rampant, with working-class Parisians reduced to bargaining for rat meat and eating bread adulterated with bone meal – bones exhumed from the catacombs that housed their ancestors. Yet even so, the bourgeoisie found it possible to continue to consume conspicuously (if rather expensively).

The national government finally capitulated to Prussia in January, 1871, and provisions were made to disband the French Army. The Paris National Guard, however, remained armed. In the elections that followed, Paris voted radical and republican, but found the countryside strongly in support of the monarchists and a full capitulation to Prussia. Part of the agreement with Prussia provided that French reparations would be financed by French, not German, financiers, who promptly informed newly elected President Adolphe Thiers that financing could only be achieved if he first eradicated the unrest in Paris. Thiers's plan was to send "the remnants of the French Army...to Paris to relieve that city of its cannons in what was obviously a first step toward the disarmament of a population which had, since September 4th, joined the National Guard in massive numbers" (p. 370). In response, the people of Paris sought to maintain their control over their armaments, pouring into the streets and onto fortifications to contest the actions of the army.

It is here that Montmartre – a symbolic center of the city – re-enters the picture. "On the hill on Montmartre," Harvey (p. 370) reports,

> weary French soldiers stood guard over the powerful battery of cannons assembled there, facing the increasingly restive and angry crowd. General Lacomte ordered his troops to fire. He ordered once, twice, thrice. The soldiers had not the heart to do it, raised their rifle butts in the air, and fraternized joyfully with the crowd. An infuriated mob took General Lacomte prisoner. They stumbled across General Thomas, remembered and hated for his role in the savage killings [of insurrectionary workers] in the June days of 1848. The two generals were taken to the garden of No. 6 rue des Rosiers and, amid considerable confusion and angry argument, put up against a wall and shot.

The hilltop at Montmartre had once again become a place of martyrdom – a point which was not lost on those who sought to build the Basilica. When the first stones of the church were laid, the connection was made explicit: "it is here where Sacré-Coeur will be raised up that the Commune began," one of the chief proponents of the Basilica proclaimed, "here where the generals Clement Thomas and Lacomte were assassinated." The Basilica would avenge those murders, and turn Montmartre once again into a holy site, and a site that would forever bury the "demons" of the commune (quoted p. 370).

If that was the function (or at least one of the functions) of the Basilica, the burying of the commune in less symbolic, more bloody means was left to fighting in the streets. President Thiers arranged a second siege of Paris in April, 1871, and reinforced it with "one of the most vicious bloodlettings in an often bloody French history." Included in this bloodletting was the massacre of communard leaders, such as Eugene Varlin, where else but on the hillside of Montmartre. "The left can have its martyrs too," Harvey intones (p. 371). "And it is on that spot that Sacré-Coeur is built." Both for atonement and to erase the history of the wildly anti-clerical communards, the movement to build Sacré-Coeur gained momentum in the year after the commune's defeat, with Pope Pius IX giving his endorsement in July, 1872. By October, the Archbishop of Paris had selected Montmartre as the site for the Basilica because "it was only from there that the symbolic domination of Paris could be assured" (p. 376). As he struggled to the top of the hill, the Archbishop proclaimed,

"It is here, it is here where the martyrs are, it is here that the Sacred Heart must reign so that all can beckon to it" (quoted p. 364).

Much debate ensued as to the devotion of public property to such a cause, as to the role that Catholic workers were to play in raising funds, and as to the symbols with which the Basilica was to be adorned. Even so, the church was finally completed in 1912, and set to be consecrated in October, 1914, when another war with Germany yet again interrupted plans. It was not finally consecrated until after World War I had ended.

Sacré-Coeur remains a powerfully symbolic site today, both to pilgrims and tourists perhaps unaware of its bloody history, and to radical protesters who know precisely what the basilica stands for. But Sacré-Coeur's representations are not always crystal clear. As Harvey (p. 381) concludes,

> [T]he visitor who looks at the mausoleum-like structure that is Sacré-Coeur might well wonder what it is that is interred there. The spirit of 1789? The sins of France? The alliance between intransigent catholicism and reactionary monarchism? The blood of martyrs like Lacomte and Clement Thomas? Or that of Eugene Varlin and the twenty thousand or so communards mercilessly slaughtered along with him? The building hides its secrets in sepulchral silence.

So how then should we understand the production of landscapes? And how should we understand both their desire to represent and their desire to hide? My own sense is that it is vital to begin with an exploration, as Harvey did with Sacré-Coeur, of the relations that go into a landscape's making. No matter how mystified a landscape may be, no matter how abstracted from the forms of place landscape representations may become (as we will see below), it is nonetheless the case that there are a set of delineable social relations – as in Johnstown, Vancouver, and Paris – that explain both how landscapes are made and how and why landscape representations circulate as they do.

An understanding of landscape production should probably therefore begin with Sharon Zukin's (1991: 16, 19) definition of landscape as a "contentious, compromised, product of society" formed through "power, coercion and collective resistance." But the important point is precisely that "landscape" fully *mystifies* that contentiousness, creating instead a smooth surface, a mute representation, a clear view that is little clouded by considerations of inequality, power, coercion, or resistance – at least until the moment when those struggles over power become overt. As Vancouver's Chinatown and Paris's Sacré-Coeur, and perhaps especially Johnstown show so well, landscape is a kind of lived, produced, and represented space. What is interesting is the relationship between the lives (and deaths), the productions and the representations, that make a landscape. As W.J.T. Mitchell (1994: 1–2) has put it, landscape:

> is an instrument of cultural power, perhaps even an agent of power that is (or frequently represents itself as) independent of human intentions. Landscape thus has a double role with respect to something like ideology.... It naturalizes a cultural and social construction representing an artificial world as if it were simply given and inevitable, and it also makes that representation operational by interpellating its beholder in some more or less determinate relation to its givenness as sight and site.

For geographers, this has meant searching below the surface of material landscapes like city blocks or national parks, "ethnic" neighborhoods and monumental buildings, as well as of paintings, photographs, gardens, and other more representational landscapes, to uncover the conditions under which a landscape is made. Geographers have done this by exploring class and gender relations, the role of race and nationality in landscape production (as with Chinatown), or by engaging in fine-grained analyses of particular events that are determinate in making a landscape (as with Sacré-Coeur). These are all types of culture wars through which landscapes are made. But it has also meant paying close attention to other kinds of battles that reveal another crucial side of landscape: landscape as representation. For representation can have a circulation – an economy – quite different (though not disconnected) from the material form landscapes take on the ground.

Representations: Or the Work of Landscape as "Scene"

A few years ago, the Smithsonian National Museum of Art in Washington, DC, opened an exhibit that sought to reconsider the nature of the images that defined the American West. Part of the goal was to show how images of heroism and conquest were propped up by (and served to mask) systems of exploitation and even genocide in the West (figure 4.8). The exhibit sought to show that the Western myth was just that, a myth. As Stephen Daniels (1993: 1) describes the exhibit, "Some images are

Figure 4.8 Tompkins H. Matson, *The Last of the Race* (1847). Native Americans were often depicted as remnants of a past landscape, justifying American manifest destiny through their passing. Prints of *The Last of the Indians* were popular in the Eastern United States. Reproduced by permission of the New York Historical Society.

described [by text accompanying them] to be less about the West than a projection of social tensions, around immigration and labour unrest, in the eastern cities where many of the art-works were produced and consumed." The reaction to this exhibition was immediate and strong. Politicians in both parties condemned the Smithsonian and threatened to cut off its funding. Museums in other cities (including St. Louis and Denver, two key locations for Western development) canceled their plans to host the show. And, in the press and on television, on the floor of Congress and in classrooms, a wild debate developed on the proper representation of history and geography – a debate that has reverberated in a series of increasingly strident battles in the culture wars around everything from the teaching of Western history, to the role of museums in promoting national culture (see chapter 1; see also Limerick 1991).[16]

What's going on? Why such a furor over the way the West was painted? How is it possible that a more truthful depiction of the West can be pilloried as an affront to the sensibilities of the nation? To answer these questions we need to move beyond the realm of landscape production and focus more clearly on the role of landscape representation in defining society, in promoting ideologies of naturalism in the manner indicated above by W.J.T. Mitchell. As Harvey's explication of the building of Sacré-Coeur makes so clear, the facts of landscape production can never be divorced from the mode and purpose of landscape representation.[17] The "iconography of landscape," to borrow a phrase from Denis Cosgrove and Stephen Daniels (1988), two pioneers in the geographical study of landscape representation, needs to be unpacked, not least to show the way that landscape itself is part and parcel of (indeed a key ingredient in) the sort of culture-as-ideology described in chapter 3.

The Landscape idea: representing ideology

Denis Cosgrove traces the landscape idea to a key period and place in European history, the Italian Renaissance. While some of the hallmarks of the landscape "way of seeing" could be found elsewhere in Europe (particularly Flanders), it was in modernizing Italy where the *idea* of landscape (as a mode of representation) was elaborated and theorized. Cosgrove (1985: 46) convincingly links this development of the landscape idea to the development of modern capitalism, showing how landscape, along with cartography, and the development of modern theater, was an important tool for the "practical appropriation of space." Particularly, landscape painting adopted the technology of linear perspective, itself a way of seeing perfected and theorized in Renaissance Italy, to create a "visual ideology" of realism – an ideology that suggested that perspective and landscape was not just *a* way of seeing, but rather *the true* way of seeing.

16 A second, related controversy erupted at the Smithsonian when it sought to stage a retrospective look at the atomic bombing of Hiroshima and Nagasaki in 1995. Even mild hints that dropping a bomb on cities full of civilians, and unleashing the destructive power of the atom may not have been all for the good, worked politicians, veterans' groups and various right-wing pundits into a frothy lather of nationalistic fervor; see Harwit (1996).
17 The fullest account of this is Duncan (1990); for a much less nuanced, and much more problematic discussion of these issues, see Barnes and Duncan (1992).

Linear perspective, as the Florentine architect Leon Battista Alberti explained it, structured the view of space so that it "directs the external world towards the individual located outside that space. It gives the eye absolute mastery over space." In essence, a painter using perspective "determines ... the 'point of view' to be taken by the observer" (Cosgrove 1985: 48). This is important because the depicted space is thus "rendered the property of the individual detached observer, from whose divine location it is a dependent, appropriated object" (1985: 49). Put another way, a realistic landscape view "is composed, regulated and offered as a static image for individual appreciation, or better, appropriation. For in an important, if not always literal, sense, the spectator *owns* the view because all of its components are structured towards his eyes only. The claim of realism is in fact ideological. ... Subjectivity is rendered the property of the artist and the viewer – those who control the landscape – not those who belong to it" (Cosgrove 1984: 26). This is important, clearly, because it shows that the landscape way of seeing is precisely a technique to render control, both ideological and material, as "natural," as part of the inescapable order of things.

In turn, as Cosgrove further shows, "landscape" was and is a particularly *bourgeois* way of seeing. Not only did linear perspective develop in urban areas (as a means of depicting the spaces of the city), but it was chiefly a result of sponsorship by the increasingly wealthy urban merchant classes. Landscape became a means of depicting not just their control over space (and, importantly, property), but also a means of representing their status and wealth. Depictions of rural villas that served as retreats from the bustle of city life, together with the active appropriation of nature that villa gardens represented, quickly came to be an essential part of the landscape tradition. For the urban elite relaxing in their country villas "landscape painting is intended to serve the purpose of reflecting back to the powerful viewer ... the image of a controlled and well-ordered, productive and relaxed world wherein serious matters are laid aside" (Cosgrove 1984: 24). Importantly, then, a central component of landscape representation is the erasure of the work that goes into making a landscape (Barrell 1980; Mitchell 1996a; Williams 1973). Rather, landscape is made to represent the supposedly "natural" order. But it is a "natural order" only made possible by the commodification of land and labor that came with the rise of capitalism in Europe.

Specifically, "the realist illusion of space ... was, through perspective, aligned to the physical appropriation of space as property, or territory. ... Landscape is thus a way of seeing, a composition and structuring of the world so that it may be appropriated by a detached, individual spectator to whom an illusion of order and control is offered through the composition of space according to the certainties of geometry. That illusion very frequently complemented the very real power and control over fields and farms on the part of patrons and owners of landscape painters" (Cosgrove 1985: 55). In other words, landscape representations justified to owners of property their status and the rightness of their rule over land. In the English Renaissance of the sixteenth and seventeenth centuries, the term "prospect," closely aligned with landscape and perspective, "carried the sense of 'an extensive or *commanding* sight or view, a view of landscape as affected by one's position'" (Cosgrove 1985: 55, quoting *Oxford English Dictionary*, emphasis Cosgrove's). Such a sense of visual *command*, according to Cosgrove (1985: 55), "reflects a period when command over land was being established on new commercially-run estates by Tudor enclosers and the new landowners of measured monastic properties." That is, pictorial command reflected control over real property. And command over real property, as Marx so clearly showed, is itself a prerequisite of capitalist development. It is the precondition for the "freeing" of labor, for turning peasants into wage laborers.

Naturalization and contestation

The "primitive accumulation" of property, and hence the development of capitalism, was a particularly bloody affair, whether we examine the enclosures of Britain and Ireland, or the usurpation of land on distant colonies by European colonial powers. It also brought with it all manner of ideological contradictions in the way peasants, workers, landowners, merchants, and factory owners alike understood their *place* in a rapidly transforming world. The landscape way of seeing, as one tool among many, served as an important technology for representing new orders as timeless and natural.

For landscape representation to work this way it must negotiate a rather complex contradiction that defines capitalism as a social system. On the one hand, "free labor" must of necessity be quite mobile. It must be available to work when and where it is needed. Capitalism cannot work without the circulation of labor (and of course laborers).[18] On the other hand, landscape views do their work precisely by freezing those they depict to the ground, making them appear as natural parts of the scene. As Cosgrove (1984: 27) explains, "when humans are represented in landscape painting they are more often than not either at repose, or, if at work, distant and scarcely noticeable figures. Their position is determined by the pictorial structure and for the most part human figures seem to be in but not of their surroundings. If they become too dominant the work ceases to be a landscape." (figure 4.9) Further, according to art historian Elizabeth Helsinger (1994: 106), in "the world of the picturesque view, labor is fixed, as a subject of representation" (when it is depicted at all).

Conversely, the viewer is the one who is mobile, because perspective renders "form and position in space . . . to be relative rather than absolute. The forms of what we see, of objects in space and geometrical figures themselves, vary with the angle and distance of vision" employed by the painter on behalf of the viewer. "They are produced by the sovereign eye" which is itself highly mobile (Cosgrove 1985: 48). Hence, in representation, lived reality is reversed. Where property ownership and development, to say nothing of the ownership and deployment of the means of production, demands a certain mobility of labor, landscape representation renders labor fixed in place. And where property implies a certain fixity in place, owners are themselves mobilized around the edge of the canvas, always outside, to be sure, but always controlling, in part through their legitimated mobility.[19]

Landscape representation thus sought to legitimate and naturalize the emerging capitalist order by erasing many of the facts upon which it was built. If the *social*

18 Marx's (1987: Part VIII) explication of the relationship between "free labor" and a monopoly on property is one of the most compelling parts of *Capital*.

19 As Helsinger (1994) explains, the very mobility of the rural poor was a new phenomenon in industrializing England and something apparently to be feared (even if it was necessary to capitalist development). For a similar argument in the context of California agriculture in the twentieth century, see Mitchell (1996a).

Figure 4.9 John Constable, *The Cornfield* (1826). Constable's painting sits easily within the landscape genre: while the traces of work (shepherding, for example) are present, those doing the work are at ease; perspective and framing are used to give the illusion of depth; and country life is romanticized for outside viewers. As Daniels (1993: 205) remarks, "various features which would have irritated local countrymen – a dead tree, a broken gate, a neglected flock of sheep – were designed to soothe urban tourist tastes." Reproduced courtesy of the Trustees, National Gallery, London.

exploitation of labor is the defining feature of capitalism, then the purpose of landscape representation was precisely to hide that exploitation by naturalizing it. The "landscape idea," therefore, can be understood to be closely linked to an emerging "European elite consciousness" of its own desired place in the world, a desire that could afford little room for those the elite exploited to retain its position (Cosgrove 1984: 1). Landscape is thus about class consciousness, about ideologically structuring the world so as to make one's place in it appear just and perhaps even divinely ordained – especially at times of great social transformation. Like all ideologies, landscape representation is not content, however, to operate only within the confines of the class that develops it. Rather, as we saw in chapter 3, ideologies function by universalizing particular meanings. In the case of landscape representation in Europe

– and later America and other outposts of European expansion – this ideology functioned not only by legitimating landownership at the expense of the working classes, but also as an important component of national identity allied with the interests of landowners, the bourgeoisie, and, to a certain extent, the middle classes. As Helsinger (1994: 105–6) explains, in eighteenth- and nineteenth-century England, this ideological move possessed no little irony:

> The aesthetics of landscape, and the activities of viewing and displaying the English place through which it was experienced, created for those who could participate in it a claim on England as their national aesthetic property. What began in the eighteenth century with the improvement, display, and representation of private property, quickly gave birth to a concept of public property....

This concept of public property is nothing short of the nation itself (chapter 10). There is an asserted congruence between the desires and constructions of landowners and the landscape of the nation. National identity is wrapped up in the estates of the landed gentry. (And, as Helsinger shows, one of the purposes of the circulation of landscape *images* was precisely to indicate to the middle classes that they, too, were invested in this landscape – were, in a sense, owners of it – at precisely the time they were clamoring for greater political representation in the state.) The interests of the elite, and to a lesser extent the middle classes, are *shown* to be the interests of everyone through landscape representation.

This issue of national identity through landscape representation is of no little importance (cf. Daniels 1993). If the desires and landscapes of a particular *class* can be shown, in landscape representation, to stand for the identity of the nation as a *whole* (and, given the constructed nature of nationality, how could it be otherwise), then what choice do those who live and toil in those national landscapes have but to *identify* with them? Actually a lot. While landscape representation is an important aspect of nationalism, it is not so hegemonic as to preclude alternative readings or other forms of resistance. Instead, landscape representations are sites of contestation, just as are the landscapes they are meant to depict. Hence, landscape representations, especially representations that seek to conflate particularity with the universality of nationhood, must constantly be propped up, supported by other ideological practices.

That such representations are vulnerable to collapse is clear from the furor over the "America as West" exhibition at the Smithsonian. It is just as clear from the fact that it has been precisely the *laborist* history at the Franklin Mill, as much as the consensus history in the city as a whole, that has so far been attracting tourists to Johnstown. The question that remains, then, is just what all this conflict and contestation, all this energy invested in both the built form and the representation of landscape, actually *means* – not just to individuals, but socially. That is the question that the next chapter seeks to answer.

5

Metaphors to Live By: Landscapes as Systems of Social Reproduction

The previous chapter explored some of the ways that landscapes – as built form and representation – are made and do their work in society. This chapter examines the ways that we apprehend, take meaning from, and ultimately consume in and through landscapes. It also explores the reason why apprehending and taking meaning from landscapes is socially important. Richard Peet (1996: 23) puts the issue this way:

> Because landscapes are partly natural, their signs are frequently long lasting, and because landscapes are the homes of women and men, they are particularly suited to the ideological task of framing the social imaginary. By recreating landscapes, filling them with signs carrying ideological messages, images are formed of past and future "realities," patterns of meaning created and changed, and, thereby, control exerted over the everyday behavior of the people who call these manufactured places their natural, historic homes; this applies to people of all classes.

"Framing the social imaginary": by this Peet means that landscapes, through the accretion of meanings over time, come to define how people think about a place (and how they think about their place in that place), how they behave in it, and how they expect others to behave. The landscape is, in this sense, "read" by its inhabitants and visitors, so as to divine the messages encoded in its signs.

For some, the fact that landscapes are meaning*ful* in this sense implies that they give off to the world a "spirit" or a "sense of place" – a *genius loci*. Such a *genius loci*, as Loukaki (1997) shows in the case of the Sacred Rock of the Acropolis in Athens, is tightly bound up in the creation, perpetuation, and transformation of myth, while myth itself is made "permanent" – or at least less vulnerable to change – by its association with landscapes. As Loukaki (1997: 325) cautions, however, it is equally clear that there is never a "single universal, unchanging truth or authenticity of *genius loci*" in any place.[1] The key methodological issue then – and one of paramount importance for those of us who want to understand the relationship between the production of culture and the production of landscape – is the ways in which the intentional meanings of the builders of a landscape clash with the myriad other meanings that may be attributed to or derived from a landscape by its "users." Given that meaning is always a product of struggle between "producers" and various "users" of landscape, it should be apparent, however, that just because landscapes can take on multiple meanings, that does not thereby mean that all meanings are created equal. For in any contest over meaning, the key issue will always be one of power. It makes little sense to argue, as Peter Jackson (1989: 177) has done, that for any landscape, "there are potentially as many ways of seeing as there are eyes to see," because, in a world riven by relations of power, that potentiality will simply never be fulfilled. The objective is to see precisely how such potentiality is always and everywhere thwarted (and therefore how meaning is controlled).

Metaphors to Live By

The degree to which landscapes are *made* (by hands and minds) and represented (by particular people and classes, and through the accretion of history and myth) indicates that landscapes are in some very important senses "authored." Hence landscape can be understood to be a kind of text (see Meinig 1979; Duncan 1990; Barnes and Duncan 1992; Duncan and Ley 1993). In fact, it seems clear that Carl Sauer himself labored under this metaphor, if subconsciously, in his landscape methodology. For what was his objective but to "read" the landscape for evidence of the culture that made it? If the reading metaphor was implicit in Sauer, it was made explicit in the 1970s by, among others, geographer Peirce Lewis (1979), in his article "Axioms for Reading the Landscape." Lewis (1979: 12) argued that a landscape was in many regards like a book – but a particular kind of book. "Our human landscape is our unwitting autobiography, reflecting our tastes, our values, our aspirations, and even our fears, in tangible form." Yet, for all his interest in how to read a landscape, and in what the book of landscape represents, Lewis seemed little interested in problematizing how landscapes were, so to speak, written. Rather, the process seems in Lewis's telling to be somewhat akin to "automatic writing," wherein the pen of the author is guided by some mysterious force larger than the author her- or himself. The author is merely a channel or medium. Thus the key word, "unwitting." Moreover, what was

---

1   This is clearly the point to be drawn also from David Harvey's (1979) discussion of the Basilica of the Sacred Heart in Paris (titled, appropriately, "Monument and Myth"), which we examined in chapter 4.

written was itself a reflection of a unitary consensus culture, as far as Lewis was concerned. He was quite explicit: "culture is a *whole* – a unity – like an iceberg with many tips protruding above the surface of the water. Each tip looks like a different iceberg; but each is in fact part of the same object" (Lewis 1979: 19). As we have already seen, such a conception of culture is hardly realistic – a point which Lewis (1979: 12) recognizes in a roundabout way when he concedes that reading a landscape is far harder than reading a book; it is more like reading a "book whose pages are missing, torn, and smudged; a book whose copy has been edited and re-edited by people with illegible handwriting." "Culture," obviously, is a product and process of struggle. How else do the "pages" of the landscape get torn and rewritten?

As the discussion of the roots of the landscape idea and the complexity of landscape representation in chapter 4 indicate, a unitary notion of culture as an "author" – and hence such an easily reconstructed *single* meaning of landscape such as Lewis posits – is too simplistic. James Duncan and Nancy Duncan (1988), therefore, have sought over the past decade to problematize this notion of reading. Their argument is that the text metaphor needs to be deepened. James Duncan (1990: 4–5) has argued, for example, that by "accepting landscapes as texts, broadly defined, we are led to examine a number of issues which have hitherto been ignored" in geography. First, we need to examine "how landscapes encode information." Second, one must understand, through an analysis of relations of power, *how* differently situated people are *able* to read landscapes. This is no easy task, since "in order to answer these questions we must go beyond a consideration of the formal semiotic or tropological properties of the landscape as a system of communication, to see the landscape in relation to both structured political practices and individual intentions."

Drawing on the post-structuralist theories of Roland Barthes (among others), Duncan and Duncan (1988) argue that reading a landscape is the province both of "experts" (like themselves) and of ordinary people as they go about their everyday lives. The text metaphor is thus not something to be approached only intellectually. Rather "reading the landscape" is something we all *do*, day in and day out. Writing with Trevor Barnes, James Duncan argues that texts "should . . . be seen as signifying practices that are read, not passively, but as it were, rewritten as they are read." More pointedly, "this expanded notion of texts . . . sees them as constitutive of reality rather than mimicking it – in other words, as cultural practices of signification rather than as referential duplications" (Barnes and Duncan 1992: 5). This notion rides on the idea of "intertextuality," an idea that "implies that the context of any text is other texts" (Duncan 1990: 4). These "other texts" in turn include everything from texts as we normally understand the term (books, legal documents, scripts, etc.) on through to "other cultural productions such as paintings, maps and landscapes, as well as social, economic and political institutions" (Barnes and Duncan 1992: 5). Everything, then, is a text, ready to be decoded, read for meanings, and rewritten in our everyday cultural practices. We are all cultural "readers" – a way of understanding landscape considerably more "active" and anarchic than that presented, for example, in my discussion of Johnstown and the controversies over establishing *the* proper meaning for its landscape.

By employing the text metaphor, geographers such as Duncan and Duncan place themselves right at the center of some of the strongest currents of contemporary cultural studies, currents that argue it is impossible to ascribe to a text anything like a stable and universal meaning. For many cultural theorists it is simply the case that we live in a world of texts, a world defined by a degree of "intertextuality," where, because any text of which we are a part necessarily refers to other texts, and because we make our way in the world by reading, often quite intelligently, sometimes rather subversively, it is both unwise and impossible to seek to discover "a" or "the" meaning of a text.[2] The text metaphor is important, therefore, because it suggests that hegemonic productions – including landscapes – are always undermined by alternative individual and collective readings. In fact, it is the very act of *reading* that *authors*. Reading itself is the productive force of meaning. The "meanings" implicit in a cultural text like landscape are therefore "multiple and positional,... there are many ways of seeing and reading the landscape" (McDowell 1994: 163). Landscape is a system of *signs*, signs that themselves may very well be unstable and open to revision.

Yet the discussions of Johnstown, Chinatown, Sacré-Couer, and the politics of representation in the previous chapter indicate some shortcomings of this metaphor. Among other things, landscape, by its very representational nature, is designed (on the ground *and* in other media, like painting) to present a single *true* perspective, and even if this is ideological and therefore partial and open to alternative readings, it is nonetheless the case that meaning is backed up by powers that cannot and should not be reduced to the status of "text." The power of property ownership, supported by the police and the military power of the state, which is so central to the construction of landscapes, is hardly something that can be adequately undermined by subversive readings and mere meaning-construction (no matter how important these practices may in fact be). What is landscape, after all, but an *imposition* of power: power made concrete in the bricks, mortar, stones, tar, and lumber of a city, town, village, or rural setting – or on canvas or photo-stock.

We may, in fact, read landscapes all the time, and we may certainly construct all manner of meanings out of them. But unless we are willing to ignore both the ideological nature and material power of "culture" and landscape, such readings make a weak foundation for political action. While it "is possible, indeed normal, to decipher or decode space," as the French Marxist Henri Lefebvre (1991: 160) argues, the further assumption that *because* we decode, all there *is to do* is to decode, "cheerfully commandeer[s] social space and physical space and reduce[s] them to an epistemological (mental) space" (1991: 61). That is, such a move transfers the weight of social action from material practice to mental exercise. It furthers the erasure of the non-textual, non-linguistic practices at work in making a landscape. Landscapes, as with other non-verbal practices and activities, are "characterized by a spatiality that is in fact irreducible to the mental realm," according to Lefebvre (1991: 62). Further, "to underestimate, ignore and diminish space amounts to the overestimation of texts, written matter, and writing systems, along with the readable and the visible, to the point of assigning to these a monopoly on intelligibility." In short, the textual metaphor runs the risk of reducing the lived and experienced to merely the thought.

2 And so we see cultural studies of walkers "reading" cities; of audiences "reading" TV and thereby subverting it; and so forth. Examples of such studies pepper During's (1993a) *Cultural Studies Reader*. See especially the chapters by Michel de Certeau, Meaghan Morris, Rey Chow, and Janice Radway.

In partial recognition of this problem geographers have sought other metaphors which perhaps better explain the lived nature of landscapes. Unlike the metaphor of text, the metaphors of "theater," "stage," or "set" within and upon which the spectacle of life plays out – as tragedy, to be sure, but just as much as comedy – suggests a realm of action and social practice that is more than just the mental exercise of reading (figure 5.1). Most simply, "landscapes provide a stage for human action, and, like a theatre set, their own part in the drama varies from that of an entirely discreet unobserved presence to playing a highly visible role in the performance" (Cosgrove 1993b: 1). In that sense, the metaphor of theater suggests a further metaphor: that landscapes are live stages for the spectacle of life. Theories of spectacle are gaining prominence in geography and other cultural studies fields (and they all rely to one degree or another on Guy Debord's [1994] aphoristic manifesto, *The Society of the Spectacle*, which we will examine more fully in chapter 6). Like landscape, "spectacle" was an important term in Renaissance Europe, where it "could mean simple display, but also something to wonder at, thus touching mystery. It could take on the sense of a mirror through which truth which cannot be stated directly may be seen reflected and perhaps distorted, and it could mean an aid to vision as in the still-uncommon corrective lenses" (Daniels and Cosgrove 1993: 58). The important point, however, is that a spectacle is something experienced, acted in, lived. But it is a lived relation of a special sort. The very notion of "spectacle" implies something orchestrated, something designed. So if we live out the spectacle of landscape then it is certainly quite plausible that we do so under someone else's direction. This same limitation plagues the theater metaphor too. While we all may be actors in the drama of landscape, it is also often the case that someone else writes the script.

Figure 5.1 Sometimes the urban landscape is specifically made over into a stage. Pioneer Square, Portland, Oregon, 1987. Photograph by Susan Millar; used by permission.

Our movements, our experiences, perhaps even our emotions, are to one degree or another scripted for us by and in the landscape.

Yet the very purpose of "landscape" – as theater, as spectacle, as a text in which we engage in our "own" readings – is often precisely to mask the relationships of control that govern the production of landscape (and, to continue the theater metaphor, the productions taking place in the landscape). How many of us actively seek out the conditions under which the shopping district or mall we frequent was made and is maintained? How often do we wonder about the conditions under which toil the carpenters, janitors, bookkeepers (and all the rest who make that landscape possible)? The "lived-relations" of landscape that the spectacle metaphor points to, while not to be minimized in their own right, are also part of a process that maintains the *illusion* of landscapes as seamless zones of pleasure: pleasure in the view that landscape affords, and pleasure in the stage for activity that it provides. The point, then, is not at all that the metaphors of text, theater, and spectacle are somehow wrong – indeed, it can be quite rightly claimed that these are metaphors we literally live by – rather, it is to understand the limitations of those metaphors, and to see how any metaphor that helps us understand some aspect of the world hides as much as it reveals. Landscapes, through their aesthetization of space, may very well be texts, and they may often be texts that revel in depictions of the good life, but they are also, always, physical concretizations of power, power that the landscape itself often works quite hard to fetishize as something else altogether. Nowhere is this clearer than in the way that landscape becomes a stage – and perhaps also a text – for the construction and maintenance of unequal relations of gender.

Gendered Landscapes

Obviously, it is not just nationalism or class relations that are propped up through landscape representation. So too are relations of gender, sexuality, and race represented, reinforced, euphemized, fetishized, and naturalized in the landscape (see chapters 7–10). To focus just on gender, and as Janice Monk (1992: 124–6) shows, nearly every monument to be found in the public landscape codifies and reinforces – often quite subtly, sometimes rather blatantly – the masculinist, patriarchal power that tries so hard to determine the shape and structure of the world. At one level, women are strikingly absent from public monuments and memorials. In Australia, for example, of more than 2,000 memorials to participation in World War I, only three (one small local memorial and two major memorials in Sydney and Melbourne) depict any women at all. In the two large memorials, "you have to look hard" to see women, according to Ken Inglis who made a study of them (cited in Monk 1992: 125). In Washington, DC, as late as 1986 only four women were portrayed in all the outdoor monuments (Gross and Rojas 1986, cited in Monk 1992: 124).

At a different level, when women *are* depicted in statues, monuments, or representational painting they are often highly idealized – and unlikely. Think of the numerous French images of fighting "maidens," breasts bared, as they defend the barricades in Paris (cf. E. Wilson 1991). "[E]ven if executed with a high degree of naturalism," according to Marina Warner (1985: 28, quoted in Monk 1992: 126), "female figures representing an ideal or abstraction hardly ever interact with real, individual women. Devices distinguish them: improbable nudity, heroic scale, wings, unlikely attributes." So while depictions of women at one level are absolutely unrealistic – fighting bare-breasted or sprouting wings at critical moments are not everyday behaviors – they are at another quite realistic: they accurately represent societal, clearly masculinist *ideals* and *ideologies* about women, ideals and ideologies designed precisely to keep women in their place.

And what kind of place is that? Feminist scholars have shown that built landscapes – the landscapes of homes, parks, shopping districts, and public squares – are remarkable in their desire to confine and control women. Take, as only one example, the development of the suburban landscape. To start with, few better examples of how landscapes are always a mix of representation and built form can be found, as nearly every history of suburbia points out. But what does this mix of representation and form *mean*? And what does it *do*?

From the outset, suburbia *as a landscape* is inseparable from suburbia *as a gendered space*. In his insightful history, Robert Fishman (1987)[3] traces the suburban residential landscape to a desire for the separation of work and home that developed among the bourgeoisie of eighteenth-century London. This desire was not innocent of gender. Quite the contrary, it was closely wrapped up in changing conceptions of femininity and masculinity. In pre-modern London – a city so closely packed it is now almost inconceivable (from center to open fields was about a one-half mile radius) – and even after London began to greatly expand in the seventeenth century, rich and poor lived cheek-by-jowl, often in the same buildings. Work was rarely separated from residence: the "identity of work and home was the basic building block of eighteenth century urban ecology" (p. 21). To live among the poor meant no loss of status to a member of the bourgeois elite. Indeed, it was often necessary to the successful prosecution of business. The degree to which homes were businesses, and businesses homes, was reflected in a quite different conception of the "family" than we in the suburbanized West have grown accustomed to (and to which our politicians pay no end of homage). Instead, "[e]ven for the wealthy elite of merchants and bankers, the family was not simply (or perhaps even primarily) an emotional unit. It was at least equally an economic unit.... Virtually every aspect of family life was permeated by the requirements of the business" (p. 29). The implications for "womanhood" and femininity, as for "manhood" and masculinity, were profound. The importance of the family as an economic unit, according to Fishman (p. 29), was "most clearly seen in the active role played by women in London commercial life. A wife's daily assistance in the shop was vital for smaller businesses, and even the most opulent merchants were careful to give their wives a role sufficiently prominent that they could participate in and understand the source of their income." Such a family/household/business structure was evident in the landscape itself. "The typical merchant's townhouse...was surprisingly open to the city. Commercial life flowed freely, so that virtually every room had some business as well as familial function" (p. 29).

---

3   Page numbers in this section refer to this book. My account of the rise of suburbia as it relates to gender, relying as it does on Fishman's incisive history, is necessarily partial. Many of the points raised in this section are amplified and developed in MacKenzie and Rose (1983).

Compare that with the common descriptions of women's lot in contemporary suburbia. As early as 1869, middle-class women – and feminist activists – such as Catherine Beecher and Harriet Beecher Stowe argued that women's role in society was as a "spiritual center and efficient manager of the home, which was portrayed as a retreat from the world for the working husband and the centre of domestic harmony" (Monk 1992: 128; see also Hayden 1981, 1984; Mackenzie and Rose 1983; McDowell 1983). This "cult of domesticity" (see chapter 8) as it has come to be called, defined middle-class femininity at least through the 1950s in the United States, and similar structures of womanhood are still often venerated through some of the characters of popular soap operas in Australia, Britain, and North America. Ideally, modern suburban women guarded the private space of hearth and home, providing a refuge from the public sphere. In all practicality such a role, as it was concretized in the landscapes of suburbia, has meant a spatial isolation of women. It has also implied an incredible "privatization" of space, as various functions of family reproduction – cooking, cleaning, childcare – are incorporated into the interior of the house, and communal strategies for such reproduction are not just downplayed, but actively designed out. They have not remained a live option for most women (or men, for that matter). The landscape of suburbia both reflects and reinforces the atomized "nuclear" family, seeking to make each family fully independent from the society around it. Suburbia thus encourages a strange form of individualism, one that is predicated on isolation – and particularly the isolation of women.

How did we get from the relatively "open" eighteenth-century bourgeois London where women were an essential (if not necessarily equal) part of the life of business, to the nineteenth- and twentieth-century suburbs where women are essentially cloistered in a landscape that works hard to preclude their involvement in anything but the business of familial reproduction (figure 5.2)? Fishman (p. 35) traces this transition to the development of a new kind of "closed family [that] contradicted the basic

Figure 5.2 Contemporary single-family home suburbia. The ideal of "houses-in-a-park" has become the norm of American middle-class suburbia. Commercial, industrial, and even educational land-uses have no place in many suburban developments, like this one in Broomfield, Colorado. The whole purpose of such developments is to create a large degree of spatial isolation. Photograph by Caroline Nagle; used by permission.

principles of the eighteenth century city." Key to the development of the new family (and of women's role in it) was a Protestant sect within the London merchant bourgeoisie known as the Evangelicals. "Members of the Established church but uncertain of its efficacy, the Evangelicals taught that the most secure path to salvation was the beneficent influence of a truly Christian family. Anything that strengthened the emotional ties within the family was therefore holy; anything that weakened the family and its ability to foster true morality was anathema" (p. 35). Hence, the traditional, mixed, urban household of the eighteenth-century London bourgeoisie was seen by Evangelicals as detrimental to morality. A new landscape needed to be created that nurtured and protected both the family and what Evangelical writer William Wilberforce called "the reformation of manners."

Such a landscape, however, was predicated on a particular ideology concerning women, an ideology that set Evangelicals apart from many others in the English middle class of the time. "On the one hand, they gave to women the highest possible role in their system of values: the principal guardian of the Christian home. On the other, they fanatically opposed any role for women outside that sphere" (p. 35). For Wilberforce, "the more favorable disposition to Religion in the female sex" seemed designed "to afford to the married man the means of rendering an active share in the business of life more compatible... with the liveliest devotional feelings; that when the husband should return to his family, worn and harassed by worldly cares or professional labors, the wife habitually preserving a warmer and more unimpaired spirit of devotion, than is perhaps consistent with being immersed in the bustle of life, might revive his languid piety" (quoted on p. 36). The city was ill-suited to such an ideology of womanhood, and hence "this contradiction between the city and the Evangelical ideal of the family provided the final impetus for the unprecedented separation of the citizen's home from the city that is the essence of the suburban ideal" (p. 38).

But for this ideal to take hold, Evangelicals (and other like-minded potential suburbanites) had to wed their ideology to a landscape form. For this they drew on the ideal of the country park and manor, with its careful manufacture of aesthetically pleasing "natural" vistas. Fishman traces the development of such a suburban, picturesque landscape ideal as it evolved in the Evangelical settlement of Clapham, about five miles from the center of London. In Clapham, houses were organized around a central common, which the settlers had remade into a "delightful pleasure ground" through careful planting of trees and shrubs in what was considered to be a "naturalistic" style (p. 55). For those who built houses at a distance from the common, the goal was to continue the landscaping style on their own land. "Contemporary drawings" of Clapham, Fishman (p. 55) reports, "show wide tree shaded lawns sweeping up from the common to Palladian houses behind which large gardens and orchards were planted. Each house added its own well maintained greenery to the whole" (see also Cosgrove 1993b). Here then is suburbia as we have come to know it: "The true suburban landscape, as seen at Clapham, is a balance of the public and the private. Each property is private, but each contributes to the total landscape of *houses in a park*" (p. 55, original emphasis). But this was a certain kind of public–private compromise. As important as the look of the landscape was its function. The houses at Clapham literally "interiorized" social life and turned it in on the family itself. "The library [in the house] and the garden outside were the Evangelical substitute for all the plays, balls, visits, and coffee houses of London. Here the closed domesticated nuclear family became a reality" (p. 56).

For a large variety of reasons, which Fishman explores in great detail, the landscape innovations signaled by Clapham (which, as he points out, were not unique, but rather exemplary), proved enormously popular – and financially successful. Such a suburbanization not only responded to changing ideologies of the family, but also served a pent-up demand for housing. Just as importantly, the development of suburbia provided an outlet for the investment of newly-won capital that the middle classes had at their disposal.[4] Hence, right from the beginning, the suburban landscape was commodified, and a central location for speculation (pp. 62–72). Once the ideal had been established, and once the family had been remade to fit the landscape, even as the landscape was remade to fit the new family, suburbia exploded, becoming, as it were, the *only* option for respectable middle-class life. And this respectability, as we have seen, was predicated on the sequestering of women in the domestic sphere. Definitions of femininity – and of masculinity – were predicated on finding a spatial form that policed the divide between public and private spheres. If landscape is a stage, then it is a stage very clearly structured to move the drama of life in particular – and not at all infinite – directions.

Landscape as Expectation: Aesthetics, Power, and the Good Life

Shopping for signs: the cultural geography of the mall

Suburban landscapes mix public and private spaces in particular and peculiar ways. They create a stage on which gender is performed in a never-ending production (see chapter 8). Likewise, shopping malls use peculiar mixes of public and private to create a different sort of stage, a stage for not only the production of identity, but its consumption too. Malls are theaters in which the spectacle of everyday life is given a new and glamorous cast (as any 14-year-old can tell you). But perhaps the text metaphor is the best one for understanding just what a mall is and what it does. Malls are landscapes that are all about signs: they are clearly *meant* to be read. As landscapes, the meaning of malls (and similar spaces like festival marketplaces) seems particularly obvious. Their job is to provide us with an exquisite sense of expectation – the expectation that through the magic of money (or a decent credit line on the Visa), one can transform one's self into anything one pleases, the expectation that one can be as glamorous and desirable as the wares on display and the people who pass by in the corridors. Malls aren't just *about* signs; they are elaborate *systems* of signs. They *are* texts. But as Lefebvre (1991: 160) has noted, "certain spaces produced by capitalist promoters [like many contemporary landscapes] are so laden with signs – signs of well-being, happiness, style, art, riches, power, prosperity, and so on – that not only is their primary meaning (that of profitability) effaced but meaning

---

4   For an analysis of the importance of the "built environment" as a locus of capital investment see Harvey (1982: chapters 8 and 12); for a specific account of this process in the production of suburbia, see Walker (1981).

disappears altogether." What does he mean by this? How can a place, built to be read, in the end be so completely illegible?

When the Park Meadows Mall opened 15 miles south of Denver, Colorado, at the beginning of September, 1996, the media hype could not have been greater. Each of the local television stations sent reporters and camera crews to cover the opening – an opening that they themselves fervently advertised on the news shows for months before the event itself. The week of the opening, newspapers published special supplements, replete with maps of the mall (both interior and exterior) and special features on the wares on display in many of the stores. These features, however, were merely a culmination. A search of electronic indexes by the Denver weekly *Westword* found that between January 1 and September 1, 1996, Colorado newspapers had run 407 stories with the world "Park Meadows" in them ("Off Limits" 1996). The stories in print and electronic media dilated on the size of the mall and its success in attracting top-name "anchor" stores like Dillards and the swank Nordstroms, and they described in breathless detail the design of the interior spaces – spaces that made this, as the corporate owner of the mall (the Hahn Company) avers, not a mall at all, but a "retail resort" (figure 5.3). Such hype, however, is not at all surprising. Now, at a time when the commodity is everything, and when corporations like Nike and Benetton can so easily make their advertising *news*,[5] it would have been far more surprising if there had been little or no media hype, if the talking heads of the media had *not* rushed to the scene of the opening, if the supposed purveyors of the news had *not* so readily acquiesced in the production of spectacle. If you lived in Colorado or Eastern Wyoming, you did not need to visit the mall to know what it is like, to understand what it is supposed to mean, and why it is so special.

I went anyway. I went to see what a "retail resort" could possibly be. As the press made so clear in its breathless reportage, the interior of the mall is fitted out to look like a ski resort. There are lodgepole pines and Douglas firs studding the hallways, peeled wood beams seem to support the catwalks of the second floor and the roof, and instead of a "food court," the "retail resort" has a "dining hall" meant to resemble the rustic cafeterias of the ski lodges a hundred miles to the west (even so, this dining hall is replete with all the fast-food franchises you would expect: beyond design features, there are no surprises in this mall). In the first months after the mall opened, the temporary main entrance on the west side was through the Eddie Bauer store.[6] Eddie Bauer is one of those stores that sells adventure and travel as fashion,

5   Commentators for the CBS television network rarely appeared on screen at the 1998 Winter Olympics without wearing at least one article of clothing marked with the Nike "swoosh." And rarely does a sports star (Tiger Woods, Renaldo, Denis Rodman) sign a promotional agreement with Nike and not have it covered in the news section of the paper. Benetton continues to make news with its controversial campaigns centered on issues such as AIDS and eating disorders. And in the United States, Coke and Pepsi have been vying with each other to secure exclusive marketing contracts with high schools and universities, all breathlessly (and conveniently) reported by local and national media. Such contracts give the soft drink maker prominent billing on scoreboards, monopolies over vending machines, and lone access to drinks dispensers in cafeterias – all in exchange for some sum of money. These agreements are taken seriously enough that on "Coke Day" the principal at a high school in Georgia suspended a student in March, 1998, for wearing a T-shirt with the Pepsi logo on it.
6   Two large department stores are being built on either side of Eddie Bauer, so no doubt the dynamics of getting from parking lot to the interior will change.

Figure 5.3 The "retail resort" theme of the Park Meadows Mall is readily apparent in the main hall, where exposed timber ceilings and flagstone fireplaces work to shape the shopper's experience and to make Park Meadows a more enticing destination than its competitors in the Denver region. Photograph by D. Mitchell.

showing how you can be an intrepid, imperialist explorer without ever leaving your range rover (except to step into the mall) – and still look good. The rugged outdoors motif of the mall hits you with a vengeance the moment you enter the Park Meadows Retail Resort.[7]

Once out of Eddie Bauer, and onto the main floor, you are confronted with a miniaturized (but still two-story) mock-up of some of the sandstone rocks that comprise the Red Rocks Amphitheater, 30 miles to the northwest (figure 5.4). Red Rocks Amphitheater was constructed to take advantage of spectacular natural rock formations by the Works Progress Administration during the Depression. It is a quite spectacular site, with the stage nestled at the base of massive standing, red stones and the lights of Denver twinkling below. The Park Meadows version was built, by contrast, to specifications laid down by a California design firm and by contractors

7   Actually, even before: the security force at the mall dresses like park rangers (complete with Smokey the Bear hats) and patrols the parking lots on horseback.

Figure 5.4 The Red Rocks Fountain at Park Meadows Mall. Designed as a "homage" to Red Rocks Amphitheater, the Fountain features cascading waterfalls, rock-climbing beavers, and periodic eruptions of steam. Note also the security guard dressed as a park ranger with a Smokey the Bear hat. Photograph by D. Mitchell.

pouring a specially formulated concrete over a chicken-wire frame. Bronze and pewter squirrels and beavers (rock-climbing beavers!) have been bolted or glued to the surface, and the whole thing, deciding that honoring Red Rocks was not enough,[8] has been turned into a fountain with water cascading down two sides. Every twenty minutes or so, the water turns off, only to be replaced by steam, whether to represent some sort of eruption (which in a presumptively sandstone environment would be fascinating), or just a gee-whiz sort of event for kids and their parents is hard to determine.

This "Red Rocks" fountain occupies the center atrium of the mall. The catwalks of the second floor skirt around it, and indeed provide places for some of the best people-watching in the mall. The facing of these catwalks, about three feet thick, makes a space for a set of murals depicting the mountain and plains scenery of

8 I never would have known the thing was supposed to be Red Rocks had the Hahn Corporation not helpfully put up signs explaining it all – while simulacrum is everything in a mall, letting consumers in on the simulacrum is the height of sophisticated marketing, these days.

Colorado. Highly stylized paintings represent each of the lines of Katherine Lee Bates's famous anthem "America the Beautiful" (the myth holds that she wrote this on the summit of Colorado's Pike's Peak in 1893, a year of exceptional depression and labor unrest):

> Oh! Beautiful, For spacious skies
> For amber waves of grain
> For purple mountain majesties
> Above the fruited plain.
> America! America!
> God shed His grace on thee
> And crown thy good with brotherhood
> From sea to shining sea.

The central idea – God shed His grace on thee – is centered directly over the main hallway connecting the swank anchor department store Nordstroms to the almost equally swank Dillards (figure 5.5). It is hard to miss the meaning: my consumption, your consumption – it is all *ordained*. The signs couldn't be clearer: we have every right to *expect* such a landscape. As Americans, it is a true manifest destiny. And we can do it all in a *park*! It is all so natural!

While the designers of the mall have stuffed it so full of signs reminding us just how natural conspicuous consumption is and should be, they have done so for a reason. Jon Goss (1993; see also Crawford 1992; Hopkins 1990; Morris 1993) has subjected the semiotics of the mall to close scrutiny (as have many others engaged in geography and cultural studies). He has especially taken care to show how, and particularly why, those semiotics are *emplaced* in the space of the mall. For Goss (1993: 20), the mall represents a particularly clear example of "the commodification of reality." He

Figure 5.5 Katherine Lee Bates's benediction of shoppers at Park Meadows Mall. Photograph by D. Mitchell.

acknowledges that "all human societies . . . recognize a class that mediates between the material and symbolic worlds," but that it is only in recent times that "this class can control both sides of this relation, and that they are able to persuade us that our 'self-concept' as well as social status is defined by the commodity." Moreover, to the degree that our relations are mediated through the commodity, then our relationship to each other is in some senses commodified as well – and in this we often readily acquiesce. We succumb to what Goss (1993: 20) calls the "magic of advertising" in which "the materiality of the commodity" is masked. Most particularly, through our consumption, and through the advertising – in media and in the space of the mall – that accompanies it, the "sign value" of a commodity has not only displaced the commodity's "use-value" but it "*has become* use value" (Goss 1993: 21, citing Haug 1986). Such sign values have a fascinating geography when they are put into circulation in the mall.

In the first place, malls are quite expensive to build. Developers thus engage in extensive market analysis – and special pleading before city councils and county commissions for tax-breaks – before deciding on where to locate a mall. Developers deploy "teams of market researchers, geo-demographers, accountants, asset managers, lawyers, engineers, architects, artists, interior designers, traffic analysts, security consultants, and leasing agents" long before they ever break ground (Goss 1993: 22). Once building begins, of course, numerous contractors, electricians, carpenters, landscapers, iron workers, brick-layers, painters, carpet layers, plumbers and concrete pourers must be employed and coordinated. When the mall opens, the owner-developers need to carefully manage the mix of tenants to "ensur[e] complementarity of retail and service functions" so as to attract the desired mix of consumers. Above all, management does not want to attract "those whose presence might challenge the normality of consumption" by making their working-class, poor, or racial status felt, for example (Goss 1993: 22; see also Goss 1992; chapter 9 below).

But even attention to such details of retail mix are not enough to make a mall "work." Analysis of consumers' movement patterns have shown that American shoppers typically will not walk more than 600 feet – which provides an outer limit of mall size, unless developers and designers can find a means to *fool* the shoppers into thinking they are not walking as far as they are (Goss 1993: 33; see also Garreau 1991, 117–18). The ultimate fear of mall owners is that customers will *leave*. "Our surveys show," one mall manager remarks, that "the amount of spending is related *directly* to the amount of time spent at centers. . . . *Anything* that can prolong shoppers' visits are [sic] in our best interests overall" (quoted in "Food Courts . . ." 1990, cited in Goss 1993: 22). Hence at Park Meadows – a mall that is really just one long rectangular box – the lower hallway gives the impression of sinuousness: one can never see more than 20 or 30 yards ahead, as the hallway turns slightly back and forth, obstructing long views. What one sees, dead ahead, is instead another enticing store only a few paces away. The hallway thus *seduces* shoppers down its length. Upstairs, one *can* see from one end to the other, but here the catwalks themselves divide and turn, opening to views of the halls below (and that fountain!), and forcing pedestrians to slide from one side of the hallway to the other, constantly bumping into stores they were not intending to visit. Along both corridors, the way is broken by oversized flagstone fireplaces (remember the "resort" theme) surrounded by rustic, slightly plush furniture. I was a little surprised not to find a collection of old paperbacks and battered Scrabble and Trivial Pursuit games filling shelves near these "lounges," presumably left by skier-shoppers who had come before me. The whole essence of Park Meadows is one of invitation, but, masked as it is, it is only an invitation to spend. The fireplaces may speak of sociability, but this is a sociability with a purpose. The shopping mall, Goss (1993: 33) rightly proclaims, "is a machine for shopping." As such, "the built environment is…physically persuasive or coercive" (Goss 1993: 31).

So it is finally in this sense that we can understand the comments by Lefebvre with which I opened this section. On the one hand, the mall is a surfeit of signs, each of which, no matter how it may be interpreted by the users of malls, serves to actively hide or mask the mall's function, which is to make money. Or if it doesn't hide that function, then it certainly naturalizes it, such that the "commodification of reality" becomes simply "God-given": "God shed His grace on thee." On the other hand, these signs ultimately become literally meaningless. The space itself is coercive, establishing the limits to life that no amount of subversive reading can undo. Subversive readings are readily accommodated within the structure of the mall itself. As I stood watching "Red Rocks" erupt, a 10-year-old or so boy walked past me in a T-shirt advising us to "Rage Against the Machine." On the back of the tee was a stylized picture of a hand about to unleash a Molotov cocktail.[9] He and his parents were on their way to join the queue at McDonald's in the "dining hall." The mall-as-landscape is indeed quite accommodating: it not only sets our expectations; it fulfills them – a quarter-pounder at a time, no matter how much we may rage against the machine for shopping.

The city as mall: modern capitalism and postmodern urbanism

Jon Goss might now disagree with my interpretation of his research on malls. In a more recent article, Goss (1996) has focused on "festival marketplaces," those historically-themed shopping districts that have become increasingly important parts of the redevelopment schemes of cities throughout the USA, Canada, and Europe. He argues that while much of the scholarly critique of these commodified spaces is correct, it is also too one-sided, because it does not pay enough attention to how these spaces are *used* by those who frequent them. He cites his own epiphany in this regard: he was at the newly opened Aloha Towers Marketplace in Honolulu one day and happened across a gay couple holding hands and watching the sunset. The open expression of homosexuality is certainly not a sanctioned behavior in most public spaces of society (see chapter 7 below), yet here it seemed unremarkable. Goss thus wonders whether the cynicism of academic critics of privatized public spaces like malls and marketplaces is warranted. As spaces open to the public, festival marketplaces are given all manner of readings by their users. And as spaces of sociability such landscapes allow for the *staging* of all kinds of activities, many of which find

9 The shirt is an advertisement for an LA rock band that preaches anarchy by cutting records for the Sony-owned Associated label. As Harvey (1989) noted (see chapter 3), oppositional culture, these days, is fully imbricated in systems of commodification.

expression in a way that has nothing to do with the dictates of the commodity or of consumption.

Or do they? Landscapes are *always* a site of struggle, a place for resistance, and a concretization of contest. That is true. But it is also true, as we have already seen, that the whole reason for making a place *into a landscape*, that is, for attempting to emplace the landscape ideal, is precisely to staunch that struggle and to make social relations appear fully natural and timeless. Indeed, we can almost say that to the degree a landscape is contested, it stops being a landscape and becomes something else – a contested space.

To understand this point, it is useful to examine in a bit more detail two contested *ideals* – two ideologies, in fact – that I think are mutually opposed to each other. These ideals, of course, are never fully achieved in practice – the fact that they are continually contested by those holding different ideas assures that. The important issue is thus how the ideals help direct social action and the social production of public space. The first ideal is "landscape" itself, and the important point to think about here is the *privatized* nature of landscape that has marked the ideal right from the beginning (as we have seen). The second is "public space," an ideal just as complex and contradictory as landscape. But here the thing to keep in mind is that the *ideal* of public space is inclusiveness and unmediated interaction (figure 5.6). The landscape (in this sense) is commodified through and through – that is part of its *ideal* structure. Public space rejects commodification – that too is part of its *ideal* structure. Landscape is where one recreates – it is literally a *resort* – and where one basks in the leisure of a well-ordered scene. Public space is a space of conflict, of political tussle, of social relations stripped to their barest essentials. A place cannot be both a public space and a landscape, at least not at the same time (even if landscapes are always

Figure 5.6 A political public space: Argyll Street, Glasgow. A main shopping street in Glasgow, Argyll Street is an important site for petitioning, leafleting, and soap-box speeches. Photograph by D. Mitchell.

sights of and for politics, and public spaces are often sights of and for pleasurable recreation).[10]

As Goss (1996) admits, malls and festival marketplaces rarely live up to their billing as public spaces, creating instead a highly controlled environment which functions, as Darrell Crilley (1993: 153) has put it, like a "theater in which a pacified public basks in the grandeur of a carefully orchestrated corporate spectacle." In such landscapes, the intrusion of undesirables – the homeless, the unemployed, or the otherwise threatening – seems to imperil the carefully constructed suspension of disbelief on the part of the "audience" that all theatrical performances (and hence all landscapes) demand.[11] Or perhaps it is a double suspension of disbelief that is at work:

> The power of a landscape does not derive from the fact that it offers itself as a spectacle, but rather from the fact that, as mirror and mirage, it presents any susceptible viewer with an image at once true and false of a creative capacity which the subject (or Ego) is able, during a moment of marvelous self-deception, to claim as his own. A landscape also has the seductive power of all *pictures*, and this is especially true of an urban landscape – Venice, for example – that can impose itself immediately as a *work*. Whence the archetypal touristic delusion of being a participant in such a work, and of understanding it completely, even though the tourist merely passes through a country or countryside and absorbs its image in a quite passive way. The work in its concrete reality, its products, and the productive activity involved are all thus obscured and indeed consigned to oblivion.   (Lefebvre 1991: 189)

Creating a city – or a part of the city, such as a mall or festival marketplace – *as* landscape is therefore important because it restores to the viewer (the tourist, the suburban visitor, or even the city resident) an essential sense of control within a built environment which is instead "controlled," as Johnstown shows so clearly, through the creative, seemingly anarchic destruction of an economy over which they may in fact have very little control. Or more precisely, it provides an illusion of control in a space so highly designed, so carefully composed, so exquisitely "set" by the owners and developers of that space that a visitor's control can only ever be an illusion.

Put another way, the built environment "must be seen as simultaneously dependent and conditioning, outcome and mechanism of the dynamics of investment, production and consumption" (Knox 1993a: 3). Yet, at this moment in time, such dynamics of investment, production and consumption must be seen in the context of a "socio-cultural environment in which the emphasis is not on ownership and consumption *per se* but on the possession of particular *combinations* of things and the *style* of consumption" (1993a: 18). That is, the landscape must (and does) function as a vast system of *signs*, signs that "advertise" meanings to their consumers – and to those watching them. The recreation of the city *as* landscape works to order all the multitudinous spaces produced through myriad investment, production, and

10   There has been an explosion of geographical research on public space since the mid-1990s. The ideal of public space is explored in Mitchell (1995a). Two recent collections give a good sense of geographical scholarship: "Public Space and The City," *Urban Geography* 17 (1996), nos. 1 and 2; and Light and Smith (1998). Feminist geographical work on public space has been particularly insightful; see Staeheli (1994, 1996); Domosh (1998).
11   This section is adapted from Mitchell (1997).

consumption decisions into an understandable whole. "Although urban space is produced and sold in discrete parcels," as Paul Knox (1993a: 28) puts it, "it is *marketed* in large packages" (see also Mair 1986). Public spaces are transformed into "mere" signs, symbols of something else, rather than valued in their own right.

A second distinction that sets landscape apart from and against public space is that landscapes, in all their seductiveness, imply another illusion: that which Richard Sennett (1994) identifies as a lack of resistance to our own "lived relations," and to our own will. In fact, more and more, our own will, as well as our own sense of well-being and comfort, seems to depend on a certain "freedom from resistance." As Sennett (1994: 310) explains, "the ability to move anywhere, to move without obstruction, to circulate freely, a freedom greatest in an empty volume" has come to be defined *as* freedom itself in "Western civilization."

> The mechanics of movement has invaded a wide swath of modern experience – experience which treats social, environmental, or personal resistance, with its concomitant frustrations, as somehow unfair and unjust. Ease, comfort, "user-friendliness" in human relations come to appear as guarantees of individual freedom of action.

This ideology of comfort and individual movement as freedom reinforces an "impression of transparency" that works to make the urban landscape knowable by erasing its "products and productive activity." "[R]esistance is a fundamental and necessary experience for the human body," Sennett (1994: 310) concludes: "through feeling resistance, the body is roused to take note of the world in which it lives. This is the secular version of the lesson of exile from the Garden. The body comes to life when coping with difficulty." The irony, of course is that in the hyper-planned urban public spaces of the postmodern city, as in the spaces of the mall, the "impression of transparency" and the ability to move without resistance is made possible only by planning for the careful overall *orchestration* of individuals' movement. Freedom from resistance in built space seems only possible if control over movement is ceded to the planners of malls and public spaces. People become comfortable by giving up their active political *involvement* in space and acquiescing instead in becoming *spectators* of the urban "scene."

This is not a completely new development, however. Sennett (1994: 347) argues that a "public realm filled with moving and spectating individuals [that] no longer represented a political domain" can be traced at least to the city of the nineteenth-century *flâneur* (a sort of traveling spectator – usually male – always viewing and observing, but rarely actively participating in and shaping the urban scene), and probably a lot earlier. It is the curious condition of the modern city, a condition only heightened in the postmodern city, that "one was and is surrounded by life, even if detached from it." And in places like contemporary Greenwich Village (where Sennett lives), "ours is a purely visible agora" (that is, a landscape) where "political occasions do not translate into everyday practice on the streets; they do little, moreover, to compound the multiple cultures of the city into common purposes" (1994: 358). In this regard, the landscape-as-leisure returns with a vengeance, creating a sort of citizenship, according to Sennett, that is *predicated* on the externalization of those deemed "undesirable." Whether this is accomplished through design or through law – both of which are as important to the landscape of the mall and festival marketplace as they are to the city street – is less important than the fact that such exclusions are seen as a wholly desirable aspect of citizenship (see chapter 10). Through landscape, politics is fully aestheticized.[12]

The Circulation of Meaning: Landscape as a System of Social Reproduction

We've come a long way, in this chapter and the previous one, in our discussion of landscape, but we have also come full circle: from the aesthetics and aestheticized politics of landscape painting to the aesthetics and aestheticized politics of the city made over *as* landscape. Both forms of aestheticization – of the built form of landscape and of its representation – were clearly important to the decline and redevelopment of Johnstown. By emphasizing the aesthetics of disaster and industry, Johnstown sought to rejuvenate itself. Inevitably whenever politics – in this case the politics of social control, of racism, and of labor unrest – is aestheticized and made into something to be gawked at, something of that politics is lost: which is exactly the point of making a place into a landscape.

And that points us to the final issue that needs to be explored in our analysis of landscape, an issue that raises again the question of just how it is that landscape functions in society. That is, we need to return for a brief moment to two important and related questions with which we began our discussions of landscape and look at them again now that we have explored many of the varied aspects of the idea and materiality of "landscape." These questions were: What is landscape? And what does landscape do? We can now give more complete (and slightly differently inflected) answers to these questions.

Landscape and the reproduction of labor and capital

As we have seen, landscape is complex and multifaceted, both a site to be struggled over and an ideology that seeks to govern our lived relations. In this sense we can see the landscape as a "vortex" within which swirl all manner of contests – between classes, over gender structures, around issues of race and ethnicity, over meaning and representation, and over built form and social use. The landscape serves all at once as mediator, integrator, and actor in these struggles. "As a produced object, landscape is like a commodity in which evident, temporarily stable, form masks the facts of its production, and its status as social relation. As both form and symbol, landscape is expected by those who attempt to define its meanings to speak unambiguously for itself" (Mitchell 1996a: 30). In this sense, the *form* of the landscape actively incorporates the struggles over it. "Landscape is thus a fragmentation of space *and* a totalization of it. People make sense of their fractured world by seeing it as a whole, by seeking to impose meanings and connections" (1996a: 31). We all *do* read the landscape, but we are not all equal in the process of "authoring" it – nor in

---

12   The best analysis of the aestheticization of politics in the realm of cultural production is still Benjamin (1968 [1936]).

controlling its meanings. Landscape representations serve precisely to create (or attempt to create) a total and naturalized environment. If the landscape is a text, then it is a very powerful one indeed. And if it is a theater or stage, then it is one in which the director is power itself.[13]

If that is what landscape *is*, then the question arises again as to what it *does*. To answer that question, it is important to remember that despite all the fragmentation, the diversity, the continual ebb, flow, and transformation of social life, we live in a world that *is* a "social totality": there are aspects of social life – political, economic, and cultural aspects – that are global and universal (or at least have pretensions to be so).[14] One of those overarching processes, contested as it undeniably always is, is the drive to accumulate capital – a drive that, as Marx rightly showed long ago, is no respecter of pre-existing social, political, economic, or cultural boundaries, or of pre-existing "ways of life." Yet the accumulation of capital can *only* occur to the degree that it *uses* those pre-existing ways of life and turns them to its own advantage. As Marx (1987: 537) put it, in a statement both admirably simple and exceptionally profound in its implications (implications that Marx himself never fully grasped): the "maintenance and reproduction of the working class is, and ever must be, a necessary condition to the reproduction of capital." On the one hand, Marx (1987: 537) argued that the reproduction of the working class – of labor-power – could be left "safely ... to the labourer's instinct for self-preservation." On the other hand, he understood (1987: 168) that such a statement was too simple. The reproduction of the working class, he argued, everywhere and always possesses an "historical and moral element," which may appear as a set of "natural" or "necessary wants," but, because it is "historical and moral," is clearly socially constructed. The historical and "moral" development of the working classes in any place – in short, its "culture" – is itself a continual site of struggle. To what degree do workers (whether called working or middle class does not matter) "need," for example, detached houses and cars; to what extent do they "need" wages sufficient for them to become constant consumers? By contrast, when is it "historically" or "morally" "natural" for workers to live in shacks and to subsist on wages of under a dollar a day? And what is the relationship between the places in which these two worlds exist?

Sharon Zukin (1991: 16) argues that landscape "connotes the entire panorama of what we see: both the landscape of the powerful – cathedrals, factories, and skyscrapers – and the subordinate, resistant or expressive vernacular of the powerless – village chapel, shantytowns, and tenements." But note that in this description, Zukin holds the two landscapes spatially separate, seeing the "high culture" of production and symbolic development as disconnected from the powerless integrity of the vernacular. In reality, each sort of landscape *depends* on the other: our ability to consume is predicated on "their" low wages and the miserable conditions that exist elsewhere. Or to use one of Zukin's own examples, the development of a landscape of skyscrapers is a product of social struggle both within and outside them: struggles over the conditions of labor and labor reproduction (who will construct, clean, and staff the

---

13 As we will see below, it is deceptive to speak of "power" in general and universal terms. Power works in and through particular historically- and geographically-specific social formations.
14 The best analyses of the world as a social totality remain Lukács (1971), and Debord (1994). This section draws on Mitchell (1994 and 1996a: chapter 1).

buildings? where will these workers live? how will they eat and with whom will they socialize?); struggles over land use (where will urban renewal, and where will gentrification occur? how strong are neighborhood organizations both where the skyscrapers are built and elsewhere in the city? what will the social costs of commuting be – and who will bear them?), and issues of race, gender, and citizenship (who will be allowed in the "public" space of the corporate plazas? how will the value of the buildings be maintained in the face of the changing demographic nature of the city?). Each of these struggles has its obverse in struggles over the nature of the places in which the skyscraper workers will live (city or suburb? small town exurb or downtown tenement?), and in the far-flung places that will provide them their sustenance (the bananas for their cereal, the shoes on their feet, the building materials for their own houses). Indeed, the answer to this second set of struggles will also be answers to the first set – and the chain of connection between and across landscapes is nearly infinite. The production of any landscape requires the constant reproduction of other landscapes in other places. The reproduction of labor-power in one place is impossible without its (always socially different) reproduction in other places.

But within this social totality, there exist important contradictions. At each place in the chain – in the building, maintenance, and staffing of the skyscraper, in the factory making Nikes or the plantation growing bananas, in the shantytowns on the banks of the Rio Grande and Harlem rivers, in the suburban tract homes of Piscataway, New Jersey, or the council houses of Paisley, Scotland – the reproduction of the inequality that makes the whole totality possible is always subject to revolt. If productive landscapes are to be maintained under capitalism (or for that matter, any other political-economic system), then possibilities for revolt must be minimized. This provides marginalized social actors with an important degree of power – indeed an essential degree because their status as a threat must always be neutralized. As a social and obfuscatory mediation, as both an input to and outcome of all these social struggles, landscapes are built as an attempt to insure this neutralization. Like culture, then, the landscape acts as a site of social integration, and therefore of social hegemony. The landscape emerges as a social compromise between threat and domination, between the imposition of social power and the subversion of social order. In turn, the very *form* of landscape results from these interactions and contested impositions. The landscape itself, as a unitary, "solid" form, is therefore a contradiction, held in uneasy truce (unless actively contested at some moment in time). Ongoing and everyday social struggle – along with all the mundane aspects of everyday life itself, like shopping, playing, and working – forms and reforms the landscape. Landscape reifies (at least momentarily) the "natural" social order. And landscape, therefore, becomes the "stage" for the social reproduction of not only labor-power, but society itself.

Yet the reproduction of labor-power remains important. By defining the reified "natural" relations of place, landscape materially affects the equation of surplus value extraction within a region (that is, it greatly affects the conditions under which firms will or will not be profitable). To the degree that social unrest, various social demands, or movements for self-determination or autonomy within a region can be stilled by pressing in on people the "naturalness" of existing social relations, surplus value can be expanded; reproduction is not threatened. If it can be successfully asserted that workers in Johnstown have no choice but to accept declining wages (because the old mills and new pollution requirements drive up costs; or because cheap foreign steel is flooding the market), to the degree that they can be convinced that making their mortgage is their own individual problem despite their employer shutting them out of a job, then to that degree, either in Johnstown itself or more "globally," capital can continue to function. The production of a landscape, by objectifying, rationalizing, and naturalizing what is really social, can have the effect of stopping resistance in its tracks. As *social* values are naturalized in place, they are historically made concrete. If, as David Harvey has argued, the landscapes of capitalism are often a barrier to further accumulation (as with Johnstown) and have to be creatively destroyed (wiping out heavy industry and sanitizing space to make it attractive to tourists, for example), it is also the case that a landscape can become a great facilitator to capital (since it determines the "nature" of labor).

Landscape as a form of regulation

Another way to think about this issue is to understand a landscape (and its constituent components) as part of a system of social regulation. Geographers such as James Duncan and Nancy Duncan (1988) have argued that landscapes should be understood not only as texts, but also as part of "discursive formations." A discourse can be defined a systematic set of statements (written or verbal), or, more generally, of signs (the implicit and explicit messages in any type of text). A "discursive formation" is the regularized, organized, routinized system of signs that exists in any particular time or place (cf. Foucault 1972). Discursive formations are obviously variable, and that is what makes them interesting. A discursive formation is therefore analogous to what could be called a "landscape formation." The important point is that "discursive and landscape formations relate not just to other discourses" – they are not only "intertextual" – "nor to power in general, but to the regulative powers of definite, geo-historical, political and economic social relations" (Peet 1996: 22). Landscapes, Peet (1996, 22) argues, as kinds of discursive formation, are, for particular historical and geographical situations "projector[s] of regulatory power" because they effectively limit the range of possible expression and representation within a discursive formation. As solid, socially powerful signs, they perform the vital function of "social regulation in the interests of class, gender, ethnic, and regional power systems."

The notion of social regulation draws on a body of ideas known as "regulation theory." Developed by French political economists in the 1970s and 1980s, regulation theory argues that rather than market equilibrium, the driving force behind the relative stability of capitalism as a social system is the "mode of regulation." The mode of regulation of any place and time is the constellation of state and civil institutions, coupled with norms and habits that encourage people to act in the general interest of economic stability. Accepting the discipline of wage cuts or interest rate hikes, coupled with religious teachings about frugality and school lessons in self-sacrifice, for example, might encourage workers to save and thereby make pools of capital available for investment in regional industries or services. Conversely, the rise of easy consumer credit, coupled with concerted advertising (and government pronouncement) that equates consumption with the good life, might (as in the 1990s) help smooth over a growing crisis of over-accumulation.[15] In either case, a particular mode of regulation (arrived at through experimentation and social struggle) defines what is known as a particular "regime of accumulation," which is a relatively stable, relatively long-term, system of capital accumulation. Any regime of accumulation is full of contradictions and will eventually become unworkable (as during the world-wide Depression of the 1930s, the Latin American debt crisis of the 1970s and 1980s, or the unfolding Asian economic crisis at the end of the 1990s). When a regime of accumulation collapses, so too does its associated mode of regulation collapse. Instability follows, and new modes of regulation governing new regimes of accumulation must be developed (as with the adoption of Keynesian macroeconomic policies in the wake of the Depression, and the imposition of "structural adjustment" in the wake of the Latin American debt crisis) (Aglietta 1976; Boyer 1990; Lipietz 1986).

Landscape is implicated in this process of regulatory change in two ways. In the first place, as Alan Scott (1988) has argued, a given regime of accumulation, coupled with the usually multiple modes of regulation with which it is associated, tend to bias development in favor of certain industries and against others (as with Johnstown and the decline of heavy manufacturing like steel-making and the rise of services like tourism and insurance-form processing) (see also Storper and Walker 1989). Similarly, the built environment often acts as a refuge for capital in times of crisis (especially crises of over-accumulation) when investment in production makes little sense. The physical landscape is thus often *built* as part of the development of, and eventual solution for, crises in the regime of accumulation (as when new mortgage systems were created in the USA during the Depression to jump-start suburban housing construction) (Harvey 1982). Second, as we have seen, landscapes themselves are a constituent part of the system of norms, habits, and institutions that regulate social life at any given moment. Indeed, landscapes are particularly important ingredients in social regulation because they are places where discourse and material practice meet – where acts of representation (about what constitutes the "good life," for example) and the material acts of living (working, consuming, relaxing) inevitably intersect. This means that landscapes should be understood as "the spatial surfaces of regulatory regimes, intended to frame social imaginaries often in definite, system supportive ways, articulated via discursive means among others, but conjoined expressly with regional and national [and now global] systems of power" (Peet 1996: 37). But such a framing of social imaginaries is always tentative and experimental. No social actor – and certainly no *collective* social actor – can know in advance just the proper mix of discipline and enjoyment, "freedom from resistance," and unpredictable social mixing that will be successful in the job of regulation. And even if they could, there is never any guarantee that they could implement their plans for spatial social regulation flawlessly and without dissent. All they can do is try to create the landscape after the image they find most desirable (Mitchell 1997).

To the degree that a landscape is both a built environment ("the homes of women and men," as Peet put it in the opening paragraphs of this chapter) *and* a system of

---

15   During the recession of the early 1990s, President George Bush took to media-covered shopping trips in hopes of convincing Americans to spend their way out of economic malaise. It has worked so well that in 1997 1.3 million Americans filed for personal bankruptcy protection (despite low inflation and low unemployment). Total consumer debt in the USA exceeded $1.2 trillion in 1997.

representation – a system of signs – it is one of the most important sites for struggle over social regulation. In these struggles, Peet concludes (1996: 23), power is maintained through the successful:

> manipulation of the image-making capacity of the socialized subject at that cognitive level where thoughts are colored by mental pictures of reality. This kind of "visualization" is most fully effected when nature and region are employed *as* signs, when the landscapes people trust are invested *with* signs, when social and political markers are taken *for* nature or history in some pure, unadulterated sense.

Landscape is part of a system of social regulation and reproduction because it is *always* an inseparable admixture of material form and discursive sign. The very value of a landscape – in structuring ways of life, in providing a place to live – is precisely this mixture of textuality and materiality.

Conclusion

So, finally, it comes down to this: perhaps "landscape" in all its fascinating complexity is best seen as a force in, and place for, the social reproduction of society. Like "culture," landscape seeks to regularize or naturalize relations between people. Like "culture," then, landscape has a political economy. And while this is not everything, it is vitally important both to how landscapes are produced and to how they function in society. As a site of social reproduction, the landscape is too vital to be left only to the study of the metaphors that guide our understanding of it (as important as those are). Rather, the key point is to see, and attempt to explain (to ourselves and to others) just how it functions – to understand its role in the culture wars that mark our lives, which, while irreducible to questions of political economy, are nonetheless inseparable from such questions. If landscape is a stage then it is a stage for many things: the politics of economic development and the politics of culture to name just two. And if landscape is a text, then it is so *because* of its very materiality – its existence as trees, shrubs, bricks, mortar, paint, canvas, and the pages of a book – not despite that materiality. But for that point to make more sense, it is important at this point to turn away from the explicit consideration of the landscape and to explore more deeply the cultural politics that takes place in and on the landscape, that *depends* on the landscape – and upon which the landscape itself unavoidably depends too for its very shape, meaning, and social function. So it is to that topic – the geography of cultural politics – that we turn in the next section of this book.

Part III

Cultural Politics

6

Cultural Politics: The Dialectics of Spectacle

The preceding two chapters focused on the sorts of political – and political-economic – struggles that make landscapes and give them their meanings. The goal was to show how particular struggles get worked out in and over the landscape, and how, in turn, representations of landscape travel through complex circuits of meaning and value. In other words, the goal was to explicate some of the processes by which "culture" – as ideas and ideologies that work to define our lives – is constructed and made a material feature of our everyday experiences. This chapter continues the theme by looking explicitly at the nature of cultural politics, but it does so by (at times) abstracting out of the built landscape to explore how representations "themselves" take on a circulatory life of their own – a life that is every bit as contested as the life of the landscape. As we will see, once again, various "culture industries" have a lot to say about the nature and meaning of these representations.[1] But they do not do so entirely under conditions of their own choosing (to turn an aphorism of Marx's on its head); instead, they work diligently to organize audiences and to control the multifarious everyday and sometimes quite spectacular acts in which people engage to create and make stick their own meanings, their own ideologies. That is, cultural construction is not simply a top-down process; rather it is organized out of the seemingly infinite variety of "resistances" in which people engage so as to maintain some semblance of control

---

1 See the discussion of Adorno and Horkheimer in chapter 3.

over the conditions of their own lives.[2] Of course, those resistancies are themselves often a product of the very culture industries they mean to undermine (as we will see later in the chapter). Understanding this contradiction is essential to understanding the nature of cultural politics. However they are resolved in practice, forms of resistance are seemingly infinite, and they are the very stuff of contemporary culture wars.

Resistance: Limits and Opportunities

What is resistance? And who engages in it? The temptation for scholars is always to define resistance as those subversive acts engaged in by their own "good guys." Acts of resistance attempt to redefine or break down the structures of power that govern resister's lives, to create a new world out of the shell of the old (as the early twentieth-century radical labor union, the Industrial Workers of the World used to say). Yet are not members of the Montana Militia in the United States, activists in Jean-Marie Le Pen's National Front party in France, racist skinheads in England, anti-immigration thugs in Rostock, Germany, or even adherents of the Japanese cult Ohm Shin Rikyo engaged in "resistance"? Certainly, apologists for English football "hooligans" during the 1998 football World Cup tried to argue that those rioting in the streets of various provincial French cities were engaging in a form of resistance – to the corrupt ticketing procedures, the hyper-commercialization of FIFA, the bumping of "true" football fans to make way in the stands for yuppies with the money to buy their way in, and so on. Are not all these acts attempted subversions of what their practitioners perceive to be systems of domination? Are they not engaged in contesting hegemony? Of course they are. Whether resistance is "good" or not depends on one's political perspective.

On a different level, numerous studies of everyday life have redefined "resistance" as *any* act that occurs in a way not fully intended by the "powers that be." When viewers reinterpret the television shows they are watching, they "resist" the dominant meanings encoded in the programs. When they shop in a manner that creates a new or transformed style, they actively resist the gender, sexuality, and class roles to which they are presumably assigned, and thereby shake up the established order. For example, Greil Marcus (1989) has explored the ways in which the late 1970s Punk movement continued a tradition of *avant-garde* resistance to mass or dominant culture that begins with the 1870 Communards of Paris (see chapter 4) and continues through Dadaist art in the 1920s (and, in the USA, aspects of the Bohemian movement), the critiques of the Frankfurt School in the 1940s (from whence we have already examined the ideas of Horkheimer and Adorno), and the Parisian Situationist International of the 1950s and 1960s (see below). As Andrew Kirby (1993: 70) summarizes, all these movements, from the Communards to the punks, "are connected via a condemnation of mass culture and a critical need to offer a radical

---

2   Resistance is used here in a slightly different sense from that used by Richard Sennett in the passages we examined in chapter 5. Sennett was interested in how people try to move through space with as little resistance – as little impediment – as possible. The term here indicates individual or organized opposition to some set of processes or relationships.

alternative." But does "resistance" to mass culture necessarily imply its condemnation? Recent studies of how people read romances, listen to music, or watch television (all forms of mass culture) show that individuals actively engage with and redefine these media as materials for the construction of everyday life – often in ways contrary to what would be expected if mass culture was simply an instrument of control that only needed condemnation. Mass culture is something to be grasped and transformed, not something to be fought straight-on. In this sense "resistance" takes on a new aspect.

Popular culture as resistance

To take just one example, Rey Chow (1993), exploring the role of rock music in East Asia (and particularly in mainland China), argues that *listening* acts as resistance in two primary ways. First, rock – especially Chinese rock – incorporates important "disjunctures" between lyrics and music. Examining a quite popular but officially frowned-upon song by Cui Jian which seemingly celebrates the historic communist Long March to Yanan, Chow (1993: 388) suggests that there is "a difference between the 'decadence' of the music and the 'seriousness' of the subject matter to which the music alludes. Without knowing the 'language,' we can dance to Cui Jian's song as we would to any rock-and-roll tune; once we pay attention to the words, we are in the solemn presence of history, with its insistence on emotional meaning and depth." Even when the lyrics are about officially sanctioned topics – or even just when they seem banal – the music can turn subversive the moment listeners *stop* listening. The collective act of dancing, of being together, and *ignoring* the message, can become threatening to established powers, perhaps because it is so hard to pin down, liable to erupt in a seeming orgy of irrationality at any moment (for what could be more irrational than *not* paying attention)? In this regard, the censorious campaigns by self-appointed protectors of morality (like US Vice-president Albert Gore's wife Tipper and her 1980s campaign to "clean up" rock lyrics) always meet their match in the blank stares of those who actually listen to the *music* more often than they read the lyric sheets included with their compact disks.[3]

Second, the miniaturization and individualization of listening has a subversive element of resistance built right into it. Chow (1993: 396) suggests that "traditionally, listening is, as a rule, public. For a piece of music to be heard – even under the most private of circumstances – a certain public accessibility has always been assumed" if for no other reason than that music has a volume that necessarily transcends the individual. The invention of headphones, and especially the Walkman, however, have drastically changed that, and this new technology has created a new form of subversion.

3   In the 1980s, Tipper Gore (the wife of soon-to-be Vice-president Al Gore) co-founded the Parents' Music Resource Center, a group dedicated to eradicating "obscene," "satanic," or otherwise objectionable lyrics from contemporary rock music. While total elimination was not possible, the PMRC was successful in convincing the Recording Industry Association of America to establish a rating system for albums similar to that used for movies, which would make many albums "off-limits" to adolescents and children.

But the most important feature of music's miniaturization does not lie in the smallness of the equipment which generates it. Rather, it lies in the *revolution in listening* engendered by the equipment: while the music is hidden from others because it is compacted, this hiddenness is precisely what allows me to hear it full blast. The "miniaturizing" that does not produce a visible body – however small – that corresponds with "reality" leads to a certain freedom. This is the freedom to be deaf to the loudspeakers of history. We do not return to individualized or privatized emotions when we use the Walkman: rather the Walkman's artificiality makes us aware of the impending presence of the collective, which summons us with the infallibility of a sleepwalker. What the Walkman provides is the possibility of a barrier, a blockage between "me" and the world, so that, as in moments of undisturbed sleep, I can disappear as a listener playing music. The Walkman allows me, in other words, to be missing – to be a missing part of history, to which I say: "I am not there, not where you collect me."

(Chow 1993: 398)

In a society like China where such emphasis is placed on the collective, but no less perhaps in Western society that so demands a disciplined individual, the Walkman provides a freedom from the conformist noise of the street: from the beseeching aural advertisements for commodities and political ideologies. Where once loudspeakers were the instrument of collective organization (as in the fascist rallies of the 1930s (figure 6.1) or in the numbing banality of contemporary action movies), the "autism of the Walkman listeners" allows them to opt out. This "irritates onlookers precisely because the onlookers find themselves reduced to the activity of looking alone. For once voyeurism yields no secrets: one can look all one wants and still nothing can be seen" (Chow 1993: 398). To the degree that Chow is correct, this miniaturization of the aural environment – with its effects on the visible economy within which people move in public – should act back on not just the "loudspeakers of history" but also

Figure 6.1 Adolf Hitler addresses a massive Nazi rally in Nuremberg, Germany (September 1933). Loudspeakers made "collective" history possible, gathering masses together in a single place to experience the same rhetoric. By contrast, the Walkman makes possible a certain collective individualism where it is never clear what message is being heard. Photograph by the Associated Press; used by permission.

the panoptical surveillance of the contemporary city.[4] If the Walkman provides a (perhaps partial) cover of invisibility – while its wearer remains fully visible – then to some degree it might just subvert (or resist) the technologies through which contemporary power is exercised: the video surveillance camera, the plainclothes police, the electronic traces on everything from credit cards to phone calls.

Note, however, that these two forms of resistance through listening (or inadequately listening) rely on a certain geography. Both demand a *public* space in which resistance can be exercised. The collective experience of ignoring official lyrics requires a place to dance, to rub up against each other in full view of others, to *create* a collective force. And the subversiveness of wearing a Walkman requires a crowd, or a crowded public space, engaged in sanctioned activities which the wearer mimics while really being engaged otherwise. For such resistancies to "work" they must occur in public spaces. Resistance really can't be private. What would be the point?[5]

This points to a significant limitation to this model of cultural resistance. Leaving aside for the moment that the sorts of resistance Chow describes require a significant accommodation to unjust structures of power (after all one must *buy* a Walkman, CDs, and concert tickets, thereby reinforcing a particular commodification of "culture" and a particular, systematic exploitation of labor), the resistance embodied in incomplete or miniaturized listening takes fragmentation and individualization as a *goal* to be achieved, rather than a problem to be overcome. It elevates small-scale tactics to the status of the only realistic mode of resistance, even though the objects of attack are anything but small-scale themselves.

Tactics and strategies

Nowhere is this limitation clearer than in a book that has become something of an icon among geographical and cultural theorists of resistance, transgression, and subversion, Michel de Certeau's *The Practice of Everyday Life* (1984).[6] There, in an oft-cited, and frequently anthologized chapter called "Walking in the City," de Certeau avers that the everyday practices of city residents who "live 'down below,' below the thresholds at which visibility begins," should be understood to be "practices that are foreign to the 'geometrical' or 'geographical' space of the visual, panoptic, or theoretical constructions" of urban planners, cartographers, policing agencies, and so forth (p. 93). Walking "is a process of *appropriation* of the

---

4   More and more downtowns are coming to resemble the controlled, constantly watched space of the mall, where surveillance cameras (and even microphones), designed to keep tabs on the activities of pedestrians, shoppers, loiterers, the homeless, etc., are ubiquitous. See Davis (1990); Fyfe and Bannister (1996, 1998).

5   There is yet another dynamic at work when we examine the role of music in public politics. Musicians, whether performing live, playing on the radio or television, or heard at the disco, create a *public* around them – people *identify* with them – and they create a "space" in which that public can form. Gill Valentine (1996) traces this dynamic in the lesbian public that has formed around the music of k.d. lang. As Valentine relates, however, the space for lesbianism that a lang concert provides is a quite contradictory one (see also chapter 7).

6   Page numbers in this section refer to this book.

topographical system on the part of the pedestrian . . . ; it is the spatial acting-out of the place . . . ; and it implies *relations* among differentiated positions . . . " (p. 98).[7] The crucial point for de Certeau (p. 101) is that the "long poem of walking manipulates spatial organizations, no matter how panoptic they may be. . . . It creates shadows and ambiguities within them." In essence, then, aspects of everyday life, like walking (or for that matter driving) are fundamentally acts of resistance – resistance to the domineering and dominating institutions that seek to order our lives.

De Certeau's (pp. 35–6) analysis rides on the distinction between small-scale, diverse, and often experimental and partial *tactics*, and universalizing, powerful, and controlling *strategies*. A strategy is:

> the calculation (or manipulation) of power relationships that becomes possible as soon as a subject with a will and power (a business, an army, a city, a scientific institution) can be isolated. It postulates a *place* that can be delimited as its *own* and serves as the base from which relations with an *exteriority* composed of targets or threats (customers or competitors, enemies, the country surrounding the city, objectives and objects of research, etc.) can be managed. . . . It is . . . the typical attitude of modern science, politics, and military strategy.

By contrast, a tactic is:

> a calculated action determined by the absence of a proper locus. No delimitation of an exteriority, then, provides it with the conditions necessary for autonomy. The space of the tactic is the space of the other. Thus it must play on and with a terrain imposed on it and organized by the law of a foreign power. . . . [I]t is a maneuver "within the enemy's field of vision," as Von Bülow put it, and within enemy territory. It does not, therefore, have the option of planning general strategy and viewing the adversary as a whole within a distinct, visible, and objectifiable space. It operates in isolated actions, blow by blow. . . . In short, a tactic is an art of the weak.   (p. 37)

As a tactic, walking takes advantage of the holes and interstices in a geographical field organized as a grid of power (overseen, for example, by the police: see Herbert 1996). Walking creates a set of stories that are subversive to the official stories of the city, undermining them, by living and transforming them (de Certeau 1984: 105–10). As a tactic, it exists "below radar," below and out of sight of the strategic vision of the state, or corporations, or the military (or whoever else it may be that controls the city).

Walking is, quite literally, incomprehensible, and it is in that incomprehensibility, according to de Certeau, that its subversiveness exists. Each footstep is a tactic that undermines the power of those who seek to control the spaces of the city:

> It is true that the operations of walking . . . can be traced on city maps in such a way as to transcribe their paths (here well-trodden, there very faint) and their trajectories (going this way and not that). But these thick or thin curves refer, like words, to the absence of what has passed by. Surveys of routes miss what was: the act of passing by. The

7 The ellipses mark points where de Certeau develops an analogy between walking and "speech acts."

operation of walking, wandering, or "window shopping," that is, the activity of passers-by, is transformed into points that draw a totalizing and reversible line on the map. They allow us to grasp only a relict set in the nowhen of a surface projection. Itself visible, it has the effect of making invisible the operation that made it possible. . . . The trace left behind is substituted for the practice. It exhibits the (voracious) property that the geographical system has of being able to transform action into legibility, but in doing so it causes a way of being in the world to be forgotten.   (p. 97)

Is this not exactly the point Rey Chow was making regarding the use of a Walkman? While listeners could be seen, their actions could never *really* be mapped. Only the traces of their movements can be seen, never can the *meaning* – especially the tactical meaning – be assessed.

Yet there is something missing in this account. De Certeau (p. 97) is interested in the myriad *individual* movements: "Their story begins on ground level, with footsteps. They are myriad, but do not compose a series." Paths cross and cross again, as atomized individuals move about the city, each in his or her *own* way tactically subverting the all-powerful geography that is meant to be imposed upon them. Strategies are undermined not through collec*tive* behavior, but through a chaotic collec*tion* of individual movements. But for a resistant movement to be effective it must surely be *social* rather than individual; and certainly social movements must engage in *strategic* resistance. To do otherwise would be simply to cede all power to those the movement opposes. If "power is bound by its visibility," as de Certeau (p. 37) hopes, it is also *made possible* by its visibility. And this is no less true of oppositional – resistant – power than of state or corporate power. Effective resistance demands something more than just individual tactics. As de Certeau himself admits, individual tactics *amount* to nothing.

Tiananmen, resistance, and popular culture in China

This can be made clear by returning again to China, not this time to the realm of pop music and music technology (though these are surely important), but instead right to the heart of the strategic city, Tiananmen Square. Cultural critic Jianying Zha (1995: 3) has written that the events at Tiananmen in 1989 have now been relegated to the status of cliché, particularly in the West. "Since 1989, Tiananmen has dominated our fantasy about China like a massive, dark, bloody cloud. . . . The images of tanks, blood, and the small statue of Liberty crumbling to dust still haunt us. In the minds of the Western public, China's face is forever tarnished: once again the distant giant has lapsed into its repressive, backward pattern, which all the money and the cheap labor markets cannot quite redeem." This picture works to preclude all complexity, Zha argues; China is rendered one-dimensional. But in the wake of Tiananmen, as Zha shows, there has been an exceptional cultural transformation, creating a nation and a city quite at odds with this uni-dimensionality. Indeed, it is quite clear that China is wrapped in its own "culture wars" in the 1990s, wars that themselves are fueled by rapid economic change.[8] But to understand these wars, we need first to look at the

8 Indeed, as I write, the paper reports that "China launches cultural cleanup," including the suppression of works by the popular writer Wang Shou (whom Jianying writes about in *China Pop*), and greater state

nature of that clichéd battle of May and June, 1989. For it is there that we can most clearly see the essential spatiality of resistance.

Tiananmen has long been the symbolic heart of Beijing and of the Chinese state.[9] Following the 1911 revolution, Tiananmen was transformed "from a closed, controlled space that both embodied and symbolized authority and orthodoxy, to an open public space in which new and heterodox functions quickly took hold" (Hershkovitz 1993: 405). In these post-revolutionary years, Tiananmen served as a central site for public protests, beginning with the May Fourth incident of 1919 (to which 1989 protesters made frequent reference). On this day, thousands of students and citizens congregated at Tiananmen to protest the adoption of the Treaty of Versailles, which ceded German colonies in China to Japan. The rally was broken up by the police at the cost of 32 arrests and one student killed. This rally was "the first of dozens of antigovernment protest movements to occur in the capital throughout the 1920s, 1930s, and 1940s.... Almost invariably these demonstrations culminated in rallies outside Tiananmen, and police consistently responded by blocking access to the area, using increasingly violent means" (1993: 406). In other words, police were used to protect the symbolic state sanctity embodied in Tiananmen. But the real "horizon of meaning" (Lefebvre 1991) that constituted Tiananmen as a place – that is, its true symbolic power to the people of Beijing and China – lay precisely in the way the Square embodied the *dialectic* between state power and resistant social movement. The iconographic meaning of the state was always a point of political contest.

After the revolution of 1949, the Square was once again enlarged and rebuilt and appropriated to the needs of the new government. Monumental official memorials to the revolution were built around the perimeter (including the Great Hall of the People and the Museum of the Chinese Revolution). In the center of the Square a new Monument to the People's Heroes was constructed, and a giant portrait of Mao was placed over the central Tiananmen gates. Tiananmen was to be "the national symbol of the People's Republic of China," but it was to be so as an *official* and *monumental* space; not a space of protest, but a space of official celebration (Hershkovitz 1993: 406–7). Even so, as early as 1976 at the death of revolutionary leader Zhou Enlai, large masses of Beijing citizens descended on the Square and "read poems, chanted slogans, and displayed banners that were both expressions of mourning for Zhou and thinly veiled criticisms of Mao and the Cultural Revolution leadership." On the annual day of mourning for ancestors (April 4), perhaps two million people gathered at Tiananmen. Police invaded during the night, and over 100 protesters were killed (1993: 409). Further occupations of the Square occurred in 1978–9 and 1986–7. Each of these, as in the Spring 1989 protests, "almost inevitably involved (and were

control over the press. According to the article, "Alarmed that China's rapid economic development has been accompanied by a parallel moral decline, the party launched the first stages of its 'spiritual civilization' cleanup campaign earlier this year.... Without accepting any responsibility for current affairs, the Chinese document [outlining the campaign] is an effort by the party to address what opinion polls say is a key gripe of average citizens: the decay of society's moral fabric in China" (Tempest 1996). The corrosive effects of economic change – the key underlying cause of the West's culture wars – also, it seems, work just as strongly in China's "Third Way." We will return to this point below.

9   In a wonderful article, Linda Hershkovitz (1993) briefly outlines the history of the Square. I draw heavily on that article in what follows.

popularly understood to involve) literal struggles over the occupation and control of the Square and the area around it" (1993: 410).

This is the key point, for control over the square did two things. First, it signified symbolic control of the center of the state. Second, it made protest public; it made protest an obvious and clear public provocation to the state itself; it made resistance to the government *visible* (figure 6.2).[10] The state had no choice but to respond – to regain control – if it was to maintain its hold on power. As Craig Calhoun (1989: 66) reports, the Tiananmen protests were developed out of a longstanding sense among intellectuals, some party officials, " 'rank-and-file' participants in the protest," and much of the public (at least in urban areas) of "cultural crisis and impoverishment" attendant upon more than a century of critical engagement with "the internationalization of culture, wrought initially by capitalist expansion and Western imperialism," and carried through into everything from the adoption and transformation of European ideas about communism and a recent fascination with contemporary Western philosophers such as Jürgen Habermas or Jacques Derrida, to the importation of

Figure 6.2 Protests in Tiananmen Square (May 1989). Photograph courtesy of Mark Avery/ Associated Press.

10   On the importance of visibility to effective protest, see Mitchell (1995a).

television shows and Japanese personal electronics (such as the Walkman) (Calhoun 1989: 55). The 1989 Beijing Spring was in crucial ways an ossification of debates about the relationship between culture and economic change. While demands for greater democratic involvement were at the heart of the Tiananmen protests, "we should not forget the element of nationalism and the sense of cultural crisis that went along with it" (1989: 66–7). While this debate had been ongoing, conducted in class-rooms, homes, journals, on TV and in the halls of government, Tiananmen thrust it to center stage. A *new* form of Chinese nationalism was being demanded from the very heart and center of Chinese nationalism. "These ideas and this sense of crisis had been widely enough disseminated before the protest movement actually got going in April that they could be taken for granted among the core of student participants" (1989: 66). The crisis for the state, then, was not just one of "democracy," it was also one of control over cultural discourse. Retaking the Square took on double urgency. As Calhoun (1989: 69) concludes, while no "demonstration or march, no spatially bounded protest could bring together enough people to define a public sphere adequate to democracy in China," nonetheless, the "role of such protests lies in setting the agenda for a much more widespread discourse. It is as such physically-bounded protests become the occasion and topic for far-flung conversations that they have their most profound effects."

The risk the protest posed to the state – as important as the direct challenge to power that Tiananmen represented – was precisely to its control over discourse, over the nature of the things discussed. Tiananmen risked up-ending the construction of what could be called a "spectator" state, a state in which the flow of information mimics the flow of production and consumption – which is a goal not only of totalitarian governments: "In the West as in China, manufactured publicity 'sells' politicians to the people; the latter respond as consumers with an acclamation of their support, but not as creative, autonomous participants in public discourse" (Calhoun 1989: 57).[11] The distinction Calhoun (1989: 69) is making here rests on that made by Jürgen Habermas (1989) "between a public which makes culture an object of critical debate and one which simply consumes it." Television and other individualizing mass media may create a public in which "citizens simply consume programming," according to Habermas; but the events of the Beijing Spring fully upset that relation by bringing resistance (to the state and organized around cultural transformation and economic modernization) into full view, in the space that is right at the heart of the Chinese state and culture itself (Calhoun 1989: 70).[12]

11 That is the dystopian ideal in any event. The analysis of "spectator democracy" in the West can be traced to Noam Chomsky and has clear resonance in Guy Debord's (1994) ideas about the *Society of the Spectacle*. Scott Kirsch (1997) has recently developed these ideas in relation to the selling of atomic bomb testing in the United States during the 1950s – a spectacular event if ever there was one. Kirsch, however, discusses the possibilities of a "dialectics of spectacle" in which counter-spectacles, like Tiananmen, are organized precisely to undermine official spectacle. David Harvey (1989a), too, makes much of this point, though perhaps more cynically than Kirsch.

12 Of course much work in cultural studies has examined the degree to which television viewers are just passive consumers of predigested messages. Much of this work has stressed viewers' active engagement with shows, and has shown that people regularly and routinely engage in alternative and even contestatory readings of the presented material. For an example, see Ang (1993); for a concise and entertaining rebuttal to such studies, see Frank and Weiland (1997). To a quite large extent, such contestatory cultural politics remains quite *private* and completely unorganized. My central point here is

When the tanks rolled into the heart of Beijing on June 4, 1989, it was to reclaim the heart of the city against a quite powerful "counter-revolutionary" movement, a movement that directly challenged the state. But it was also a movement to regain some semblance of control over "culture."[13] "All but the most technocratic or cautious party-loyal Chinese intellectuals...felt that China's modernization was in need of a cultural vision," according to Calhoun (1989: 66). "However real the economic gains might be [before Tiananmen], they were either in jeopardy or even pernicious if not accompanied by a sound vision of Chinese society and culture. This was essentially the point where most students and intellectuals thought they had a crucial part to play." And "after the disaster at Tiananmen," adds Jianying Zha (1995: 46), intellectuals now "feel that they have lost even the power to describe China." This is the case because "the Chinese intellectual is waking up to one common fact: no longer is the government the only thing they must deal with. Now they must reckon with the forces of commercialism." For it was just that – the culturally corrosive effects of commodification – that the Tiananmen massacre did little to slow. As Zha (1995: 202) shows in her collection of essays on cultural transformation in China, after Tiananmen, "a sense of fatigue and cynicism about politics seems to pervade Chinese society" and so "for the time being at least, the majority of the population have happily turned away from politics and geared their energies to making money and living better." This passion for "making money and living better" and the transformation of economic laws that have made it possible, have unleashed forces of societal transformation the Communist Party may not have reckoned with. While many intellectuals in China fret about the inroads of Western-style popular culture, many others do little but profit from it. Yet even as China continues its "March Toward the Market" (as one Party slogan has it), each step of that march, like the Long March to Yanan, can be achingly difficult – and often surreal.

Zha recounts the story of how a group of artists, some of whom "only a few years ago, had displayed experimental works in major Chinese museums," planned to stage a major exhibit in Beijing's McDonald's. Their goal was precisely to *sell* art to ordinary people. The art was heavily indebted to Pop Art trends in the West – greeting cards, for example, depicted such things as "a bizarre creature with the body of a dragon, the head of Donald Duck, a foot in a Nike sneaker, and claws clutching a stack of dollar bills, against a Ming vase pattern" – and its goals were clear: the show was entitled "New History: 1993 Mass Consumption." While Zha wondered whether the artists were creating the "Whopperfication of Chinese Art," the artists themselves seemed to have no doubts. They kept reminding her that they were not even producing "works"; instead they were making "just *products*." The organizers of the show, however, failed to inform the Beijing police of their intentions, and the police, noting the show's proximity to both the end of the Party Congress and the approaching anniversary of Tiananmen, feared trouble. They arrested the organizers, banned the show, and filled McDonald's with undercover

---

that *organized* resistance must be public, and it must claim what I call a *space for representation*; see Mitchell (1995a).

13   This is one of the main points made by Zha (1995). Her other point is that in some very surprising ways this culture war was lost by the state, as we will see in a moment.

agents to assure no one tried to stage it anyway. As Zha (1995: 111–12) summarizes, "The irony, of course, is that these artists really meant no harm. They'd like to make a stir, but only the sort of stir that would get their 'products' sold. . . . In the past four years, the cultural scene in China has changed a great deal, but certain things won't change for a long time to come."

The culture wars in China are ironic, indeed. While there may be a new freedom for cultural experimentation in China, a freedom closely aligned to the commodification of culture (in all its guises: Zha also details newspapers' new use of nudity to sell issues), it exists in relation to a system of political power that is changing at a different speed. And besides, as many in China admit, this new "freedom" is itself already compromised: "Sure we're freer than before," one of Zha's (1995: 202) friends tells her, "we have the freedom to gyp our fellow men now." Yet the changes this "freedom" indicates should not be discounted: since 1992, commercialization has "exploded onto Beijing like a great tide, shaking up old structures, breaking down old habits and alliances, smashing old illusions and romanticisms. . . . The city has turned into a giant bubbling pot with everyone pushing and shoving, trying to get a piece of the action. Energies, hopes, dreams – the exuberance has returned. But it is different than 1989: in some fundamental sense, Beijingers have never looked and felt so alone" (1995: 16–17). Perhaps this is what the "resistance of the Walkman" has inevitably wrought: the commodification of social (and political) life, while liberating in some senses, is fundamentally a resistance of the private, of the individual. And if that is the case, then the transformations in China, both during and after the Beijing Spring of 1989, give a whole different inflection to the idea of "cultural politics."

Cultural Politics

What should be clear from the foregoing is that while the story of Tiananmen shows how important collective, political action remains, de Certeau's ideas about the dialectical movement between control and appropriation of space by *individuals* remains likewise important (if ultimately too optimistic). His ideas point to the potential subversiveness of everyday life. Moreover, the corrosive effects of the commodity compound this subversiveness by wrenching changes in the cultural economy that no state can fully control. But is this politics? That, of course, depends entirely on how we define "politics."

The dictionary I keep next to my desk is telling in its definition of "politics." Here is what it says: "The science of government; that part of ethics which relates to the regulation of government of a nation or state for the preservation of safety, peace, and prosperity; political affairs, or the conduct and contests of political parties."[14] You can almost see the barriers going up: politics is confined to government and political parties. Where is there room for the sorts of issues we have been discussing in this book? Clearly they are not "politics," at least in the sense given in this dictionary. But here is also where we realize the *power* of the idea of "cultural politics." The very act of understanding the cultural as political is transgressive of common sense – or of the policed boundaries that are meant to govern our lives. A new sense of "politics"

14   *The New Webster Encyclopedic Dictionary of the English Language*, 1978: Politics.

thus emerges. At least when we are talking of the politics of the less powerful, the counter-hegemonic, and the everyday, then "politics" are acts that transgress, acts that throw into question the "taken-for-granteds" of social life. Cultural politics, then, are contestations over meanings, over borders and boundaries, over the ways we make sense of our worlds, and the ways we live our lives.

Peter Jackson (1989: 4) derives this sense of cultural politics from the realization that "unitary culture" is nothing more than a myth. "That the cultural is political follows logically from a rejection of the traditional notion of a unitary view of 'culture,' and from the recognition of the plurality of cultures. If cultures are addressed in the plural (high and low, black and white, masculine and feminine, gay and straight, urban and rural) then it is clear that the meanings will be contested according to the interests of those involved." Our earlier discussion of how "culture is politics by other means" (chapter 1), however, suggests an even more basic sense of cultural politics. Where Jackson sees contest between groups (and this is important), the very act of *creating* cultures is always and everywhere political – and inescapably so. The question then is one of how these politics proceed; and, related, of what constitutes *meaningful* cultural politics.

Cultural politics as "resistance"

Cultural politics works from both the top down and the bottom up. The power to implement certain meanings, ways of seeing, or policies about education, art, movies and television, and so on, are every bit as political as efforts to resist and transgress those implementations. To get at the complexity of cultural politics, however, it is worth while beginning from the bottom up, and discussing the resistant and transgressive sorts of cultural politics that many practitioners of cultural studies and cultural geography (myself included) find so attractive. The goal here will be to seek out the meaningful, and to place that against the limits that any cultural politics must face.

"[R]esistance does not inevitably take the form of active struggle," according to Jackson (1989: 59). But, counters Tim Cresswell (1996: 22), "resistance seems to imply intention – purposeful action directed against some disliked entity with the intention of changing it or lessening its effect. The resistance of an action therefore appears to be in the intention of the perpetrator, in the eagerness to overcome or change some obstacle." At issue in this seeming difference of opinion is precisely what constitutes *meaningful* and *effective* action. Now both of these terms are indefinable in the abstract; instead, they can only be defined empirically, and often after the fact. Whatever the intentionality of a particular act, it may have all manner of unintended consequences that, *de facto*, make the act one of resistance. Or to put that another way, "resistance" can exist outside the intentions of those practicing it, but only if it is (usually later) *organized* as resistance, or *given meaning* by some influential group or another *as* resistance. Cultural politics thus operates at the level of material practice; but it also, and importantly, operates at the level of discourse.

The Centre for Contemporary Cultural Studies, for example, went to great pains to describe various subcultural "rituals of resistance" in Britain in the mid-1970s (Hall and Jefferson 1976). Peter Jackson (1989: 59) summarizes their work as follows:

By "rituals," a coherent set of actions is implied the meaning of which and purpose of which are symbolic rather than purely practical, and which are routinized in the sense that they can be practised almost unconsciously. These rituals include various styles of dress and patterns of verbal and non-verbal behaviour the adoption of which implies an attitude of resistance to those in power.

It is actually an open question as to whether these rituals really did "imply an attitude of resistance," beyond, perhaps, simply the resistance implied in shock. Or as Jackson (1989: 59) notes, "Whether such 'rituals of resistance' can be regarded as truly *strategic* is a matter of some debate." There is little debate, however, that such practices constituted the sorts of *tactics* described by de Certeau. And there is even less debate that skinheads and punks, for example, were engaged in an act of *transgression* as described by Cresswell. Cresswell (1996: 21) defines "transgression" as "literally, 'crossing a boundary,' " and he notes "transgression, and the reaction to it, underlines those values that are considered correct and appropriate" in larger society. He thus sees transgression as distinct from resistance in that it "does not, by definition, rest on the intentions of actors but on the *results* – on the 'being noticed' of a particular question" (see chapter 7 below).

Yet resistance circulates in discourse, too, so the *organization* of transgression by critics such as those associated with the Centre for Contemporary Cultural Studies into a *thing* given the name "rituals of resistance" helped transform transgression into resistance – at least to the degree that these ideas (and others like them) penetrated popular media and hence popular discourse (which they did to a surprising degree). In this sense, such critics – and their popularizers in the media – act as part of the "critical infrastructure" of "culture" that we discussed in chapter 3. Recall that we defined the "critical infrastructure" as those influential actors who are able to define a particular moment, to organize an "audience" for it, and to show us how it fits our own lives and gives meaning and coherence to them. Such an "infrastructure" works as much from the bottom up as it does from the top down: the "critical infrastructure" is not just composed of those purveyors of meaning who teach yuppies the value of gentrified neighborhoods or the middle classes the value of emulating the rich (in housing style, choice of clothing, etc.). Rather, it is also composed of those who seek to organize all the disorganized, tactical "rituals," and other coping mechanisms of youth, of workers, of radicalized women, of people of color, into a clear *movement* – a movement with the shape and structure of something permanent that changes not only how we live, but perhaps the balance of power obtaining in society.

Punks and carnivals: strategies of inversion

Take as an example the incredible impact of the Sex Pistols (1976–8) not just on rock music, but on cultural life more generally. In his remarkable book *Lipstick Traces: A Secret History of the Twentieth Century*, Greil Marcus (1989: 3) makes much of a recollection by Elvis Costello of his days "back when he was still Declan McManus, a computer operator waiting for his train to Central London." McManus had seen the Sex Pistols on their first TV appearance (December 1, 1976), and recalls his experience the next day: "On the way to work, I was on the platform in the morning and all the commuters were reading the papers when the Pistols made headlines – and said FUCK on TV. It was as if it was the most awful thing that ever happened. It's a mistake to confuse it with a major event in history, but it was a great morning – just to hear people's blood pressure going up and down over it." The weight of Marcus's book, however, is to show just what "a major event in history" the Sex Pistols were, even if they were thought up as "a joke" by their manager Malcolm McLaren – a major event because it was first so transgressive and *then* so intentional, even if always accidentally so. The result was indeed important: people took notice. But so was the way Punk was organized and reorganized into a *movement*, even if short-lived and frequently coopted. "The record that was to change the world": that is how Marcus describes "Anarchy in the UK." This was a record – and a movement – that was both an act of transgression and resistance, even if now, twenty years on, body-art and piercings, disaffection and mainlining are so middle-class and bourgeois as to be boring. And even if the whole point was simply to make money.[15]

In this regard it is probably invidious, in the realm of cultural politics, to make hard-and-fast boundaries between categories such as "resistance" and "transgression," and as I will argue in a moment, between alternative culture that is somehow "real" and that which is commodified. For it is always problematic to draw boundaries between, say, "resistance," and "co-optation," especially in a world, like ours, where there simply no longer is any life outside of commodity production (see especially Frank 1997a; Debord 1994). That is, the power urging conformity and social control can often be turned in on itself; commodities – like records and concerts, like articles of clothing and magazines – can become not necessarily "sites" for resistance, but certainly tools for it. It all depends on how they are used. Similarly, there may very well be a transgressive or resistant *potential* in walking in a city or watching TV in a certain way, but it will always remain only a potential until it is organized and made into a *strategy*. That is what cultural politics is all about: strategizing in the realm of practice and meaning to create new worlds, new histories, new ways to live. Or conversely, strategizing to preserve the old.

The Sex Pistols and the Punk movement that flowed from the band were transgression at its rawest: Punk was precisely about impurity, about breaking down borders (between audience and performer, for example, or between professional and amateur, between health and disdain); and it was about shock. In this regard, the Sex Pistols' act tapped into the suppressed (and repressed) history of "carnival," those popular festivals of transgression during the European Middle Ages that ritually turned the world on its head (see Bakhtin 1984; Burke 1978; Cresswell 1996: 121–33; Jackson 1989: 79–80; Stallybrass and White 1986). "Such things as carnivals, fairs, and everyday life," Cresswell (1996: 78) writes, "are a powerful set of tools for subordinated culture that constantly undermine the presumptions of elite culture. The inversion of symbolic domains of 'high' and 'low,' for instance, pokes fun at the establishment and irritates the agents of dominant culture." Now listen to how Marcus (1989: 67) describes the Punk scene:

---

15   Or is that an exaggeration? Recall the furor that greeted the celluloid depiction of Scottish drug users, *Trainspotting* (1996), when many interpreted that film as glorifying heroin use (even if it really did the opposite).

As people in the Roxy heard the Adverts, or the two girls and three boys who made up X-ray Spex, or the balding teenage Beckett fan who sang for the Buzzcocks – all people who had climbed up out of the Sex Pistols' first audiences – there was a reversal of perspective, of values: a sense that anything was possible, a truth that could be proven only in the negative. What had been good – love, money, and health – was now bad; what had been bad – hate, mendacity, and disease – was now good. The equations ran on, replacing work with sloth, status with reprobation, fame with infamy, celebrity with obscurity, nimble fingers with club feet, and the equations were unstoppable. In this new world, where suicide was suddenly a code word for meaning what you said, nothing could be more hip than a corpse. . . .

Punk in this sense *was* a carnival, where the celebration was of the "use value, profanity, and incompleteness [that] temporarily dethrones the sacred, the complete, and the distinguished" (Cresswell 1996: 78). Punk was dangerous – unless it could be contained. For Punk "changed history" precisely to the degree it was "noticed" and recognized as a subversive inversion – where audience became performer, and neither were very good – and to that degree it became, for too short a period, clearly an act of resistance: to the state, to the norms of employment and unemployment and their associated ethic of work, to Art and Music, and, to a much lesser extent, to commodification and commercialization.

Note, however, Cresswell's important caveat about carnivalesque moments: they *temporarily* invert the world: the moment is either officially limited (as with Mardi Gras) or their subversive power is reabsorbed into dominant structures of power and ordered norms of culture. Ritual carnivals had long been a part of the European cultural calendar. Carnivals institutionalized what has been called a "license in ritual"; that is, it was a time in which inversions of the social order were sanctioned – but also contained by their very nature as temporary. Even though Carnival often took place in the streets of the city, it nonetheless took place in a "world apart." This inversion of the "normal" social order created an incredible, but also quite cathartic, "tension between 'social control' and 'social protest'" (Jackson 1989: 80). Carnival thus substituted a temporary spectacle of inversion for a more permanent revolution in the social order. Carnival was – and is – a means of letting off steam.[16]

Even so, there are enough instances of the resistance implicit in Carnival to cast at least some doubt on the degree to which we might want to see Carnival as *merely* a means of controlling dissent. Indeed, Carnival was often a key moment in the active transformation of society. That is why Peter Stallybrass and Allon White (1993) (drawing on and developing the work of Bakhtin) take pains to show the means by which the old medieval European carnivals were increasingly brought under control – if not outright closed down – as the industrial revolution took hold and a period of more "modern" social order developed. In the period from 1850 to 1890, fairs and carnivals, ritualistic wakes and other public uses of the streets were canceled, closed, or intensely sanitized throughout Europe. While Stallybrass and White's point is that many of the ritualistic transgressions of Carnival were *displaced* and not eliminated with "the attack on Carnival," they nonetheless show a host of ways in which

16 For a contemporary example, think of the American college ritual of Spring Break in Daytona Beach, Palm Springs and Mazatlan, "carnivals" that are now so ritualized as to be an annual feature on MTV.

Carnival was driven underground – or to the margins of the geographical and social order. In England, for example,

> the sites of "carnival" moved more and more to the coastal periphery, to the seaside. . . . The seaside was partially legitimated as a carnivalesque site of pleasure on the grounds of health, since it combined the (largely mythical) medicinal virtues of the spa resorts with tourism and the fairground. It can be argued that this marginalization is a *result* of other, anterior processes of bourgeois displacement and even repression. But even so, this historical process of marginalization must be seen as an historical tendency distinct from the actual elimination of carnival.   (Stallybrass and White 1993: 291; see also Shields 1991)

Notice what Stallybrass and White are saying. The carnivalesque is really never eliminated; instead its form and location are changed, perhaps made "safer" and more ordinary. "In the long process of disowning carnival and rejecting its periodic inversions of the body and the social hierarchy," they explain, "bourgeois society problematized its own relation to the power of the 'low,' enclosing itself, often defining itself, by its suppression of the 'base' languages of carnival" (Stallybrass and White 1993: 292). But Stallybrass and White make a key argument at this point. They argue that the displacement and suppression of Carnival was certainly a process of spatial marginalization, but it was also *temporal*. If Carnival had relied on a ritualized seasonal cycle "which had once structured the whole year" (because Carnival was a particular *time* as well as a place), then its suppression meant that the carnivalesque was "no longer *temporally* pinned into" that cycle, and thus could "erupt" at any time "from the literary text, as in so much surrealist art, or from the advertisement hoarding, or from a pop festival or a jazz concert" (1993: 292).

So "Carnival" can live on, and it is unpredictable; but it also seems quite well-tamed: in the seaside town to which one might resort for a "dirty weekend," in the Ferris wheels and roller coasters along the boardwalk, and in the touring summer music festivals, carefully staged and choreographed. Stallybrass and White (1993: 292) conclude: "Carnival was too disgusting for bourgeois life to endure except as a sentimental spectacle." But that seems to assume that "spectacle" itself is a one-way street, and not a dialectical moment of potential transgression. And that just might not be a safe assumption to make: Punk, for example, was such an important act of transgression and resistance precisely because it was – it became – such a huge *spectacle*, a spectacle that changed Punk from an underground *movement* of resistance into a hyped and quite accessible *event*. On the idea of spectacle, then, a whole new complication in understanding cultural politics – and the geography of that politics – comes to the fore.

Spectacle and resistance

The rumors of the time held that Malcolm McLaren, the inventor and manager of the Sex Pistols, used to be connected with something called the Situationist International (SI), a radical Paris group of the 1950s and 1960s. It was that rumor that got rock critic Greil Marcus on the case, and what he found was an incredible lineage – in affinity if not always intent – between a number of European avant-garde, radical-art groups in the twentieth century (and before). From the Communards of 1871 Paris, through the Dadaists of the 1910s and 1920s Zurich and Berlin, to the Situationist International, Marcus traces a wild history of history-making on the fringes of power, sometimes intentional and sometimes not.

The work of SI was most certainly intentionally resistant, but it was often not clear what exactly it was resistant to. Theorists affiliated with SI argued from the beginning that theirs was a project to change the world, to recreate the "situations" in which we lived. Primarily, the "situation" of postwar Europe was one of relative affluence, and with it came the "problem of leisure," which was really the problem of boredom: "raging and ill-informed youth, well-off adolescent rebels lacking a point of view but far from lacking a cause – boredom is what they all have in common" (*International Situationiste*, 1958, quoted in Marcus 1989: 52). A world too safe, too sanitized, too stultifying was being built throughout Europe (and of course the United States), and the "spectacle" was just one manifestation of that ordered and controlled world.

For Guy Debord (1994: 20), the person perhaps most closely associated with SI, "the spectacle is the permanent opium war waged to make it impossible to distinguish goods from commodities." More forcefully, he argues (1994: 45) that,

> The image of the blissful unification of society through consumption suspends disbelief with regard to the reality of the division [of society] only until the next disillusionment occurs in the sphere of actual consumption. Each and every new product is supposed to offer a dramatic shortcut to the long-awaited promised land of total consumption. As such it is ceremoniously presented as the unique and ultimate product.

Importantly, the commodities Debord (1994: 29) refers to are not only the tangible things we buy directly at the store – disks, toothbrushes, cars – and which define the meanings of our lives through our identification with them; but these commodities are also images that we buy and buy into, images produced like commodities to define our lives for us. "Commodities are now *all* there are to see; the world we see is the world of the commodity. The Spectacle is *capital* accumulated to the point where it becomes image" (1994: 24).

By the 1990s it was not unusual to talk about how we live in a "national entertainment state," a state in which the image of things more and more comes to stand for its actuality, and in which large conglomerates (like Time-Warner and Disney-Capital Cities) try their damnedest to tell us what to think, and to ensure that our leisure time is always *productive* (of profit, and for them).[17] But in the late 1950s, such trenchant critiques of leisure, entertainment, and the "situations" of everyday life were less common. Debord's signal contribution was to show just how deeply implicated in our everyday lives were the *images* of life produced for us by capital and the state, and to show how the resulting *boredom* – a boredom derived from an increasing alienation not just from nature or the means of production (as traditional critiques of capitalism have it), but from every aspect of our own lives – was both the norm, and the fulcrum upon which revolutionary change could be leveraged. "The spectacle's function in society is the concrete manufacture of alienation," Debord (1994: 23) claimed. His

---

17   An excellent examiantion of the "National Entertainment State" can be found in the special issue of *The Nation* by that name: June 3, 1996.

point was not that the "situations" and "spectacles" established to entertain and pacify us, designed to reinforce the hegemony of consumerist capitalism, were *completely* hegemonic, but that the "society of the spectacle" created new sets of *relationships* between people, and between people and the institutions of capital and the state, relationships that meant we now had to think and act within and through the very terms established for us *by* the spectacle. Debord (1994: 12) argued that in the society of the spectacle, "all that once was directly lived has become mere representation," but that it was not necessarily the case that *all* life is representation. The spectacle was therefore quite complex: "the spectacle is not a collection of images; rather it is a social relationship between people that is mediated by images." To put that another way, spectacles create situations within which people must live their lives, and relate to each other. The way to regain control of life, then, is quite literally to remake the situation, transform the images, counter the spectacle with even more spectacular spectacles. As spectacle and image are transformed through such actions, so too will relationships between people be reconfigured.

Now at one level Debord provides a straight Marxist account of the power of commodities and the need to transform the conditions and reasons for their production. But on another level, he makes an argument that takes as its roots not (only) struggles over the length of the working day or the ownership of the means of production (which were key struggles for Marx), but also the need for taking hold of spectacle itself, of the need to counter "official" spectacle with a spectacle of one's own making. Situationist International saw its job as one of fanning the flames of resistance (of both everyday and more spectacular varieties) into a full-scale spectacle in its own right. Debord claimed of SI: "Where there was fire, we carried gasoline" (Marcus 1989: 176). SI's driving question was a clear one: "How do people make history, starting from conditions pre-established to dissuade them from intervening in it?" (1989: 178). One of SI's answers was to engage in continual acts of *détournement*, which involved the appropriation of images and artifacts – particularly images and artifacts of popular culture like movies and comic strips – and ripping them from their context or transforming their dialogue and speech-bubbles to make them mean something wholly different. *Détournement* was the practice of taking the images and spectacles that were the society of the spectacle and warping them into critique (figure 6.3). Another means for subverting the dominant spectacle and for transforming situations was the *dérive*, which involved "a drift down city streets in search of signs of attraction and repulsion" (1989: 168); in other words, a somewhat aimless mission of transforming the meanings of the spaces – the situations – in which we live our lives. And so we are back to "walking in the city" as a form of resistance, but now with this difference from the sort of walking celebrated by de Certeau: SI saw the *dérive* as intentional and organized, as a dialectical relationship with the spectacle and a means to both transgress and subvert that spectacle with a spectacle of one's own.

If the images that defined the society of the spectacle were images of plenty and leisure, then SI sought to organize boredom, alienation and anomie (exactly those traits that so worried many sociologists of the 1960s) into something productive – something productive of new situations, new spectacles, new geographies and new "cultures." The overriding pessimism of Debord's book *The Society of the Spectacle*, then, was a "pessimism of the intellect"; but it harbored within it an incredible

Figure 6.3   A classic *détournement*. Here American film-cowboys, little boys playing, ecclesiastical art, and even a computer punch card are all made to shill for revolutionary theory. From André Bertrand, *Le Retour de la colonne Durutti* ("The Return of the Durutti Column"), a widely circulated underground poster from 1966 that was splashed on the walls of Strasbourg University. The Durruti Column was a regiment of Anarchists who fought in the Spanish Civil War, headed by Buenaventura Durruti (note the difference in spelling from the Situationist International's version). Now the Durutti Column is (inevitably) a rock band.

"optimism of the will."[18] Where the spectacle sought the continual purification of space and society, of history and possibility, SI sought continual transgression and

18   The phrases are from an aphorism by the Italian Marxist and theorist of cultural hegemony, Antonio Gramsci (see chapter 2).

even the sort of productive filth that became such a hallmark of the Punk move-ment.[19] Resistance in a world governed by spectacle implied the need to create a spectacle of one's own.

And the Situationist International had their chance – in May 1968 when mass student protest transmogrified into a total, if ultimately unsuccessful, critique of French society. As a small avant-garde Paris faction, SI was really little known, even though it had staged a few rather spectacular interventions into popular culture. Some of those who helped found SI, for example, "invaded" Notre Dame Cathedral during the Easter service in 1950, leading to news reports around the country and the world. And a year later the same group stormed the Cannes film festival in a bid to get one of its movies shown. But mostly SI (and its predecessor, the Lettrist International) contented itself with obscure transformations of poetry, the production of experimental films, and drinking to excess in the cafes of the Saint-Germain-des-Prés district of Paris. SI would likely have remained obscure had not a set of almost accidental events allowed it to burst onto the international scene in the Paris uprising of May 1968.

Paris's May '68 actually begins in Strasbourg, Spring '66, when a group of students intent on "destroying" the student union were elected to run it.[20] With a rather large budget now at their disposal, the students contacted SI during the summer seeking guidance on how to undo the power they now had. Even though the waves SI made in the fabric of the spectacle society were by this time taking place "only in its journal," it sent as advice the words of Debord: "A revolutionary organization must remember that its objective is not getting people to listen to speeches by expert leaders, but getting them to speak for themselves" (quoted in Marcus 1989: 415). The students thus produced a manifesto: "On the Poverty of Student Life," which argued, as Greil Marcus (1989, 416) has put it, "in the society of the spectacle, the student was the 'perfect spectator,'" and which went on to call for a new relationship to the world, one in which not just students, but anyone "who has no power over his own life and knows it" (quoted in 1989: 417) strove "to create a new situation" in which that absence of power was no longer true – a new situation in which everyone grabbed hold of the conditions of their own lives and "détourned" them.

The response by conservative professors, many students, the university adminis-tration, Strasbourg city officials, and the French State "could not have been more extreme if the student union had spent its money on guns" (Marcus 1989: 418). Each group in its own way shrilly denounced the student leaders for misappropriating funds and for betraying the public trust. The reason for such a reaction was fairly straightforward, and it was anticipated and repeated throughout the world during those years – in the Free Speech Movement in Berkeley in 1964, in the rise of the Black Panthers next door in Oakland a couple of years later, and in Abby Hoffman's Yippee antics in Chicago and Washington a few years after that (to name just a few): those content with the *status quo* anticipated the likely course of events. "On Monday

19   On the transgressive qualities of filth more generally and especially as it relates to controlling women, see Cresswell (1996), chapter 5.
20   This account is based on Marcus (1989), 413–31. Accounts of Paris '68 are legion. See the bibliography in Reader and Wadia (1993); the effects of the May '68 uprising are usefully explored in Henley and Kerr (1989).

people began to question rules and regulations, the next day the institutions behind the rules, then the nature of the society that produced the institutions, then the philosophy that justified the society, then the history that created the philosophy, until by the end of the week both God and the state were in doubt and the only interesting question was the meaning of life" (1989: 419).

Within six weeks, though the student union had done nothing illegal, the French courts closed the university and disbanded the union. As one partisan summarized, at Strasbourg, "a situation was created in which society was forced to finance, publicise and broadcast [through the funds of the student union] a revolutionary critique of itself, and furthermore to conform to this critique by its reactions to it" (quoted in Marcus 1989: 420). The Strasbourg revolt percolated (with more than 300,000 copies of "On the Poverty of Student Life" quickly printed) until it surfaced again at the suburban Paris University of Nanterre in the spring of 1968, where a small group of students continually disrupted classes by shouting SI slogans at their (usually leftist) professors. As tensions mounted, students elaborated their critique from one of the irrelevancy of education as then structured, to a wider critique of the university and society as a whole[21] – which itself escalated into violent confrontations with the police (figure 6.4). The Communist Party called a one-day general strike to protest police

Figure 6.4 Students battle with the police during the May 1968 Paris uprisings. Coupled with a general strike involving more than 10 million workers, the student revolt shocked the French state to its core and threatened to radically transform the "situation" in Paris and throughout France. Associated Press photograph; used by permission.

21   Again, the parallels with the Berkeley Free Speech Movement are clear. For a history and geography of that event, see Mitchell (1992b).

brutality (and to argue for higher wages), and this strike in turn exploded into a full-scale, indefinite general strike involving more than 10 million workers. But this was not just an ordinary strike. "The workers who occupied their factories and soldered the doors closed were not acting in solidarity with the people rioting in Paris; like the people in Paris, they were taking the breakdown of authority as a chance to act for themselves.... [In the strikes and riots] there was only public happiness: joy in discovering for what drama one's setting is the setting, joy in making it" (Marcus 1989: 428).

By the time French President Charles de Gaulle restored order in the streets at the end of May (conceding educational reform and pay raises), something new – if only temporary – had been created: "commodity time stopped in May, free time moved too fast to keep or master" (1989: 430); boredom had been banished to the outer reaches of the suburbs and countryside. A new situation – if again only a temporary one – had been created that united people, and united them in public space, creating a transgressive world, perhaps never solid enough to become a new *order*, but at least one in which spectacle was set against itself. While, as Marcus notes, the history of May '68 is "almost invisible" now, it created a "moment," a time and a place where history was made under conditions when it never should have been (after all the story of France after World War II was one of economic success and relative affluence). It was a lot like that moment on British television in 1976 when the Sex Pistols said "FUCK." It didn't make history as we usually think about it, perhaps, but it made history all the same. And it did so by radically transforming the cultural geographies within and through which we live our lives.[22] In that regard, it was a lot like May '89 in Beijing, another "moment" quickly suppressed in official history, another moment, according to Jianying Zha, that is just as soon forgotten by many of those who were there as they get on with their lives of finding new ways to transform situations.[23] Paris '68, the Sex Pistols, and Tiananmen all "made history" (and geography) because they so thoroughly disrupted the carefully made and manicured "culture" – or situation – to which we were meant to acquiesce and in which we would be content.

Conclusion: Culture War as a Geography of Spectacle and Transgression

"You can't dismantle the master's house using the master's tools."[24] That has become almost a mantra of many of those who look at forms of resistance. Yet, Debord's

---

22   David Ley (1996) provides ample evidence of this by tracing the Situationist movement's impact on youth culture at the end of the 1960s, and through that, on the gentrifying cities of North America and Europe in the 1970s and 1980s. The "Dionysian" goals of the Situationists (and similar groups) helped "a life-style of liminality, of anti-structure" to take root "in counter-culture enclaves in the inner city, and its influence passed into the aestheticism of the professional middle-class who followed them" (p. 333). This was an aestheticism, however, fully shorn of the incisive economic critique and political edge of Debord's (1994) Situationist manifesto.

23   But it is different, therefore, than the uprisings of Eastern Europe later in 1989, uprisings that did, in the end, radically, suddenly, and permanently transform the situations of millions upon millions of people.

24   The phrase is Audre Lorde's.

point in *The Society of the Spectacle* is that we *have no choice* but to "use the master's tools" if we want to do any dismantling. We need to retake and reshape commodities – because "commodities are now *all* we see." We have to work within a form of history that is not of our own making and make it our own. We need to use that history – and especially that geography – to make a new "situation," to make, as the Industrial Workers of the World used to say, a new world "out of the shell of the old." Transgression is paramount.

But in cultural politics – in the politics of culture – when does "transgression" become "resistance"? Is walking through Tiananmen listening to a Walkman enough? Does that suffice not just to make history, but to remake geography too? For, as Henri Lefebvre (1991: 54) has argued, a "revolution that does not produce a new space has not realized its full potential; indeed it has failed in that it has not changed life itself. . . . " This fact is intuitively, if not explicitly, understood by all manner of social movements contending on all manner of cultural fronts. The point is that the contest over "culture" *is* a contest over space – over its control, its production, over who is allowed in and who is kept out, and over what the nature of acceptable activities is to be in that space, over what constitutes a pure space filled only with acceptable behaviors, and what constitutes transgression of that putative purity. The production of new (cultural) spaces is a complex dialectic. The next four chapters map some of the fractures – of sexuality, gender, race, and nationalism in particular – through which this dialectic operates. As we will see in each instance, the production of new spaces (and the maintenance of old) is crucial to the transformation of society (or the protection of society as it now exists).

7

Sex and Sexuality: The Cultural Politics and Political Geography of Liberation

The Geography of Sex

If some form of visibility in public space is essential to the production of "culture" and for cultural politics – and if it is especially important for engaging in resistance to hegemonic social relations – then this is no less true for sex and sexuality. That might seem a contradictory statement: after all, what could be more private than sex and one's sexuality? If there is a geography to sex, isn't it a private one, consisting of bedrooms, private conversations with friends and lovers, frank (or not so frank) discussions within the household between mother and daughter, father and son? One of the signal contributions of academic cultural studies – and now their adoption into geography – has been to point to the obvious, to show just how "public" sex and sexuality always are, and thus how they are always and everywhere contested in and through the public sphere and public space. But this visible publicity is not only of the most obvious sort: the commodification of sex and the pursuit of pornography, for example (as important as they may be). It is also a publicity that allows, through negotiation, political struggle, acts of bold transgression and timid acquiescence, for people to create sexual identities for themselves.

All this might seem a particularly *contemporary* issue. After all, it has only been 30 years since the famous Stonewall Riots in New York City that many mark as the

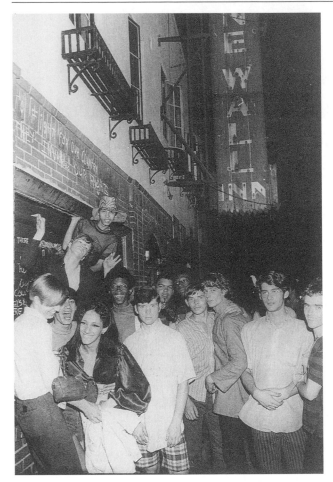

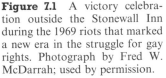

Figure 7.1 A victory celebration outside the Stonewall Inn during the 1969 riots that marked a new era in the struggle for gay rights. Photograph by Fred W. McDarrah; used by permission.

beginning of the Gay Liberation movement (figure 7.1). It has only been in the last two or three decades that nudity and sex acts have become commonplace in film (and to some extent television). Read newspapers from the 1970s or earlier and you will not find the sort of frank sex-advice that appears daily now. The so-called "sexual revolution," and its significant transformation by AIDS, is only a generation old. Surely, sex is only very recently "public." To use the current metaphor, before the 1960s, in the Western world, at least, sex and sexuality were very much "in the closet." Or were they?

At the most obvious (but perhaps least remarked) level, heterosexual sex and sexuality have always been quite public. Take the very public marriage ceremony with its various ritual fertility rites, for example, or the simple acceptability of straight couples kissing in public.[1] The selling of sex – through commercial advertising and prostitution – has also long been conducted in public space. And, of course, the great battle for contraception and greater freedom for sexual experimentation at the turn of

1   Queer scholars often describe this congruence of obviousness and transparency as a condition of "heteronormativity," using the term to point to the ways in which heterosexuality as a *norm* is encoded

the twentieth century relied not only on public debate, but also on considerable doses of street theater. But let us return to what many still consider "transgressive" or immoral, sexuality – homo- and bi-sexuality. By examining it, we can see the strange ways in which sexuality is always overtly public and still oddly invisible.

In a book incredible both for its insight and for its use of fragmentary and fugitive sources (underground newspapers, oral histories, crosswise readings of mainstream media), George Chauncy (1994) has shown just how public sex – and particularly gay sex – was in New York City before the Depression. His book, *Gay New York*, is a compelling account of how men constructed for themselves a world of transgressive sexuality that was at once quite open and quite fluid (if also contested). The "closet" which now seems such an obvious part of gay sexuality, Chauncy argues, had to be actively constructed. Chauncy shows that the gay male world in New York was one strongly structured by class, in which homosexual encounters among working-class men were often dissociated from gay sexual identity.[2] The fluidity of this arrangement – in which some working-class men could engage, often quite openly, in gay sex without necessarily adopting a "gay persona," while others worked hard to become self-styled "queers" and "fairies" – created a world in which homosexuality to some degree flourished.

Significantly, it flourished in particular *spaces* in the city, spaces that provided locations in which men could forge or remake their sexual identities. Far from being spaces well out of the public eye, many were quite public indeed – cabarets and bars of the Bowery, theaters of Harlem, public parks and restrooms – and some even became important tourist attractions. In much writing about gay life in America and Europe, there has arisen what Chauncy (1994: 3) calls a "myth of invisibility" that asserts that "even if a gay world existed [before Stonewall], it was kept invisible and thus remained difficult for isolated gay men to find." However, Chauncy (1994: 3) continues, "gay men were highly visible in New York, in part because gay life was more integrated into the everyday life of the city in the prewar decades than it would be after World War II – in part because so many gay men boldly announced their presence by wearing red ties, bleached hair, and the era's other insignia of homosexuality." Gay men frequented many of the same bars and other public and semi-public spaces as other members of the working class and bohemian circles. One should not read into this relative openness, however, a complete acceptance. On the contrary, brutal policing of gay men and gay sex waxed and waned with changes in government and public opinion, and incidents of gay-bashing were common and rarely punished. "The history of gay resistance" to these countervailing pressures, according to Chauncy (1994: 5, emphasis added), "must be understood to extend beyond formal political organizing to include the strategies of everyday resistance that men devised in order *to claim space* for themselves in the midst of a hostile

---

into our everyday lives and the spaces we occupy – and the ways in which it is a norm that is so prevalent and unquestioned as to be (for many) fully oppressive.

2   In this Chauncy builds on work by Foucault (1978) and others, who argue that homosexuality as an *identity* was "invented" around 1870, when a change in discourse about sexual "inversion" led, as Eve Kosofsky Sedgwick (1993: 245) puts it, to a new "world-mapping by which every given person...was not considered necessarily assignable...to a homo- or hetero-sexuality, a binarized identity full of implications, however confusing, for even the ostensibly least sexual aspects of personal existence" (see also Sedgwick 1990).

society." Gay men, in other words, needed to create and maintain a "gay world" in the otherwise straight city. Sexuality and space were – and are – indivisible.[3]

What did this world of gay men look like? Where was it located? How did it change over time? Chauncy spends nearly 400 pages answering these questions, so I can only give the briefest outline here. In the first place it must be recognized, as alluded to above, that sexual identity is itself fluid and changing. To think in terms of a strict opposition between, for example, gay and straight, erases the reality of most people's sexual lives, desires, and fantasies. Within the "gay world" of prewar New York, for example, not only were there self-identified homosexuals (who called themselves "queers") there were also "fairies," whose sex interests may or may not have been other men, but who evinced a certain level of "effeminacy" in their character. Finally, there were those men who engaged in gay sex, but who identified themselves as heterosexual. The "dichotomous system of classification, based . . . on sexual object choice" had to be actively constructed: it is an historical, cultural artifact (Chauncy 1994: 21). Until quite recently, Chauncy convincingly argues, sexuality was constructed in terms of *gender* more than in terms of *sexual activity*.[4] By understanding prewar sexuality in terms of gender, Chauncy is able to show not only how a gay world was publicly constructed and maintained in New York, but also how present-day ideals of masculinity and femininity were developed and now are policed.

Second, Chauncy (1994: 23) details the "topography of gay meeting places" in New York, showing the importance of bars, theaters, bathhouses, rooming houses, and public parks, to "the social organization of the gay world and homosexual relations generally." He explores the "tactics by which gay men appropriated public space not identified as gay – how they, in effect, reterritorialized the city in order to construct a gay city in the midst of (and often invisible to) the normative city." Yet it was also quite visible too. In the Bowery (New York's Skid Row, an area of cheap bars, flophouses, cabarets, and transiency), gays, among many others, created a "spectacle" of themselves both for the amusement of "slumming" locals and tourists, and so as to create a haven of acceptance for themselves. Drag shows, same-sex dance halls, and prostitution (both gay-male and heterosexual-female) vied both for a spot in the public eye and against various moral crusaders seeking to clean up the city. The Bowery was particularly home to numerous "flamboyantly effeminate 'fairies,'" engaged both in the sex trade and in showing off to themselves, creating in the process a "gay male society [that] was much more fully integrated into working class culture than middle class culture" (1994: 34). This was a working-class milieu where "normal manhood" was defined less by whom one had sex with than by how one comported oneself, both on the streets and in the bars, and in the sex act. The emergence of a "queer identity" according to Chauncy, was as much a part of a middle-class redefinition of heterosexuality, coupled with the bourgeois sanctification of the family as a private oasis in the public city, as it was an inevitable outgrowth of the desires of gay men. The middle-class created and policed a spatial and

3 In geography the key work on sexuality and space to this point is Bell and Valentine (1995b). The introduction and bibliography to this volume provide a sense of the scope and vibrancy of this work.
4 We will examine gender more closely in the next chapter. While it is in some ways false to divorce sexuality from gender, I think it important to keep them apart for now because each social construction raises a different (if interconnected) set of geographical issues which deserve attention.

sexual "apartheid" in the city: manhood was in part predicated on the sequestering of women in the home (as we saw in chapter 4 and will revisit in the next chapter), and on the exhibition of male "virility" in public, especially as middle-class men's own professional jobs demanded less and less of them in the way of physical activity.

What should be clear from this all-too-brief synopsis of Chauncy's major thesis is that the construction of sexuality, like the construction of gender, is a contested *process*; it is formed in *relationships*, rather than as a stable, immutable thing. And it should also be clear, that like any other social relationship, sexuality is inherently *spatial* – it both depends on particular spaces for its construction and in turn produces and reproduces the spaces in which sexuality can be, and was, forged. For many men (and women) in New York before World War II, Chauncy shows, "privacy could only be had in public": bars, toilets, and dark corners of parks all became scenes for sexual encounters, especially for members of the working classes who often lived in overcrowded apartments that afforded no opportunity for privacy at all (1994: chapter 7). These spaces were well known, certainly to men seeking gay sex and spectacle, but also to crusading moralists seeking to shut them down. (These quite public spaces were coupled with more private [but commercial] gay bathhouses that served as centers of gay sociability, but drew an even greater degree of attention from reformers because they were sites of frequent, and often anonymous, sexual encounters between men.)

The "gay world" then, as a set of spaces in the city, was always in danger of destruction. Gay political power, therefore, was forged through yet another spatial strategy: the development of gay residential enclaves in Harlem and Greenwich Village (forerunners, in some ways, of today's gay neighborhoods in places like the Castro in San Francisco) (figure 7.2). There and in other places around the city, gays

Figure 7.2 Castro Street on an early Sunday morning (January 1999). The center of gay life in contemporary San Francisco, the Castro is, as we will see in this chapter, part of a quite complex urban geography of sexuality in San Francisco. Photograph by D. Mitchell.

developed a politics of camp and kitsch, of respectability and studied degeneracy. And in some senses, it may have been their very visibility and success in carving out a gay world in New York that led to the eventual "exclusion of homosexuality from the public sphere" during the Depression. In a transformation with clear parallels to our own moralistic times, an

> anti-gay reaction gained force in the early to mid-thirties as it became part of a more general reaction to the cultural experimentation of the Prohibition years and to the disruption of gender arrangements by the Depression. As the onset of the Depression dashed the confidence of the 1920s, gay men and lesbians began to seem less amusing than dangerous. A powerful campaign to render gay men and lesbians invisible – to exclude them from the public sphere – quickly gained momentum. (Chauncy 1994: 331)

In some senses, a "closet" was constructed into which gays and lesbians were forced – at least until Stonewall.

These spatial metaphors – "gay world," "closet" – are important, because they provide a window on the actual spaces in which sexual identities are formed, policed, and transformed. The exclusion of public homosexuality in no way indicated the end of a *space* for homosexuality. Rather it indicated an important transformation of the spaces within which sexual identities are formed – in which the *relations* through which people forge their identities take place. The destruction of a public gay world in New York meant not just that gays "went underground," but that the very means by which "gayness" and "straightness" and everything in-between (who has access to whom, who is part of what world, how oppositions between homo- and hetero-sexuality are policed and negotiated) – was established on a very different spatial basis.[5] The purpose of the remainder of this chapter is to explore just how integral space is to sexuality, and hence to explore how that space is structured, how it is contested, and how it is transgressed.

Geographies of Sexuality

The preceding stories about the gay male world in New York might leave the impression that sexuality is an issue of homosexuality, a "gay issue," and that, beyond that, the construction of a "gay world" is a man's project. Neither of these is the case, of course. Just as gay sexuality is constructed (and performed) in space, so too is straight sexuality and all the shades of sexuality emanating in all directions from these two convenient labels. And just as men produce and occupy space, just as male spatial relations structure social relations, so too do women. The key issue, of course, is power. Gay sexuality has become an important focus of study precisely *because* it is powerfully coded as "transgressive" to "normal"

5   In many ways, Chauncy's depiction of a gay world being superseded by a gay closet relies on overly simple spatial metaphors. As Michael Brown (1996: 768) points out, the important point is that worlds and closets were fully intertwined during the period Chauncy is discussing. "Chauncy's own evidence ... seems to presume that there was a braided simultaneity of gay closets and gay worlds mapping through each other in New York City between 1890 and 1940."

sexuality.[6] And "gay *men's* space" has garnered attention in part because of gay men's greater visibility (*as* men) in the public sphere and in relatively successful gay enclaves in New York, Boston, London, San Francisco, and elsewhere.[7] The trick for cultural geography is to read sexual spatiality through this lens of power both to see how norms of sexuality are constructed, and how they are maintained. The description of "Gay New York" above is meant only as a first glimpse at just how intriguing and important such a project is.

The starting point for studies of sexuality, according to Eve Kosofsky Sedgwick (1993: 247), is the obvious one: "people are different from each other." She sets out a list of obvious reminders about this difference, noting that sex may be more or less important in different people's lives; that it may have a more or less great impact on their formation of identity; that sexual acts can be of innumerable varieties and mean innumerable things; that some people see sex as a means for identifying with others, while others see it as a means of exploring their selves; that some people see sex and sexuality closely entwined with issues of gender, but that others do not; and so forth (Sedgwick 1993: 249–50). But while "difference" may be the overriding fact of sexuality, it is also the case that these differences are themselves *socially organized*. And in the contests over that organization we can begin to see how issues of sexuality are strongly caught up in the culture wars of this and past times. It is these wars in fact, which are often wars of territory (as we will see in the next section), *through* which sexuality is socially organized.

Difference itself is scary to a lot of people, and so, unsurprisingly, sex and sexuality have become one of the keenest fronts in the culture wars. At its most basic, such a fear of difference is expressed in the oft-heard phrase, "I don't care *what* other people do, as long as I do not have to see or hear about it." Such a sentiment, at its most benign, aligns itself with a liberal and libertarian philosophy of individual rights that argues "anything goes" as long as it does not impinge on the rights of others, in this case defined as the right not to have to think about sexual activities different from one's own. The argument asserts that what occurs in private is of no concern to anyone but those engaging in that activity. Actions in public, however, must conform to the dictates of the "normal" or hegemonic society. Yet the very savageness with which cultural battles over sexuality are fought – in the media, on the streets (through such practices as "queer-bashing"), in the courts, and by the police – quickly give the lie to the sharp divide between public and private that such sentiments demand. The most obvious example is the ridiculous policy instituted by the Clinton Administration concerning gays in the US Military. Under the so-called "don't ask, don't tell"

---

6   As Sedgwick (1993: 260) caustically remarks about the search for "gay genes" and hormonal combinations that "produce" homosexuality (and thus which could be treated through some technological intervention), "If I had ever, in any medium, seen any researcher or popularizer refer even once to any supposed gay-producing circumstances as the *proper* hormonal balance, or the *conducive* endocrine environment, for gay generation, I would be less chilled by the breezes of all this technological confidence." Or on the cultural front: "Advice on how to make sure your kids turn out to be gay, not to mention your students, your parishioners, your therapy clients, or your military subordinates, is less ubiquitous than you might think" (Sedgwick 1993: 258).

7   As we will discuss more fully later, Castells (1983) has argued that lesbians are less "territorial" than gay men, but recent work by Tamar Rothenberg, Gill Valentine, Ann Forsyth and others has shown this may not be the case.

policy, gays may serve in the military, as long as they keep their sexual orientation absolutely private. That is, they may serve if they agree to suppress a very fundamental part of their own selves.[8]

In Colorado in 1992 voters passed an initiative that made it illegal to extend rights (in housing, employment, schooling, etc.) on the basis of sexual orientation. Proponents of the initiative argued that it would prevent gays, lesbians, and bisexuals from being granted "special rights" (whatever those may be); but the text of the initiative made it plain that its supporters wanted to make it the position of the state government (and its subdivisions) that homosexuality and homosexual behavior would not be tolerated. The initiative set off a storm of public debate as to what right gay men and women had to their "lifestyle." The arguments only intensified as the initiative was challenged in court and eventually made its way to the Supreme Court, which decided in the summer of 1996 that the Colorado initiative was unconstitutional because it unfairly excluded some citizens, by dint of the way they engaged in sex, from due process before the law by making it impossible for them to claim they had been discriminated against.

This decision came as a partial surprise if only because a scant decade earlier, the Court had ruled (in a decision that still stands) that state governments had the right to regulate sexual behavior *in the privacy of one's home*. In *Bowers v. Hardwick*, the Court argued that anti-sodomy laws were perfectly constitutional because there was a "compelling governmental interest" in preventing sodomitical acts (which include both anal and oral sex by gay or straight people, as well as mutual masturbation between people of the same sex). Police power extends right into the bedroom. If that is not clear enough evidence that what "they" do in private has indeed long been a concern of the state (and there are plenty of people who will work to assure that it stays as such), then consider the spate of "defense of marriage" acts passed by state legislatures and the US Congress (the latest of which was signed into law by President Clinton). These laws had nothing to do with "defending" marriage. Instead, they were designed to assure that gays could *never* marry. Responding to a case working its way through the Hawaiian court system that may legalize marriage between same-sex couples, state after state has passed laws which make a gay marriage consecrated in any other state null and void within their own borders. These laws contravene the "full-faith-and-credit" clause of the US Constitution that assures that states will recognize each other's laws and policies. But that, of course, is precisely the point.

In the United States, public battles over "acceptable" sexuality are the quintessential culture wars, with one side arguing that what is at stake are "immoral lifestyles" and acts which are "abominations before the Lord." On the other side, discourses about personal rights, human dignity, and defense of minorities prevail. In between, all manner of arguments rage, from within more liberal churches which accept homosexuality as legitimate, but still refuse to give positions of authority to sexually active gays (as with the American Presbyterian Synod), to debates within the gay community itself over whether being granted the right to marry will co-opt the more radical agenda of transforming societal sexual mores.

---

8   This policy is even more of a sham than it appears, because it is still illegal for military personnel to engage in any homosexual act. They may be gay if they are celibate.

Such contestations over the role of the state in people's sex lives are not limited to the United States. In Britain, police have raided private parties where men were engaged in consensual sadomasochism, arguing that intervention was necessary for "health reasons" (see Bell 1995). And the Thatcher government weighed in in 1988 with a section of the British Local Government Act that forbade local authorities from the "promotion of homosexuality" because it was a "pretended family relationship." As Jon Binnie (1995: 189) points out, such official positions, though perhaps legislatively weak, have "served an important ideological purpose as part of the wider Conservative family values agenda in which homosexuality was seen as one root cause of the moral decay of the nation." But they have also led to a significant political mobilization of gay- and sex-rights activists and their allies, assuring that issues of sexuality, and its *place* in society, remain a crucial focus of debate and struggle.

The very severity with which we prosecute these debates over sexuality in the public sphere indicate the degree to which understandings of sexuality are being revolutionized. Whereas it was once simply common sense that one's sexuality was a product of nature, it is now considered by many that sexuality is itself something we actively *perform* (Butler 1990, 1993, 1994). On the left, this generally means that people create and recreate their sexual selves in public and private rituals and activities, and that the very performance of sexuality indicates at once its fluidity, its *social* (as opposed to only *natural* and *personal*) construction, and its subversive potential.[9] Relations of power are right at the center of this mode of theorizing. On the religious right, by contrast, this sense of fluidity and construction indicates that homosexuality is a "lifestyle choice" – and an immoral one at that. By contrast, heterosexuality is seen as fully, and exclusively, natural, wherein any deviation ought to be corrected or punished. In this case, not a theorization of power, but the exercise of power, stands at the center of the religious right's understanding of sexuality as performance.

This exercise of power extends itself into the spaces we occupy. The construction of a gay world in prewar New York may be seen "as the 'queering' of space through its active appropriation" (Bell et al. 1994: 32). But if that is so, the underlying assumption is that space is *a priori* sexually coded as straight: "public (straight) space remains the original: the real space which gay space/queer space copies or subverts. It is as though it was there first, not produced, not artificial, but simply *there*" (1994: 32). The point here is that "straight space" must itself be produced and maintained, just as much as gay or queer space must be. If the production of space is accomplished through social struggle, then it will not do to assume that all spaces are *a priori*, and without effort, straight. The key is to see space as dialectically constructed through the give-and-take between contending (sexual) interests and (sexual) social formations.

Yet most spaces in the Western world are *hegemonically* straight. A "sexual order" is enacted in and through spaces – whether these spaces are the public spaces of a

9   Many commentators on the left remain quite agnostic about the degree to which sexuality is biologically determined, agreeing that there very well may be some genetic, hormonal, or other component to sexuality. But their point is usually that the question of biological determination is moot. The real question is how to construct a society in which difference is not only tolerated (and certainly not medicated or healed) but actively encouraged in the name of equality and justice.

festival marketplace (see Goss 1996), the (putatively) private space of the bedroom, or the in-between space of a bar or coffee shop. The importance of sexually transgressive acts in normatively straight spaces cannot be overestimated. They "queer" a socially purified space, unsettling commonsense notions about how sexuality and place intermingle. In particular, organized, disruptive transformations of everyday space, such as when Queer Nation stages same-sex "kiss-ins," "reveal . . . the socially constructed nature of sexual identity and sexually identified spaces," even if those spaces are only *implicitly* coded as sexual (Bell et al. 1994: 32). Struggles over sexual identity, then, produce space. So too do certain spaces produce sexual identity, but not necessarily in any simple way. Referring to the performance of sex, Glen Elder (1996: 757) argues that as a spatial practice, it takes place "at many scales (including the body)"; the same is clearly true of performing sexuality. Queer Nation makes its interventions in response not just to some local homophobia, but as part of a strong cultural reaction to the global epidemic of AIDS, the national and international reaction to the "sexual revolution," the consequent re-sequestering of (non-commodified) sex, and the quite local geographies of sexual identity and practice.

Space and Sexuality in Capitalism

Nor do they make their interventions in a world devoid of the structuring power of capital and capitalism, a point that many gay activists are at pains to make clear (for example, Geltmaker 1992).[10] Larry Knopp (1992: 652) has argued that the production of sexuality, like the production of space, is intimately linked to the "spatial dynamics of production, consumption, and exchange (including particularly class struggle) under various phases of capitalist development." These links create a "range of possibilities for sexual practice and sexual identity formation that confront people in their daily lives, as well as to people's struggles, individually and collectively, to negotiate and shape these possibilities." At the most philosophical level, this linkage between sexuality and capitalism is expressed through what Henri Lefebvre (1991) calls the domination of "abstract space." This abstract space is not the same as the sorts of "purified" spaces alluded to above. Rather, it is a space defined by the *abstraction* of lived social relations from their material, everyday contexts, and their replacement by *images* and *representations* of those relations – images and representations organized pursuant to some goal (like profit-making). In the case of sexuality, "in its natural form, the sexual relationship implies a certain reciprocity; at a later stage this bond may be abstractly justified and legitimated in a way that changes it into a social reality (often wrongly described as 'cultural'). Physical reciprocity is legalized as contractual reciprocity, as a 'commitment' witnessed and underwritten by authority" (1991: 309). In other words, what was once an exchange between individuals, based on pleasure, love, or mutual usefulness, is transformed into a societal

10   There are, of course, quite different interpretations of gay relationships to capitalism: "Gay culture . . . is anything but external to advanced capitalism, and to precisely those features of advanced capitalism that many on the left are most eager to disavow. Post-Stonewall urban gay men reek of the commodity. We give off the smell of capitalism in rut, and therefore demand of theory a more dialectical view of capitalism than many people have the imagination for" (Warner 1991: 17, note 21; see also Warner 1993).

system of exchange, based on the desire to uphold certain societal norms and interests – and reinforced by, among other things, state-supported marriage contracts. "The representation of sex . . . takes the place of sex itself, while the apologetic term 'sexuality' serves to cover up this mechanism of devaluation" (1991: 309).

This transformation is important, according to Lefebvre (1991: 309–10), because it devalues a "culture of the body" in favor of the increased valuation of exchangeable parts: "'erotogenic zones' (as assigned by sexologists), 'organs' of reproduction, and the like." Under capitalism, which relies on the production of abstract space in which all relations are the abstract relations of exchange, the "body as represented by the images of advertising (where the legs stand for stockings, the breasts for bras, the face for make-up, etc.) serves to fragment desire and doom it to anxious frustration, to the non-satisfaction of local needs" (1991: 310). The production and distribution of commodities, of course, stands ready to sublimate this frustrated desire to its own needs. And "[t]his is especially true of the female body, as transformed into exchange value, into a sign of the commodity and indeed into a commodity *per se*" (1991: 310).

Declaring that the over-representation of sex in current, highly commodified art has become boring, a critic in the *New York Times* has made this connection plain:

> The really up-to-date obsession is not sex, but consumption, the locus of lust having shifted from the bed to the shopping mall and superstore. Shopping malls are larger, more continuously populated spaces devoted to the incitement of desire than topless bars ever will be. Attraction is more powerful at the mall, hearts beat faster, boredom is less common, action more likely, fulfillment of desire more frequent, and every man there is potent by virtue of having a few bucks in his pocket. Art photographers have done their bit to kill off interest in sex, but commercial photographers have been far more instrumental in effecting the shift to possessions. . . . Advertising and fashion photography are the safest sex of all: the merchandise comes with implicit promises, there is always the hope that the photographic aura is included in the price, and if it is a lie, at least it's not life threatening. (Goldberg 1997)

Desire, whether fulfilled (or more likely delayed or sublimated) by sex or by shopping, relies on the construction of *objects*: the body, the perfume bottle, the sleek stereo. And the construction of objects demands appropriate places: the mall, certainly, but also the sorts of liminal spaces associated with romantic or dirty weekends, with the suspension of the ordinary (see Shields 1991). "Typically," Lefebvre (1991: 310) notes, "the identification of sex and sexuality, of pleasure and physical gratification, with 'leisure' occurs in places specially designated for the purpose – holiday resorts or villages, on ski slopes or sun-drenched beaches" and in city night-club districts. Space is thus divided, sex and sexuality is localized, creating an uneven development of sites of pleasure in and through which commodified relations hold sway: space and place must themselves become commodities within the circulation of desire as it is regulated by the circulation of capital.

The central irony of contemporary capitalism is that "[a]s spatial barriers diminish so we become much more sensitized to what the world's spaces contain . . . . The local availability of material resources of special qualities, or even marginally lower costs, starts to be ever more important, as do local variations in market taste . . . " (Harvey 1989a: 294–5). That is to say, variations in place are themselves a condition of market growth. Market segmentation, like the division of labor, leads to transformed geographies, with specialized, "niche" markets growing up in particular locations, and with these locations in turn become a means to attract ever more capital investment. Places "sell" themselves (or parts of themselves) as a means of guaranteeing their own continuance (Kearns and Philo 1994). Savvy entrepreneurs, city managers, and development authorities, possess the relative "power" to alter spaces "in such a way as to make them more rather than less attractive to highly mobile capital" (Harvey 1989a: 295).

If that is the case, then the development of "identity politics" has served as an important means for situating places within the global economy, creating a sense of distinction and difference that sets this city apart from that one. This is so precisely because "identity" can itself be commodified. The rise of "lesbian chic" and "gay lifestyles," according to Peter Jackson (1995: 107), may simply "represent a cynical commodification of our current 'gender troubles,' making a fast buck from the ambiguities of our contemporary gender and sexual identities." The point is that the remarkable rise of gay and lesbian neighborhoods (see below), like the construction of a "gay world" in early twentieth-century New York, can be, and has been, enfolded into capital circulation and accumulation, becoming an important cultural "sphere" into which the logic of exchange-relations holds sway. For many purveyors and purchasers of chic sexual styles, "[t]heir interest in gender and sexuality is little more than shopping for style: aiming for an affluent, youthful market where transgressive sexualities and blurred gender identities are the latest fashion, a form of 'cultural clothing' that can be abandoned at the first sign of real gender trouble" (1995: 108).

There is an even more basic sense in which capitalism and sexuality intertwine. Normative heterosexuality, according to Larry Knopp (1992), is a productive relationship under capitalism. Terming the relationship between patriarchal capitalism and heterosexism "complex," Knopp (1992: 658) argues that the control of "sexual behavior [has been] a means of regulating fertility and, hence, a major facet of the reproduction of labor power. This is especially true if the individuals being controlled are women. Indeed heterosexism, like patriarchy, has everything to do with how the reproduction of labor power is organized under capitalism"[11] However, as Knopp continues, biological reproduction is only one facet of the reproduction of labor power. The other side is the day-in-day-out "reproductive" work in the household (cooking, cleaning, shopping, etc.) that makes it possible for a laborer to return to work day after day.[12] With the advent of industrialism, the domestic sphere was more clearly hived off from the sphere of waged work, the former "staffed almost exclusively by women," and the latter by men (1992: 658; see also Fishman 1987). Women's reproductive work in the household in essence subsidizes (largely) male waged work. The benefits to capitalism are obvious. But so too are there benefits to men: "Because women and women's workplaces (the home) now depended on male wages for their

11 Without denying their at least partial validity Michel Foucault (1978: 5–6) gently mocks such analyses of sexual control and capitalists' needs as overly functional.

12 The literature on the connection between "reproductive labor" and (so-called) "productive labor" under capitalism is extensive. For work by feminist geographers, especially that relating to women's work and the debates over how to theorize it, see Bondi and Peake (1988); McDowell (1983); Massey (1994: chapter 9); and Kobayashi (1994).

economic survival . . . the domestic sphere represented a significant new arena for the exercise of male workers' otherwise limited economic power. Men's control of space and their power over women thus became very intimately intertwined" (Knopp 1992: 658). Men had a vested interest, in other words, in maintaining a system wherein the home became the "site of unprecedented levels of exploitation" for women (1992: 658).

How does all this implicate capitalism in the perpetuation of normative hetero-sexuality? Among other ways, the uneven relationship between men and women, where one was a "bread winner" and the other an unwaged worker who subsidized that breadwinning, could not be easily replicated in either same-sex couples or in transitory sexual relations (either hetero- or homosexual). Two-women households lacked the economic advantage of a better-paid male worker. Two-male households lacked the advantage of a subordinated domestic partner – unless one of the men was willing to undermine normative notions of masculinity in order to serve his partner.

But there is a contradiction at the center of this "sex-gender system" (Rubin 1975). As Knopp (1992: 659) outlines, the creation of "separate spheres" for male and female labor created new forms of sexual subjectivity for men and women. For women, escape from domination meant escape from male domination and the con-struction of "relationships of cooperation with other women" centered on the "pri-macy of use-values over exchange values in the domestic sphere." Even so, "[w]omen's lack of economic power . . . and their role as uncompensated providers of sex, love, and domestic labor to men, prevented them (in most cases) from asserting complete independence from men." Hence, "lesbianism could only play a part in women supporting one another if it did not threaten the unequal power relationship between women and men" (1992: 659). For men, by contrast, whose lives centered on the daily selling of their own labor power, escape from domination implied the creation of "leisure" and personal free time – time bought with the wages they received from selling their labor at the workplace. Caught up so fully in relations of exchange, therefore, the "male definition of personal life turned sex (like nearly everything else) into something very close to a commodity. It was something to be objectified, traded for, and consumed" – and this certainly included homosexual relationships. Yet insofar as which gay relationships among men were possible, it was only, as noted above, if "one or both partners in a gay relationship den[ied] at least some aspect of traditional gender roles" (1992: 659). The upshot was *both* a demand, within capitalism, for gender and sexual conformity, *and* the development of spaces to explore other sexual options, as George Chauncy's *Gay New York* shows so well. As Knopp (1995: 155) concludes:

> As sexual experiences in particular became increasingly dissected, categorized and com-modified . . ., the possibility of new (but socially disruptive) sexual experiences being profitably produced also increased. The proliferation of commodified homosexual experience, for example, led to a homosexual *consciousness* among some people, and this was very threatening to the heterosexualized gender relations of the industrial city.

But so too was heterosexuality dissected and commodified at precisely this time: for the transformations in the city that allowed for (commodified) homosexual *identities* likewise allowed for (commodified) heterosexual identities. Sex and sexuality were indivisible from their (usually urban) markets. If the city provided a place for voyeurism, eroticism, and exhibitionism *because* it allowed a place for anonymity (the anonymity made possible by establishing relationships in terms of the anonymous exchange of the marketplace), then it did so for a range of sexualities and a range of sexual experimentation (even if these were always and everywhere the focus of intense contestation).[13]

Gay and Lesbian Neighborhoods as Spaces of Cultural Exploration and Politics

It is in this context that the development of contemporary gay and lesbian neighborhoods should be placed. But, as the preceding discussion makes plain, it should be kept in mind that the contradictions that arise from within the dialectic of capitalism and sexuality themselves provide a set of *opportunities* for capital and capitalists. "Culture" cannot be divorced from economics, politics, or any other "realm" of social life, and this is especially apparent in the rise of numerous postwar "gay ghettos" in the Americas, Europe, Australia, and New Zealand. Perhaps the most prominent of the postwar gay neighborhoods is San Francisco's Castro Street, where by the 1970s a remarkable politics collided with transformations in the commercial and industrial worlds to create a neighborhood important not only for its path-breaking organization of political power, but also for its exceptional urban vibrancy.

Gay neighborhoods: ghettos or liberated zones?

The Castro in the immediate pre-AIDS period was a fabulous place. For a relative of mine from Boston, it was something of a gay Utopia, a place of pilgrimage, and delight; for a high-school friend in the late 1970s, the Castro was everything our suburban Bay Area town was not: it was a place where he could lose himself so as (in the California words of the day) to find himself. Just living in the area of the Castro, where it appeared with great frequency on the local nightly news in all its splendor (and, following the assassination of gay city supervisor Harvey Milk and Mayor George Moscone, grief), gave my friend the courage to "come out" – not at all an easy task at our quite conservative high school. In both these cases, the Castro stood as a beacon, as a "shining city on a hill," as Frances FitzGerald (1986) put it – and not only for gay people either. While my experiences were different than my gay high-school friend, I remember looking to the Castro as a place of liberation, of political possibility. And I remember crying desperately when Harvey Milk was killed, tears that turned to rage when his murderer was let off lightly on a manslaughter charge: the Castro had become a place of possibility, a

---

13   This commodification of sexual experimentation, of course, is every bit as apparent in straight "red light districts" as it is in gay districts. On the importance of anonymity and the role of "strangers" in the construction of sexual identities, see Sennett (1994).

"liberated zone" not just for gay men, but for many others also who saw in the transformation of the Castro the beginnings of a transformation of society, even as the assassination of Milk suggested such a transformation would not come easy. The construction of a gay community, a "city within the city" as Manuel Castells (1983: 162) put it, showed among other things a new way of urban living: "it has shown the city the streets are for people, that urban culture means gathering together to play in public places, that music, politics and games can intertwine in a revitalizing way, creating new media for messages and establishing new networks of communication."

The clearest expression of this "new media" is really the quite old one of parading in the streets. The annual San Francisco Gay Freedom Day parade (held to commemorate the New York Stonewall Riots of June 27, 1969) draws as many as 300,000 participants and spectators. Hundreds of gays, lesbians, and their supporters parade through the streets of the financial district, down Market Street and through the Castro – in often outrageous costume, and as members of groups as diverse as Dykes on Bikes, the Gay Freedom Day Marching Band, and Parents and Friends of Lesbians and Gays – to both the cheers of the crowd and the derision of groups protesting the immorality of homosexuality. Since the early 1980s, this parade has been overlain by the specter of death by AIDS giving it an aura of both celebration and mourning, defiance and sorrow, but also giving the gay community an important foundation for an even more trenchant cultural politics than one founded solely on the apparent liberatory hedonism of sexual freedom (see below) (figure 7.3).[14]

Figure 7.3 ACT-UP (AIDS Coalition to Unleash Power) marches in the 1989 San Francisco Gay Freedom Day parade, adding a trenchant radical politics to the mix of hedonism and celebration that typically marks the day. Photograph by Rink Foto; used by permission.

14   A good description of the 1978 parade may be found in FitzGerald (1986), 25–36.

Even more carnivalesque than the Gay Freedom Day parade in San Francisco is Halloween. Centered not so much in the Castro, but in the older, partially queer neighborhood around Polk Street, Halloween has become an event quite like the carnivals discussed in the previous chapter: it functions as a time of reversal, when social conventions are flouted, when normal hierarchies are disrupted, and when people give themselves license to try on new identities, new personas. By the late 1970s, Halloween in San Francisco (and a number of other cities) had "become a major festival where straight and gay people share their fantasies of 'crossing over,' dressing as in a contest of imagination, aesthetics and humour, and parading along Polk and Castro streets in a night of joy, drinking, laughing and dancing in the streets under the outraged eyes of a nervous police force..." (Castells 1983: 162). Here politics, aesthetics, and outrageous humor, all become inseparable: and the mix is so powerful, in fact, that some communities have begun to eliminate just this carnival- esque aspect of Halloween and to "return" it to the children's holiday it is "sup- posed" to be.[15]

Gay Freedom Day parades and Halloween carnivals, for all their importance in displaying the power of the gay and lesbian community and for queering, at least for the moment, the hegemonically straight spaces of the city, are themselves fraught with deep internal political questions and schisms. In Montreal, for example, the Gay Pride parade had traditionally been confined to the city's gay neighborhood. In 1991, gay activists associated with Queer Nation and ACT-UP broke away from the main parade and marched through downtown. Their argument was that gay life was "ghettoized" and needed to be brought more fully into the everyday spaces of the city. In response, the organizers of the 1992 Pride parade established a set of ground rules for parade participants which outlawed cross-dressing, nudity, and eroticism (see Bell and Valentine 1995a: 14–16). The rationale was clear: the organizers of the parade felt that overly outrageous (or to some, offensive) displays would endanger whatever political gains gays and lesbians had made in Montreal and Canada, a real danger at a time of AIDS-induced backlashes against "deviance" throughout North America. The response by ACT-UP and Queer Nation activists, however, was simple defiance, taking to the streets in "irreverent combinations of identities... including fags posing as dykes, dykes dressed as clone fags, and bisexuals pretending to be fags pretending to be lipstick lesbians" (Namaste 1992: 9, quoted in Bell and Valentine 1995a: 15). For one activist, the contest was clearly over space. The rules established for the 1992 parade indicated that "drag queens are permitted in certain spaces among certain people, at certain times...." The "wrong" type of people in the "wrong" places at the "wrong" time threatened not just "straight" society (the hegemonic ideal of normative heterosexuality) but also "respectable," incremental political and cultural change in the gay community itself: "Clearly, the activist focus on the idea that drag is everywhere threatens precisely the borders and limits [of acceptability]" (Bell and Valentine 1995a: 15).

---

15 A case in point is Boulder, Colorado, where during the 1980s upwards of 20,000 people would converge on its gentrified pedestrian shopping district on Halloween night in an act of collective revelry. By the early 1990s city and county police, under the direction of the city council and local merchants, put an end to the carnival, establishing a set of roadblocks at the edge of town to keep revelers from Denver and area suburbs away.

These borders and boundaries are certainly social, but they are also geographical. Many in San Francisco referred to the Castro not as a "gay ghetto" but as a "liberated zone." Either name, however, indicates the degree to which gay social identity is wrapped up with control (and contest) over particular places. It is worth turning our attention for a moment to the construction of these places – and the importance for both maintaining and transcending these borders – so as to better see the relationship between place, sexuality, and cultural-political transformation.

How did San Francisco's Castro Street become a "mecca" for gay men (and to a lesser extent lesbians)? The origin stories usually begin with San Francisco's development as a frontier and sailing town – a city of men and very few women – in which tolerance of all manner of vices was a necessity. San Francisco has maintained and protected "tolerance" ever since. In reality, moral, often violently moral, crusades against all those who were different (Chinese, gays, blacks, Latinos, Beats, and so many others) were just as much a part of San Francisco's development as they were of other cities. As late as the early 1970s, police regularly raided gay bars and drag shows (FitzGerald 1986: 36–40). Even so, San Francisco's function as a port city, especially during World War II, coupled with its strong bohemian undercurrents, made the city more attractive to homosexuals than many other American cities and towns.

Gay-identified bars and clubs developed over time in several neighborhoods (figure 7.4). The Tenderloin, between the financial district and city hall, developed in the first half of the twentieth century as San Francisco's "skid row" – a place in which all

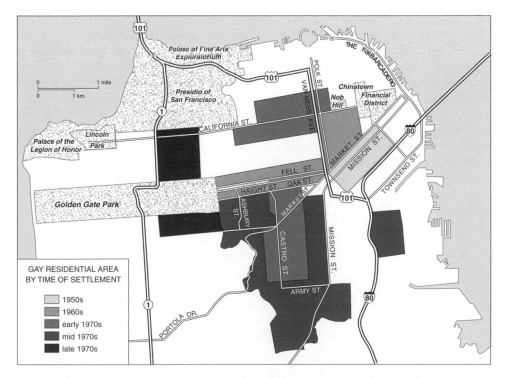

Figure 7.4 Gay neighborhoods in San Francisco. Map redrawn from Castells (1983).

manner of outcasts, deviants, and misfits gathered, and where informal "police zon-ing" tolerated otherwise intolerable sexual and social behavior (Castells 1983: 145)[16] By the 1950s, with the development of a gay night-club district in nearby Polk Street, the Tenderloin specialized in drag bars and the "rough trade." Polk Street developed as a tonier district, organized especially around the "effeminization" of gay men, many of whom worked in the service professions. For straight society, Polk Gulch (as *San Francisco Chronicle* columnist Herb Caen called it) was the place to find high-class, unthreatening, and often stereotype-confirming gay society displayed in public. By the 1970s, the fading, deindustrialized warehouse district South of Market street – now a prime site of gentrification, then not yet threatened by the wrecker's balls of urban "redevelopment" – became "the raw, as it were, to the cooked," refined Polk district (FitzGerald 1986: 33). South of Market (inevitably called SoMa when it became trendy) was a place where bathhouses specializing in casual and perhaps anonymous sex vied for space with leather bars, punk concert halls, and occasional up-market restaurants feeding off all the cultural ferment. In between the develop-ment of Polk Gulch and the South of Market area, the tourist sex-district of North Beach, home to the Beats in the 1950s, also became a center of gay nightlife.

For gay men in postwar San Francisco, bars and clubs "were the focal points of social life for gay people; and networks were constructed around these bars: a specific form of culture and ideology began to emerge"(Castells 1983: 141). Yet such net-works are quite different from a "gay ghetto" or a "liberated zone." Especially with repeated police raids of gay bars and clubs, such networks and relationships were often fleeting and unstable – and not particularly powerful. "There were networks, but no community-places, [and] no territory," according to Castells (1983: 154).[17] "The critical moment," in the creation of gay cultural and political power in San Francisco, therefore "was the transition from the bars to the streets, from nightlife to daytime, from 'sexual deviance' to an alternative lifestyle" (1983: 141).

Castro Street provided just such a territory. As late as 1970 the Castro was not identified as a gay neighborhood. It was still largely Irish-American, but out-migra-tion to the suburbs had been prominent since the end of World War II. Coupled with San Francisco's declining importance as a port and industrial zone, and its recom-position as a center for financial and other services, the Castro saw a long period of disinvestment and decline. But by 1978, the Castro had become a "neighborhood… like other [gentrified] neighborhoods except that on Saturdays and Sundays you could walk for blocks and see only young men dressed as it were for a hiking expedition" (FitzGerald 1986: 34). The Castro, vibrant at night to be sure, was also

16   On informal police zoning of skid rows around the country – and a call to return to such practices so as to spare "respectable" neighborhoods the spectacle of homelessness, public sexuality, and other "unwanted land uses" – see Ellickson (1996).

17   In this regard, it is worth considering again George Chauncy's (1994) discussion of the construction of a gay "world" in pre-World War II New York: To what degree did this "world" of bars, tearooms, YMCA dormitories, and flophouses constitute an effective *territory* in which gay men could forge their identities? To what degree did it impart to gay men the power to control their own destiny? For if exercising power is a function of controlling some space or place, then to what degree did this require full and *permanent* control over a space larger and more varied than furtive gay meeting places? Chauncy goes some way towards answering these questions in his discussion of the development of Greenwich Village in *Gay New York*.

very much a "daytime" place, which, despite the crowded lunchtime bars, the twenty-four hour cruising and the perhaps one hundred thousand gay tourists who came each summer, was a place in which people went about their ordinary lives: doing laundry, shopping for groceries, riding the bus to work, or going to the bank. And they did all this as fully "out," open, unabashed gay men.[18] Between 1970 and 1978 a complete transformation of the Castro district had been effected.

Many commentators trace the beginnings of the Castro as a gay neighborhood to the opening of Harvey Milk's camera shop on the street in 1972. While two gay bars connected to the nearby Haight-Ashbury hippy district preceded Milk to the Castro, Milk was a political dynamo who more than anyone else turned the Castro into the "liberated zone" it became by 1978 when he was assassinated.[19] For Milk, the Castro became a base for gay political power, certainly, but, at least in the early years it was also a base for a more general neighborhood politics. Milk's early campaigns, especially as he was constructing his political base, stressed neighborhood organizing (often against city hall), revitalization, and development. A populist, Milk sought support among the elderly, poor, and minorities who were increasingly squeezed out of affordable housing by downtown redevelopment and gentrification. Yet just the sorts of qualities that made the Castro desirable for these constituents – affordable housing, organized resistance to large-scale redevelopment – also made it attractive to more and more gay in-migrants, which in turn fueled runaway gentrification and speculation.

The cheap, relatively attractive, and sound housing of the Castro was as appealing to gay in-migrants – because of its potential for renovation or preservation – as was the prospect of an "out" lifestyle. Speculation and development was feverish in the early years of the 1970s. Business transactions on Castro Street increased by 700 percent between 1968 and 1978 according to some estimates (FitzGerald 1986: 46). Housing prices skyrocketed. Not only were long-time residents forced out of the neighborhood, but so too were many less well-off gays financially excluded. A further effect of the gentrification was a degree of "spill-over" into surrounding communities, creating tensions between gay gentrifiers and those pushed out or struggling to hang on in the face of rising rents and property taxes. For example tensions were apparent among both African Americans in the Hayes Valley on one side of the Castro, and along the Delores Street boundary of the largely Latino Mission district on the other (Castells 1983: 167).[20]

For Peter Jackson, this trajectory of gay neighborhood development implies a need for both gay activists and for social theorists to develop better links to other struggles for social justice. On the one hand, gay gentrification clearly displaces numerous poor, often minority, residents. On the other hand, many gay men and women are themselves poor, people of color, or otherwise subject to systematic oppression on grounds additional to their sexuality. These issues "demand to be taken seriously by the gay community if it is committed to repairing the range of social inequalities that

18   In the early years, the Castro was very much a men's place. By the mid-1980s, however, the gender composition had begun to change somewhat and more women, both gay and straight, were seen on the streets.

19   Milk's biography is Shilts (1982); see also the film, *The Life and Times of Harvey Milk.*

20   Lawrence Knopp has conducted a series of studies on "gay gentrification"; see Lauria and Knopp (1985); Knopp (1990a, 1990b).

characterize contemporary society, not just those that are defined in terms of sexuality" (Jackson 1989: 128).[21] For Knopp (1992: 665), the point is to understand how "gay identity and accumulation goals can intertwine." For him, the "irony ... is that the often place-based identities upon which ... struggles [over sexuality] are predicated owe their existence in large measure to the universality of exchange relations and the spatial dynamic of capitalism that results in the creative construction of new and subtly differentiated places" (1992: 666). In addition to the complicity the development of gay space may have with strategies of capital accumulation (and hence with the perpetuation of unjust social structures in other realms of life besides sexuality), gay space may prove a double-edged sword, as "the concentration of [sexual social] movements and subcultures in urban space has made it easier to both demonise and control them" (Knopp 1995: 149). By necessity, then, gay politics has to move from a focus on the production of a gay culture to a clear political movement. Not only in the pre-Stonewall era, but also in the current climate of a strong movement against sexual deviancy on the part of the religious and political right, gay territories "could not remain ... cultural, Utopian communit[ies]; either walls had to be elevated around the free city [i.e. the gay "liberated zones"] or the entire political system had to be reformed" (Castells 1983: 145). That is, gay sexual politics has to quite literally remake the contemporary landscape, molding it after an image of relative freedom – either that or it has to accept its ghettoization as the price of safety. This is exactly why gays in San Francisco and elsewhere have seen themselves not just at the forefront of expanding their *own* rights and carving out a space for their *own* lives, but of a societal transformation, emanating out of gay enclaves, but not confined to them, that queers not just the space of the city, but the politics of society too.

That, then, is the signal importance of events like Gay Pride marches, kiss-ins, and radical appropriations of "straight" space by queer activists associated with groups like ACT-UP and the Lesbian Avengers. The very goal of radical, dissident sexual social movements such as these is the production of transformed spaces, and hence transformed social and cultural relations. But so too is this the result of the inexorable growth of gay enclaves and neighborhoods around the world. And *that* is why the backlash – in places like Colorado, in laws like Article 28, and in debates over the advisability of gay marriage – has been so virulent. If sex is cultural, then sex wars are cultural wars – both wars of attrition and wars over space.

Lesbian territoriality

Many analysts of gay neighborhood development have written explicitly about gay *male* neighborhoods, arguing that lesbians, presumably like women generally, do not

21 Andrew Kirby (1993: 75) disagrees, arguing that "it is both naive and presumptuous to argue that a collective defined in terms of sexual orientation should act monolithically to accept a 'map of meaning' defined by those with a different political agenda, such as concern for neighborhood displacement." Apparently, for Kirby, sexuality should be completely cordoned off from other aspects of social life. Kirby suggests that while strategic alliances with other political movements might be a good idea, it makes no sense to build extra-sexual concerns into a movement based on contesting societal sexual norms. This, rather than Jackson's, is the position that seems naive, as Larry Knopp's work makes plain.

really control space, do not really engage in territoriality in the same manner as men. In a rather essentialist manner, Manuel Castells (1983: 140), for example, has argued that since, "on the whole they are poorer than gay men and have less choice in terms of work and location," lesbians "tend not to concentrate in a given territory" or "acquire a geographical base for their political organization." Instead, they tend to establish "social and interpersonal networks" designed to further "their own rich, inner world" – networks that are aspatial in that they do not clearly trace well-defined territories. Gender, rather than sexuality, is the key variable in structuring gay women's lives. In her analysis of the Castro, Frances FitzGerald (1986: 56–7) makes much the same claim: "While gay men built businesses, gay women built communes – both literally and figuratively speaking.... Liberated gay women, in other words, turned out to be archetypically women, and gay men in the Castro turned archetypically men – as if somehow their genders had been squared by isolation from the other sex."

FitzGerald's point was in part that gay men and women had grown apart in the early years of the Castro (though they seemed to be coming back into spatial contact by the early 1980s, especially in response to the AIDS crisis), and there is certainly a great deal of validity to the argument that gender is of great importance in understanding differences between gay male and lesbian spaces. As numerous studies have shown, for instance, women's use of public space is highly curtailed by the very real fear of violence, and by the long history of women's ideological exclusion from the public sphere itself. When women do appear in public they are often politically invisible (E. Wilson 1991; Marston 1990; on violence against women in public space see Pain 1991; Valentine 1989). And as we saw, what made neighborhoods like the Castro so politically important was precisely gays' ability to occupy public space and make their presence *visible*. Even so, a number of studies have recently given the lie to the assumption that lesbians are not "territorial," that lesbian neighborhoods do not exist in any coherent spatial sense.

One such neighborhood is the Park Slope area of Brooklyn, New York. While there is certainly a set of lesbian styles or "codes" that announces their presence in public space (Bell et al. 1994), it is largely "word-of-mouth" that "lures women to a 'lesbian neighbourhood'" (Rothenberg 1995: 169). "When I first moved here five or six years ago," one Park Slope resident has recalled, "I couldn't walk down the street without saying 'she's gay,' 'she's gay'" (1995: 169). Tamar Rothenberg found in her study of the neighborhood that Park Slope was largely a *residential* rather than a *commercial* or *institutional* community of gay women. Park Slope was described by many of Rothenberg's (1995: 172–3) informants as "an area where lesbians live," but there seemed to be a fairly weak sense of an "organized community," despite a handful of social organizations and newsletters. There were few lesbian-identified cafes, bars, bookstores, or community centers. Manhattan remained the center of gay social life for most lesbians. Like their male counterparts, however, many lesbians were engaged in the gentrification process, a process that has pushed the gentrification frontier into surrounding neighborhoods, such as Windsor Terrace and Prospect Heights, leaving displaced residents – gay and straight alike – in its wake. "As Park Slope gentrifies, the physical community expands," according to one resident. But many "[w]omen are being outpriced by rent increases.... We're the ones who lead gentrification, without even knowing it" (1995: 178). Despite the negative effects (for some) of lesbian-led gentrification, and despite the relative lack of lesbian commercial and institutional ventures, Park Slope has become, for lesbians, something akin to gay male districts like Manhattan's Greenwich Village or San Francisco's Castro: "Being a dyke and living in the Slope is like being a gay man and living in the Village; it's part of the coming out process" (quoted in Rothenberg 1995: 179).

Gill Valentine (1995; see also Peake 1993; Valentine 1993) found a similar sense of lesbian residential territoriality in her studies of a smallish unnamed city in central England, but here there exists "an invisible ghetto." In this town, there "are no public expressions of lesbian sexualities; no mark on the landscape that 'lesbians live here.' It is a lesbian space only to those in the know" (Valentine 1995: 99). The lesbian neighborhood, then, is surreptitious, where once again word-of-mouth seems to be the important factor in attracting newcomers – newcomers who stay, perhaps, because despite its "invisibility" it functions *as* community: "it feels very much like a community," one of Valentine's (1995: 97) informants remarked, "because there are so many dykes around here. It's nice to be able to walk round to people's houses and feel there are quite a few of them in a small area." There is an "institutional base" for this community, but Valentine (1995: 102) notes that it is insecure and peripatetic. For the most part, particular venues are hired for specific events – parties, dinners, and the like. In addition, various support groups have been established, but each tends to reflect "the fragmented nature of 'the scene' " rather than integrate it.

The upshot of this surreptitious, fragmented spatiality is the creation of a set of what Valentine (1995: 97) describes as "lesbian spaces . . . produced or claimed through collective imaginings and sometimes fantasies focused on social networks, individual celebrities and specific sites." Such a rendering would seem to confirm Castells' and FitzGerald's point: that gay men claim visibility in public space, while gay women seek to minimize that visibility. But as Ann Forsyth shows, that need not be the case. The semi-rural region around Northampton, Massachusetts, has become somewhat famous as a "lesbian mecca." "Country music fans gravitate to the Grand Ole Opry," intoned *Newsweek* in 1993, "painters dream of Provence and ski bums settle in Aspen. Lesbians have a mecca, too. It's Northampton, Mass. a.k.a. Lesbian-ville, U.S.A." (Kantrowitz and Senna 1993, quoted in Forsyth 1997). Northampton is a "visibly lesbian space," marked by an annual Lesbian festival, a lesbian and gay business guild, a lesbian archive, lesbian galleries and exhibits, same-sex wedding and birth announcements in the local paper, and a worldwide web page (Forsyth 1997: 39). "The population may not have large amounts of political and economic power, but it is hardly underground," Forsyth concludes (1997: 42).[22] Forsyth describes a vibrant community of lesbians (and to a lesser extent gay men) throughout the Connecticut River Valley region of western Massachusetts that by the 1990s was serving as a magnet to gay in-migrants. There is a concentrated core of lesbian businesses in downtown Northampton and frequent gay and lesbian activities at

---

22   Forsyth implies in her article that the "invisibility" of lesbian neighborhoods may itself be as much an artifact of research methods as of lesbian desires or political disempowerment. She relates how reviewers of her paper thought it unethical that she explore the public face of lesbianism, or name names of activists, even though those same activists readily appear in the local and national media, produce newsletters and newspapers for public – not just lesbian – consumption, and are themselves quite open and visible in their actions. "[T]o try to hide a very public population, that has sought out publicity, can in fact be interpreted as implying that lesbians and gays *should* be hidden."

nearby colleges and universities. The region also possesses a set of "comfortable public spaces" in which lesbians can be "out" in public – holding hands, sitting intimately together, and so forth (Forsyth 1997: 46). In short, in both Park Slope and Northampton, spaces quite analogous to the Castro or Greenwich Village have been carved out of larger hegemonically heterosexual spaces, giving the lie at least partially to the sense that gay women, unlike gay men, do not produce and control spaces conducive to their own sexual identities.

Sexual Politics

Even so, such spaces are not utopias, and even if they were, they represent such small fractions of global space that both their impact on society as a whole and their longevity might be quite tenuous. In the first place, as Wayne Myslik (1996) argues, one of the ironies attendant on the construction of gay and lesbian neighborhoods has been that those very neighborhoods become the primary site for anti-gay violence. Second, and following from the first point, such neighborhoods must constantly be protected and maintained, against threats of anti-gay violence, to be sure, but also against transformations in the urban land market that might make many residents of gay neighborhoods vulnerable to dislocation. And finally, activists must guard against homophilic sexual politics becoming ghettoized – they must seek to expand their activism outwards to engage other aspects of social life and other places, too.

In Boston, for example, gay, lesbian, and bisexual Irish Americans sought permission to march as part of the annual St. Patrick's Day parade in conservative South Boston in 1992.[23] The struggle to gain admission to the parade was carried out in the media and the courts, with the Gay and Lesbian Irish Group of Boston (GLIB) eventually winning admittance to the parade. GLIB was greeted by jeers and threats by the largely Irish American audience. The crowd held signs declaring that "God Will Punish Perverts," "God Said Kill Fags," and "What's Next 'Rights' for Child Molesters?" (figure 7.5). While gay activists saw the Boston March as producing a "radical impact" on the "cultural meaning" of the parade, it was clear that many Irish Americans saw gays' participation as a threat not only to their sexuality, but to their ethnic identity as well (Davis 1995). One of the parade organizers argued that "[t]his is geography. This is coming into South Boston for the sole purpose of disrupting us.... This is not a sincere movement" (Davis 1995: 301). And a conservative city councillor urged "the gay, lesbian and bisexual group of trouble makers who hate the Catholic Church and its teachings...[to] raise their own money, organize their own parade, and apply for a permit to march in downtown Boston to express their sexuality" (quoted in Davis 1995: 301). In other words, organizers of the St. Patrick's Day parade and its supporters sought to police the boundaries of acceptable sexuality in certain places, maintaining that an aggressive heterosexuality had a prior claim to the streets of South Boston, and asserting that GLIB had no right to these spaces, even if they might just have the right to be elsewhere. Ethnicity, religion, and sexuality all had their places, organizers seemed to be saying, and to

23   In this they followed the lead of the New York Irish Lesbian and Gay Organization, which sought in 1991 to march in that city's parade.

Figure 7.5 Protesters at the 1992 Boston St. Patrick's Day parade. Photograph by Peter Erbland; used by permission.

disrupt or transgress the established order was simply out of the question (see Cresswell 1996). The point for GLIB was just the opposite: "What was really wild about South Boston was that we really didn't need to carry any signs. We didn't need to do shit. Just being there was being in their face" (quoted in Davis 1995: 301).

That "in your faceness" seems to have been at least somewhat successful. Davis (1995: 302) notes that by 1993, GLIB's inclusion in the parade was met "by fewer jeers, fewer projectiles and more cheers and waves from apartment windows and the crowds along the streets." Even more importantly, this confrontation and others like it in other cities have led many "to re-define what it means to be Irish in America . . . [to] re-examine the Irish past and [to] rediscover a history of tolerance and inclusion" (1995: 302). Transgression of normative spaces, then, and the politics of sexuality that necessarily goes with such a transgression, can have profound impacts (even if these impacts are always partial and tenuous).

The politics of AIDS: grief, anger, memory

Such an understanding of the inseparability of spatial and sexual politics is precisely what guides radical gay and lesbian groups like ACT-UP, Queer Nation, and the Lesbian Avengers. It is also responsible for the often outrageous, celebratory, and spectacular nature of much gay activism. Yet there is an edge to the carnivalesque, which after all is also often closely associated, in time and space, with the masque of death. For gay activists, the spectacle of sexual politics cannot be divorced from the specter of AIDS.

The politics of AIDS, as it has intersected with the politics of sexuality, has radically transformed gay politics as a whole – but so too is it indicative of changes throughout the polity, as Michael Brown (1997) has made clear with his examination of the connections between AIDS politics and radical citizenship. While this trans-formation is evident throughout the varying networks of AIDS activism – from health activists, to promoters of needle exchange, to hospices – it is perhaps most succinctly crystallized in the form of the NAMES Project Memorial Quilts, a now multinational project to commemorate the names and lives of those killed by the disease. In October 1996, the United States Quilt was displayed in its entirety for perhaps the last time – on the Mall in Washington DC, the "nation's front yard," as the *New York Times* (1996) put it (figure 7.6). As many as three-quarters of a million people came to see the more than 37,000 panels of the Quilt. In conjunction with this showing were numerous candlelight vigils, the national convention of the Parents and Friends of Lesbians and Gays, and a meeting of the Latino/Latina Lesbian and Gay organization. The Quilt itself is a moving memorial. Friends and families construct panels, often including memorabilia and photographs from the lives of the now-dead. Perhaps most affecting is the sheer number and diversity of people killed by AIDS, coupled with the incredibly personalized nature of this public display of grief and celebration.

Figure 7.6   The AIDS Memorial Quilt being laid out on the Washington Mall (October 11, 1996). Perhaps three-quarters of a million people came to wander among the 37,000 panels of the quilt. Photograph by Ron Edmonds/Associated Press; used by permission.

But what exactly does the Quilt do, and in what ways is it political and transgressive? Among other things, the Quilt makes public, normalizes, and universalizes the
grief and mourning attendant on the AIDS crisis. It is a monument to memory, but it
is a monument designed to show victims of AIDS as more than just victims: they are
friends, lovers, and community members, sometimes prominent and well-known,
sometimes relatively obscure. People memorialized in the Quilt are made unremarkable; they are made just like you and me. Yet they are also in every way quite
remarkable; they are sometimes outrageous, full of camp and kitsch, sometimes
quiet and closeted, sometimes well known in localities or the nation, often anonymous to all but a few close friends.

Many activists find the Quilt to be at best a diversion from the necessarily con-
frontational politics necessitated by AIDS and homophobia. Yet, as Brown (1997:
161–4) shows, the Quilt is itself a strong statement of cultural politics because it
makes public what is usually thought of as private: grief and mourning. In fact, it
makes such grief and mourning something of a public spectacle, bringing them out of
the dark recesses of the private and into the glare of the public. In this regard the
AIDS politics manifested in the Quilt are like sexual politics more generally: they seek
to transgress and transform the boundaries between public and private so as to more
radically transform the conditions under which not just gay men and women, but
everyone else, lives their lives.

Such political gestures begin first with decisions over where to display the Quilt.
The display on the Washington Mall was hardly neutral: this is the site, after all, of
the most significant political demonstrations in the country, the place where Martin
Luther King called together more than a quarter-million people for a massive
demonstration for Civil Rights in August 1963 (the largest political rally to that
point), and the location of numerous demonstrations and rallies since.[24] In Vancouver, British Columbia, the Canadian NAMES Quilt was displayed in May, 1993,
before several thousand visitors at the British Columbia Enterprise Hall, built by the
conservative Social Credit government for the 1986 World Expo. Indeed, it was
precisely the "arch conservative political culture" embodied in Enterprise Hall that
led NAMES organizers to choose it as the venue for the Vancouver display. The
antipathy many in the gay community felt for the Social Credit government and its
policies towards gays and AIDS more generally, "took the form of spatial appropriation" – precisely the sort of *détournement* advocated by the Situationist International (see chapter 6). "Because of its association with the Social Credit party, the
venue . . . resonate[d] within the gay community. . . . It was not merely gay appropriation of a public space, but of a site that signified homophobic and neoconservative
cultural politics in British Columbia during the early years of the AIDS crisis"
(Brown 1997: 166–7).

Such a *détournement* of cultural spaces, cultural memory, and cultural politics is
precisely why the Quilt is such an effective site of politics. "Cultural memory

---

24 Recently, for example, both the predominantly African American "Million-Man March," and the
predominantly white "Promise Keepers" brought hundreds of thousands of men to the Mall to publicly
profess their "atonement" in the eyes of the nation and of God. Since neither event was ever very clear as to
precisely what was being atoned for, nor what *these* particular men were guilty of, these were political
statements of an order quite different than the rallies against the Vietnam War, or in favor of a woman's
right to abortion, to say nothing of their differences with an event like the Quilt display.

generated by this memorial to a controversial epidemic can be seen as inherently political," according to Marilyn Sturken (1992, quoted in Brown 1997: 163–4):

> it defiantly marks the human toll of the epidemic and says: We must mourn these lives lost, challenge the homophobia that worsens the AIDS epidemic, and fight the policies that make prevention and treatment so difficult. Yet cultural memory is by no means a simple, liberatory act of negating official history or creating a "united front." The AIDS quilt is the locus of a clash of identity politics, where issues of race, gender, sexuality, and class are in conflict. The cultural memory generated by the quilt is often subsumed into historical and national narratives, and becomes part of the controversial marketing of the quilt. The quilt raises fundamental issues around the politics of public commemoration, such as for whom memorials are created and to whom they belong, and how a memorial defines who is forgotten.

The cultural politics of the Quilt – like the cultural politics of sexuality – is therefore quite complex. What is certain, however, is that it is inseparable from the geographies it both creates and contests, just like the politics of sex more generally.

In pre-World War II New York, a "gay world" was created out of the intersecting politics and economic realities of working-class urban life, middle-class reform, the development of mass entertainment and media, and the struggles of gay men and women to find a place for themselves in the city. Contemporary gay worlds, though perhaps different in their contours from the "Gay New York" of the past, are made through quite similar processes. Transgression, experimentation, the dead weight of hegemonic norms (and their continual reinforcement), the unexpected eruption of disease – all these come together to create not just *a* gay world, but many intersecting gay *worlds*. But so too do they also construct the "straight" world, even if such constructions seem perversely invisible.

Conclusion: Sexual Worlds

The politics of sexuality cannot, as we have seen, be divided from other political, economic, and social currents of the day. Sexuality both exists in and is contradictory to the demands made by capitalist social relations on family, community, and individual. Like gender, race, and nationality (to which we turn in the next three chapters) the politics of sexuality should not be studied as if they were somehow separate from political economic structures – as both Lawrence Knopp's and George Chauncy's work shows so well. But neither should they be reduced to these relationships of political economy. Rather, the whole point of trying to understand any aspect of identity as socially constructed is precisely to see just how complex matters are. Understanding identities – sexual, racial, or gendered – as socially constructed also demands that we understand the spaces in and through which such identities are performed – and how, in turn, the performance of identities, circumscribed as such performaces must be by so many social forces, are themselves productive of certain space, geographies, or "worlds."

That is why each argument that I have made in this chapter has been presented through specific examples. To understand the *general* forces at work in structuring sexuality, it is essential to understand the specific instances in which sexuality is constructed, performed, and reproduced. George Chauncy's *Gay New York* is only the most exemplary instance of how the general (large categories like "gay" and "straight," the slow process of revaluing sexual difference in new ways, etc.) and the specific (the actions of particular men, the role of morality reformers in New York, etc.) come together to create the "world" in which we live. The specific events in New York before World War II, in the Castro in the 1970s, or in the Connecticut River Valley in the 1990s radiate in space and in time to transform not only how we think about such things as sexuality, but how we act it out too. Being gay or straight or anything else is a different thing at the end of the 1900s than it was at the beginning. That much is obvious.

What has been less well recognized, by scholars as well as everyday folks, is the degree to which such changes are both dependent upon and a continual force of change in the "worlds" in which we live – in the very nature of the public and private spaces that provide the stage for our lives. I have tried to point in this chapter to some of the forms that the spatial politics of sexuality takes. What should have been apparent throughout this chapter is that sexual worlds cannot be divorced from structures and politics of gender. The next chapter, therefore, turns to an explicit consideration of gender.

8

Feminism and Cultural Change: Geographies of Gender

In the preceding chapters, I have stressed through examples and historical explanation how the tools and concepts developed and deployed in cultural geography help us to understand the relationship between political movements, societal changes, political economic structures, and the production of "culture." I have also tried to make it clear that social change and political action drive intellectual development. Such has particularly been the case in feminist theorizing in general and feminist approaches to geography in particular. As Mona Domosh (1996a: 411) remarks, "feminism was not a mode of analysis borrowed from some other social science where its implications had already been thought through; rather, it developed out of the direct political imperatives of the women's liberation movement of the 1960s, a movement that based its politics on personal experiences." That politics, of course, arose out of very specific cultural, economic and political contexts – out of a congruence of political forces that conspired to transform not only the ways we understand women and their place in society, but also femininity and masculinity and the nature of politics and political change. The eruption of what is sometimes called "third-wave" feminism in the late 1950s and 1960s, launched a series of cultural skirmishes and battles that are still being fought in the media, legislative bodies, streets, and villages around the world.[1]

1   The history of feminism in the USA is often divided into three periods: the agitation of the 1840s that eventually resulted in the signing of the "Declaration of Sentiments" at Seneca Falls, New York, in 1848

As I drafted the preceding paragraph, for example, I was listening to an installment in a long-running series of reports on National Public Radio (a non-commercial American radio network dedicated to news and cultural programming) about the struggles – in the household, in wider society, and in the minds and hearts of women (and men) – over the "appropriate" role in society for women of childbearing age. Are working outside the home and motherhood incompatible, these reports ask over and over again. Or is there some "happy compromise" between the demands of motherhood and women's desire for the fulfillment, independence, and security that paid work and career development bring? This debate, like the others that have come before it, is depressing in its refusal to question the societal structures that put *women* in the position of always having to make such choices, while allowing men much greater degrees of freedom in pursuing intellectual and professional development.[2] There is rarely any question as to whether fatherhood and career ambition are compatible. It is particularly depressing that such debates carry such force a full 30 years after women took to the streets – and worked at home – to demand equality in matters political, familial, and social. But it is nonetheless indicative of the ferocity with which the culture wars over gender have been conducted in recent years. That a discussion of whether women are "natural" homemakers is even on the table is clear testimony to the effectiveness of the "backlash" against feminism that has gained ground over the past several years in the United States and other industrialized countries (Faludi 1992). Such a backlash, in turn, was only made possible by the even clearer gains made by feminism in the postwar era – the sorts of gains which, as Domosh indicates, led to transformations throughout society, including, of course, the way various academic disciplines understood their objects of study. This is certainly the case in cultural geography. In this chapter we will explore these changes in society and academic practice both to see the relationships between them, and to come to a fuller understanding of what a feminist cultural geography is – or could be.

In chapter 5 we saw the ways in which the creation of a suburban landscape was bound up in – and reinforced – the transformation of women's roles in industrializing society. In chapter 7, that issue was again raised as we discussed the intersection of sexuality and industrial capitalism. In both instances, women were shown to be at least partially "sequestered" in and behind certain kinds of spaces, not as some part of a grand conspiracy, but as the outcome of all manner of social decisions made by all manner of collective and individual actors. A set of social-geographic *structures* were thus created which had, and have, the effect of both reproducing and reinforcing

---

(the Declaration called for equal rights for women); the birth-control and women's vote movements of the turn of the century (a movement with its roots in the earlier wave of feminism, and which eventually resulted in the enshrinement of women's right to vote in the Constitution); and the (global) feminist movement that began in the 1950s, intensified in the 1970s, and which today is still working itself out in social policies and practices. Some commentators have argued that the "third wave" has ended and we have now entered into a "postfeminist" phase of history since, they argue, women are now equal and the "need" for feminism no longer exists. Such a reading of contemporary history requires one to believe that, in the "developed" world at least, women are both formally equal to men and treated as equal in practice, a belief that is delusional at best.

2   They are also depressing in the degree to which questions of class and race are rendered invisible in the discourse about "proper" roles of women.

certain cultural norms, societal forms, and spatial realities. The maintenance of these structures then becomes a goal of those they benefit, who often want them to be understood not as *social* structures, but as *natural* orders. Yet, as we have also seen throughout this book, simply because a set of social structures are reproduced, that does not make them invulnerable to change. Instead, movements of resistance, well-organized or chaotic, collective or fragmentary, tend to arise to combat and under-mine these structures – and the people who benefit from them. When "situations" become unbearably taken-for-granted, then people often take it upon themselves to find ways to upset the *status quo*. This is a dynamic process, so any movement of resistance is likely to call up its own opposition, an opposition bent on reinforcing precisely the *status quo* that is under contention, hence the severe "backlash" to feminism. The result of this *danse macabre* between contending forces is sometimes the radical transformation of society, sometimes the squashing of resistance, and usually simply the ponderous, incremental change by which social formations evolve. If the women's movement of the 1960s and 1970s threw into question the role that women were to play in industrial and postindustrial society, then the sort of backlash that developed in the 1980s and 1990s sought to reinforce what has come to be known as "traditional" female roles, and traditional "family values." Hence all the fretting in the media as to whether women are at all capable of working both inside and outside the home – and over who wins and who loses if they choose to do so.

This chapter explores the geographic politics that lie behind these culture wars in the sphere of gender, and it seeks to show how these politics have structured the agenda of feminist geography. The chapter focuses on three primary and interrelated concerns. One is an exploration of the constant formation and transformation of the boundary between public and private space. The second is a reconsideration of "space" itself. And the third is a reformulation of how we think about gender. I draw on each of these reformulations in the last part of the chapter to explore what a feminist analysis of "landscape" could be. As we will see, any feminist analysis will always be contested, not only from those opposed to feminism, but from within feminism itself. That being the case, I present two contrasting feminist analyses of the politics of landscape representation. The main point of the chapter, therefore, is to build on the ideas about the performance of identity and the spatiality of resistance outlined in the previous two chapters to show not only how "gender" is produced and reproduced through particular spatial configurations, but also how, like sexuality, gender and gender politics are themselves productive of the spaces – or "worlds" – in which we live. Finally, and as with the other chapters of this Part, the analysis will show that the important questions for cultural geography remain ones of context; they remain questions about the conditions (geographic, social, political, economic) under which "culture" – in this case the "culture" of gender – is produced.

Public and Private: Gendered Divisions of Space

The opening paragraphs of this chapter perhaps render understandable one of the great culture *non*-wars of the late 1990s. In October, 1997, several hundred thousand men, organized by the Colorado-based religious group, the Promise Keepers,

Figure 8.1 Some of the hundreds of thousands of men gathered on the Mall in Washington, DC, reaffirming their commitment to their families as part of the massive Promise Keepers rally in October 1997. Photograph by Associated Press/Greg Gibson; used by permission.

gathered on the Washington Mall to publicly reaffirm their "commitment to their wives and family" (figure 8.1). Founded by Bill McCartny while he was still coach of the University of Colorado football team, the Promise Keepers during the previous five years had filled sports stadiums in cities around the USA with men gathered for highly successful pep-rallies-cum-revival-meetings. It had also organized countless hundreds of men's study and counseling groups around the country. For several years, the Promise Keepers had been tapping into the networks of religious activists organized through the various fundamentalist churches and institutions. In doing so, "PK" (as its adherents call it) had gained access to an already organized "audience" (see chapter 3) for its message and had activated that audience as a means for reconfiguring public debates about gender and family in America. In Colorado itself, McCartny and the Promise Keepers had long been controversial not only for their message – that men needed to recommit themselves to their families by reasserting their "leadership" over moral, religious, and economic matters, and that women should necessarily surrender "leadership" to their husbands – but also for their links to solid institutions of the political religious right such as Focus on the Family and for McCartny's outspoken support for anti-gay and anti-abortion movements.

The October rally in Washington, however, was almost uniformly portrayed in the national media as a fully "non-political" event, one in which good, dedicated men were gathering to profess their faith in God and their desire to be good husbands and fathers. The "non-political" label was taken at face value by much of the media despite the Promise Keepers' public pronouncements that the goal of the rally was to "take back our country for Christ" and that the organization was beginning to plan for rallies on the steps of every statehouse in the country on January 1, 2000. Still, the *New York Times* could report that the men at the Washington rally "tend to steer away from political issues; instead they talk about 'relationships' and that is where the Promise Keepers will try to make their mark" (Goodstein 1997a). These relationships are defined in a very particular way. According to one rally-goer, the Promise Keepers loved everyone – even Jews, just "as long as they were Christians" (quoted in Goodman 1997a). And as for the professed goal of the rally, men recommitting themselves to their families, that too was defined in a peculiar and pointed way. According to Tony Evans, long affiliated with the Promise Keepers, men should not "ask for your role [as leader of the family] back, I'm urging you to take it back. Treat the lady gently and lovingly, but lead" (quoted in Goodstein 1997b).

Leaving aside the highly constricted definition of "politics" at work in the national coverage (see chapter 6), and also leaving aside for the moment the fascinating construction of masculinity the Promise Keepers relies on, what is *also* apparent in Promise Keepers' success and the concomitant lack of critical attention in the mainstream media is the degree to which gendered divisions within families and within society at large are simply taken for granted (and actively reinforced) by many, many people. "Men and women have never been anything less than equal in God's eyes," one woman PK supporter argued in the *Hartford Courant*, "and God knew what He was doing when He set up the model for marriage with a loving and caring man at its head and a wife who is his partner and helpmate. Real women are not threatened by this model, but freed and empowered to fully develop all their womanly potential" (Solimene 1997). The important point for us, however, is that such taken-for-granted assumptions about the naturalness of gender divisions are themselves both reflected in and reinforced by gendered divisions of space – divisions of space that remained quite invisible in all the coverage of the Promise Keepers' rally or in the ongoing stories on National Public Radio about working women and the family.

Gendered spaces have been a key theme of feminist geography since the 1970s, a decade that saw a flourishing of research on the geographical and architectural reinforcement of traditional gender roles.[3] This research developed out of women researchers' own engagement with the questioning of gender roles associated with the rise of the women's liberation movement of the 1950s and 1960s.[4] It was also the result of the maturation of the huge postwar suburban expansion, a boom based on the "historical aberration" of the one (male) earner nuclear family as the predominant family type (as the architecture critic for the *New York Times* puts it: Muschamp 1997). That is to say, the suburban boom created massive tracts of housing, in Europe and Australia as well as North America, designed precisely to enshrine the "wife and mother" both in the house and as the chief provider of purposely privatized "services" (such as transportation, family shopping, community building, etc.). Indeed,

---

3   A good introduction to the literature is Werkele et al. (1980).
4   For a quite telling personal recollection of how women's awareness of the oppressive nature of suburban and urban space led to new research on the relationship between space and gender roles, see Abu-Loghod (1974). The classic account of women's sequestration in suburban domestic architecture is, of course, Friedan (1963).

the religion writer for the *Atlanta Journal and Constitution*, seeking to show how much one wife of a Promise Keeper has changed since her days as a National Organization of Women activist, sets the scene as follows:

> In her 20s in Boston, Jean Stinebaugh was a NOW woman. She went to meetings of the National Organization for Women and strongly advocated equal rights, equal pay and free expresssion for women. At 47, Stinebaugh is a Promise Keeper's wife. She has daughters 18 and 10 and lives in a traditional red brick two-story house in Alpharetta with fresh flowers on the table, family pictures on the wall and a porch overlooking a back yard where birds sing.   (White 1997)

The suburban landscape is the perfect metaphor, it seems, for the sort of family structure the Promise Keepers advocates. And it is the polar opposite of what a "NOW woman" would presumably want.

Architecture and gender roles

What then is the relationship between women's desires, women's lives, and architectural form? Much of the research on the relationship between women's desires and changing societal roles and architectural and urban form has been historic in nature, seeking to understand how differentiated male and female roles were incorporated into and reproduced by changing architecture and urban design. Some research, however, has looked at the contemporary effects of spaces like suburbia on job opportunities, women's (and girls') self-fulfillment, and range of life-opportunities. It is worth looking at each type of research in turn, because together they have led to yet another important focus of feminist geographical work – explorations not of gender roles, but of the very constitution of genders themselves.

As we have already seen (chapter 5), the "sequestering" of women in the home was itself a product of changing ideologies of domesticity associated with the rise of the bourgeoisie – ideologies that some have called the "cult of domesticity" or the "cult of true womanhood" (Lerner 1980; Welter 1966). So hard were these ideologies pushed, and so entrenched did they become, at least among those with access to the bourgeois media, that by the end of the nineteenth century, in such purveyors of taste and proper behavior as women's magazines, "there was no accepted role for women outside this model, and consequently there was no dwelling type based on other roles. Even historians and social scientists of the time insisted that the nuclear family had always existed, everywhere the God-given state for human beings" (Rock et al. 1980: 87, citing Westermarch 1889). Books of architectural drawings, along with illustrations in turn-of-the century magazines, worked hard to shape domestic space to reflect and reinforce this ideal. There were then, just as there are now, dissenting voices; but these voices, while arguing for radical changes in domestic architecture to accommodate the *needs* rather than the putative *roles* of women, nonetheless did not usually "conceive of domestic problems in a way that took full account of the larger economic and political issues underlying them" (Rock et al. 1980: 88).

These "economic and political issues," as Linda McDowell (1983: 62) has made clear, are often rooted in class. The very ideal of domesticity, she argues, glosses over the fact that in Britain, for example, "almost a third of all women... have been in paid employment since 1881." To the degree that the domestic ideal for the middle class may have implied a more leisurely existence, it is only because such women have "depended on the labour of [their] working-class sisters." For McDowell (1983: 62), then, the focus should be on the *changing* relationship between "patriarchy and the organisation of domestic labour," which would lead to "questions about why and which areas of reproduction became socialised and which became privatised...." It would also demand "a more satisfactory focus than the over simple dichotomy between the public and private sectors, work and home, that is common in much feminist urban analysis." In other words, McDowell (1983; see also Brownill 1984) sought to shift the debate from one about domestic *ideals* to one about the lived relations of women's lives – lives made complex by the fact that, all ideology of the home as retreat from the demands of the workaday world aside, "production and reproduction [are] *part of a single process*" under capitalism.

This issue of "reproduction" is crucial. But "reproduction" itself carries many meanings, ranging from biological reproduction to the reproduction of labor power, to the social reproduction of the social conditions of "immediate life" (as Engels put it). The key point is that these three spheres or realms of reproduction are intimately connected. Indeed, at one level they cannot be divorced from each other: the conditions of biological reproduction are dependent on the reproduction of everyday life, and under capitalism, at least, the reproduction of everyday life is itself fundamentally dependent upon the reproduction of labor power. Causality runs in both directions, however, so the reproduction of labor power is itself dependent upon the other two realms of reproduction. One of the key contributions of feminist – and particularly socialist feminist – work in the 1970s and 1980s was to show that despite the degree to which these realms of reproduction are bound up with each other, the exact nature of their configuration was a matter of historical – and, importantly, geographical – development. Within industrial capitalism, for example, it makes all the difference in the world when neighborhoods are built to reflect and reinforce a growing separation between public and private spheres, whether or not those neighborhoods are ever "perfect" in their control of women's and men's lives.[5] That is to say, the very form of the landscapes within which reproduction, in all its guises, must take place is strongly determinative of the form that such reproduction will take.

It also makes all the difference in the world precisely how the space of the house itself is designed. In the first place, the home of the industrial era enshrined the family as a private entity, sufficient unto itself. It thus also enshrined privatized domestic labor, labor done on the whole by women. With each wife and mother sequestered in her own kitchen, doing her own laundry, and subject, by the turn of the twentieth century, to the hectoring demands of "efficiency experts" who desired to design the home so as to extract the most possible labor out of women, women found themselves isolated from the very community they were supposed to be the foundation of (see Rock et al. 1980). Feminist and socialist critics of the time were unsparing in their condemnation of the suburban house form. For example, Constance Austin, who

5 For a study of the blurred separations between public and private in a working-class district of Birmingham built at the height of the era of industrialization, see Brownill (1984).

designed the socialist Llano del Rio east of Los Angeles, called the traditional home "inconceivably stupid" because it both maimed women and confiscated their labor with no just compensation (quoted in Hayden 1980: 104). Others were just as unsparing, and sought to design, in the face of a political economy that seemed to demand the privatization of women's labor, communal living and working spaces.

These socialist ideals were themselves hardly free of gendered divisions of labor. In an article on socialist-utopian architectural alternatives to the privatized home, Delores Hayden (1980: 106) reprints a drawing of the communal dining room at the Oneida Colony in 1870 (figure 8.2). While men and women, boys and girls, all sit together at the tables laden with food, it seems to be only women and girls engaged in serving.[6] Even so, because such cooperative colonies stressed the introduction of labor-saving technologies and cooperative work arrangements, Hayden (1980: 117) suggests that "women's overall hours of work were limited. Rather than being on call day and night, like the average wife and mother, most utopian socialist women had the leisure to develop their interests – reading and writing, participating in musical or theatrical performances, developing friendships, enjoying amorous relationships." That is, women more nearly approached the degrees of freedom traditionally accorded men in industrial society, which, as we saw in the previous chapter, afforded a greater amount of room for social and sexual experimentation. But as we also saw, and the reason such experiments in living were most advanced in socialist colonies, such experimentation by women undermined the "traditional" nuclear family that provides the unacknowledged subsidy to capital for the reproduction of labor that is

Figure 8.2 The dining room of the Oneida Colony, 1870. Note that even in this egalitarian community, it is only women and girls doing the serving. Source: *Frank Leslie's Illustrated Weekly Newspaper*, April 9, 1870.

6   Contemporary tour guides at Oneida stress that men and women shared most work tasks; yet it is also the case that there were clear gendered divisions in some of the work.

so necessary to continued capitalist economic development.[7] The transformation of the shape of the home advocated in utopian and socialist communities, therefore, portended transformations not only in the gendered roles that women were meant to play in society, but also in the functioning of the economy. Conversely, the continual reassertion of the domestic ideal by the mainstream in both words and house-design served to shore up a system predicated precisely on the exploitation of women.[8]

The spatial entrapment of women

When socialist feminists in the 1970s and 1980s resurrected the critiques of housing style lodged by socialist feminists at the turn of the twentieth century, it was no accident. Rather, in the wake of the suburban explosion of the postwar era, it was a concerted attempt to imagine alternatives, and to theorize the conditions under which such alternatives could be made reality. The structural features maintaining women's inequality were not confined to the home itself, many feminist geographers argued; they were part of the total *landscape*. The development of this idea took two main forms. The first was a critique of the gendered nature of the built environment (of which a critique of domestic architecture was a part). The second, which we will explore later in the chapter, was a critique of the way the very idea of landscape itself was masculinist.

If the historical development of suburbia was in many ways predicated on changing notions of female domesticity (as we have seen), then in the postwar period further transformations of women's roles in society – most notably the increase in women's participation in the paid labor force as a result both of women's movement agitation and structural transformations of the economy that made lower-waged female labor desirable to many firms – have further remade, but not undone, the gendered divisions of space that mark metropolitan areas in the developed world. In a study of "back-office" labor in the San Francisco Bay Area, K. Nelson (1986) found that managers of "clerk-intensive" back-office firms were limited as to where they could locate their operations by the dynamics of *local* labor markets. By contrast, those firms that employed higher-wage technical and research labor chose sites from within the whole metropolitan region. Since back-office firms relied heavily on female labor, and since it was commonly assumed that "women who work outside of the home have shorter journeys to work," it was therefore assumed by back-office managers that they had to locate near the labor supply (Nelson 1986: 152). With the automation

---

7   The trajectory of the Oneida Colony is a perfect case. Founded as a communist cooperative, its growing success as a producer of silverware led first to the hiring of outside labor, next to the privatization of its economic functions (and the sale of its stock on public exchanges), and finally to the abandonment of communal living.

8   This is not to say that the subordination of women by men can be entirely explained by the functional requirements of capitalism. Rather, it is to argue that capitalism reinforces and exploits that subordination, whatever its origin. The geographical complexity and numerous contradictions of contemporary families in patriarchal, capitalist society are explored in Aitken (1998). Aitken's book makes it abundantly clear that the functioning of families can never be *reduced* to their ideal function in capitalism. But neither can they be divorced from capitalist social relations: capitalism, patriarchy and the family are mutually and complexly imbricated in each other.

of many clerical functions, and hence with a need for more highly educated labor, however, the locational constraints on clerk-intensive businesses have ironically intensified. Nelson (1986) found that Bay Area managers preferred locating near new suburban developments because the available female labor supply is "more likely to be relatively well educated and similar in race and class to employers compared to women living in central cities." Moreover, "the individualistic consumerist ideology prevalent in middle-income suburbs is also attractive to employers." According to one manager, "it is very important to people here to maintain the lifestyle they have chosen," and thus women workers are less likely to cause trouble on the job. Additionally, in new subdivisions, there is a large pool of women returning to the labor force after starting a family but whose primary responsibility remains to the household. For these women, "wage work occupies a secondary place in their lives" and hence wage demands are not as high as they might be. Finally, in the suburbs there are fewer well-developed formal and informal means for child-minding or other "women's" duties than in central cities (where, for example, extended-family networks are both more common and less spatially dispersed). Taken together, these lifestyle and structural constraints on women's lives in the suburbs reinforce the notion that their wage-earning is secondary to their roles as wife or mother, no matter how necessary to the household their income may be (Nelson 1986: 157–8).

Couple these factors with the already-mentioned shorter journey to work for many women (a journey that must be shorter because it is usually women rather than men who must be available to collect sick or injured children from school, to pick them up from day care or be home when they get home after school, and who typically prepare the evening meal and do other necessary housework) and this suggests to many researchers that women are "spatially entrapped," and thus form a ready supply of highly-educated, skilled labor available at low prices. Kim England (1993), however, argues that such analyses are, at best, too simple. In fact, England found in a study of Columbus, Ohio, "that women conventionally viewed as being the most spatially entrapped (married women with dependent children) actually had longer commutes than categories of women who, theoretically at least, should have been the least spatially entrapped (never-married women without children)" (1993: 240).

Instead, England (1993: 238) argues that the key issue is to understand the changing "stretchability of spatial relations" of women. "If a woman's particular job is as necessary as her residential location," England writes, "then no matter how much distance between the two increases, she will maintain the connection and simply elongate her journey to work" as far as possible. Such a statement, of course, begs all manner of questions, as England recognizes. What happens when spatial relations are "stretched" to the breaking point? She argues (1993: 239) that any individual woman will assess her own situation and determine that "some sociospatial relations are more necessary than others. A job which initially was unnecessary may acquire a certain necessity over time. Some women continue to work close to home, even though they no longer 'need' to . . . while others have long journeys-to-work even though (theoretically) they should only be able to support short commutes. . . ." Yet in the absence of any analyses of what the *societal* pressures might be on women who make these decisions, with no analysis of the ways that *men's* labor is more highly valued than women's, such an argument fails to answer the questions it raises (see Hanson and Pratt 1994, 1995). It returns us, in fact, to the endless and depressing debates about the "appropriate roles" for women and mothers with which I opened this chapter. But most particularly, England's study fails to answer questions about generally accepted notions of women's responsibility to the private sphere, and men's greater societal access to the public – societal norms that themselves have a huge impact on the nature and value of women's employment.

Both the discussion of spatial entrapment and the discussion of the relationship between architecture and gender roles – like the debates over the goals and meanings of the Promise Keepers – indicate the degree to which gendered boundaries between "public" and "private" are continually negotiated, reinforced, and reformed. Communal living arrangements sought to de-privatize the spaces in which domestic labor was performed. The viability of the more "public" space of the back-office depends on the maintenance of a more "private" (and privatized) space of the home – a private (and privatized) space governed by patriarchal gender norms. The ability of back-office firms to be profitable is to some extent reliant on the social maintenance of particular, privatized, spatial forms of domesticity. An unfunny (because all too indicative of the true state of gender relations) joke making the rounds in the presumably socially liberated San Francisco Bay Area in the late 1980s put it this way: "A woman's place is in the home. And she should go there right after work." A clearer indication of the spatial entrapment of women, and of the nature of the continuing struggles over domesticity and publicity – over the nature of public and private spaces – would be hard to find.

Breaking open public space

One effect of the social reinforcement of domesticity – and the private sphere – as part of the long history of suburban development and expansion was to code the public spaces of the city as "masculine." It seems almost natural that the world is separated into "separate spheres" for men and women. For the former a public space of public social interaction: the space of the city; for the latter a private sphere of domesticity, emotional bonds, and the maintenance of family: the space of home and suburb. Indeed, such a division of space (and of labor) lies behind the Promise Keepers' claim to value women for the unique roles they play in the family. Women are the keepers of family and morality. They provide a refuge to which men return after facing the temptations of the city. "The city," Elizabeth Wilson (1991: 5–6) writes, "offers untrammeled sexual experience; in the city the forbidden – what is most feared and desired – becomes possible. Woman is present in cities as temptress, as fallen woman, as lesbian, but also as virtuous womanhood in danger, as heroic womanhood who triumphs over temptation and tribulation." Or at least that is how femininity (and masculinity) has been socially *constructed* in the public spaces of the city. Public space is no place for (real, moral) women. Better for them is a house in the suburbs with freshly cut flowers on the table and birds chirping in the backyard.

To point to the social construction of these *images*, however, is not to deny that being a woman in the public spaces of the city *is* dangerous.[9] Much feminist political

9   Geographers such as Gill Valentine (1989) and Rachel Pain (1991) have explored women's fear of danger in public space and how that structures their involvement in the public life of the city. It is important

organizing, in fact, has been directed at breaking open the public spaces of the city so as to allow women in, either by working to assure safety or to transform the structure of the very spaces themselves. This has been the goal of the annual "Take Back the Night" marches that have become important in cities and on college campuses in North America in the last two decades. Take Back the Night events are a combination of political protest, support-group speak-out, and spectacle, each aimed at drawing attention to the dangers of rape faced by women both in public spaces and in the more "private" space of home, dorm room, fraternity party, and workplace. Mostly, though, the goal of Take Back the Night marches is to assert women's presence on urban streets after dark. Through the strength of numbers, through chants and speeches, women claim their rights to the streets. The very act of having to gather in large numbers to show that they belong indicates the degree to which women are excluded – often quite violently – from public space. But if rape (or the fear of rape) is one means of exclusion, it is not the only one. Indeed, some feminists have argued that the very public sphere, and by extension urban public space itself, is predicated on the exclusion of women – both physically and ideologically.[10]

Such exclusion of women, Wilson (1991: 9) argues, stems from our "deepest philosophical and emotional assumptions, the unconscious bedrock of western culture." Here, "the male–female dichotomy has . . . damagingly translated itself into a conception of city culture as pertaining to men. Consequently, women have become an irruption in the city, a symptom of disorder, a problem: the Sphinx in the city." Wilson is speaking of individual women, but Take Back the Night seeks to organize that "symptom of disorder" and turn it back on itself, showing that while it is not particular *men* who are to blame for women's effective exclusion from public space, it *is* particular constructions of masculinism (which are themselves wrapped up in more general systems of patriarchy). For Wilson (ibid), as (implicitly at least) for Take Back the Night, the goal is to remake the city from what she calls "the worst of all worlds" where we have "danger without pleasure, safety without stimulation, consumerism without choice, monumentality without diversity" to one where social life is founded on a basis of equality and inclusion, rather than inequality and exclusion.[11] As Nancy Duncan (1996b: 132) puts it, the "feminist slogan 'Take Back the Night' should be seen as a suggestion not for women to disregard personal safety, but for all of us who can (not just women) to organize . . . to transform public spaces and make them safe and accessible to everyone at night as well as during the day."[12]

to remember that a woman is in greater danger of abuse and rape at home than she is in public, but that the fear of violence in public space is not at all unfounded.

10   This exclusion is never complete and always contested. In fact, there is a good deal of contention as to the degree to which women have in fact been excluded from, for example, playing the *flâneur* on urban streets; see Domosh (1998).

11   In her critique of Take Back the Night events, Katie Roiphe (1993) disputes this claim. She argues that Take Back the Night precisely reinforces "safety" *at the expense of* not only stimulation, but also women's own strength. Roiphe's argument falters, however, in its perverse unwillingness to admit that rape is a very real fear that *does* structure how women act and are perceived in public space.

12   In fact there has been a great deal of contention as to what men's role in Take Back the Night marches ought to be. Some organizers argue that the march should be a time and a place for women exclusively, while others argue that the consciousness-raising function of the march has to be extended to men to be effective. I have benefited from reading Jennifer Katz's (1997) unpublished paper.

Take Back the Night dramatically demonstrates both the ambiguities and the importance of public space for social and cultural life. And it demonstrates also the degree to which public space, as part of the built environment in which we live and give meaning to our everyday lives, is produced and structured through struggles over gender itself. Feminist geographers have therefore begun to unravel the gendered construction of public space. Early research, such as that by Pain (1991) and Valentine (1989), has examined the role that gender violence plays in excluding women from the public sphere. Broader critiques of the exclusivity of public space – relying, in particular, on the insights of Nancy Fraser (1992) – have re-evaluated Jürgen Habermas's (1989) famous analysis of the bourgeois-democratic public sphere. Sallie Marston (1990), for example, has re-evaluated the notions of public inclusiveness that inspired the "founding fathers" of the United States. Marston has shown how these notions of inclusiveness were actually based on a quite constricted notion of who counted as a "legitimate" member of the "public," and therefore who had the "right" to engage in political discourse in public space. Marston notes that not only were most men excluded (because they were not property owners, they were the wrong race, or because they were foreigners), but *all* women were not legitimately a part of what was supposed to be an "inclusive" public space. If citizenship is a function of engaging in public discourse, then the structural constraints on women in public space all but precluded their ability to be citizens – a point made obvious by the long struggle to gain formal voting rights for women.

Lynn Staeheli has extended into the present these arguments about gender, citizenship, and their relationship to the construction of "the public" by focusing on women's political activism and by challenging the very importance of "public space" to political action. Where some (like myself) argue that to be effective, politics must be made visible in public space (Mitchell 1995a), Staeheli (1996) shows that the structural constraints on women's participation in the public sphere have encouraged the development of alternative spaces of citizenship and hence a reconsideration of the historically developed boundaries between public and private. Staeheli argues that it is a common mistake for social theorists to confuse the *content* of some action with the *material* space in which that action occurs. That is, we often too easily assume that public actions must take place in public space and private actions in private space.

It is better to understand both spaces and actions along continua from more public to more private and to realize that the degrees of publicity of actions and spaces do not necessarily vary together (figure 8.3). Indeed, Staeheli shows that activists have long known this. Just as, on the one hand, events like gay kiss-ins and mothers' public breast-feeding campaigns throw into question the sexist and heterosexist nature of public spaces by bringing putatively private actions into them, many activists have found that the putatively private spaces of their everyday lives – home and workplace, for example – are the best loci for public political action (organizing, letter-writing, etc.). For many women, Staeheli (1996: 615) writes, "conducting their political activism from their home [is] a way of overcoming...constraints" on their time implied by their roles as mothers, wives, and workers, as well as activists. "There is no *necessary* reason why actions that are intended to affect broad economic, social, or political relations must be taken in public spaces" (1996: 609). The important point is that women's political activism itself has challenged taken-for-granted notions about

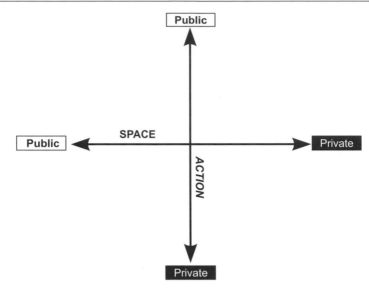

Figure 8.3 Lynn Staeheli argues that instead of understanding both spaces and actions as existing along the same public-to-private continuum, we need to see how the public or private nature of spaces and actions may not vary together. This schematic representation makes it clear that public actions can take place in private spaces and vice versa. Staeheli's contention is that understanding *how* different kinds of space are used for different actions is essential to understanding women's political involvement. Source: Redrawn from Staeheli (1996).

there being a clean separation between public and private spheres and spaces. What is interesting is how public and private are continually defined in relation to each other through specific political actions and activities. "The shifting constructions of public and private," Staeheli (1996: 605) says, "become something to be *explained*, rather than dismissed."

If feminist analysis, such as Staeheli's, has questioned the very notion of what constitutes public space – that is, if one of its key points has been precisely to question the dividing line between public and private – then it has also clearly begun to challenge just what it is that constitutes "politics" too. Of course, the redefinition of politics has been a founding tenet of feminism, as the slogan "the personal is the political" indicates. Taking for granted that public space is often highly controlled and surveyed, and that it is from the start an exclusionary space in which women are in many ways made unwelcome, Mona Domosh (1998) has shown that women have long been adept at inventing new forms of politics that fit into the interstices of the socially constructed geographies of control that govern the spaces they occupy. Domosh points out rightly that what is at issue in debates over the social geography of public space is not that they are controlled by all manner of social rules and norms (and by actual policing); but rather the question is one of which norms and rules they are to be controlled by. That question, Domosh (1998: 211) avers, is answered as much by observing everyday practices in public space as it is by studying the violent struggles that may occasionally result from conflicting norms about public space. Drawing on de Certeau's notion of "tactics" (see chapter 6), Domosh argues that the "polite politics" of everyday life expose how women formed an "ongoing opposition" to the de facto rule of men in the streets of New York City in the late nineteenth century. Domosh thus studies published drawings of well-heeled white women, blacks of both sexes, and others parading in the streets of the city in the 1860s. She analyzes the various exchanges of looks, the pointed ironies in the texts supporting the drawings, and the general social climate of the time to show how women, African Americans, and other marginalized people engaged in a form of "micropolitics" which, when all added together, "disrupted at the same time as it supported bourgeois standards" of proper behavior in public space. That is, while it appeared to almost all observers that women and blacks were simply succumbing to the dictates of the social order – trying to live up to what was expected of them as members in good standing of the bourgeoisie – they were in fact being "transgressive to the established norms." That they were doing so, however, "was only evident in the smallest of ways, and only to those who understood the complex and contextual script of polite performance" (Domosh 1998: 223). In sum, Domosh argues that such small transgressions invite us to rethink the nature of the public–private boundary and to begin to see women as users and transgressors of public space in the nineteenth century. A new definition of politics allows for a revaluation of women's public political action.

While Domosh is no doubt correct in her analysis, and while the focus on women's everyday life in the public spaces of the city is vitally important, it is hard to see where such a singular focus on micropolitics gets us. How do such minute transgressions add up to any difference? Domosh does not say, though she does argue that studying the micropolitics of gender and space provides a window on the " 'tactics' that many of us, who cannot afford the emotional and spatial distance required of an oppositional politics, embody in our everyday transgressions" (1998: 224). No longer is it so important that the "personal is political"; now it seems to be enough that the political is personal. If studies of public space that focus on conflict and confrontation have tended to overlook the importance of the everyday for structuring women's (and men's) lives in public space, then Domosh's analysis commits the opposite sin.

Rethinking Space

So far in this chapter I have discussed the spaces of home and street, of public place and suburban neighborhood. Feminists, and feminist geographers, have long been involved in social movements designed to transform and make more acceptable these spaces, to remake them less after an image of patriarchy and more after an image of a more gender-equal world. Yet feminists, and particularly feminist geographers, have also been concerned to redefine "space" itself. Consider this passage from geographer Gillian Rose (1996: 62):

> ... what if the insistence that there is a real space, that there is a real which is neither imagined nor symbolic, a real which is quite untainted by the imaginary or the symbolic, is not a statement of plain commonsense fact at all, but a hope, a desire? What if this real, this claim that there is a real space, itself depends on desire, is itself an imagined fantasy? A desire for something safe, something certain, something real? A fantasy too of something all-enveloping, something everywhere, unavoidable, unfailingly supportive: space?

In which all things could be charted, positions plotted, dwellings built and inhabited? And was itself a dwelling, secure? What if that space, that real space, was a dream, an old dream, a most basic dream? Would this space be dreamt as territory? Would this be the plenitudinous space which geography assumes, in which everything has its space and no space can be occupied by two objects simultaneously? Might this be the actual space of the real world which can be fully analysed scale by scale, from a satellite maybe, or a hotel tower, each scale with its own real structures, scale after scale nesting one within the other in infinite regress, the latest addition to the scale of the body, in a series which hopes to constitute a totality? Whose desire, whose space would this be? Who would constitute it? Who would dwell within it, and how?[13]

Rose's goal is to question the distinction between "real" and "non-real" spaces, by arguing that no space is free from human intent, human desire, and human imagination. She follows the French social theorist Luce Irigaray in arguing that "space" is more complex and less easily described than that which can be plotted on a map or delineated on the ground. Rather, "space is the medium through which the imaginary relation between the self and the other is performed." The imaginary, in turn, is not the opposite of "the real." Instead, "the imaginary" is a psychoanalytic term that refers to a person's (a subject's) negotiation of a symbolic world it can never fully know. Our relations are "imaginary" because they must necessarily be filtered through our own minds and made knowable to us. Yet "the imaginary" is also always social and symbolic: it is structured by the dominant discourses of the day. In a phallocentric world, the imaginary of the feminine is necessarily more constrained than that of the masculine. Yet it is constrained not only in discourses, but in the "spaces" in which women and men must live.

For Irigaray, Rose (1996: 62) argues, "the master subject constitutes himself through the performance of a particular space."[14] Note here the slightly different inflection given to both "space" and "performance" compared which our discussions in chapter 7. If there we suggested that space forms something of a stage for the performance of identity, here Rose and Irigaray suggest that it is *space itself* that is "performed." Space is thus ever-mutable, unstable, a function as much of desire and power as of bricks and mortar. The "master subject" defines "himself" through the performance of a certain *kind* of space, according to Irigaray (1985a: 166, quoted in Rose 1996: 62): "It is ... by distance and separation that he will affirm his self-identity." And this space of distance and separation is one that "he" must always maintain, for "if he arrived at the limits of known spatiality he would lose his favourite game, the game of mastering her" (Irigaray 1992: 42, quoted in Rose 1996: 62). Rose argues that to see the sorts of relationships Irigaray is concerned with as *space* is more than just metaphorical, because "to describe these images as metaphors at all assumes an economy of substitutable solid objects and reiterates 'the privilege granted to metaphor (a quasi solid) or metonymy (which is much more closely related to fluids).' Real space then contains a certain fixity, concreteness,

13   Rose is most directly critiquing Neil Smith (1993).
14   "Master subject" goes undefined in Rose's article as it does in much work of this sort. The clear implication is that the "master subject" is the person or social entity with, as we put it in an earlier chapter, "the power to define." If this "master subject" is never a particular, identifiable *man*, it is nonetheless clear in Rose's and Irigaray's accounts that it is socially constructed as *male*.

solidity," a limiting factor, according to Rose, that not only goes against any radical notion of what *space* is, but also against the mainstream of human geographic theory over the past two decades (1996: 67, quoting Irigaray 1985b: 110). Since control over others is effected by assuring that there is no space that such an other can perform, no space in which she can be, Rose argues, it is doubly important that we do not limit our notion of just what constitutes space. Rather, a progressive feminist geography would seek out new forms of space, new spaces of resistance. It would seek out and seek to reinforce space "that is not only multiple, composite, heterogeneous, indeterminate, and plural," but also "space the dimensions of which cannot be completely described, defined, discoursed" (Rose 1997: 188). It cannot – and should not – be described and codified, because to do so is to automatically exclude – to act as a "master subject."

Such a questioning of the boundary between the "real" and the "non-real" has its roots not only in feminist theorizing, but also in the concurrent postmodern and post-structuralist reassessment of the bases of Western philosophy. One primary pillar of Western philosophy has been what could be called a "Cartesian spatial order" defined, as Benjamin Genocchio (1995: 35) puts it, by "tribes of grids, binaries, hierarchies and oppositions." As Rose put it above, Western metaphysics relies on an assumption of the existence of an "actual space of the real world which can be fully analysed scale by scale." Space is seen to be "absolute" and "abstract" in that it exists simply as the container for social action, for events and processes, and for things (Smith 1990; Lefebvre 1991). Space is the unchanging backdrop against which life is played out. While Henri Lefebvre's (1991) philosophical de- and re-construction of such Cartesian notions of space is perhaps the most accomplished, Michel Foucault's (1986) brief comments on the subject have drawn the most attention (see Soja 1989). In place of the homogeneous, empty, absolute, and abstract space of Cartesian metaphysics, Foucault suggests it is more interesting and more accurate to understand the world as a set of overlapping "heterotopias" – spaces of multiplicity or spaces of difference. They are spaces that are *simultaneously* home to conflicting performances. And they are *utopian* in the sense that they are not spaces of containment and control, but rather of experimentation, fluidity, and disorder. Foucault does not deny that the Cartesian ordering of space has had real effect. Indeed, the bulk of his work was geared towards analyzing the various geographies of control modernity had invented. Rather he argues that there has always been a sub-history at work in the interstices of these geographies of control, a history of resistance that itself emerges in and against the dominant order as a set of "counter-sites." In conventional geographical terms, Cartesian space represents just that: *space*; and heterotopias can be understood as *place*, as the sites we not only live *in* (or on) but which we make our own by investing them with meaning – meaning that varies by social and spatial position.[15]

For Elizabeth Grosz (1995),[16] to think of "place" in this way, while also investing it with a radical feminist politics, is to reclaim the idea of *chora*, a term developed by Plato to mean "place," "location," "site," etc. Yet, Grosz (p. 48) notes, *chora* "also contains an irreducible, yet often overlooked, connection with the function of

---

15 The best recent geographical analyses of "place" have been by Doreen Massey (1994).
16 Unaccompanied page numbers refer to Grosz (1995).

femininity, being associated with a series of gender-aligned terms – 'mother,' 'nurse,' 'receptacle' and 'imprint-bearer.'" *Chora* is a kind of space but it is one to which one cannot attribute "any specificity [because] it would immediately cease to have its status as intermediary or receptacle and would instead become an object (or quality or property)....It is thus the mother of all qualities without in itself having any" (p. 49). If this sounds like the empty abstract space of Cartesian thought, the difference is that *chora* is also "inherently transformable, open to the specificities of whatever concrete it brings into existence." It is "steeped in paradox, its quality is to be quality-less, its defining character that it lacks any defining feature" (pp. 49–50).

Grosz's point is that *chora* is a kind of *feminine* space, and as such can be reclaimed by *feminists* as they search for some means to replace the Cartesian sureties about "real" space that have collapsed in the wake of postmodern critique. She avers (p. 54) that, "conceptions of spatiality and temporality have rarely been the explicit object of feminist reflection: they have always appeared somehow above the more mundane concerns of day-by-day politics, too abstract, too neutral and self evident...." Yet, as she goes on to argue (p. 54), "it has...become increasingly clear that the organization and management of space – the projects of architecture and regional planning, among others – have very serious political, social and cultural impact, and in a sense cannot but be of concern to feminists." Like Rose, Grosz turns to Irigaray to help navigate the new senses of space opened by the collapse of belief in a fixed, unchanging "real" space. The important point that Grosz takes from Irigaray's work is that *men* have built a world for their own purposes and in doing so they have sought to "take up all (social) space themselves," allowing to women the secondary role of becoming "guardians" of that space (p. 55). Women are thus "contained" within "a building which they did not build, which indeed was not even built for them," and the result is "a homelessness within the very home itself" (p. 56). The connection to our discussions of domestic architecture, the landscapes of suburbia, and the sequestering of women is obvious; but Grosz's argument about "homelessness within the home" is meant to indicate something far larger than the physical spaces in which we live: "This enclosure of women in men's physical space is not entirely different from the containment of women in men's conceptual universe..." (p. 56). To undo one means undoing the other, and both imply imagining new kinds of space; they require reclaiming *chora* and the construction and celebration of heterotopias that, while real sites, are sites not only of mixed spaces, but also mixed conceptual universes:

> The project ahead, or one of them, is to return women to those places from which they have been dis- or re-placed or expelled, to occupy those positions – especially those that are not acknowledged as positions – partly in order to show men's invasion and occupancy of the whole of space, of space as their own and thus the constriction of spaces available to women, and partly in order to be able to experiment with and produce the possibility of occupying, dwelling or living in new spaces, which in their turn help generate new perspectives, new bodies, new ways of inhabiting.   (p. 57)

The question such a desire raises, of course, is one of politics: if space cannot be described and defined, if it is always, as Rose says, only a desire or dream, then how can an effective politics of opposition to "men's invasions" be developed? For are not these "invasions" part of the social make-up of actually existing spaces, whether public or private, spaces themselves that provide a foundation for, more than just a backdrop to, the social actions of men (and women)? Precisely *what* must be reconstructed? Is it enough to just "imagine" a new *kind* of space? Or must we also engage in the difficult work of transforming the geographies – the situations – in which we live? These questions are of special importance when we turn to the third area of concern for this chapter: the ways that at the same time as social and geographical boundaries are being questioned and at the same time space itself is being retheorized, so too have feminists undertaken the task of retheorizing just what is meant by "gender" itself.

Space and the Cultural Construction of Femininity and Masculinity

Gillian Rose is certainly cognizant of the difficulties of *simultaneously* questioning the nature of space and gender. By assuming that space is not real, one may underestimate the real effects of space. In the midst of critiquing the "time geography" popular in the late 1970s and early 1980s for not understanding fully the constraints on women's lives, Rose (1993: 34–5) quotes June Jordan's argument that there is:

> a universal experience for women, which is that physical mobility is circumscribed by our gender and by the enemies of our gender. This is one of the ways they seek to make us know their hatred and respect it. This holds throughout the world for women and literally we are not to move about in the world freely. If we do then we have to understand that we must pay for it with our bodies. That is the threat. They don't ask you what you are doing in the street, they rape you and mutilate your body to let you remember your place. You have no rightful place in public.

Rose takes this as an indication that, historically, the public sphere has been constituted as "masculine" – and it has been policed, by men, as such. Yet, public space's "masculinization through a certain policing of bodies means that every new body requires disciplining in order to guarantee [public space's] reconstitution" (Rose 1993: 37). Hence, events like Take Back the Night represent collective, public disobedience of the taken-for-granted codes of public space, and, of course, of women's place in that space. But they also represent a reconfiguration of the very categories of "masculine" and "feminine," of "man" and "woman." And it is in response to this that many geographers have turned to examining the role that space plays in the cultural construction of not just gender *roles* but *gender* itself.

Social space is experienced bodily. It follows, then, that the production of space (like that explored in the two sections above) at the same time serves to produce certain kinds of bodies. Such an abstract idea makes sense, however, only if we understand "bodies" to be both the physical embodiment of particular people, and a culturally constructed set of ideas and ideals about what is bodily proper for men and women. That is to say, there is an intimate relationship between the social construction (and policing) of space, the cultural construction (and policing) of gender, and the ways we comport ourselves, the experiences we have, and, at least to some degree, the very morphology of our physical bodies. I say "to some degree" because just as productions of space are always contested, just as there is never a single, purely determinate force that makes space after *its* own image, so too we are not simply the result of the external forces – cultural norms, social pressures – working on us. As physical, biological beings – and as stubborn individuals – we are always formed as a result of the dialectical interplay of social forces, biological "givens," and personal desires and actions. Building on early feminist work in geography concerned with analyzing the social construction of "separate spheres," building on arguments about the role of public and private spaces in the construction of the self, and most importantly building on a strong tradition of what could be called "cultural" feminism, cultural geographers have begun to explore these relationships between space, social pressures, gender, and the body in interesting ways.

The first point of departure is the recognition that women's and men's bodies have been historically understood in quite distinct ways in Western society. Women have been more closely identified with their bodies (and nature) than have been men who have more easily transcended the body and bodily experiences, removing themselves from the vulgarities of nature. By contrast, as Linda McDowell (1995: 79) notes, feminist scholars have begun to understand the ways that "women's bodies [are] the sites and expressions of power relations." They recognize "that female bodies and the attributes of femininity mapped onto them, including variants of passive heterosexual desire, are social constructions or productions, constituted and produced by the effects of power and self-surveillance" (McDowell 1995: 79; cf. Brumburg 1997). That this self-surveillance, and these relations of power, have profound effects on the way that girls and women shape their bodies, McDowell notes, is "well-documented." The same point also holds true for male bodies, if under different social circumstances.

As McDowell recognizes, such pronouncements have little meaning if they remain at such a high level of abstraction. Or as Henri Lefebvre (1991: 61) argues, the importance of "the body" is that it mediates between mental (more or less individual) and social realms. "But one may wonder what connection exists between this abstract body...and a practical and fleshy body conceived of as a totality complete with spatial qualities (symmetries, asymmetries) and energetic properties (discharges, economies, wastes)." To put that another way, while it is sometimes important to understand the abstract processes creating abstract "bodies" (i.e. *the* body – a phrase of disappointing regularity in current cultural geographic work), to understand bodies *only* in this way, rather than understanding how these abstractions are connected with *real*, physical, "fleshy," *people*, makes the same mistake as seeing all space as abstract and undifferentiated.[17] The key then is to understand the specific relationships between bodies – and notions of masculinity and femininity that attach to them – and specific geographies.

In general, many feminists have begun to understand "gender" as a "regulatory fiction" in society (Butler 1990). It is "regulatory" in that gender is constructed and policed as a means for regulating the relations between people. It is a "fiction" because, first, it cannot be assumed that gender is something that naturally adheres to any individual person or individual body, and second, because the discourse and

17   Lefebvre makes this point in the midst of a complex critique of the psychoanalytic theories of Jacques Lacan. For a discussion of Lefebvre and Lacan see Gregory (1997).

politics of gender is only one among many social forces at work in shaping people and bodies. Recent work in feminism has thus subjected the very category "woman" (and by extension "man") to close scrutiny, arguing that it is a chaotic category, one that cannot possibly contain all that it is meant to. Other feminists worry that the deconstruction of "woman" as a political project will inevitably lead to the deconstruction of feminism, since feminism will no longer have an object around which to organize its politics or analyses. "The logical outcome of post-modern feminism is post-feminism," according to one skeptic (S. Jackson 1992, quoted in Valentine 1997: 66). Whatever the validity of that complaint, the importance of the move to understand gender as constructed and as a form of social regulation is that it makes obvious just how complex our notions of male and female, and masculine and feminine are. It also opens up the possibility that the social construction of the categories, along with their "performance" by particular socially-situated actors, is profoundly spatial. Masculinity and femininity certainly vary regionally (think of the differences between womanhood in Adelaide as compared to Addis Ababa). But it is even more importantly the case that gender is *spatially constructed* in that it is constructed in and through particular social spaces (however defined).

Femininity and the frontier

To take just one example, Jeanne Kay (1997) has argued that the relationship between female bodies, femininity, space, and nature on the American Mormon frontier was profoundly complex. On the Mormon frontier, the standard equation of women with passive nature and therefore with domination is quite misleading.[18] She begins by acknowledging that "some of the oldest, most widespread, and durable metaphors for landscape and Nature invoke the female body: the land as the Great Mother in any of her many guises, wilderness as an enticing temptress available for the frontiersman's wooing or taking, or dangerous, uncontrollable Nature as hag or fury" (Kay 1997: 361). Women's experiences in pioneer Utah settlements as Mormon life and religious doctrine were being developed were shaped by their interaction and identification with, and acceptance and sometimes rejection of, the land, the developing community, and religious teaching. "The mid nineteenth century Cult of Domesticity, or Cult of True Womanhood, to which the chaining of bourgeois white women to lives of useless domesticity has been attributed, was profoundly modified in frontier Utah by the perceived need for the faithful to be productively employed in the region's economic development" (Kay 1997: 367, citing Lerner 1980; Welter 1966). Possessing strong beliefs in the Utah landscape as the new Zion, many Mormon women conceived of themselves as active participants in the "subduing" and "conquering" of nature, in the work of transforming wild nature into a productive landscape. As Kay argues, such self-conceptions make it extremely difficult to make simple associations between gender and nature; the very specificity of experience mediates against any such simple claims. It also makes it difficult to see women themselves as, like nature, passive and ready to be subdued. By focusing on the ordinary lives of ordinary – if often marginalized – women in ordinary places, she argues (1997), the exceptional

18 For the leading critique of such an equation, see Merchant (1980).

complexity of the "co-production" of gender and place or space can be recovered. Femininity – the social construction of "womanhood" – thus takes on a different cast in developing Mormon towns, than it did, say, in the suburban drawing rooms of eighteenth-century London or the communal workshops and dormitories of Oneida, New York. "Gender," in other words, is always in a state of social construction – social construction that varies over time, space and circumstance.

Masculinity and femininity embodied

"Gender" is also wrapped up in the shape and shaping of human bodies, and this is just as true for men and masculinity as it is for women and femininity. Much writing on the "corporeality" of gender, sexuality, and race "move[s] quickly past arms, legs, torso and head on [its] way to a theoretical agenda that requires something unknowable or unknown as an initial premise" (Foster 1992, quoted in Cream 1995: 32). By contrast, Doreen Massey (1996: 109) (among others) has suggested that it is important to understand social performances such as masculinity and femininity *as lived*, "for philosophical frameworks do not 'only' exist as theoretical propositions or in the form of the written word. They are both reproduced and, at least potentially, struggled with and rebelled against, in the practice of living life." That is, the goal for work such as Massey's is to show how "philosophical frameworks" are quite literally inscribed on the bodies of people – through, for example, their desire to attain some socially acceptable form of masculinity, femininity, and the "look" associated with those.

Much of the imagery of popular culture, in fact, is geared towards displaying what it is – and what it means – to be male or female, meanings that are continually negotiated through the medium of popular culture itself. Thus the comic strip character Cathy can complain about how even in women's magazines, articles on how it no longer matters what a woman looks like (because desirable femininity is now defined by what a woman does on the track, ski slope, or basketball court) can be immediately followed by an article on how to lose ten pounds quickly to fit into the sheerest of bathing suits and look good on the beach (figure 8.4).[19] Popular culture products like magazines, TV shows, and advertising are particularly powerful forums for displaying cultural ideals about gender, but it is in everyday life that such ideals are enacted (or contested). Whether in the world of the steel mill, the high-tech office, or the space of leisure defined by television, there is always "a convergence of desires/ interests between a certain sort of masculinity [and femininity] and a certain sort of capital" (Massey 1996: 116). This is not to say that masculinity and femininity are somehow simply functional to capitalism – no more than sexuality is – but it is to say that capitalism, as a system of social reproduction, is impossible without constantly negotiating (and thereby changing) gender. Nor, for that matter, is "gender" possible outside of the structuring pressures of capitalism (or any other political-economic system).

Indeed, our bodies themselves are actively *shaped* by the steady demands and pressures of a capitalism defined by constant technological revolutions. The recent

19   See the "Cathy" for August 9, 1998.

Figure 8.4 "Cathy" (August 8, 1998); used by permission of Universal Press Syndicate.

academic interest in "the body," according to Felicity Callard (1998), has had the effect of promoting exciting new theorizations about the relations between bodily morphology and the porousness of boundaries ("between the real and the artificial, the organic and the inorganic, the authentic and the simulacrum" [Chambers 1993: 56, quoted in Callard 1998]), and interesting speculations about bodily fragmentation. Yet it also has the effect of often ignoring the material social processes that *produce* that boundary-questioning and fragmentation (1998: 395). As early as the mid-nineteenth century, Marx pointed clearly to the processes at work in the fragmentation and "hybridization" of workers' bodies: "[Manufacture] converts the worker into a crippled monstrosity ... the individual is divided up, and transformed into the automatic motor of detailed operation, thus realising the absurd fable of Menenius Agrippa, which presents the man as a mere fragment of his own body" (Marx 1987, quoted in Callard 1998: 396). The difference in Marx, as compared to many recent theorizations of "the body" (in all their abstract non-specificity) is that Marx was clear that the object to be understood was precisely "fractious and unruly links, cuts, appropriations that characterise the structures enjoining labourer and machine, labourer and labourer, labourer and collective labourer," and perhaps most importantly, bodily labor (which both produces and disfigures bodies) and capitalism's incessant construction out of those bodies of bodiless abstract labor against which all things are measured (1998: 397).

Moreover, gender identities, and the bodies to which they are attached, are very much fields of profit (Harvey 1998). At the most basic level, the faster new images of gender can circulate, the faster that new desires for the reconstruction of one's self can be internalized, then the faster new clothes, new make-ups, new cars, new exercise equipment, and new foods can be sold. The fashioning of self is more and more a function of the purchasing of commodities designed to aid in this process.[20] At another level, a level often in objective contradiction to this pressure towards rapid change, is the degree to which, as we have seen, the construction of particular *roles* – and hence particular, socially sanctioned body types (muscular, relaxed, "brainy," nurturing, etc.) – associated with particular genders allows capital to take advantage of locally uneven wage-levels, levels disaggregated by gender (as well as sexuality, race, etc.). The definition of genders – the socially accepted and socially contested definitions extant at any time or place – is thus a result both of political economic forces and interests (such as new marketing strategies [see Frank 1997a]), *and* the context within which the political economy must operate. In turn, the shaping of bodies as certain *kinds* of men and women is a social project without which capitalism or any other political economic system would be impossible (figure 8.5).

Marx made much of the ability of workers to reproduce themselves. He also showed how struggles between capital and labor over the length of the working day and week were very much struggles by workers to control their own bodies – to assure enough time to fully recuperate after work, to develop faculties allowed to atrophy because of the type of work done, and so forth. Struggles over wages and the conditions of work, therefore, are struggles over the shaping of bodies.[21] "Body politics" – the politics of fitness, leisure, sport, and social development – has a long (and not always salutary) history in socialist politics. One of the goals of feminism is

Figure 8.5 Maurice Glickman, "Construction." The celebration of labor is also the celebration of a certain kind of body in this Depression-era woodcut in South River, New Jersey. Photograph from the National Archives, Washington.

20 A good polemical analysis of various aspects of this process is Frank and Weiland (1997).
21 Massey (1996) makes a similar argument but expands it to include the psychic benefits of a varied and not overly-controlled life.

to advance this politics in ways more amenable to the varied means of not just men, but of women too.[22]

If carving out *time* for the fashioning of bodies against the steady pressure of work and media is an important aspect of social struggle over gender, so too, of course, is the carving out of a *space* for recreation. Just as with the need to create spaces for the expression and development of sexuality, gender needs space to develop, change, or be reproduced. Consider, as just a couple of examples, the development in recent years of women-only gyms and outing clubs, or the long historical availability of men's clubs, cigar lounges, and sporting arenas. *Contra* the arguments made above (by Rose and others) about the need to reconceptualize space itself and not necessarily rely on an assumption that "space" is something material, it is of course the *material social relations* of space that govern just how space for recreation (like space for production) is regulated. This is a point that Gillian Rose accepts (even if she wants to theorize a form of geography that moves beyond it) and one that she develops in interesting ways when she explores that most traditional of cultural geography concerns: the landscape.

Gender and the Visual Landscape

Social constructions of gender, together with sexuality and (as we will see in the next chapter) race, have been instrumental in determining the shape, importance, and meaning of public and privates spaces – of physical landscapes. And the cultural politics of space that has resulted is also clearly a cultural politics of masculinity, femininity, and "the body." It follows, therefore, that other realms of discourse and social life will not be unaffected by the politics and productions of gender. One of the other realms worth thinking about is the ongoing reconsideration, in geography and related disciplines, of the very *idea* of landscape (as a particular kind of representation; see chapter 4). In this regard, "landscape" serves as a codification of what could be called the "visual field" – that which we see when we look around us. Cultural geographers, drawing on both feminist work in cultural studies and cultural interpretations of intellectual history, have begun to interrogate this visual field to understand its changing cultural construction (Nast and Kobayashi 1996; Gregory 1994: chapter 1). Martin Jay (1992) has described vision as "the master sense of the modern era." And as Derek Gregory (1994) and David Livingstone (1992) variously show, geography has long considered itself a specifically *visual* discipline. For geography, vision – the process of looking so as to know – is intimately connected with fieldwork and the depiction of the landscape. As we have seen "landscape" is a particular "way of seeing"; and to understand the landscape, geographers have "learned from looking" (to slightly modify Peirce Lewis's [1983] phrase). The landscape itself has been understood, as Vidal de la Blache put it, as "what the eye embraces with a look" and as "that part of the country that nature offers up to the eye that looks at it" (quoted in Gregory 1994: 39). To look, one must go into the country; one must spend time "in the field" cataloguing, assessing, exploring (cf. Stoddart 1986).

22 In this regard, the related project of theorizing "ableist" geographies is of great importance; see Chouinard and Grant (1996).

Gillian Rose (1993) has subjected this tradition of visualization and fieldwork in geography – and particularly cultural geography – to a vigorous feminist critique.[23] If the process of "learning from looking" relies on finding ways to create a distance between viewer and viewed (as we saw in the case of landscape as a way of seeing in chapters 4 and 5), then, Rose argues, such a process relies fundamentally on the feminization of Nature. Fieldwork is condemned by Rose (p. 70) as masculinist in that "geographers become stronger men by challenging Nature" in the field and by establishing "fieldwork as a particular kind of masculine endeavor" (see also Sparke 1996). But, Rose (p. 72, quoting Hart 1982: 29) goes on to say, such a relationship to feminized nature is not a simple, direct one of rape, domination, or conquest. Instead, mixed with the desire to dominate nature, is "a strong sense of pleasure in the 'complex, surprising, exciting, and utterly magnificent world we live in.'" Relying on a landmark essay by J.K. Wright (1947) on the place of the imagination in geography, Rose (p. 73) argues that what geographers really possess as they view the world around them is an "uneasy mix of pleasure, mystery and fear in the face of Nature" that is best "represented by the alluring but dangerous feminine figure of the Siren. The gaze of the fieldworker is . . . equivocal, intimate and humbled, as well as distant and dominative."

Such an ambivalent relationship to the object of the "gaze" is clear enough as geographers engage in fieldwork. But it is also there in studies of landscape representations such as paintings, engravings, and photographs. What is necessary, then, is a critique of these ways of seeing and knowing as themselves socially constructed – a project well under way in the sorts of landscape studies produced by "new cultural geographers" like Stephen Daniels and Denis Cosgrove. As Rose (p. 87) summarizes, such studies "argue that the gaze of the fieldworker is part of the problematic, not a tool of analysis." Hence, cultural geographers have increasingly turned to examining how landscape images themselves are, and have been, constructed not by individual artists or scholars, but by the long development of a "visual ideology" of landscape (see chapter 4 above). But, Rose (p. 87) correctly notes, "questions of gender and sexuality have not been raised by this newer work."[24] And it is here that we can really see what Rose (p. 86) calls "the uneasy pleasures of power" made available by "looking at landscape." Indeed, "the structure of aesthetic masculinity which studies landscape is inherently unstable, subverted by its own desire for the pleasures that it fears" (p. 89).

Yet Rose begins more modestly. Rather than jumping into arguments about masculinity and pleasure, she begins by showing how new cultural geographic approaches to landscape have confirmed the very ideological nature of landscape that they seek to uncover. Geography's visuality, she argues, "is not simple observation but, rather, is a sophisticated ideological device that enacts systematic erasures"

---

23 Unaccompanied page numbers in this section refer to Rose (1993). While much of Rose's critique is excellent, it is consistently marred by her refusal to understand and examine historical changes in geography. Thus statements made by male cultural geographers in 1920, 1939, 1959, and 1968 are presented as if they are universally ascribable to geographers working in cultural geography in the 1990s. If nothing else, such historically sloppy analysis underestimates the impact that feminist cultural geographers *have* had in cultural geography as a whole.

24 That lacuna has begun to be addressed in the past few years in the work of geographers such as Rose herself, Catherine Nash, David Matless, and the contributors to N. Duncan (1996a).

(p. 87). Combined then with the deceptive quality of the landscape and its representations, this selective vision of geographers has profound effects on how we understand gendered relations to the land. To make her point Rose subjects Thomas Gainsborough's painting "Mr. and Mrs. Robert Andrews" (figure 8.6) to an imaginative and compelling interpretation. This painting is something of an icon in new cultural geography, appearing in several studies as the depiction *par excellence* of how landscape painting serves to codify particular ways of seeing and controlling the land.[25] The standard new cultural geography discussion of this painting draws on John Berger's (1972: 107) important comments in his book, *Ways of Seeing*. The painting celebrates landownership and the freedom that entails for the landowners. It also erases from view any real sense of the work that makes the landscape depicted. While the hay in the fields has been mown and stacked, there is no sense of the conditions under which this was done. It is obvious that Mr. and Mrs. Andrews did not plow and cut the fields, but who did? By so clearly erasing the evidence of not just work, but its social conditions, the painting helps to naturalize capitalist property ownership and the rights of the owners.

But, as Rose rightly notes, there is more to the painting than that. "It is possible to prise the couple – 'the landowners' – apart, to differentiate between them," Rose (p. 91) says. While

Figure 8.6 Thomas Gainsborough, "Mr. and Mrs. Robert Andrews" (ca. 1748). This painting has become an icon of "new" cultural geography, appearing in countless books and articles (and now here!). Gillian Rose's feminist reading sheds new light on the politics of the painting – and cultural geography. Reproduced courtesy of the Trustees, The National Gallery, London.

25 Among other places it can be found in Daniels (1989); Daniels and Cosgrove (1988); Gold (1984); Short (1991).

both figures are relaxed and share the sense of partnership so often found in eighteenth century portraits of husband and wife, their unity is not entire: they are given rather different relationships to the land around them. Mr Andrews stands, gun on arm, ready to leave his post and go shooting again.... Meanwhile Mrs Andrews sits impassively, rooted to her seat with its wrought iron branches and tendrils, her upright stance echoing that of the tree directly behind her. If Mr Andrews seems at any moment able to stride off into the vista, Mrs Andrews looks planted to the spot. This helps me to remember that, *contra* Berger, these two people are *not* both landowners – only Mr Andrews owns the land.   (pp. 91–3)

The important point, Rose argues, is that "landscape painting... involves not only class relations, but also gender relations" (p. 93), which, I would add, precisely reflects the construction not only of discourses and visual representations, but the social structuring of the landscape – the "built environment" – itself, as so clearly shown in the discussions of suburbia and domestic architecture, above. An important avenue of research, then, would be one that examines the ways in which such landscape representations refract and reflect constructions in the physical landscape, one that explores how the gendered constructions of each are often (though perhaps not always) mutually reinforcing, not just of property relations and gender roles, but of particular notions and habits of gender itself.

But Rose takes her argument in a different direction. Instead she seeks to show that a "gaze" upon a "landscape" inevitably "structures" that landscape as feminine, and thus equates Woman with Nature. This association, which Rose argues was especially strong in nineteenth-century allegorical landscape painting (which relied heavily on depictions of idealized natural landscapes populated with nude female figures), allowed the (male) viewer both a sense of control (because the landscape and female nude were fixed in place while the observer was free to move and observe at will), and a "kind of sensual pleasure" (p. 97). Landscape painting thus encapsulates

(hetero)sexual fantasies of both artist and spectator. It is the imagined and desired sexuality of the female nude that is offered to the (implicitly masculine) spectator.... This means that the sensual topography of land and skin is mapped by a gaze which is eroticized as masculine and heterosexual. This masculine gaze sees a feminine body which requires interpreting by the cultured knowledgeable look; something to own, something to give pleasure.   (p. 97)

"Learning from looking" takes on a whole new meaning. But, Rose argues, "there is a great reluctance among geographers to engage critically with this masculine pleasure, even though the pleasure in the landscape encountered during fieldwork is... frequently admitted (even erotic pleasure is conceded)" (p. 99).[26]

Rose concludes her re-evaluation of the landscape traditions in geography by arguing for a cultural geography that understands "sexuality in the field of vision" (J. Rose 1986) in psychoanalytic terms that draw particularly on the work of Jacques Lacan and on advances in feminist film studies. Rose (pp. 103–4) approvingly quotes

26   Rose further argues that the recent "textualization" of landscape – the development of text metaphors for understanding landscape – attempts "to deny the phallocentrism of the geographic gaze" by creating a false "critical distance" between interpretation and interpreter (p. 101).

Laura Mulvey (1989: 19) to the effect that while "the gaze" is always contradictory (in its pleasures and purposes), it nonetheless constitutes

> Women as image, man as bearer of the look.... [I]n a world ordered by sexual imbalance, pleasure in looking has been split between active/male and passive/female. The determining male gaze projects its fantasy onto the female figure, which is styled accordingly.

Following Lacan and his feminist interpreters (such as Elizabeth Grosz [1990]), Rose asserts that the "feminine subject" (not any particular woman) is defined by "lack" – particularly by lack of "a sexual organ" – at least on first look.

> The look is...central to subjectivity, and the active look which sees the mother as lacking rather than simply different is phallocentric. The active look is constituted as masculine, and to be looked at is the feminine position. But this is not a coherent look: narcissistic identification with the powerful, pre-Oedipal, phallic (m)Other and voyeuristic fascination with lack remain, and so the look "oscillates between memory of maternal plenitude and memory of lack." (Rose 1993: 104, quoting Mulvey 1989: 14)

For geographers the important point is that "these connections between identity and vision suggest why visual pleasure recurs in geographical discourse: it is a fundamental part of the masculine subjectivity which shapes and is constituted through that discourse. And geography's pleasure in landscape can be interpreted through psychoanalytic terms across which the gaze is made – loss, lack, desire and sexual difference" (p. 104).

Visual pleasure is thus masculine pleasure, and "this is cultural geography's erotics of knowledge" (p. 109). Catherine Nash (1996), by contrast, suggests that such a rendering of visual pleasure as masculine cannot be sustained. She accepts (1996: 149) that "pleasure in research, writing or looking at landscape or the body is political," but argues that it is not thereby completely unacceptable. By focusing on women's depictions of male bodies as landscape, she shows (1996: 151) that feminist psychoanalytically-based film theory, such as that on which Rose bases her argument, tends to equate vision and representation directly with "generalized notions of masculinism, imperialism and oppression" and that "the simple suggestion that landscape representation is ideological, or visually oppressive, suggests an ahistorical condemnation...rather than attention to the particular effects of images in specific and finely differentiated social contexts."

Diane Baylis's photograph *Abroad* (figure 8.7) makes Nash's point. By drawing on conventions of landscape representation, and the erotic pleasures they afford, but by making a man's body – and particularly his genitals – the focus of attention, *Abroad* upsets the "arbitrary and constructed authority of figuring the female body as nature. It is as easy in this instance to find curves in the male body to correspond to the apparent rounded forms in the natural landscape. This frees the body-landscape metaphor from any essential equation between nature and femininity" (Nash 1996: 160). Nash's point is *not* that such associations between nature and female (or feminine) do not exist; rather it is that they are constructed in historically and geographically specific ways that overly generalized psychoanalytic theories shed no light on.

Figure 8.7 Diane Baylis, *Abroad* (1992). As Catherine Nash shows, the relationship between the body, the landscape, and erotic pleasure is complex and cannot be reduced to a function of the masculinist "gaze." Reproduced with permission of the artist.

Not only that, but the male body-landscape *is* pleasurable and an object of erotic desire in *Abroad* – for women and men alike. Where Rose (1993: 101) sees "learning from looking" – "the logic of the gaze and visual pleasure" – constantly reinforcing masculine heterosexuality, Nash argues that this is not necessarily so. Female and feminine heterosexual pleasure is possible; as is a homoerotic gaze. "To picture the male body as landscape is not simply to invert customary gendered positions within a scopic regime but to suggest other pleasures and subject positions which are not determined by this regime" (Nash 1996: 161). Moreover, it might just be the case that "a radical politics of visual pleasure may in some cases entail and endorse objectification" because "neither landscape nor looking is redundant or inherently oppressive" (1996: 167).

Conclusion

Nash's point is that what needs to be understood is the specific *politics* that "engender" both particular readings of aesthetic representation and the physical appropriation and use of space. That, of course, has been precisely the political point of feminism – and it has been the driving force behind its development in geography. If Take Back the Night marches sought to refigure public space as safer for women, then Gillian Rose has likewise sought to clear a similar space in the discipline of geography. Yet the politics of the body, or pleasure, or the privatization or publication of space is fraught with contradictions. To what degree are the "polite politics" that Domosh describes an effective means for undermining the masculine control of space? To what degree does the renegotiation of publicity and privacy that Staeheli describes among women activists throw into question the taken-for-granted notions of what constitutes "politics" in the first place? And how does the continual circulation of "the body" and gender within capitalism structure the ways in which we can and can not take control over the production of our own selves?

All of these are crucial questions that illustrate, as Domosh says, how feminism develops out of "direct political imperatives." They also illustrate the ways in which the construction and reproduction of gender – as it is encoded in the space of the city and the space of the body – is a geographical project. It is a geographical project in which issues of domination, violence, resistance, and justice are front and center (as Take Back the Night shows). Yet it is also a project in which ideas and practices of pleasure are claimed and contested. And finally, it is a project in which the culture wars of the day – over gender roles, over "leadership," and over the right of women and men to determine the structures and spaces of their own lives – are always at the surface. The obvious assumption behind the evolution of domestic architecture, the development of "pink collar ghettos," or the endless debates about whether and how much mothers should work outside the home, is that everyone "has their place" in the world – and that place is somehow "naturally" ordained. The struggles of feminists – in geography and in the streets – has been to upset that assumption and to show how wrong it is.

The notion of "everyone in their place," obviously, is not confined to questions of gender. The same dynamic of asserting and seeking to control people by constructing a "natural" place for them is just as visible and important when we consider another vector of social differentiation: race. The next chapter explores the cultural geographies, and cultural politics, of race. It shows that the desire to "place" everyone is little more than the desire to control.

9

"A Place for Everyone": Cultural Geographies of Race

Race as a Geographical Project

Race, like gender and sexuality, is a geographical project. Race is constructed in and through space, just as space is often constructed through race. As a geographical project the co-production of race and space is never uncontested, and thus the spatiality of race often needs ordering and policing. Such policing manifests itself in all manner of quite ordinary – and sometimes extraordinary – ways. Consider the following example, and you can see just how ordinary the geographical policing of race is: it only becomes extraordinary when we stop to think about it in any reasonable way. On December 3, 1995, Theresa Seamster, a 44-year-old black woman from Denver was evicted from the Greeley Mall in northern Colorado for wearing "gang colors." Seamster had gone to the mall with three friends, one of whom was an elderly woman with Alzheimer's disease. After spending nearly two hours there (and after the four had spent about $750), Seamster was approached by a mall security guard and informed she would have to remove the blue scarf she was wearing on her head if she wished to remain in the mall. The guard was enforcing an unposted – indeed, unwritten – rule that forbade the wearing of scarves of certain colors. When Seamster refused to remove the scarf, the security guard called in help to escort Seamster and her elderly friend out of the mall. Seamster insisted on first collecting her two other friends who were waiting at a store on the other side of the mall. As the women were escorted across and eventually out of the building, a crowd of onlookers gathered, creating a sense of humiliation in Seamster and her friends. When Seamster complained of their treatment by letter to the mall manager, the letter went unanswered. So did calls from reporters about the incident. The Greeley police chief, however, did comment, saying that he generally supported the policy: he called the wearing of gang colors a "detriment to the atmosphere" of the city.[1] Yet he also argued that the mall needed to be more careful in its enforcement of the policy. "The lady [Seamster] does not necessarily fit the profile of a gang member. If I had a group of eight or ten kids flashing signs and wearing bandanas, they'd be gone. But that's a totally different situation" (Witcher 1995).

"Profile" is everything. What is this "profile"? Clothing style, of course, but also, and obviously, skin color. It hardly needs saying that a middle-aged white woman would not have been treated in the same manner: she would have drawn no attention at all, no matter what the color of her scarf. Such "profiling" on the basis of age, skin color, clothing type, and the like, is a growing – and increasingly controversial – practice by both private and public police forces. Numerous attempts have been made to outlaw "gang colors" in various jurisdictions – often with humorous results. Mike Davis (1990: 318, note 30) tells of the attempt to outlaw gang colors in Fontana, California, which was stymied when someone pointed out that to do so would be to outlaw two-thirds of the colors in the American flag! Usually profiles are more complex and rely on some combination of clothing, skin color, and location. What might be tolerated in one place (black kids hanging out in a poor, black neighborhood), might become suspect elsewhere (black kids hanging out near a rich, white neighborhood). What is clear is that no matter how complex the "profiles" become, at their root is an elementary classification of people on the basis of skin color. Skin color, in the most racist of ways, becomes destiny. For Theresa Seamster and her friends, that destiny was humiliating treatment at the hands of the security guards at the Greeley Mall. For thousands of urban kids, it means a life of unrelenting harassment at the hands of cops seeking to enforce "quality of life" initiatives.[2]

I can tell you the story of Theresa Seamster's trip into and out of the Greeley Mall because I used to live not too far from Greeley, and a Colorado weekly newspaper, *Westword*, ran a story about it. That this story was *not* picked up by the national news media suggests, to some extent, just how ordinary such occurrences are. What is it, then, about "race" that calls up such reactions, that makes such unreasonable behavior on the part of security officers, mall owners, politicians, and the like, so commonplace? An easy answer would be that this story is less about race than it is about suburban fear, about the loss of community contact that is both cause and effect of the sequestering of the middle class behind walls of their own making (see Davis 1998: chapter 7).[3] But such an explanation leads to many more questions than

1 The California-based owner of the mall says it opposes the local rule against "gang colors" and has asked the Greeley Mall to refrain from enforcing any unwritten policies.
2 "Quality of Life" is the name given to urban campaigns to "clean up" streets and public spaces by strictly enforcing loitering and anti-gang color laws, passing new laws outlawing seemingly innocuous behavior like sitting on a curb, washing motorists' windows or hawking newspapers, or cracking down on public drinking. Many of these campaigns trace their roots to an influential article published in 1982 by two criminologists, James Q. Wilson and George Kelling.
3 T. Coreghesan Boyle's (1995) novel about suburban Los Angeles evocatively explores just this point. This argument is also taken, as we will see, in fully racist directions by cultural conservatives.

answers, not least because it seems to minimize the role of "race" in the production of fear. But if we acknowledge that "race" is a key factor in people's fear of each other, then we have to ask precisely what "race" is – and what it is not. Is it something innately, biologically, part of one's body, something natural and immutable? Is it purely a figment of society's imagination, a collective fantasy about difference? Is it a fact, or a factor, of identity? And is that identity therefore individual or collective? And, again, *why* and *how* is "race" a geographical project (as I so blithely declared it was in the first sentence of this chapter)?

These are questions geographers (and countless others) have been asking for more than two decades now.[4] But they are questions of a much longer pedigree. In this chapter we will explore the biological and social arguments about what, exactly, race might be, and then see how our *ideas* about race are made very real "on the ground." In other words, as Peter Jackson (1989: chapter 6) has shown so well, there are important, historically and geographically constructed "languages" of race and racism. The key issue we will address is precisely how those languages are dependent upon, even as they give rise to, specific *kinds* of space – specific sites and places – both for their development and reproduction. Languages of racism do not exist in a vacuum: they are effected on the streets of cities, in the fields of the countryside, and in their large-scale spaces of migration that make up the contemporary world. But since these spaces are themselves both socially constructed and open to constant challenge and revision, we will also explore in this chapter precisely how race and geography are policed, by and for whom they are policed, and, hence, again, how and why geography and race are dependent, in so many ways, on each other.

In other words, we will raise yet again the questions so crucial to cultural geography raised in chapter 3: *Who* reifies particular cultural meanings (in this case race)? *How* are these reifications solidified and enforced? *Whom* do they benefit, and whom do they harm? *In what ways* are they contested both in everyday practices and in more spectacular fashion? And, most importantly, *under what conditions* are these reifications made and reproduced? As Robert Miles (1982: 64) has argued, "the basis of racism is to be found not in the attribution of meaning to phenotypical difference, but in identifying the economic, political, and ideological conditions that allow the attribution of meaning to take place." Like the idea of culture – and the practices that support that idea – the idea of race is powerful only insofar as it organizes people's activities, actions, and ordinary lives in particular ways for the benefit of particular people, classes, or social groups. This chapter will explore these questions in more detail, focusing on "race" as one of the key ideologies and sets of practices – like gender and sexuality – that structure all of our lives. First, we will look at what race is, and what it isn't. Second, we will explore a particularly pernicious use of the idea of race – one that associates it with degrees of intelligence and other forms of abilities – and explore how such an idea is underpinned by a quite remarkable geographical vision. Third, we will show how such visions themselves will have currency only to the degree that they are "fixed" in particular spaces. We will take a look at the obvious case, apartheid, but it should be clear that our compass is wider:

4   Perhaps the earliest, and angriest, explicit critical discussion of the geography of race as a project of social control is Bunge (1971); see also Jackson (1987b); S. Smith (1989).

the race idea circulates through all manner of other kinds of space. These spaces are as instrumental in transforming the social and geographical structure of space as space is in reproducing the very idea of race.

Indeed, in the contemporary world, there is not a space that is not saturated with the poisoned blood of "race" through and through. bell hooks (1992: 345) has written that she is frequently astounded at how "the discourse of race is increasingly divorced from any recognition of the politics of racism." My goal in this chapter is to never forget the politics of racism. Instead, no matter how technical the discussions of race may become, I want to keep at the forefront of our attention the fact that it is simply impossible to address issues of race without also addressing issues of racism.

The Vagaries and Vulgarities of Race

"Race" in Western ideology

"Race" seems so obvious. What could be more straightforward than the color of people's skin, the shape of their face, the texture of their hair? There can be no doubt that the physical appearance of people varies and that these variations seem to be associated, over the long history of human development, with particular regions, giving rise to broad similarities and differences between peoples. There seems to be a regularity of skin type (etc.) by region: people from particular parts of the world tend to look similar to each other (figure 9.1). Racial difference is

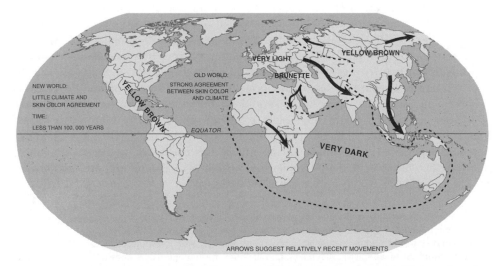

Figure 9.1 The correlation between place and race is taken as given in much Western thought – and it has been dutifully reproduced in cultural geography textbooks. Here, in a book from the 1960s, a simple correlation between skin color and climate is taken as given, and differences between racial features – or features that seem out of place – are explained as the result of migrations. Source: George Carter, *Man and the Land* (New York: Holt, Rinehart and Winston, 1968: 24).

undeniable.[5] Yet as obvious as those regional similarities and global differences may be, they are also deceptive. There seems to be little regularity of *co-variation* of particular traits within and across populations. As Jared Diamond (1994: 85) has pointed out in *Discover* (a popular science magazine), the way that "races" are classified is "a matter of personal preference" among scientists. In a series of examples, Diamond shows just how idiosyncratic racial classification is: if classification is made by such traits as fingerprints, then one group would combine "most Europeans, black Africans, and east Asians;" another would be comprised of "Mongolians and Australian Aborigines;" and a third would consist of "Khoisans and some central Europeans" (Diamond 1994: 87). If, instead, we looked at the ability to easily digest milk, one grouping would be of northern and central Europeans, Arabs, and some West Africans; the other would consist of most other Africans, east Asians, American Indians, southern Europeans and Australian aborigines. Imagine checking to see how these criteria co-vary with others such as skin color or hair-type and you can see how ridiculous the notion of racial classification is. Diamond (1994: 88) provides the clincher:

> One method that *seems* to offer a way out of the arbitrariness [of "race"] is to classify peoples by degree of genetic distinctness. By this standard the Khoisans of southern Africa would be in a race by themselves. African blacks would form several other distinct races. All the rest of the world's peoples – Norwegians, Navajo, Greeks, Japanese, Australian aborigines, and so on – would, despite their greatly differing external appearance, belong to a single race.[6]

"Race" is thus little more than the vagaries of the popular and scientific imagination; it provides no means to classify human populations. "The straightforward biological fact of human variation is that there are no traits that are inherently, inevitably associated with one another. Morphological features *do* vary from region to region, but they do so independently, not in packaged sets" (Shreeve 1994: 58). Given that "straightforward biological fact," the particular ways that humans have been classified have been free to vary with the changing political and social winds. Hence the longstanding historical debates on just how many races there are (three? four? five? twenty?), and just how these races should be hierarchically ordered. So too the pernicious arguments about the degree to which pathological behavior is "associated" with particular "races" (see Williams 1994). In short, what no biologist, eugenicist, geneticist, supremacist, or polemicist has been able to show is that there is any coherent way to define similarities *within* groups and differences *between* groups on the basis of physical and genetic variation.

5   For a brief, accessible discussion of the geographical basis for the division of humans into subspecies – and of the ontological status of "subspecies" in the first place – see Gould (1985a).
6   Diamond's own research is interesting in connection not only with questions of race, but also environmental determinism (see chapter 1). A staunch anti-racist and anti-biological determinist, Diamond continues to search for mono-causal answers to questions of human social difference. His recent Pulitzer Prize-winning book, *Guns, Germs, and Steel: The Fates of Human Society* (1997), is nothing if not a sophisticated development of the environmental determinist thesis (stripped of its racism). The problem is that by using environmental determinism to contest biological determinism, Diamond allows almost no possibility for the social efficacy of society itself. For Diamond the argument seems to be that since it is a fallacy to rely on biology (especially "race") for understanding social difference, then we *must* rely on environment.

To put that another way, and as my use of the popular science magazine *Discover* indicates, there is broad acceptance in the scientific community, at least, that there is no such biological thing as "race."[7] Dividing humans into groups, on the basis of some combination of physical and genetic traits, simply does not make sense. And when variation in those traits is further tied to such reified attributes as "intelligence," "character," or "ability," claims about race become even more dubious. Indeed, the very absurdity of such claims can easily be seen in historical tracts on race – tracts that are to our ears quite unsophisticated in their discussions of difference. Consider the following statements from biologist Charles White's "An Account of the Regular Gradation in Man, and in Different Animals and Vegetables" (1779):

> Captains and Surgeons of Guinea ships, and the West India planters, unanimously concur in their accounts, that negroes sweat much less than Europeans: a drop of sweat being scarcely ever seen upon them. Simiae sweat still less, and dogs not at all.   (Quoted in Gould 1985a: 288)

> Ascending the line of gradation, we come at last to the white European; who being most removed from brute creation, may, on that account, be considered as the most beautiful of the human race. No one will doubt his superiority of intellectual powers; and I believe it will be found that his capacity is naturally superior to that of every other man.   (Quoted in Gould 1985a: 289)

Note the context. White draws on the accounts of slave-traders and colonial planters to make his case, an obvious indication of the nature of the "economic, political, and ideological" conditions of which Miles spoke in the passage cited above. And note, too, the degree to which such sentiments have been repeated over the years. In the first half of the twentieth century, the geographers Ellen Churchill Semple (1911) and Glenn Trewartha (1926) would both note how Africans' "economy of sweat" make them particularly suited for manual labor.

That "race" is a fact of nature is deeply embedded in Western consciousness, but it is one that derived from a European encounter with the world in which European superiority was not just asserted, but actively maintained through the use of guns and weapons of torture. Why? As historians such as Sidney Mintz (1974, 1985; see also Miles 1982: chapter 5) have shown, slavery, for example, solved a particular material problem – one of labor shortages in the expanding colonial domains of the Americas. This is not to say that all manifestations of racism can be directly mapped onto economic necessity. It is to say, however, that a look at the material conditions of society goes a long way in *explaining* the need for racial distinction.

How colonial powers – or dominant groups in contemporary society – explain racial difference to themselves is another matter. Ideology is often most effective not on the objects of that ideology (racialized people, for example) who can see through it right

---

7   A little more than a decade ago, Peter Jackson (1987a: 17) wrote that while the social construction of race was widely accepted in the natural and social sciences, "it has yet to penetrate public consciousness and to influence the realm of common-sense understanding." That is less the case now, as debates over how best to classify by race in the USA census attest. If my own students' comments are anything to go by, then it seems that even early in university education students are repeatedly exposed to critical deconstructions of the idea of race. Nonetheless, matters of popular knowledge about race are quite complex and hardly perfect, as the discussion below of Herrnstein and Murray's (1994) *The Bell Curve* makes clear.

away, but on the people in power as a means of justifying their actions (Scott 1985). Ideology also has the material effect of organizing allegiance in particular directions. For example, in the case of "race," blacks are often constructed as a "common enemy" of *all* whites, which is a means of masking differences in material interests *between* whites. That is, "race allegiance" is developed and exploited as a means of convincing some in society to "buy into" their own exploitation by transferring the cause of that exploitation to a third party identified as "naturally" different, and socially suspect. Important strains of ideology in the West, have, therefore, been structured on the notion that differences in society – between whites and blacks, Europeans and Asians, even rich and poor – actively reflect, indeed are determined by, not social conditions, but by our biology. Obvious physical differences are *reified* into largely immutable classes that represent not only amounts of melanin, but also levels of intelligence, physical prowess, cultural attributes, and so on (see Gould 1981: 24).

The earliest uses of the term "race" in the English language indicate that it referred to distinct classes or categories of things, but the distinctions were not seen to arise from biology. Not until the end of the eighteenth century did the idea of race take on its biological, physical connotations, as "race" was used to make sense of both European history and expanding colonialism. By the 1850s, it was fairly well accepted, in the centers of imperial power at least, that "what set populations apart was not so much their history as their physical appearance" (Miles 1982: 10). As Europeans tried to come to grips with their encounters with different peoples the world over, and as they sought to justify their own drive to dominate those peoples, a complex debate developed on the origin of racial difference. The question was not so much *whether* innate biological differences existed between people – differences that were directly responsible for social, cultural, and intellectual ability – but *from whence* these differences arose.[8] Drawing support from the biblical story of Adam and Eve, monogenists argued that all humans were descended from a single original couple, but that different races had declined – fallen from grace, really – to different degrees. Attributions of cause for this degeneration (which whites were seen to suffer from the least) were varied, but usually centered on some environmental factor: biological determinism had its roots in environmental determinism.[9] Such beliefs in environmental degeneracy were deeply held. Stephen Jay Gould (1981: 39) tells of the president of the College of New Jersey (now Princeton), who "hoped that American blacks, in a climate more suited to Caucasian temperaments, would soon turn white." "Race" in the monogenist formulation, therefore, was not entirely immutable, even if many argued that change would occur too slowly to make much difference in the affairs of the world.

By contrast, polygenists argued that races were distinct biological species (or, in more modern formulations, that racial distinctions were apparent in the evolutionary ancestors of humans and were then carried through into human evolution) (Coon 1962; see Gould 1985b). Evidence in support of this view ranged from body shape and

---

8   The classic – and classically racist – geography text is Ellsworth Huntington's (1915) *Climate and Civilization*. This book, which went through a number of subsequent editions, is worth reading for assessing the length to which proponents of racist geographies go to support an essentially unsupportable case. In this regard *Climate and Civilization* is a telling precursor to *The Bell Curve* (discussed below).

9   Much of this debate was conducted in neo-Lamarckian terms. See Livingstone (1992) and chapter 1 above.

type to the size of skulls.[10] For the nineteenth-century Swiss-American natural historian Louis Agassiz, like so many others of his time, the existence of different races implied the need to rank those races in terms of natural intellectual and cultural ability.

> There are upon the earth different races of men, inhabiting different parts of its surface, which have different physical characteristics; and this fact . . . presses upon us the obligation to settle the relative rank among these races, the relative value of the characters peculiar to each, in a scientific point of view. . . . As philosophers it is our duty to look it in the face.   (Quoted in Gould 1981: 46)

For some, a look at the face of the race showed that there were three distinct and immutable races: Caucasoid, Negroid, and Mongoloid. Others added two more: American Indian, and Pacific Islanders. A cultural geography textbook from the early 1970s adds "Negritoid, Bushmanoid, Australoid, and Papuan-Melasian" (Broek and Webb 1973: 88). Still others, seeing in the face of race impressive variation, and finding that biological and genetic facts were actually poor support for dividing humanity by three or five, argued for many, many more. By the time he had finished his studies of cranial capacity, for example, the American nineteenth-century craniologist Samuel Morton had divided humanity into twenty-two separate and distinct races (Gould 1981) (table 9.1).

Whatever the nature of these arguments about the number of races, about the proper criteria for distinguishing one race from another, and about the evolutionary (or Godly) origins of racial difference, scientists of the nineteenth century largely agreed on several basic propositions, as Robert Miles (1982: 13) summarizes:

> (i) the physical appearance and behaviour of individuals was an expression of a discrete biological type which was permanent; (ii) cultural variation was determined by differences in biological type; (iii) biological variation was the origin of conflict between both individuals and nations; and (iv) "races" were differentially endowed such that some were inherently superior to others.

Combined with Social-Darwinist ideas about the cultural survival of the fittest (and thus the "natural" basis for rule and domination),[11] such fundamental beliefs were a powerful inducement to the exercise of power. They also provided a handy excuse for dismissing white historical culpability for oppression and genocide. Even so (or perhaps especially because of that) such ideas were largely accepted as common sense well into the mid-twentieth century with biology, sociology, and geography textbooks of the 1970s (and 1980s) still faithfully reflecting the received wisdom about the separate races that inhabit the globe – even when they forthrightly admitted that

---

10   Gould's (1981) *Mismeasure of Man* is devoted to examining the distortions this scientific effort produced – distortions that ranged from outright fakery of data to the more interesting subconscious skewing of results to fit a predetermined outcome.

11   As we saw in chapter 1, important social theorists such as Herder argued strongly against such notions in the late eighteenth century. The fact that such voices of opposition existed – and were strongly registered – should serve as a sufficient caution in assuming that a *dominant* way of thinking in a particular era and place is the *only* way of thinking.

Table 9.1   Morton's final summary of cranial capacity by race

Races and Families	N	Cranial capacity (IN^3)			
		Largest	Smallest	Mean	Mean
Modern Caucasian group					
Teutonic Family					
Germans	18	114	70	90 ⎫	
English	5	105	91	96 ⎬	92
Anglo-Americans	7	97	82	90 ⎭	
Pelasgic Family	10	94	75	84	
Celtic Family	6	97	78	87	
Indostanic Family	32	91	67	80	
Semitic Family	3	98	84	89	
Nilotic Family	17	96	66	80	
Ancient Caucasian group					
Pelasgic Family	18	97	74	88	
Nilotic Family	55	96	68	80	
Mongolian group					
Chinese Family	6	91	70	82	
Malay group					
Malayan Family	20	97	68	86 ⎫	
Polynesian Family	3	84	82	83 ⎭	85
American group					
Toltecan Family					
Peruvians	155	101	58	75 ⎫	
Mexicans	22	92	67	79 ⎭	79
Barbarous Tribes	161	104	70	84	
Negro group					
Native African Family	62	99	65	83 ⎫	
American-born Negroes	12	89	73	82 ⎭	83
Hottentot Family	3	83	68	75	
Australians	8	83	63	75	

Note: Using cranial capacity as his yardstick, Samuel Gould divided humanity into an impressive 22 separate races. The numbers in this table are not to be trusted. As Stephen Jay Gould has shown, Morton's measurements do not bear up under scrutiny: he had the habit of adjusting his results to fit the outcome he wanted. Morton's taxonomy, therefore, stands more as a testament to nineteenth-century racial ideology than it does as an accurate rending of differences between humans.
Source: Reproduced from Gould (1981: 55).

such a belief was "nonsense." A good example is the 1973 cultural geography text-book, *A Geography of Mankind*, by University of Minnesota professors Jan Broek and John Webb. The authors begin their chapter on "Race: Biological Facts and Social Attitudes" by stating clearly that "classification of human races is difficult, if not impossible," and that "biologically speaking, mankind is a single subspecies (*Homo sapiens sapiens*);" yet they still devote 11 pages to a discussion of "the main racial stocks," "the present distribution of the races," and so forth. Much of this

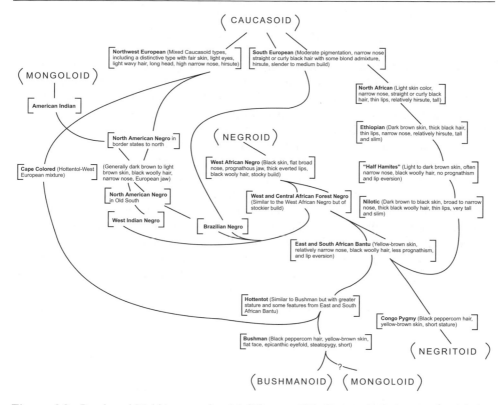

Figure 9.2 Broek and Webb's map of racial difference. This diagram indicates genetic variation from a presumed "true Negroid." The lines, according to the authors, indicate "scales of increasing and decreasing Negroid gene frequency," not "lines of descent." Note that Caucasians are placed in a superior position in the diagram. Source: Broek and Webb (1973: 91).

discussion is given over to associating particular physical features, such as facial shape, hair type, and skin color, with particular regions. We are told where the "'true' Negroid" and the "'classic' Mongoloid" are to be found (West Africa and Mongolia), and where groups with "decreased frequency" of Negroid or Mongoloid genes live, but are warned that "it is not so easy to divide the Caucasoid people into distinct subgroups living in separate regions" (Broek and Webb 1973: 81–92) (figure 9.2). Since the authors provide no compelling anthropological or other arguments for spatial variation or racial groups, offer no evidence about the degree of homogeneity in phenotype or genotype among peoples of particular regions, and indeed argue that in most regions phenotypic variety is the rule rather than the exception, it is hard to see what the point of these pages is, other than to reinforce, even if critically, the notion that distinct biological groups do indeed exist on the face of the earth. But that is an idea that has come under increasing attack in the biological sciences in the past several decades (as even the authors of the textbook under discussion admit).

The arguments against "race"

The majority of biologists and geneticists simply no longer accept that "race" has any scientific validity at all. The arguments in favor of a biological basis to race fail in two places: at the level of phenotype and at the level of genotype. Racial classification is usually based on phenotype – the surficial physical characteristics of an organism (skin color, hair type, size and shape of various body parts) that provide the most common basis for dividing people into distinct races. The problem, as we have seen, is that phenotypic traits do not vary consistently together. Stature and skin color, hair type and nose shape – it is impossible to consistently associate changes in one trait with changes in another. As we have also seen, this fact led many who would divide the world into discrete races based on phenotype to continually further divide the human pie into smaller and smaller pieces, hoping thereby to create coherent and cohesive racial populations. They never did. Phenotypic chaos is the rule since *each* phenotypic variation exists along a continuum, and thus the classification of individuals into groups must find a way to slice coherently through variation in nearly infinite dimensions. Exceptions to whatever classifications are formed will not prove the rule, as the old saying goes, they will *be* the rule. "One consequence is that any attempt to identify 'races' by reference to phenotypical variation can only ever produce overlapping classifications and not distinct categories," as Miles (1982: 14) puts it. This is so in part because phenotypic variation is not a simple expression of genotypic variation (genotype is the genetic "code" of an individual). Genotype "programs" for a range of phenotypic expression, and the resulting "look" of an individual is a complex result of biological foundation (the genotypic "code"), biological chance (the contingent expressions of that "code"), and environmental and social influence. The important point, however, is that the sheer abundance of difference cannot be classified into distinct groups at the level of phenotype.

Can it at the level of genotype? Not in any coherent fashion, as the *Discover* Magazine article makes clear. We can arbitrarily choose a particular gene (or maybe even a small gene sequence) and parcel out humanity on the basis of that gene. But as soon as we choose another bit of genetic code we end up with a completely different classification. The problem is exactly the same as with phenotype. So, unless we are willing to believe that the genetic basis for some particular trait (sickle cell resistance or lactase tolerance, for example) is more important than all the other genetic traits that make up our biological endowment, then it is simply impossible to divide humanity into discrete genetic packages on anything but the most arbitrary grounds. Geneticists recognize this and argue that "race" is a term that can only be used to describe "populations which differ in frequency, or in prevalence, of some genes" and hence the exact population of any particular "race" will vary depending on the genes studied (quoted in Miles 1982: 15). Yet even this definition of race falters as anything more than a handy heuristic for whatever limited scientific study happens to be in progress, since genetic variation *within* a "race" so defined is greater than the average difference *between* populations. Hence, whether one divides one race from another at point x rather than at point y, z, or any other point in the total genetic endowment – or whether one divides races at all – is completely arbitrary. A "matter of taste" as one geneticist puts it (Bodmer 1972: 90, quoted in Miles 1982: 16). What is more, as Jared Diamond's *Discover* article quoted above makes plain, even any *regional* coherence to "race" falls apart – note the similarities in such traits as the ability to digest milk between such geographically distant populations as east Asians and southern Europeans and the differences that occur over small areas in West Africa.

Most simply put, then, there is *no such biological thing as race*. "Race" is both the classic "chaotic concept" – a concept that is meant to contain far more than it possibly can – and the classic reification – the "thingification" of a process or relationship. Even so, there are few concepts – chaotic or not, reified or not – as powerful as "race." The belief in race, fervently held, fervently acted upon, has been the maker of history and a maker of geography, whether that history and geography is one of colonialism and slavery, housing and urban development, economic exploitation, or education funding. It also insinuates itself in the whole history of Western literature and social thought. There may not be any such *thing* as race, but that does not mean that "race" is not a very real fact in all our lives (whether we are part of a privileged or oppressed group). Racial *differentiation* (as opposed to innate "difference") must therefore be understood "as a product of power *struggle* rather than as something imposed by white society and passively accepted" by people of color (S. Smith 1989: 8). The lack of a biological basis for race, in addition, does not mean that racialist thinking, and whole arguments built atop the fallacy of race, are not still current in contemporary society. Quite the contrary.

The Bell Curve and Racism's Geography

I mentioned at the outset of this chapter that an awful lot of effort goes into the policing of the boundaries of race. It clearly must, as we can infer from the discussion above. If there is nothing natural about race – if there is no basis in nature for a racist social order – then it must be socially maintained. This policing takes innumerable forms as it works through our everyday lives. These include everything from racist lending practices by banks that make it difficult for racial minorities to obtain loans or to move to the neighborhoods of their choice, to employment practices, to the actions of the police, to the way from the earliest ages we are taught to talk to each other. But these everyday practices have also to be supported and reinforced at the level of overt ideology and political action. Immigration laws are obvious examples (consider, for example, the changes in British immigration policies as African and Caribbean colonies won their independence), as are the changing rules of asylum and citizenship on the European continent (see chapter 10). The role of public discourse, especially as it is amplified in and by the media, is also important. Even more important is the way that public discourse intersects with the geography of place so as to structure "common sense" about "race."

In the United States, perhaps the most prominent recent example of racialist, and clearly racist, public argument – an example that understands the geography of difference to be absolutely central to the social development of the country – was Richard Herrnstein and Charles Murray's (1994) book, *The Bell Curve: Intelligence and Class Structure in American Life.*[12] To understand the importance of geography to the racist argument presented in *The Bell Curve*, it is first necessary to examine that racist argument itself in some detail.

The Bell Curve's *Racist Reasoning*

Despite the fact that the mainstreams of biological and even social science have rejected the notion that race has any roots whatsoever in the natural world, Herrnstein and Murray's scurrilous account of the "cognitive ability" of different groups in the United States (and to a lesser extent elsewhere), became a huge media event. The major American newsweeklies, *Time, US News and World Report*, and *Newsweek*, all carried feature articles and debates on Herrnstein and Murray's arguments. The *New York Times Magazine* put Charles Murray on its cover and wondered if he was the "most dangerous conservative in America." The *New Republic* (October, 1994) devoted a whole issue to an article derived from the book and no fewer than nineteen separate commentaries on it. Murray was a frequent guest on television and radio talk shows (Herrnstein died just before publication). Herrnstein and Murray plainly saw their work as an important argument against social policies such as affirmative action, welfare, and equality of opportunity in schooling. *The Bell Curve* refueled debate in America on just these issues – and the racist discourses that support them – right at the moment (1994) that radical cultural and economic conservatives were wresting power from the slightly less radical conservatism of the Clinton Democrats who had been elected in 1992.[13] To the question of what material conditions make racism possible at any given moment, the answer in this case must look towards, among other things, the declining real wages of American whites (particularly men), the continued, and continually questioned, obvious fact of disparate life chances for blacks, whites, Asians, and Latinos, the continued immigration of people of color to the United States, particularly from Latin America and poorer regions of Asia, the "race panic" that set in after the 1992 Los Angeles rebellion, the emergence of prison construction as a dynamic growth industry, and a redistribution of wealth in American society from bottom to top, most marked in the attack on welfare (Muwakkil 1995). This was the world into which *The Bell Curve* was launched – and upon which it hoped to have an incisive impact.

The Bell Curve was not favorably received in much of the early commentary on it; indeed, perhaps the majority of the commentary was highly critical.[14] What is remarkable, however, and what makes the book such an important indicator of how "race" remains a key weapon in the culture wars, is that the book was taken seriously at all (see Gates 1995; Lind 1995). It is remarkable because Herrnstein and Murray's argument is slipshod and their obvious racism puts them in league not with the putative mainstream of American culture, but with the racist right of the KKK and the Aryan Nation, more deserving of scorn than serious analysis. Their use of

---

12   Unaccompanied page numbers in the sections that follow are from this book.
13   Herrnstein and Murray were fairly coy in their arguments about these issues in *The Bell Curve* itself, but were much more openly hostile to such social policies in their *New Republic* article.
14   Two volumes collect analyses of *The Bell Curve*: Fraser (1995) and Jacoby and Glauberman (1995).

sources and evidence borders on the intellectually dishonest, as any relatively attentive reader can see.[15] But more than that, they simply fail to document most of the claims that they make (their common ploy is to say either that documentation would take too much space [p. 23] or that they will support their points later in the book [p. 24] – which they never adequately do). Despite their explicit recognition of the fact that correlation does not equal causation (and correlation studies are the backbone of the book), the authors regularly *imply* just the opposite. To take just one example: "High intelligence also provides some protection against lapsing into criminality for people who are otherwise at risk" (p. 235). Such a statement – made in a chapter introduction designed for those readers who want to understand the author's points "at the simplest level" – does strongly *suggest* a causative relationship between intelligence and criminality, and the authors do nothing anywhere else in the book to dispel that implication.

More fundamentally, *The Bell Curve* is simply incoherent, as any argument that bases itself on unvarying genetic difference between arbitrary groups must be. This does not slow Herrnstein and Murray down a bit as they insist – and repeat over and over – that while an individual's membership in any group (be it class, race, ethnic, or otherwise) does not matter one whit to their chances of being "intelligent," one's membership in a group (be it class, race, ethnic, or otherwise) is the single most important determinant of one's probable intelligence.[16] Such an amazing argument is laid out something like this:

1   The authors argue that there is some innate thing called "intelligence" which can be captured through standardized tests and which can be expressed as a single number (called *g* for "general factor"). In popular accounts, "IQ" is freely substituted for *g*. This *g* is argued to be "substantially" genetic in origin: anywhere from 40 to 80 percent of the variation in *g* is explained by genetic variation.[17]

2   Herrnstein and Murray aver that genetic IQ not only varies by individual, but also varies in a regular manner by group.   (See especially pp. 298–311)

3   At the beginning of the book, these groups are classes. The authors argue that the upper classes are composed of the "cognitive elite" who have risen to their top of the political and economic hierarchy through sheer intelligence. The corollary is that the "dumb" and "very dumb" (as Herrnstein and Murray call them) sink to the bottom, there to wallow in their stinking habits of crime, illegitimate childbirth, menial labor or unemployment, and welfare dependency.

15   Numerous commentators – collected in the Fraser (1995) and Jacoby and Glauberman (1995) volumes – point to Herrnstein and Murray's consistent denigration – or non-citation – of studies that contradict the ones they favor. For excellent studies of Herrnstein and Murray's use of sources – and the bankrolling of their favored studies by disreputable eugenicist foundations – see Jacoby and Glauberman (1995), Part II.

16   Herrnstein and Murray's contradictions are particularly clear when discussing Latinos: The term, they concede, includes innumerable people of "highly disparate cultural heritages and a wide range of racial stocks." But even so, "their tests generally fall about one-half to one standard deviation below the national mean." The group does not exist as a coherent group. The group exists as a coherent group. Both. See Hernandez (1995).

17   Both Fraser (1995) and Jacoby and Glauberman (1995) devote considerable space to showing just how poorly Herrnstein and Murray use their statistics, how they misrepresent the evidence such statistics present, and how they often draw conclusions from the numbers wholly at odds with what the numbers say.

4 In both cases, one's genes determine one's ascent to the summit or descent into the abyss.[18] Intelligence is coded in one's DNA. There is nothing you can do about it. But since genetic coding varies within as well as between groups, there is no reason to assume that dumb parents will *always* produce dumb or dumber children.

5 The odds that dumb parents will produce dumb offspring are increasing, however, as geographical separations between classes prevent intermarrying: more and more, "cognitive elites" breed with "cognitive elites;" the dumb breed with the dumb.   (pp. 101–5).[19]

6 Beginning with chapter 13, Herrnstein and Murray argue that g varies regularly not only by class, but also by ethnic group (for which they mean "race"). They point out that African Americans, as a whole, consistently score 15 points lower than white Americans on standard IQ tests. While scores for both blacks and whites have risen over the years, that gap has not closed.[20] The authors therefore argue that the *average* African American is simply – and naturally – not as intelligent as the *average* white American. "Translated into centiles," IQ testing shows that "the average white person tests higher than about 84 percent of the population of blacks, and that the average black person tests higher than about sixteen percent of the whites".   (p. 269) Unfortunately for whites, Asians out-score everyone.[21]

18 Herrnstein and Murray place a great deal of weight on the claim that intelligence is 40 to 80 percent heritable, and they typically use an estimate of 60 percent as what they hope will seem a reasonable middle ground. They further argue throughout the book that intelligence is negatively associated with pathological behavior (indeed, that is one of their main points). However, they also admit that cognitive ability "almost always explains less than 20 percent of the variance... usually less than 10 percent, and often less than five percent. What this means in English is that you cannot predict what a given person will do from his IQ score.... On the other hand, despite the low association at the individual level, large differences in social behavior separate groups of people when the groups differ intellectually on average. We will argue that intelligence itself, not just its correlation with socioeconomic status, is responsible for these group differences" (p. 117). As Stephen Jay Gould (1995: 19) points out, the assumption that intelligence is 60 percent heritable means that we must understand that genetic intelligence *at best* accounts for 12 percent of observed variation between groups, and "often" only three percent. Moreover, the best R^2 the authors report is .16 (in an appendix where it would not be noticed by many), thus suggesting the "goodness of fit" of the regression equations upon which their whole argument is built is not very good at all.

19 In Parts III and IV of their book, Herrnstein and Murray strongly imply that the cognitive sorting they describe for classes also works between races. Or, more simply, there is little opportunity for cross-racial marriages. In fact, between 1960 and 1990, according to census data, interracial marriages increased by more than 800 percent. That is, the elimination of Jim Crow and formal laws governing miscegenation, have led to greater racial mixing. As we will see, Herrnstein and Murray really want to return us to the pre-1960 days rather than, as they claim, find ways to encourage mixing between races and classes. See Lind (1998).

20 Actually, the authors concede that the gap is remarkably variable according to which studies are consulted (pp. 289–90). That is, the studies don't really support the strong claim that the black–white gap in IQ is largely invariable.

21 The authors again concede that *universally* test scores have been rising steadily since they were invented, "sometimes as much as a point a year for some span of years" (p. 308). This means one of several things: (a) IQ tests *do not* actually measure intelligence – the tests are flawed and the rise in scores is an artifact of the test itself (this conclusion must be drawn by those who want to argue for a genetic control on intelligence); (b) "environmental factors" are more important than genetic factors in determining intelligence, and the world-wide rise can be attributed to changes in the environment (such as more universal and better education); or (c) people are evolving *really fast* (this conclusion must be drawn by

7   These "racial" differences are *real* (they say something significant about the natural abilities of African Americans as a whole), according to the authors, because "race" itself is real. Racial differences in skin color, hair texture, "cognitive ability" and a host of other factors are there in the genes (p. 297). In other words, differences in phenotype are classifiable into groups and are mapped directly from differences in genotype – differences that themselves vary regularly between groups in a way that is more significant than all the within-group variation in these genotypes and phenotypes. Racial groups have ontological validity and are not just an artifact of statistical (or other) clustering.[22]

8   In the end it does not matter whether the "real differences" between races are genetic or environmental (though the authors argue they plainly *are* genetic); the important point is that they are, like race itself, *real* and that fact must be faced squarely (p. 312). But these real differences are differences between *groups* and thus say nothing about *individuals*.

9   Indeed, statistical studies show that when controlling for IQ, African Americans have a *better* chance of graduating from college and entering a profession than do whites of the same cognitive ability.

10 Unfortunately, as a group African Americans are "dumber," and therefore few of them are simply smart enough to do as well as whites in college and professions (indeed, for "dumb" blacks – which the authors have already declared are the majority – there is "nothing they can learn that will repay the cost of teaching" [p. 520]).

11 These differences in cognitive ability, and their relative distribution within and between groups (including races) will not be influenced "much" by "outside intervention." They will be altered, however, by what the authors call "dysgenic pressures" which include higher birthrates among people of lower intelligence and immigration policies that allow in people of the wrong groups. The logical corollary (though one the authors shy away from) is that the only means to improve cognitive ability is by countering dysgenic trends with eugenic ones. That is, some *individuals* and some *groups* must both be encouraged, and others must be discouraged, from having children.

This is a truly incredible and appalling argument, and one, quite frankly, I did not think it any longer possible to make – at least not in circles beyond those circumscribed by the National Front, the Aryan Nation, the Ku Klux Klan, or the

those who would want to retain a faith in IQ testing *and* in genetics as the most important determinant of intelligence. Hernnstein and Murray understand these issues, but argue instead that (a) since the rise is universal, there is no chance that blacks will ever "catch up" with whites and Asians, and therefore IQ tests still measure innate differences between groups; and (b) that the rise is a temporary aberration: "No one is suggesting, for example that the IQ of the average American in 1776 was 30 or that it will be 159 a century from now." Moreover, they argue, "at any point in time, it is one's position in the distribution that has the most significant implications for social and economic life...and also for the position of one's children" (p. 309).

22   Hertnstein and Murray provide no evidence for their claim. They just argue that it is common sense to know that racial difference in skin color indicates some other, more fundamental difference. They also dodge the issue in some places by claiming they will "classify people according to the way they classify themselves." But to then draw conclusions about the *natural, biological* tendencies of such self-identified groups is simply perverse.

"scholars" at the Holocaust-denying Institute for Historical Revision. Herrnstein and Murray do make it, however, in a book published by a quite respected New York publisher, and they do it all under the cloak of dispassionate science.

Beyond the fact that the authors' own data do not show what they pretend they do, the book itself is founded on a fallacy, namely, the fallacy of "race" that we have already explored. Such fallacies and bad scholarship in *The Bell Curve* have been well exposed. The general incoherence of the argument has been well scrutinized by others, and the book has been found to be not only poorly argued, but fundamentally dishonest in many instances (see Fraser 1995; Jacoby and Glauberman 1995). And yet it seems to me that one reason the book found a ready audience (and not just a critical one – see the commentaries in *The National Review*) is not necessarily because of the scientific vision the authors projected, but because of the *geographical* one.

The Bell Curve's *Racist Geography*

Underlying, and supporting the whole structure of the argument in *The Bell Curve* is a vision of what America "should be," and what it should be seems to be a highly nostalgic world of small towns and authentic urban neighborhoods where everyone "knows their place." It is a world in which the social order perfectly reflects the natural order of intelligence (as Herrnstein and Murray define it), and everybody is properly valued as to their real social and natural worth because they are "where they belong."[23] Herrnstein and Murray establish their nostalgic geography by first exploring the dystopian direction they see the USA heading (because as a society, it fails to recognize the importance of "natural" and "immutable" cognitive difference). That dystopic world looks something like this:

It is marked first and foremost by an almost ineluctable dysgenic tendency. As we have seen, Herrnstein and Murray argue that "intelligence" is a largely "natural" or genetic attribute of individuals, that it is highly impervious to change by environmental factors, that it is correlated strongly with particular groups (such as races), that group–intelligence correlations are strengthened through geographical isolation and "in-breeding," and that intelligence, including "group average intelligence," is highly associated with particular behaviors (ability to make money, criminality, legitimacy and illegitimacy, etc.). Indeed, the dysgenic tendency is being *strengthened* as the "cognitive elite" more and more separate themselves out from the rest of society and work to create – purposely or not – a "custodial state" in which the elite tries to protect itself by ever stricter control over the "duller" masses. Rank fear of the growing black and Latino underclasses and their supposedly violent ways is leading elites, Herrnstein and Murray aver, to ever more fully separate themselves from society, retreating into their compounds from which they direct the ever more harsh policing of the masses. Such tendencies are evidenced in everything from the growth in prison construction and strict policing, to intolerance towards homeless people, to the continual and growing spatial concentration of the underclass. This vision actually

23 For excellent discussions of the ideological relationship between space and "natural" orders, see Cresswell (1996); Sibley (1995).

has much in common with critiques of the current social geography of urban areas by scholars and activists on the Left (e.g. Davis 1990; Mackenzie 1994), except that Herrnstein and Murray explain the evolution of what they call a "high-tech, more lavish version of the Indian reservation" (p. 526) by reference to the putative "natural intelligence" of different groups in society. It's not the *only* outcome towards which such "natural" differences must lead, but it is currently the predominant one.

It should be noted, however, that with the exception of this one reference to an Indian reservation, Herrnstein and Murray nowhere directly link the evolution of the high-tech reservation system (or any alternative to it) to race itself; they only link it to differences in "mental ability." But no reader can help but remember that the authors have already spent more than a hundred pages explicitly linking "cognitive ability" to race, and putatively showing that African Americans, among others, just aren't smart enough (and never will be). What they see as the probable future is one in which African Americans and Indians and anyone else "not especially bright" will live in a world apart, and in a geography of quite dehumanizing conditions.

That makes their alternative all the more intriguing – and the racial geography in it even more obscene. In their final chapter, titled "A Place for Everyone," Herrnstein and Murray suggest that the cognitive elite should develop policies that take as their inspiration a time past when good Americans realized and *valued* innate differences between people. "In a simpler America, being comparatively low in the qualities measured by IQ did not necessarily affect the ability to find a valued niche in society. Many such people worked on farms" (p. 536).[24] The authors define "valued" in the following way: "You occupy a valued place if other people would miss you if you were gone. . . . Both the quality and the quantity of valued places are important. . . . If a single person would miss you and no one else, you have a fragile hold on your place in society, no matter how much that one person cares for you. To have many people who would miss you, in many different parts of your life and at many levels of intensity, is a hallmark of a person whose place is well and thoroughly valued" (p. 535). That's a stunning argument if you remember the context – "a simpler America." When was that?

One "blueprint of the good society" to which Herrnstein and Murray refer might be the period from 1890 to 1915, according to Jacqueline Jones (1995: 82–3; see also Wickham 1995). "While the country was undergoing a process of urbanization and industrialization, the majority of black people were domestic servants and agricultural workers (that is, they worked at jobs befitting their low mental abilities, in the parlance of *The Bell Curve*)."[25] But this was the time of Jim Crow, of race riots against Asian and African Americans in northern cities, and of the often violent

---

24 Similar arguments concerning the natural order of place in a "simpler America" have been made in other realms, too. Law scholar Robert Ellickson (1996), for example, has proposed tackling the problem of chronic homelessness by instituting programs of "informal zoning" (reinforced by police practices) in which each member of society is kept in her or his "proper place" – for the homeless, that means they will be kept, forcefully if necessary, on Skid Row, where "they belong."

25 If Herrnstein and Murray seem a bit coy on the implications of their research, one of the authors they approvingly cite is not. Michael Levin of the City College of New York says, "Race difference shows that whites aren't at fault for blacks being down, and making whites pay for something they're not responsible for is a terrible injustice. Eliminating affirmative action is the first step. Next – please, yes, if only – eliminate the Civil Rights Act" (quoted in Miller 1995: 165).

restriction of Latinos to "their side of the tracks" in the Southwest. Herrnstein and Murray persist in their delusional geography, nonetheless. In urban neighborhoods of the golden past, they argue, "anyone who wanted to have a place in the community could find one in the local school boards, churches, union halls, garden clubs, and benevolent associations of one sort or another.... Someone who was mentally a bit dull might not be chosen to head up the parish clothing drive but was certainly eligible to help out" (p. 537).

If that model of interaction between the smart and the dumb – the black and the white – in America seems a bit fanciful, Jacqueline Jones suggests another model which fits the author's argument much better, but which they may have shied away from. "On the plantation, blacks and whites coexisted in a relatively peaceful way (though the peace was always enforced with violence or the threat of it)" and the division of labor – between those who could "head up" and those who could "help out" – was as clearly drawn as it was inclusive.

> The slave plantation operated on the principle that all low-IQ persons (i.e., blacks) could work productively and should be taken care of accordingly – a virtue in any society. If we extrapolate from Herrnstein and Murray's analysis – and understand the planter as a paternalistic smart white man overseeing lots of hardworking black males and fecund "wenches," and controlling the "Nats" predisposed to violent crime or rebellion – then the slave plantation takes on a more benevolent, or at least socially useful, cast.   (Jones 1995: 86)

Such is the result that Herrnstein and Murray's analysis of race, IQ, and society, combined with their complaints about a reservation state, gets us.

Perhaps Herrnstein and Murray would not go quite that far, but it is hard to see where the line should be drawn between the kind of "value" they define as important in society, and the way that slave owners "valued" their slaves (figure 9.3). After all, a hard-working slave would surely be missed by many if she or he escaped or died. Knowing the dangers of making clear these historical antecedents for the world they want to construct, Herrnstein and Murray instead promote a vision of world order that perhaps could best be called conservative multiculturalism. In this vision people recognize that "cognitive partitioning will continue; [i]t cannot be stopped," and that "inequality of endowments, including intelligence, is a reality" (p. 551). The roots of a "liberal and just society" (p. 388), therefore, lie in people coming to appreciate their own natural endowment – and learning to respect and appreciate others'. As neo-conservative cultural commentator Andrew Hacker noted, such a vision of the just society has roots in such ancient philosophers as Plato and Socrates, and in more modern philosophers such as Edmund Burke. In Hacker's (1995: 107) words,

> If all of us can be led to accept our "appointed place," the result will be personal happiness and social stability. Those of high ability and deserved responsibilities will be able to find cheerful and deferential servants to mow their lawns and clean their homes. We will also have a class of skilled and reliable artisans, who take pride in their callings. In addition, they will charge appropriate fees, realizing what is their rightful due. And if governance follows the Burkean model, citizens will grant that rule belongs to those best able to conduct matters of state. In return, all will be honored and respected for jobs well done, without condescension on one side or envy on the other. To which

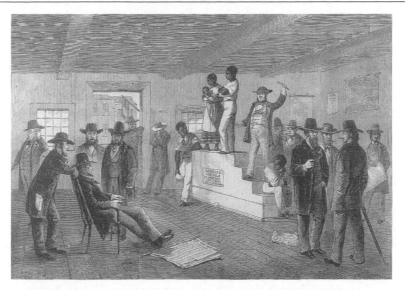

Figure 9.3 Determining the "value" of a human being in New Orleans. Also on auction here: estates and pictures. Herrnstein and Murray suggest that the value of people depends on whether (and how much) they would be missed when they die or move on. It is never clear in *The Bell Curve* where the authors would draw the line between the world depicted here and the one they want to create. Source: *Leeds Anti-Slavery Series, No. 16.*

must be added a further *Bell Curve* corollary: if members of some races are found, on average, to be less suited for responsibilities, they should accept this as nature's dictate and not human artifice.

Such a vision of a "liberal and just" society has had many adherents, but they have often made a much more explicit account of what "place" in such a world must imply.

"Clear-headed thinkers" pursuing such a Burkean universe understand that if it is the case that some are simply naturally inferior to others, then daily contact between people of different castes is best avoided. The best model of the world Herrnstein and Murray hope to see constructed is thus, beyond doubt, apartheid South Africa. Here, for example, is South Africa's Minister of the Interior, Dr. T.E. Dönges, in the debate over the Group Areas Act (a crucial component of apartheid), in May, 1950:

Hon. Members will realize what it must mean to those groups, always to have to adopt an inferior attitude, an attitude of inferiority towards Europeans, to stand back for the Europeans, where they live alongside the Europeans, but if we place them in separate residential areas, they will be able to give expression to their full cultural and soul life, and that is why we say that separate residential areas must be established. (Quoted in Western 1996: 86)

It's easy enough to see the disingenuousness of these remarks – full cultural and soul life, indeed! It's not much harder to see the same disingenuousness in Herrnstein and Murray's professed concern for the ability of "each human being" to find their proper place in society: "It is time for America once again to try living with inequality, as life is lived," they intone in the final sentences of the main part of their book:

> understanding that each human being has strengths and weaknesses, qualities we admire and qualities we do not admire, competencies and incompetencies, assets and debits; that the success of each human being is not measured externally but internally [i.e. genetically]; that of all the rewards we can confer on each other, the most precious is a place as a valued fellow citizen.   (pp. 551–2)

Perhaps Herrnstein and Murray, like Charles White and Glenn Trewartha, might like us to value blacks for their "economy of sweat," or perhaps like the racist South African Dönges they really are interested in the full development of the "soul life" of people presumably less intelligent than themselves. Either way, theirs is a fully racist geography, and so it is important to turn to an examination of just how that geography has played itself out in practice.

Apartheid and the Geography of the Race Idea

While analysts like Herrnstein and Murray keep debates about race alive by obscuring their fallacious basis, social policy, economic development, and so much else remains predicated on the *assumption* that "race" is a real thing. As that is the case, it is especially important for geographers to turn their attention to the *idea* of race, for the circulation and powerful reinforcement of that *idea* is decisive in how we organize the world. A focus on the geography of the idea of race shows how race, like culture, can be *made* very real "on the ground" through a series of spatial strategies designed to make the reification of race a fact, if not of nature, then of society. Groups *are* formed in society. Group membership *can* be quite determinant in such things as social opportunity, education, income, and the power to effect change. But this is not because of some natural, genetic sorting process, but rather because of the workings of social power. The policing of race – of group difference – relies not only on such arguments as those made in *The Bell Curve*, but also in the sorts of social policies, and the sorts of geographies, that works like *The Bell Curve* seek to create.

Nowhere is this clearer than in the system of apartheid that ruled South Africa until 1991, and which was decisively eliminated – as a constitutional tenet of South African life – with the election of Nelson Mandela and the African National Congress in 1994. Apartheid literally means "apart-ness" – the creation of separate spaces for separate races in South Africa. It rests on and makes possible what John Western (1996) famously called "the power of definition" – that social ability to name (a group, a group's place in society, a person) and make that name stick. To define one person or one group as "dumb" or as "low in cognitive ability" is, as we have seen, a powerful ideological tendency. But there is nothing inherent in the defining process that makes definitions "stick." Rather, that is a question of power. On the one hand, as Lefebvre (1991: 44) put it, "ideology only achieves consistency by intervening in social space and in its production, and by thus taking on body therein. Ideology *per se* might well be said to consist primarily in a discourse upon social space." On the other hand, while space itself, through its built form and codes of conduct, has the effect of sorting and dividing, or assuring people do or do not mingle, such control is never perfect, and must be policed both ideologically and through raw exercise of power itself (through violence, incarceration, etc.). In short, space and spatiality *make* "race," to the degree that they require the separation of peoples into groups and reinforce ideological notions about race. Or, as Kay Anderson (1987: 584) has put it concerning Vancouver's Chinatown (see chapter 4), "racial ideology [is] materially embedded in space... and it is through 'place' that it has been given a local referent, become a social fact, and *aided in its own reproduction*" (emphasis added). In this regard, geographical "isolation," the factor most commonly adduced as the prime cause in phenotypic and genotypic variation between groups, *does* make a difference in the construction of "race," but not at the level of biology. It is a key fact in the *social* construction of races.

Apartheid effected this social construction and gave race "its local referent" through a series of laws that regulated the movements and actions of people of different "races" at three primary scales.[26] At the most immediately personal level, interaction between people was controlled through the "microsegregation" of every-day space – buses, toilets, beaches, seating at stadiums and theaters, elevators, and the like (Western 1996: 61) (figure 9.4). This "petty apartheid" sought to assure that no informal contact between the "races" went unregulated, and it saturated every aspect of life. At the urban scale, apartheid divided the space of the cities into separate residential areas for each racial group (figure 9.5). Enforced in part through the Group Areas Act of 1950 (and its successors), this level of segregation was effected through restrictions on the sale of homes across race lines, and through an extensive program of urban planning, including the destruction of whole residential neighbor-hoods if they were occupied by the "wrong" race (Kruger 1992). At the regional and national scale, apartheid operated through the creation of "homelands" for different racial groups and the enforcement of "pass laws" which regulated the movement and

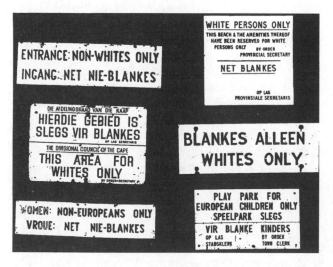

Figure 9.4 Signs of petty apartheid. In Apartheid South Africa, space was partitioned right down to the level of the beach, park, and toilet. Photo-montage by Mike Bostock, Henry Holt Company.

26 I use the past tense in this paragraph because the legal basis for apartheid has been removed. That does not mean that apartheid as a spatial system has somehow simply disappeared.

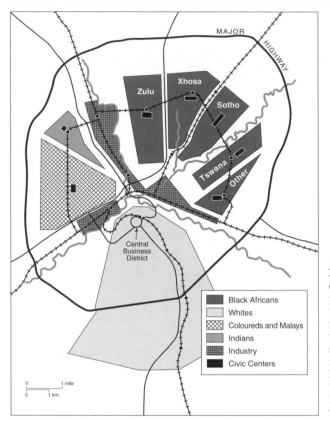

Figure 9.5 Using a set of principles laid out by the Durban city planning department, John Western suggests that the dream of an ideal apartheid city looked something like this. Such perfect separation and symmetry was never fully achieved under apartheid, but urban space was nonetheless radically sorted. Source: Redrawn from Western (1996: 91).

settlement of non-whites (figure 9.6). Together these scales of "apartness" were meant to solidify on the ground a "perfect system of control," as Jennifer Robinson (1990) has called it, in which white domination was made manifest and reinforced through a clear geographic strategy. Segregation was a form of domination; it had no other purpose (Western 1990: 60).

It was also a means of reinforcing difference. If apartheid apologists saw segregation as a means of allowing for the full development of each race, then that was only a poor euphemism for the goal of complete separation between the races – the goal of a clear spatial strategy for creating and enforcing that which simply was not there in "human nature." At the urban scale, racial group residential areas were created (with whites arrogating to themselves the most desirable areas, of course) and reinforced through environmental means – the creation of solid barriers between groups, such as superhighways, rail-lines, empty tracts of land, or, less optimally, fences and walls – and through the unrelenting *physical* policing of people who were "out of place." Among black South Africans, fine distinctions were made between ethnic groups and separate areas were set aside for Xhosa, Zulu, Sotho, Tswana, and others. No such distinctions were made between various white ethnicities, despite a long history of animosity between, for example British- and Dutch-descended South Africans. The goal, obviously, was control through division, and control was meant to be a *white* (minority) project. "Race" was thus a precondition for the division of space in South

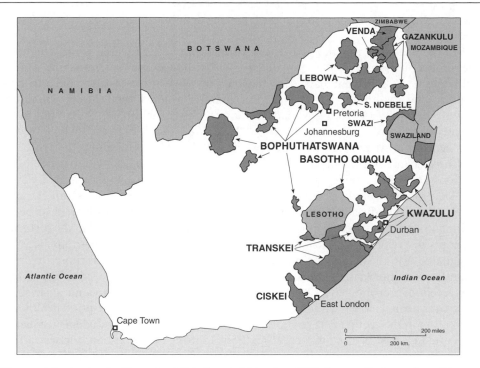

Figure 9.6 A plan for "homelands" in South Africa (ca. 1975). Source: Redrawn from Western (1996: 67).

Africa, but it was also very much an outcome. Whites were whites (even if there were class differences); but blacks were a lot of things, each of which needed to be provided with its own space in which to develop a full "cultural and soul life."

The details of life in the different group areas of South Africa under apartheid are well known. Whites could live very well indeed (even accounting for differences of class status), reserving for themselves the best lands, the best views, the best schools, and the best neighborhoods. They could, as John Western (1996: 309) has put it, choose to believe that "nonwhites and their problems...have been put at a distance" and that they had thereby "lessened the potential for 'friction'" between races. In the black homelands and the non-white townships and squatter settlements, by contrast, conditions were (and are) bleak. In the Transkei in the 1970s, for example, some two-thirds of the households were *never* able to produce enough food to be self-sufficient; 70 percent of the remainder only produced enough for self-sufficiency during good years. Child malnutrition hovered around 12 percent and infant mortality around 25 percent. Movement to urban centers in search of work was an economic necessity for black males in the homelands, just as black labor was necessary to the functioning of the "white" South African economy (Western 1996: 289). Such was made abundantly clear in 1976 when the minister for Bantu administration and development "stated that the only reason for which black Africans were permitted in 'white areas' was to sell their labor." And the pass laws, designed to assure that blacks did no more in "white areas" than sell their labor, were vigorously policed. In 1975–6 alone, 1 of every 25 black Africans in putatively "white" South Africa was prosecuted for infractions of the pass laws (Western 1996: 291).

In urban shantytowns things are in fact somewhat better for non-whites than they are in the homelands – but not much. Of the houses in the townships around Johannesburg 85 percent had no bathrooms in 1975; three-quarters did not have ceilings; and two-thirds did not have hot running water. Despite rapid population growth, the South African government allowed only 5,500 houses to be built in the already overcrowded Soweto between 1970 and 1983: densities in the mid-1980s were between 10 and 15 people per house (Goodwin 1984: 98). Throughout the 1980s, the South African government increasingly relied on the private sector to provide housing for non-whites, a policy that did nothing but intensify housing shortages. By 1991, the Development Bank of South Africa estimated, about 7 million South Africans lived in informal dwellings; the "official" housing shortage was estimated to be 1.2 million (Saff 1994). These figures were exacerbated by, on the one hand, the historical attempts to "remove" and relocate people of the "wrong" race from group areas not designated for them; and on the other, continued high rates of rural to urban migration among black South Africans. Together these trends have led to appallingly low levels of nutrition in both the homelands and the townships and such social deprivations as lack of schooling, high unemployment rates, and poor healthcare. Education in the group areas and townships was bad enough that students frequently boycotted classes, protesting lack of textbooks, broken facilities, and understaffing. Occasionally these boycotts led to full-fledged protest movements and riots (as in Cape Town in 1980: Western 1996: 327–31). Were Richard Herrnstein and Charles Murray to transport their study of IQ to South Africa, they would no doubt maintain that any differences found between "races" was a product of bad genes rather than any environmental or social factor. And their brand of "conservative multiculturalism" would tell us that it is best that the various peoples of South Africa continue to pursue, as they always have, the separate development of their full cultural and soul life. They, like apartheid's planners, would urge that everyone keep in mind that there really is a proper place for everyone.

Unfortunately for Herrnstein and Murray and for apartheid's supporters, but not for most South Africans, the overthrow of the Afrikaner government and the legal dismantling of apartheid have shown that there are other, better paths to development. But even so there is not much cause to hope that the vast disparities in wealth, education, nutrition, and the like between whites, coloureds, and blacks in South Africa will be quickly overcome. Rather, as Grant Saff (1994) has shown, the reality is that as space is being "deracialized," at the same time it is being resegregated on the basis of class. Saff (1994: 382) points to two simultaneous processes at work in the post-apartheid city. The first is a process of *desegregation* of white suburbs and urban enclaves. Desegregation "is characterized by the in-migration of blacks [and other non-whites] of an income status equal to or higher than those [whites] moving out." The process can work the other way too. Saff (1994: 385) reports that in Cape Town, whites have begun to move into a formerly Malay area, gentrifying property and forcing out lower-income Malays.

The second trend is towards the *deracialization* of space. Here the process is one of "the expansion of townships or informal settlements onto the boundaries of, or within, 'white' municipal areas" (Saff 1994: 382). As he points out, "while spatially the racial impress of the apartheid city is changed by this process, it has little social effect on these new black residents, as they are excluded from access to virtually all the facilities and social institutions (such as schools) within the 'white' areas." White resistance to deracialization, these days, tends to be expressed in class rather than race terms. For example, one white petitioner against the appearance of black squatter settlements noted that:

> The issue is standards and not race since we already have several black families living in Presidents Park.... We strongly object to the siting of squatter shacks right on the doorstep of our R200,000 homes which will be devalued to the extent that they will be unsaleable [*sic*] at any price. (Quoted in Saff 1994: 388)

What apartheid established, in other words, was a geography of privilege that worked not only to police the boundaries of wealth – to establish the spatial form in which the reproduction of inequality was possible – but to do so by simultaneously establishing and policing the geographical boundaries of "race." With no existence in biology, "race" was *created* and *maintained* through the geography of apartheid. The legal dismantling of the apartheid system, as important as it is, is only one step in the process of "deracializing" society and space, not the deracialization as represented by squatter incursions into "white" areas, but the sort of deracialization implied by the need to dismantle the policing of socio-spatial *boundaries* established for the sole purpose of *creating* and *naturalizing* exactly that which is not the least bit "natural:" race. Such a project in South Africa, as elsewhere, will be one of also dismantling the *class* privilege that has historically attended being "white" (see Roediger 1991).

Conclusion: Space Makes Race

The moral of the story of apartheid should be plain: As a geographical system it used space to quite literally construct and maintain hard-and-fast boundaries between "races." That is, it constructed on the ground precisely that which could not be constructed in our bodies: clear distinctions between us. It should also be plain that the legal destruction of apartheid does not imply the end of "race" in South Africa. Far from it. As in America, race is built into the ground, in housing and neighbor-hood patterns, in funding of schools, hospitals, and other necessities of life (Massey and Denton 1993). As Susan Smith put it in 1989, in a statement little undermined by the collapse of apartheid a few years later, "racial (racist) exclusivity may be less a legacy of the past and more a strategy for the future in advanced industrial eco-nomies" (S. Smith 1989: viii). This is so because, among other things, one of the contradictions of contemporary capitalism is that it is an incredible force for homo-geneity at the same time as it is an incredible force for heterogeneity.[27] As the relations of capital expand, putting everybody on the same footing as buyers and sellers of commodities (their own labor power; Big Macs), there is simultaneously the need for distinction between and within people not only to accord with ever more

---

27   A now classic, if often incomprehensible, account of this issue is Appadurai (1990); see also chapter 10 below.

complex divisions of labor, but also as a means of guarding against advancing costs of labor power (see chapter 3). The "racialization of labor" (Jackson 1992b) is one means by which difference can be organized to the benefit of capital by creating castes and classes in which decent pay is somehow "unnatural," or "undeserved." Apartheid surely operated on this assumption, but such racialization is part of a more general process in which "capital uses racial, national and sexual categorization to differentiate between groups of workers, splitting the labour force, and permitting the super-exploitation of certain sectors" (Castles, with Booth and Wallace 1984: 98, quoted in S. Smith 1989: 8). As Susan Smith (1989) argues, this "unequal dispensation of economic rights" finds a corollary and seeks its legitimacy in unequal distribution of other rights, particularly those of citizenship.

It is in this sense that "race" may be understood as a "strategy" for advanced capitalist societies: if race can be seen as a *natural* basis for unequal access to rights (as Herrnstein and Murray assert), if race can be presented as a commonsense reason why some in society are meant to be more privileged (with money and in the eyes of the state), then such inequality is made to appear as pre-ordained, as simply the natural order of things (S. Smith 1989: 8).[28] In other words, the continued definition and redefinition of "race," refracted through unceasing political and economic struggle over the power to define both people and space – their being *and* their place – must be predicated on keeping alive clear distinctions in social practice precisely *because* they do not exist in biological fact. All the references to "can be seen" and "made to appear" in the preceding sentences are a clear indication that what we are dealing with here is nothing "natural" at all; it is instead the power to define, the power to reify, the power to make the social into the natural.

If race is a social practice, then, the spaces in which we make that practice are crucial. To approach this issue from a slightly different angle than the preceding paragraph, consider the relative ability, in white-dominant society, to move about, to travel. Metaphors of movement and travel are very much the rage in contemporary social theory (see Cresswell 1997), drawing often on the insights of James Clifford (1992: 111), who has argued that the metaphor of "travel" within and between cultures is valuable because it comes laden with images of "gendered, racial bodies, class privilege, specific means of conveyance, beaten paths, agents, frontiers, documents, and the like." That is, thinking about relationships between peoples as relationships of "travel" keeps at the forefront the hierarchical order of the world in which we live, for it is by movement within and between those hierarchies, and across the boundaries that delineate one "culture" from another, that the possibility of cultural creativity, resistance, and transformation opens. "Travel, in this view, denotes a range of material, spatial practices that produce knowledges, stories, traditions, comportments, musics, books, diaries, and other cultural expressions" (Clifford 1992: 108). In apartheid South Africa it meant pass laws.

For the USA, bell hooks (1992: 343–4) worries that Clifford's notion of travel "would always make it difficult for there to be recognition of an experience of travel that is not about play but is an encounter with terrorism. . . . To travel, I must

28 This is precisely the issue under contention in one of the key "culture wars" in the contemporary United States – the ongoing debates over affirmative action in America. The argument is that somehow disadvantaged groups have not *earned* a place in universities, jobs, etc.

always move through fear, confront terror." As a black woman, hooks knows just how much her own travel is circumscribed by the racialized and gendered spaces in which she must live, work, and move. "All black people in the United States, irrespective of their class status or politics, live with possibility that they will be terrorized by whiteness" (hooks 1992: 345).[29] By contrast, "in white supremacist society, white people can 'safely' imagine that they are invisible to black people since the power they have historically asserted, and even now collectively assert over black people accorded them the right to control the black gaze.... Since most white people do not have to 'see' black people (constantly appearing on billboards, televisions, movies, in magazines, etc.) and they do not need to be ever on guard, observing black people, to be 'safe,' they can live as though black people are invisible and can even imagine that they are also invisible to blacks" (hooks 1992: 340).[30] They can live so, that is, until some event erupts into their consciousness – like the collapse of apartheid in the wake of continual demonstrations and organizing, or the more sudden Los Angeles rebellion in 1992 – and forces them to come to grips with the specific racial geographies that have been created (see Davis 1990, 1998).

hook's comments need to be put in context. Her point is not that whites understand themselves as *simply* invisible. Rather, it is that they continually try to construct for themselves a world in which they are *in fact* invisible to blacks. Fear of black people is crucial here. The aim has been – and is – in white racist societies to create and maintain a world in which whites have near total freedom of movement precisely because blacks do not. The "travel" of whites is predicated on the sequestration of blacks. It is precisely here, then, that Herrnstein and Murray's desire for a world organized around some putatively natural "place for everyone" gains its greatest, and most horrific, currency.

This construction of a "place for everyone" – a place that whites could move freely and invisibly across – was also, of course, precisely the practical problem faced by apartheid's planners. How should that "terrorism of travel" be institutionalized so that knowing one's place became as natural as Herrnstein and Murray would like it to be? And, simultaneously, how could certain forms of travel across the hard and fast boundaries of space – to work, for example, in the shops and factories of the city or the homes of the suburbs – be controlled so as to retain the essential hierarchies enforced through the division of space? How could the travel of the racial "other" be controlled such that it became impossible for blacks (and other racial groups) to burst their bounds and spill into spaces where they "do not belong?" South Africa's pass laws, which attempted to govern the movement of blacks across putatively "white" space, but which contained no similar provisions for whites, was an attempt to answer just these questions, but so too is the construction of what Mike Davis (1998: 359–422) describes as a new "social ecology" for cities such as Los Angeles. This

29   These issues have had frequent hearing in the United States Supreme Court, most recently concerning the right of a black man to walk unmolested by the police through "white" neighborhoods in San Diego (*Kolender v. Lawson* 461 USA 352 [1983]). That such a right would have to be affirmed by the Supreme Court is some indication of the degree to which it is a right honored in the breach rather than in the practice.

30   This was just the point that John Western was making above about how apartheid made it possible for whites in South Africa to imagine that they had "distanced" themselves from the problems they attributed to non-whites.

"ecology," predicated on abject (and largely racial) fear, seeks to re-order the city into a series of more or less contained spaces of control.

The point is bigger than that, however, for the issue is not just one of control. Rather, as we have seen, at the most fundamental level, control over the production of space – the ability to create space in particular ways – also lends to powerful groups the ability to actively *create* race. That is, "race itself" – that social reification, that ideology masquerading as nature – is made "real" on the ground through the maintenance of spatial boundaries. If "race" is something that does not exist, then it is always something that *is made* to exist through specific (if contested) practices and policies. And it is something that is ideologically supported through the work of defining and redefining just what it is that is "natural."

The eviction of Theresa Seamster from the Greeley Mall in December, 1995, for wearing gang colors might be seen simply as an example of stupid and overzealous policing. There is no doubt it was that. But given the context, amid debates about the relationship between race and crime, while the arguments about Herrnstein and Murray's desire to put everyone in their place were still raging, and at a moment in American history when fear is the reigning principle by which space is being divided, sorted, and ordered, it would be a mistake to attribute Seamster's experiences to mere anomaly. Instead, they show the degree to which "race" itself is a project of the ordering and controlling of space – and of ordering and controlling the movement (or "travel") of people. For many whites, safety is defined precisely by making others invisible. And if that is not completely possible, then efforts can at least be made to assure that everyone knows her or his place, that movements are strictly controlled so that the lives of the privileged are not unduly disrupted. Theresa Seamster's "mistake" was that she put herself "out of place" by showing up at the mall with the "wrong" clothes, the "wrong" friends, and, most importantly, the "wrong" skin color. She had no *rights*.

10

Geographies of Belonging? Nations, Nationalism, and Identity in an Era of "Deterritorialization"

Why did it seem so *wrong* for Theresa Seamster to be seen in public, dressed as she pleased, doing as she wanted? Why is it still so contentious when black people in America claim what is their *right*? Part of the answer to those questions surely has to do with the continual reproduction of the proper "places for everyone" explored in the last chapter, but part must also have to do with the nature of the American nation more generally. Who counts as an American?, Theresa Seamster's case forces us to ask. What does an "American" look like, and what rights is one entitled to? These questions, so haunted as they are with the politics and geography of race, are hardly unique to the United States. Consider the identical questions for England: What is "Englishness"? Who are "English"? What do they look like? Where are they to be found? There are, of course, no easy answers to those questions, but perhaps a rather stark image will help us see who is *not* English – at least in many people's minds.

Look at Ingrid Pollard's photograph (figure 10.1) of a black woman out for a walk in the English countryside, pausing to admire the view of rolling hills, fields, and wood-lots so evocative of rural England. Accompanying the photograph is a stark text: "...feeling I don't belong. Walks through leafy glades with a baseball bat by my side..." Pollard's work asks what it means to belong, what it means to be excluded – often violently – from the England that is her home, and indeed what it means for her to be "at home" in the first place. Much of Pollard's work, in fact, is designed explicitly to ask *who* has the right to the land, who can call the land "home." Other

. . . feeling I don't belong. Walks through leafy glades with a baseball bat by my side . . .

Figure 10.1 Ingrid Pollard, from *Pastoral Interludes* (1984). Reproduced by permission of the artist.

work of Pollard's calls into question the stereotypical construction of identity, by questioning why blacks are always associated with the urban and how therefore black people will always be considered strangers in the English countryside (figure 10.2).

These are important issues because, as Phil Kinsman (1995: 301) suggests, when "a group is excluded from . . . landscapes of national identity, . . . they are excluded to a large degree from the nation itself."[1] Pollard's art raises just that issue and makes viewers confront taken-for-granted assumptions about the relationship of landscape – in this case the English countryside – and identity – in this case the identification of "English" with "white." Her photographs and texts bring "race" and "nation" together in startling ways by questioning "dominant representations of black people within national history" while at the same time forcefully testifying "to their continued presence within national life" (Kinsman 1995: 307). In other words, Pollard's

1   The following account of Ingrid Pollard's landscape photography is drawn from Kinsman's essay; see also Matless (1998).

... it's as if the black experience is only lived within an urban environment. I thought I liked the LAKE DISTRICT, where I wandered lonely as a Black face in a sea of white. A visit to the countryside is always accompanied by a feeling of unease, dread ...

Figure 10.2 Ingrid Pollard, from *Pastoral Interludes* (1984). Reproduced by permission of the artist.

photographs force us to face precisely the question of who is included and who is excluded in the land, and how these exclusions and inclusions both shape and reflect on-going constructions of not only national identity, but also national*ism*.

The purpose of this chapter is to pursue the questions Ingrid Pollard raises with her art, and to interrogate the cultural politics to which these questions give rise. The first question arising from her startling images (developed more fully in the first section below) is that of "nation." What kind of a space is the nation? Consider Indian novelist Arundhati Roy's (1998: 18) answer to that question:

There's no such thing as an Authentic India or a Real Indian. There is no Divine Committee that has the right to sanction one single, authorized version of what India is or should be. There is no one religion or language or caste or region or person or story or book that can claim to be its sole representative. There are, and only can be, visions of India, various ways of seeing it – honest, dishonest, wonderful, absurd, modern, traditional, male, female. They can be argued over, criticized, praised, scorned, but not banned or broken. Not hunted down.

And yet people do "hunt down" "authentic" national identity. Or should I say that people often and violently hunt down those they consider a threat to the authenticity

– the purity – of the nation? While national identity is at one level all about "belong-ing," it is also all about exclusion, about keeping out those you do not like and identifying yourself largely in terms of who you are not. It is about establishing a purified link between "blood and soil."

Yet on the other hand Roy is absolutely right. And what she claims for India is true for everywhere else: there can only be struggles over the nation, that is, over the shaping of "culture" in space. Nation, nationalism, and cultural identity are never anything fixed, only always contested – and always intimately linked to the structures of power that govern our lives. And when national identity is brought into contact with the politics of race, gender, sexuality, and class, it can be understood as nothing more than an on-going struggle – a culture war – over the determinants of social identity.

But "nation" and "national identity" are fluid and contested in another way too. The very status of the nation-state as a coherent scale of social, political, economic, and cultural power is, at the moment, up for grabs. Think of superstates-in-formation like the European Union, or global economic institutions like the Multilateral Agree-ment on Investments that discipline, in favor of global investors, national policies on everything from environmental regulation to wages. Either of these, and any number of others that could likewise be mentioned (GATT, NAFTA, the IMF) suggest that global imperial power is being transferred, at least to some degree, from particular, powerful nation-states, to a particular, powerful international *class*. While the work-ers of the world are as far as ever from uniting, the global capitalist class has learned to speak almost as one voice as they seek to reconfigure the spaces of the globe to make them ever more hospitable to their own desire for the endless accumulation of capital. In such a world what is the status of the "nation" and its spatial form, the nation-state?

For many cultural and political analysts the answer to that question has been to assert that we live in an era of "deterritorialization." Everything from capital to pollution is now global in scope, and cultural identities are themselves more and more constructed out of the new opportunities, the new flows of peoples and goods, the new reach of the media, each of which is global in scale, than they are out of some rooted attachment to territory. That may be so, but consider this too: racist nationalism, and the violence that it brings, has been on the rise, not the decline, in Europe since 1989; in Canada, Britain, Spain, and countless other places separatist nationalists continue to gain adherents; in the United States stringent new anti-immigrant policies have been enacted with only a little murmur of protest and "English-only" and anti-bilingual education laws have met with unprecedented success; in India, as Arundhati Roy hints, Hindu nationalism continues to grow in force and violence; while in Pakistan, Muslim nationalism does the same. How can we account for this rise in nationalist sentiment right at the moment when objective transformations in the global political economy coupled with a global "communications revolution" would seem to suggest it ought to be withering away?

That is the second question raised by Pollard's art (and developed in the second main section below). It asks about the status and importance of cultural identity under conditions of "deterritorialization," conditions which, as we will see, are actually not all that new. What does it mean to be a migrant? How do people understand their place in the world when places themselves seem to be ever more fluid? In fact, we will see that such a claim – that places are ever more fluid – does not adequately describe what is happening, spatially, over the globe. It is more accurate to understand every *de*territorialization as simultaneously a *re*territorialization, perhaps at a different scale. Neither territory nor space simply dematerialize, and so neither do identities come untethered from the spaces that give them shape. What is changing is the geography through which power operates. The place to begin an interrogation of that changing geography of power, however, is back at the "nation," since, for all the talk of deterritorialization, we still do very much live in a world of nation-states.

Nations and Nationalism: Territory and Identity

In 1991, the year after Unification, there were about 1,500 reported cases of right-wing violence in Germany, much of it directed against Turkish "guest workers" and other "foreigners." The next year, the number was 2,200. A governmental crackdown on extremist groups in 1993 led to a decline in violence, but by 1996, the number of reported racist crimes had again climbed to over 2,300 (Birnbaum 1993; *New York Times* 1998; Traynor 1997). Some of the crimes attracted global attention, such as the January, 1996, arson attack on a hostel in the northern city of Lubeck that killed ten immigrants and asylum-seekers (including four children). Four young men with ties to extreme-right groups were originally detained in connection with the attack, but were soon released when police diverted their attention to a Lebanese resident of the hostel. That resident was later acquitted after defense attorneys successfully argued that the police had been biased in their investigation and had ignored crucial evidence linking racist Germans to the crime. One of the original detainees has since confessed to the crime (Traynor 1996; Staunton 1998). Other, less spectacular, crimes are simply part of the low-grade race war that haunts the depressed housing estates of German industrial states, particularly in the east, where racists have attempted to create "foreigner-free" zones, while their political parties have campaigned on slogans such as "Criminal Foreigners Out" (Karacs 1998). Perhaps the general attitude towards "foreigners" (such as Turks, northern Africans, Asians, and "Gypsies") on the part of the racist German right (both its violent and more "respectable" wings) is best summed up by Oliver Handl, the leader of the Young National Democrats, the youth group of the far-right National Democratic Party: "I can't just take a goose and put it into a chicken shed with a sign around its neck saying: I am a chicken. It's still a goose. It's the same if you give a Turk a German passport. He's still a Turk in my eyes. He's got a totally different mentality to me" (quoted in Staunton 1998).

Violence and wholeness: Germanness and Heimat

Is such violence, and such an exclusive sense of what it is to be "German," something inherent in "Germanness" itself? Is it a product of the unique ethnic character of the German people? Or, by contrast, is such violence the preserve of only a "tiny minority" that seeks to assert its will and domination by constructing a particularly virulent form of German nationalism, creating a set of myths about the German nation that is neither accurate nor healthful? Is, in other words, German nationalism and its associated violence, just an "invention" of the racist right, used as a means to exclude those they do not like from the landscape of Germany?

Such questions in fact present too simple an understanding of the complex phenomenon of national identity and of nationalism.[2] While violence against "foreigners" seems attributable to only a "small minority" of Germans, the fact is that exclusionary politics deeply infects even the mainstream political movements. But that does not mean it is somehow a "natural" attribute of "the" German people. Rather, "Germanness" is a point of struggle, a continuing battle over just how the German nation is to be socially constructed. An examination of those battles, placed within a discussion of theories of "nation" and "nationalism," will help us understand just what is at stake not only in Germany, but anywhere identity is linked, in one manner or another, to place – which is to say, everywhere.

Only a year after the reuniting of Germany, a town in Saxony (in the former GDR) had already declared its intention to make itself *ausländerfrei* (free of foreigners), and throughout Germany a virulent debate on what it is to be properly "German" has been raging for more than a decade now (see Peck 1996). There is a specific political or legal context within which these debates must be understood. While Germany has had exceptionally liberal asylum laws since the end of World War II, "German-ness" – the ability to be or become "German" – has, until the spring of 1999, been legally and culturally a matter of "blood." More formally, in Germany for 86 years, laws of consanguinity have governed citizenship. "Germans" were not only ethnic Germans in Germany, but also those "ethnic Germans" from elsewhere in Eastern Europe deemed to have a "historic right of return" to their *Heimat* (roughly, homeland). That is, anyone who can claim to have "German blood" could become a German citizen. For those who didn't have "German blood," citizenship was next to impossible.

Until 1999, somewhere around 10 percent of the residents of reunited Germany could never become citizens. They were largely darker-skinned immigrants, arrived in Germany as either "guest workers" (*Gastarbeiter*) or asylum-seekers. Many traced their family's residence in Germany for generations. In contrast, "ethnic Germans" who had little or no historic connection at all to the German state, were not only given generous resettlement aid if they desired to "return," but were also quickly eligible for citizenship. *Ausländer* status was determined not by where one is from so much as by one's skin color or ethnicity.[3] "Blood" was everything – it determined your rights within the German state. The imagined German nation remained one that was ethnically, purely German. Germany was the *home* of Germans – and not of anyone else. The citizenship laws of Germany, while hotly contested throughout the

---

2　And they are questions that should not be seen as limited to Germany. The ascendancy of xenophobic nationalism is a phenomenon across Europe (France's far-right parties, in fact, have had even greater electoral success than Germany's) and the globe. Germany merely presents a particularly stark and vexatious case.

3　As Peck (1996: 485–6) points out, there is a hierarchy of "at homeness" in German contemporary society that looks something like this: first (West) Germans, then former East Germans, then Ethnic Germans, then German-Jews, then "Noble Foreigners" (Western Europeans, Scandinavians, fair-skinned Americans), then *Ausländer* (Turks, Southern European guest workers, other Mediterraneans, Roma and Gypsies, Africans, etc.), and finally Vietnamese in the former GDR.

post-World War II period, served to codify this sense of national belonging. And such a sense of belonging – and exclusion – was deeply felt. Turks, Africans, and other "guest workers" knew they never could become "German" in a cultural sense. "'Germanness' is not perceived to be an open or permeable category" by either Germans or "foreign" residents, according to the anthropologist Andrea Klimt (1989). Indeed, she goes on, "none of the migrants I knew, regardless of class, generation, or degree of 'integration' considered the prospect of 'becoming German' to be desirable, realistic, or even imaginable" (Klimt 1989, quoted in Peck 1996: 484).

This may be changing. On May 7, 1999, the German parliament voted by almost two to one to replace the "law of blood" with a "law of territory." The new citizenship law grants German citizenship to nearly anyone who was born to parents resident in Germany for at least eight years. Adult "foreigners" too are now eligible to apply for naturalization after the eight-year waiting period (Benhabib 1999). While these changes in citizenship law are heartening, it is also the case that the German nationalist Right – including factions in the "respectable right" of the Christian Democrats – have used this liberalization in the treatment of "foreigners" as a nationalist rallying point, seeking not to amend, but to reinforce, notions of Germany purity.

Such a notion of German purity derives from a long history of imagining a German *Heimat*, a history that obviously reached a peak during the Nazi era when ideologies of "blood and soil" were made state policy, but which has only been greatly complicated since then, first with the division of the German state and then with its reunification (figure 10.3). *Heimat* is a particularly complex notion. Contrasting *Heimat* with its opposite, *Fremde* (roughly, "strange"), Heidrun Suhr (1989) notes that "both terms imply far more than simply 'homeland' or 'a foreign place.' 'Heimat' also connotes belonging and security, while 'Fremde' can refer to isolation and alienation" (quoted in Peck 1996: 484). Or as Jeffrey Peck summarizes, "as a word without equivalent [in other languages] *Heimat belongs* to the Germans, to a specific past and tradition that are linked to common values, ideals, customs, and locations. To be able to participate in this *Heimat* requires an identification that is at least ethnic, if not racial." But *Heimat* does not just "belong" to Germans; Germans *belong* to *Heimat*. That is its resonance: *Heimat* is "belonging." David Morley and Kevin Robins (1996: 459; see also Morley and Robins 1995: chapter 5) perhaps summarize the point best:

> Heimat is a mythical bond rooted in a lost past, a past that has already disintegrated ... It is about conserving the "fundamentals" of culture and identity. And, as such, it is about sustaining cultural boundaries and boundedness. To belong in this way is to protect exclusive, and therefore excluding, identities against those who are seen as aliens and "foreigners." The "other" is always and continuously a threat to the security and integrity of those who share a common home. Xenophobia and fundamentalism are opposite sides of the same coin.

Hence, at least to some degree, increasing violence against guest workers and other *ausländer* mirrors rising insecurity over German identity – and economic health – that accompanied reunification.

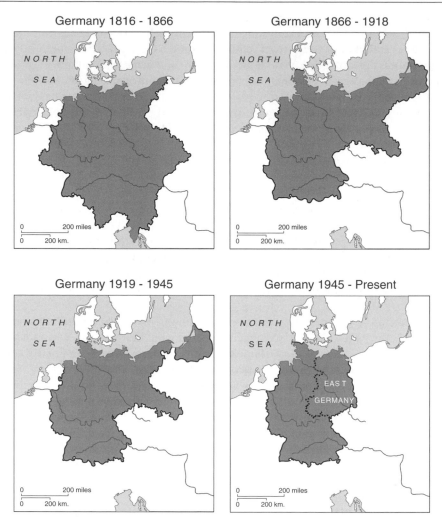

Figure 10.3 The changing borders of Germany (1815 to the present). Each map represents the maximum extent of the German State for each period. Cartography: Michael Kirchoff.

Economically, Chancellor Kohl promised that with reunification, East Germany would become "a blossoming landscape," and yet the reality has been significant *disinvestment* in the East, with productive capacity being either abandoned or consolidated in the West. The "recurrent features of the East German landscape are deserted factories, rusting industrial dinosaurs lying idle and empty as they await their fate in the privatization lottery" (Fulbrook 1994: 213). Culturally, there are significant differences between *Wessis* (West Germans) and *Ossis* (East Germans). Where the destruction of the Berlin Wall brought the ecstatic hope (for some) of once again forging *ein Volk*, the reality has been one of continued, if contested, difference, with the relative economic poverty of the East creating a sense among many *Wessis* that *Ossis* and all they stand for are somehow inferior (Fulbrook 1994). And on the

part of *Ossis* there has been a forceful reassertion, at times, of their separate identity –
an identity now constructed, as often as not, through the nostalgic consumption of
East German goods and a growing hatred directed against both *Wessis* (who are
perceived by *Ossis* as smug and privileged) and *Ausländer* (who are perceived to be
taking jobs and benefits from East Germans) (Talbot 1994).[4] Against this backdrop
of resentment and fear significant landmarks of the German *Kulturnation* – Wartburg
Castle (where Luther translated the New Testament), for example, or the museums
and landmarks of Berlin (figure 10.4) – are being restored so as to better serve as
"symbols of continuity" in the German nation, and as indications of how the
government is investing in the East German economy "by attracting quantities of
Western tourists" (Fulbrook 1994: 213). *Heimat* is made to stand for both the
economic and the cultural health of the German nation.

And yet *Heimat* does not just innocently exist as some German yearning for place.
It is an "invented tradition" that has always to be maintained and reproduced –
sometimes violently.[5] The *reassertion* of a unified German cultural nationalism in the

Figure 10.4   The newly rebuilt Reichstag. Originally built in the 1870s as Germany was solidifying
as a nation-state, the Reichstag reopened again as the seat of Parliament in April 1999, serving as
evidence both of reinvestment in the East and the continuity of the German state and nation.
Photograph by Christoph Schuster; used by permission.

4   Karacs (1998) indicates the degree to which the argument that *Ausländer* are taking jobs from "real"
Germans is a lie. In Magdeburg, for example, where unemployment approaches 25 percent, foreigners only
constitute 3 percent of the population.
5   The classic accounts of "invented traditions" of nationalism are in Hobsbawm and Ranger (1983).
Anthony Smith (1996: 119) argues that calling modern nationalism "invented traditions" does a disservice

wake of the quite uneven and divided reunification of Germany has unleashed strong recidivist currents, currents that draw for their force on a long history of ethnic nation-building – a history that has a conflictual and contradictory relationship to the forces of modernization. By the mid-nineteenth century in Germany, for example, the myth of a Teutonic homeland was connected in part to a strong, romantic critique of capitalism.[6] As expressed by the sociologist Wilhelm Riehl in a series of books published in the 1850s, the recovery of the German *Heimat* allowed for the development of a countervailing force to the materialist individualism that capitalism promoted. For Riehl, *"Heimat* [was] much more than a patriotic sentiment: it [was] a physical topography with specific customs and idioms, in short the memories particular to Germany, embedded in its soil"* (Schama 1995: 116). That is, it was a *landscape*, an indissoluble link between people and place, culture and nature.[7] In contemporary Germany, such a critique of the individualizing force of capitalism remains strong among *Ossis* – who can no longer turn towards socialism to combat it. For many, the remedy to rapacious market capitalism lies in the ethnic community of Germans, and to their ties to the land, to *Heimat*.[8]

For Riehl in the nineteenth century, the essential natural ingredient in this bond was the German forest. The woods "were in some mysteriously indeterminate way an essential element of the national character; they were, as Riehl put it, 'what made Germany German'" (Schama 1995: 116). Simon Schama traces this woods-worship through the development of the German Reich in the 1870s and into the Nazi era, showing how the bond between German people and the lands of which they were a part was strengthened again and again by all manner of reference to mythical and mystical pasts, pasts linked ethnically and directly to the original "German tribes" who so vexed the Roman empire. In each of these the survival of the nation was tied directly to the survival of "the folk" and the specific landscapes within which they lived – landscapes that had to be protected from invading hordes, lest the German people themselves be overrun. For Riehl, and for his later followers, German forests were "the heartland of [German] folk culture...so that a village without a forest is like a town without any historical buildings, theater or art galleries. Forests are games fields for the young, feasting-places for the old" (Schama 1995: 114). The preservation of German forests was also the preservation of the German folk.

The "invented tradition" that governed German romantic nationalism, and that still governs many strands of German nationalism today, was one that therefore assumed an unbreakable bond between landscape and culture. Hence, speaking of the Nazi state, Schama (1995: 119) notes that "it is...painful to acknowledge how ecologically conscientious the most barbaric regime in modern history actually was. Exterminating millions of lives was not at all incompatible with passionate protection

---

to the actual intellectual, political, and ideological work involved in creating nationalism. He suggests instead that what is work in most nations is the *rediscovery* of an "ethnic past." We will come back to this distinction below.

6   Simon Schama (1995) connects this romantic critique of capitalism also to the writings of Thoreau, Ruskin, and Carlyle.

7   The complex politics and ideologies that structure the relationship between national identity and landscape for the case of England and the USA are explored in Daniels (1993) and Matless (1998).

8   I do not mean to imply that *Heimat* is a specifically *Ossi* phenomenon. It is far more complicated, and far more deeply implicated in the *Wessi* sense of self, to make such easy associations.

of millions of trees."[9] Indeed, each was mutually supportive of the other. "Heimat is an ominous utopia," Morley and Robins (1996: 459) write. "Whether 'home' is imagined as the community of Europe or of the national state or of the region, it is drenched in the longing for wholeness, unity, integrity" – unity, integrity, and wholeness that can only be maintained through the active (and violent) exclusion of *Ausländer*, as the recent history of racist politics and violence in not only Germany, but France, Britain, and the United States, clearly indicate.

Nation

What should be clear from this discussion is that "nation" is itself an "imagined community" as Benedict Anderson (1991) so famously put it. That is, nations are *represented* as spaces in which members of the nation have a strong bond with each other, a bond that trumps whatever differences (of class, gender, or religion, for example) may divide people within the nation one from another. And yet this bond can only be *imagined*; it can never actually be *known*, because the collectivity that forms the nation is too large to allow any one person to know more than a few of her or his fellow nationals. The notion that the community of the nation can only ever be imagined is important for understanding the ontological status of nations: it turns us away from the assumption that nations are somehow a *natural* result of a common *people* or *folk* and their relationship to a particular place, and towards the sense that nations are contested and thus a particular materialization of power and ideology.

Yet the language of "imagination" can be limiting. If, as Anderson (1991: 11) says, the thing to understand is how loyalty to some notion of (exclusive) community is generated, how links are forged between "the dead and the yet unborn" for whom the nation is to be a binding force, then the focus must be not just on the "imagining" (as important as that may be) but also the *practices* and exercises of power through which these bonds are produced and reproduced. The questions this raises are ones about who defines the nation, how it is defined, how that definition is reproduced and contested, and, crucially, how the nation has developed and changed over time. For "the nation is not a once-and-for-all, all-or-nothing, concept; . . . historical nations are ongoing processes, sometimes slow in the formation, at other times faster, often jagged and discontinuous, and some features emerge or are created, while others lag" (A. Smith 1996: 108). The question is not what common imagination *exists*, but what common imagination is *forged*. Nations can only ever be argued over, never "hunted down," as Arundhati Roy says.

But that just begs the questions of what, exactly, a nation is. Does it tell us anything at all to say that a nation is an "imagined community," even one that is forged, discontinuous, or "ongoing"? Anthony Smith (1996: 106–7) suggests that "nation" should be understood as an "ideal type" (generally subscribed to by both political nationalists and political theorists) that describes "a named community of history and culture, possessing a unified territory, economy, mass education system and common legal rights." Most nations do not achieve this ideal and so "nation" must

9   Some recent geographers, conversely, have concerned themselves with the dubious project of disassociating Nazi ecological theories from the brutality of the Nazi regime; see Rollins (1995).

also be understood as both an abstract construction (an imagined community) and a historical reality (a struggled-over people and place). That is, the key question is one of just what the relationship is between the ideal and the place. Nations, therefore, "can be seen as both constructs or visions of nationalist (or other) elites, but equally as real, historical formations that embody a number of analytically separable processes over long time-spans" (A. Smith 1996: 108). If that is the case, then each of the components of the ideal type – the community of history and culture, the territorial base, the construction of a national economy, the role of education (and, now especially, media), and common legal rights – have to be examined in historical and geographical context. This, then, is an empirical issue, one that can only be addressed through the study of particular nations at particular moments in their construction.

Even so, some general principles can be noted. Etienne Balibar (1996), for example, argues that the forces of capitalism ineluctably shape the historical and geographical context within which nations develop. While it "is quite impossible to 'deduce' the nation form from capitalist relations of production," it is nonetheless the case that the "privileged status of the nation form derives from the fact that, locally, that form made it possible... for struggles between heterogeneous classes to be controlled and for not only a 'capitalist class' but the *bourgeoisie* proper to emerge from these..." (Balibar 1996: 134). That is to say, ideologies of national solidarity have often been used both to dampen struggle between classes and to create a form in which capitalism and the bourgeoisie more generally could develop. And, during the long modern era, *nation-state*s developed as the scale at which the global economy was regulated and through which particular local economies were integrated (see N. Smith 1990). Most particularly, Balibar asserts that with capitalism came the construction of a "national-social state" that assured the reproduction of the relations of capitalism by " 'intervening' in the very reproduction of... the formation of individuals, family structures, the structures of public health and, more generally, the whole space of 'private life'... the result of which is entirely to subordinate the existence of the individuals of all classes to their status as citizens of the nation-state, to the fact of being 'nationals,' that is" (Balibar 1996: 137).[10] What developed, particularly in the European nation-states that evolved alongside the rise of European capitalism, was a particular kind of *identification* with the "national" – an identification defined by one's relation to the (social) *state*. National identity thus is related to the formation of certain kinds of individuals, individuals related to one another through the mediation of a special kind of community – the state.[11] It is in this sense that it is not enough to see a nation as an *imagined* community; rather it is also a community constituted through the institutionalization of practices of citizenship and socialized reproduction.

Yet, Balibar (1996: 138) goes on (echoing Anderson), *"Every social community reproduced by the functioning of institutions is imaginary,* that is to say, it is based on

---

10   Clearly, Balibar is describing the production of a particular *scale* of belonging and identification, a scale functional to the development of nationally-based capitalism.

11   This argument has parallels with Jürgen Habermas's (1989) discussion of the development of a bourgeois "public sphere" as a force in the mediation of the relations between state and society during the ascendancy of capitalism. See Calhoun (1992).

the projection of individual existence into the weft of a collective narrative, on the recognition of a common name and on traditions lived as the trace of an immemorial past (even when they have been fabricated and inculcated in the recent past)." And "in the case of national formations, the imaginary which inscribes itself in the real in this way is that of the 'people.'" Balibar (1996: 138) argues that "the people" is the community which "recognizes itself...in the institution of the state...." Yet such recognition is only possible because the state produces that community as *a people* in the first place. It should be obvious that the contemporary "national question" is thus a question of belonging, a question of who is included as part of the collectivity described by the "national-social state," a question of who the people are – and of what rights *different* people within the state have (see also Marston 1990). This is precisely Ingrid Pollard's question – and Theresa Seamster's too.

The point, then, is that nations and national identity are produced in specific historical and geographical contexts as means of producing a certain kind of loyalty, or sense of belonging, between people (a certain *identification*). Nations are both "imaginary" and all too real. But what then is nationalism?

Nationalism

The standard definition of nationalism is that of "a feeling of belonging to the nation." It is also the desire or aspiration to equate the nation with a particular territory, and to thereby secure sovereignty for the people of the nation (Johnston et al. 1994: 405). Yet, "nationalisms are not just phantasmagoria of the mind; as systems of cultural representation whereby people come to imagine a shared experience of identification with an extended community, they are historical practices through which social difference is both invented and performed" (McClintock 1996: 260). Such social difference is often not at all innocent. That is why Theodor Adorno (cited in Borneman 1998: 221) argued back in 1966 that "barbarism" – the "principle of Auschwitz" – is directly related to nationalism. Indeed, he argued, "a reawakened nationalism" was the first precondition for a return to the principle of Auschwitz – and hence why the violent developments in contemporary Germany are so important. And that too is why Young National Democrat Oliver Handl's denial that his nationalism was the same as that of the Third Reich could not be more wrong. "Every time I say I'm a nationalist," he notes, "other people bring up the Third Reich. But I was born in 1975. What has it got to do with me" (quoted in Staunton 1998)?

Nationalism has certainly been a force for evil on the scale Adorno indicated. But it is more complicated than that. Most generally, nationalism can be seen as "an ideological movement for attaining and maintaining autonomy, unity, and identity on behalf of a population deemed by some of its members to constitute an actual or potential 'nation'" (A. Smith 1991: 73). Given that definition, it is hard to avoid the conclusion that nationalism – and nationalist movements – are ubiquitous. Nationalism, wrote Tom Nairn in 1974, "is among other things a name for the general condition of the modern body politic, more like the climate of political and social thought than just another doctrine" (Nairn 1996: 80). Despite the current wave of "globalization," this is still the case. Indeed, as Nairn points out, nationalism is in part a product of the insecurities of national middle classes (insecurities, I would contend, that are often heightened, rather than diminished, as a response to globalizing processes). In their insecurity national middle classes turn to "the masses" for support, organizing their consent by "taking a kindlier view of their general 'culture'" and promoting populist understandings of the roots of the nation itself (Nairn 1996: 85). Nationalist movements the world over have at least this in common: they are "idealistic"; they always "imagine an ideal 'people' (propped up by folklore studies, antiquarianism, or some surrogate for these)." This, of course, was precisely Johann von Herder's project (see chapter 1 above). Moreover, nationalism "always search[es] urgently for vital inner, untapped springs of energy both in the individual and the mass" (Nairn 1996: 86). That is, nationalism is itself an organizing and energizing force; it is a set of ideologies about what a nation *can* be. Most importantly, nationalism organizes the masses around the idea of a space to be defended, a space that is the very embodiment of national sovereignty.

But is "the desire to bring cultural and territorial imperatives together," as Nuala Johnson (1995: 100) defines nationalism, really all to the bad? Recall from chapter 1 that for Herder (who actually coined the term nationalism), developing a sense of cultural (or national) identity implied a project of cultural pluralism – what we now might call "multiculturalism." And recall too that the liberal philosopher Isaiah Berlin positively equated Herder with "all regionalists, all defenders of the local against the universal, all champions of deeply rooted forms of life" (quoted in Livingstone 1992: 124). Countless socialists, like Raymond Williams (chapter 2 above), have likewise drawn on a localist, rooted sense of identity as a mainspring of their politics – and of their objections against the depredations of a globalizing, abstracting economy. Finally, some of the most important social movements, and some of the most radical social formations, of the second half of the twentieth century have been, at least in part, nationalist in aim and scope. Consider, as just a few examples, the nationalist liberation struggles in Africa, from Jomo Kenyatta's nationalist movement and the Mau-Mau rebellions in Kenya to Nelson Mandela's African National Congress; the radical nationalism of the Black Panthers and the American Indian Movement in the United States; and the struggles for self-determinacy among the Palestinians, Basques, Kurds, and the Ogoni of Nigeria (see Watts 1997; Hammer 1996). None of these movements or formations was (or is) without its recidivist aspects; but neither were any wholly reactionary. In any of them there remains room for the development of what Doreen Massey (1994: 146–56) has identified as a progressive, or global, sense of place that understands identity not in terms of some unchanging history or tradition, but *in relation* to other places, other identities. A progressive sense of place and identity is predicated as seeing that identity and that place as part of a web of interconnections with other places and identities, a web defined not by exclusion and sameness, but by interdependence and difference. As Paul Gilroy (1992: 197) remarks, "the invocation of nationality and ethnicity corresponds to real political choices and to the wider field of political struggle."

These "real political choices" are invariably inflected with the politics of gender and race. "Despite many nationalists' investment in the idea of popular unity," Anne McClintock (1996: 260) notes, "no nation in the world grants women and men the same access to the rights and resources of the nation-state." Typically, the nation is equated with the "family," which McClintock (1996: 262) argues "offers a 'natural' figure for sanctioning national *hierarchy* within a putative organic *unity* of interests." That is, nationalism tends to incorporate inequality (in terms of gender, and as Frantz Fanon [1986] has shown, race) right at its center, naturalizing it as an inevitable aspect of national unity. For Fanon (1986: 141–2, quoted in McClintock 1996: 265), "militarization and the centralization of authority in a country automatically entail the resurgence of the authority of the father." This is true too of liberatory nationalist movements. "All too frequently, male nationalists have condemned feminism as divisive, bidding women to hold their tongues until after the revolution" (McClintock 1996: 281). Therefore, McClintock (1986: 281), concludes, "the question thus remains for progressive nationalism: Can the iconography of the family be retained as the figure for national unity, or must an alternative, radical iconography be developed?" Can there be a progressive nationalism – a "nationalism that gives vital expression to popular memory and [that] is strategically essential for mobilizing the populace" (McClintock 1996: 282) – that is built not out of sameness and hierarchy, but difference and equality?

The point is that nationalism, like national identity or "the nation" itself, is not inherently *anything*; it is what it is *made*. Nationalism is "chameleon-like, for it can accommodate itself to such diverse socio-territorial backgrounds as authoritarian collectivism (e.g. fascism and right-wing movements) and democratic movements struggling against domination by another nation, state or empire" (Johnston et al. 1994: 405). And so the question is really one of *how* nationalism is made, and how it situates itself in the world at large. Yet when we turn to that question, we have to set our sights on scales both larger and smaller than the scale of the nation-state.

Flows and Networks: Deterritorialization and Identity

All this talk of *Heimat*, of territorial nationalism, of violence against "foreigners" of all types,[12] and yet we live in a time of "globalization," a time of instant communication, a time when trade barriers are being smashed and Europe is unifying, a time when, as *The Economist* (1998: 19) puts it, "you cannot help but feel that the march to a 'borderless world' is proceeding briskly." If nationalism is the intersection of both cultural and *territorial* imperatives (as Nuala Johnson maintains), then what is its status at a time when the dominant geopolitical and geo-economic trend seems to be one of *deterritorialization*? What kind of "belonging," if any, is possible in such a world?

Networks

The notion of deterritorialization – and the associated idea of deterritorialized identities – has become the subject of a great deal of debate in cultural studies (and,

---

12   The Los Angeles County Commission on Human Relations reports that in 1995 there were 995 hate crimes reported in the county: 559 racial attacks; 338 on the basis of sexual orientation; and 118 motivated by religious hatred; in 1996 attacks on blacks increased 50 percent. In a single two-year period (1993–5) there were five vicious racist murders of African Americans in Southern California (Davis 1998: 405–9).

of course, in the world at large). From the perspective of power, for example, Paul Gilroy (1992: 188) argues that "neither political nor economic structures of domination are still coextensive with the borders of nation-states." The old territories that seemed to define our lives seem less relevant than they once were. Instead, we live in a world defined by a "space of flows." In Manuel Castells's (1989: 6, my emphasis) telling, this space of flows "dominates the historically constructed space of places, as the logic of dominant organisations detaches itself from the social constraints of *cultural identities* and local societies through the powerful medium of information technologies." Not only the economy, but social identity too is uprooted as new systems of communication *and* new systems of power are constructed that seem to span, rather than reinforce, the traditional power of the nation-state. We now live not in a local, or even national, society, but as "nodes" in a "network society" (Castells 1996; Thrift 1995).

But this is nothing new. A hundred and fifty years ago, Marx and Engels (1998 [1848]: 39) saw much the same thing:

> The bourgeoisie has through its exploitation of the world market given a cosmopolitan character to production and consumption in every country. To the great chagrin of reactionists, it has drawn from under the feet of industry the national ground on which it stood. All old-established national industries have been destroyed or are daily being destroyed. They are dislodged by new industries, whose introduction becomes a life and death question for all civilized nations, by industries that no longer work up indigenous raw material, but raw material drawn from the remotest zones; industries whose products are consumed, not only at home, but in every quarter of the globe. In place of the old wants, satisfied by the productions of the country, we find new wants, requiring for their satisfaction the products of distant lands and climes. In the place of the old local and national seclusion and self-sufficiency, we have intercourse in every direction, universal interdependence of nations.

As Marx and Engels indicate, even *local* identities are completely caught up in a web of global interdependence, in structures of power and domination that span nation-states (even as they are organized through them). They have long been "nodes" in a network.

Or as the Jamaican-born and raised Stuart Hall (see chapter 2 above) wryly summarizes, the very hallmark of "Englishness" – heavily sugared tea – was only made possible by the construction of an imperial *network* of labor and commodity exchange:

> People like me who came to England in the 1950s have been there for centuries; symbolically, we have been there for centuries. I was coming home. I am the sugar at the bottom of the English cup of tea. I am the sweet tooth, the sugar plantations that rotted generations of English children's teeth. There are thousands of others beside me that are ... the cup of tea itself. Because they don't grow it in Lancashire you know. Not a single plantation exists within the United Kingdom. This is the symbolisation of English identity – I mean what does anybody know about an English person except that they can't get through the day without a cup of tea. Where does it come from? Ceylon-Sri Lanka, India. That is the outside history that is the inside history of the English.

There is no English history without that history. (Hall 1991: 48–9, quoted in Crang 1998: 70–1).[13]

This is the history of empire-building, of conquest and colonization. "Englishness" – or any other modern identity – has been made possible only by the simultaneous development and destruction of other places and people, the uprooting of whole continents and their reconfiguration into webs of interrelations that link places together and make possible the global circulation of goods, capital, and people.

But this is not to say that the European slave trade, for example, wrenched people from some "authentic," "primitive," hermetic existence and threw them into the modern world of long-distance networks and relations. Quite the contrary. At the dawn of the trans-Atlantic slave trade, West Africa was already knitted together as a network of empires, kingdoms, and trading blocks. Important trading cities exchanged not only among themselves but exported ivory, gold, cotton, and spices to other parts of Africa, Southwest Asia, and by the early fifteenth century, Europe. Portuguese traders took commodities back to Europe, but they also brought back fantastic tales of wealth.

By the middle of the fifteenth century, the Portuguese had opened a small market in African slaves, who were sent to Europe mostly as domestic servants. Such a trade in human chattel tapped into indigenous West African markets in domestic slavery, but as European colonial development of the Americas increased in scope, the consequent demand for labor radically transformed the structure of African slave-systems (Levine et al. 1989). Between the middle of the sixteenth century and the end of the nineteenth, at least ten to twelve million African slaves were transported to the Americas, with most headed to Central and South America. Some, like the ancestors of Stuart Hall, of course, ended up on the sugar plantations of Jamaica, growing, harvesting, refining, and packing the sugar that became so central to the English diet (Mintz 1985). Others, perhaps Theresa Seamster's ancestors, were settled on plantations in the American South, there to make possible the mercantile and, eventually, industrial development of the United States.

The international slave trade not only benefited European shipping companies and plantation and mine owners; it also enriched some African traders well placed to reap the benefits of capturing and selling slaves to the Europeans. "In response to increased European demand, the West African ruling elite stepped up the hunt for suitable human merchandise, which meant increased – and increasingly lethal – regional warfare, carried out with European firearms" (Levine et al. 1989: 25). In addition to regional warfare, the amplified slave trade induced a large migration of coastal West Africans to the interior, depleted the ranks of skilled artisans, and flooded the continent with cheap European imports, all of which served to increase West African dependency on Europe.

The actual transportation of African slaves to the Americas was a brutal affair. At least one in six died on the journey from disease, suicide, and violent handling by

---

13 For an excellent history of the sugar trade that makes just the links Hall is referring to, see Mintz (1985). On the link between the English landscape and the plantation landscapes of the West Indies, see Said (1993), especially chapter 2.

ships' mates and officers. But the voyages, and subsequent dispersal of slaves throughout the Americas had another effect:

> The enslaved African men, women, and children transported to the New World came from different parts of the continent, from distinct societies and cultures. They spoke an array of languages and carried with them a variety of customs and beliefs. But many enslaved Africans also shared common skills and fundamental assumptions about the nature of religion, culture, kinship, and social life. They built upon these commonalities as they began the long and painful transition to a new, specifically African-American culture.... This process, so crucial to the history of the New World, commenced the moment they boarded the slave ships, as they began out of necessity to overcome their differences, as they cooperated toward the common end of survival in a strange land.
> (Levine et al. 1989: 27)

New identities, that is, were *forged* out of the violent processes by which a truly global market – or network – was constructed. This was a market and network *of* people and *built by* people, and in which people were treated little differently from other commodities.

This is precisely Stuart Hall's point: to understand the construction of "English" identity, one must attend to the network of relations established by the African diaspora. But one cannot stop there, for "Englishness" is also a product of complex Asian Indian, Chinese, and of course European diasporas, and of the historical-geographical and geopolitical contexts that both gave rise to and were made possible by them.

Cultural flow and social reproduction

Identity thus exists as a nexus, a meeting point, not as an unchanging "thing" rooted to place, and with each historical upheaval, each new conquest, each new round of "time-space compression," identity itself is radically transformed. For the cultural theorist Arjun Appadurai (1990: 301), this means that with each round of geopolitical and geo-economic change, "the problem of reproduction in a deterritorialized context" is raised anew. How, he asks, is any identity (like "Englishness," "Blackness" or "Indianness") socially reproduced (see also Gilroy 1993)? How are identities forged and maintained?

For Appadurai, such questions indicate the need to attend to the fact that the global cultural economy is a "disjunctive order": "the complexity of the current global economy has to do with certain fundamental disjunctures between economy, culture and politics" that need to be better understood (Appadurai 1990: 296). As a starting point, Appadurai suggests we need to understand that there are five dimensions to "global cultural flow." He calls these dimensions "scapes" (see chapters 4 and 5): ethnoscapes (configurations and flows of people), mediascapes (media and images), technoscapes (technology), finanscapes (capital), and ideoscapes (ideologies). The suffix "scape" is employed:

> to indicate first of all that these are not objectively given relations which look the same from every angle of vision, but rather that they are deeply perspectival constructs,

inflected very much by the historical situatedness of different sorts of actors: nation-states, multinationals, diasporic communities, as well as sub-national groupings and movements...and even intimate face-to-face groups, such as villages, neighborhoods and families. (Appadurai 1990: 296)

The idea is to understand the "ever fluid" global configuration ("scape") of each of the five dimensions (people, media, technology, capital, and ideology).[14] It is also to explore the tension between these scapes. For as Appadurai notes, what is at work is a "scalar dynamic" in which each configuration at each moment structures how and where new flows and new configurations will occur. Global cultural flows, Appadurai (1990: 301) argues, "occur in and through the growing disjunctures between" the various "scapes." He admits that "there have been some disjunctures between the flows of these things" at "all periods in human history" (as the history of slavery makes abundantly clear), but what sets the current epoch apart is that "the sheer speed, scale and volume of each of these flows is so great that the disjunctures have become central to the politics of global culture." This is what he meant when he indicated that questions of social reproduction are to some degree also questions of *de*territorialization.

For many, these heightened tendencies towards deterritorialization, these tendencies towards a global reach for everything from capital to television shows, indicate the "end of the nation-state." They imply the construction of a highly homogenized, and not-very-democratic "McWorld," where we all eat the same things, watch the same shows, and pursue the same desires the world over. They indicate a world in which social reproduction is more and more the product of homogenized commodity consumption. For Benjamin Barber (1992: 59–60), the only thing standing in the way of this "McWorld" is the equally undemocratic "holy war" – or *jihad* – waged by "rebellious factions and dissenting minorities at war not only with globalism but with the traditional nation-state." Barber calls these "holy wars" "parochial," suggesting that they are localist in intent and chauvinist to the core.

Yet as Appadurai makes clear, the flows of capital and commodities rarely simply produce homogeneity. Rather, these flows are increasingly marked by a radical geographical and social *unevenness*. The current "technoscape," to take just one example, hardly constructs a uniform world. Consider the following image:

> Jumbos have enabled Korean computer consultants to fly to Silicon Valley as if popping next door, and Singaporean entrepreneurs to reach Seattle in a day. The borders of the world's greatest ocean have been joined as never before.... But what about those they fly over, on their islands five miles below? How has the mighty 747 brought them greater communion with those whose shores are washed by the same water? It hasn't, of course. Air travel might enable businessmen to buzz across the ocean but the concurrent decline in shipping has only increased the isolation of many island communities.... Pitcairn, like many other Pacific islands, has never felt so far from its neighbors. (D. Birkett, quoted in Massey 1994: 148)

---

14 Our discussion of "landscape" in chapters 4 and 5 shows that Appadurai's indication that "scapes" are "ever fluid" is, at best, naive. Better is his notion that "scapes" represent particular *configurations* at given places and times.

We may be able to communicate across the globe by e-mail with just a press of a button, but as we do, "somewhere in sub-Saharan Africa, there's a woman – amongst many women – on foot, who still spends hours a day collecting water" (Massey 1994: 149). *This* is the reality of "reproduction in a deterritorialized context," a reality marked not by the end of territoriality, but by increasingly unjust reconfigurations of space.[15]

For others, therefore, the "end of the nation-state" really implies a reconfiguration of space. Like Appadurai, David Held (1996: 408) understands the contemporary world to be constructed out of a series of "disjunctures." He defines these disjunctures as " 'gaps' between, on the one hand, the power of the nation state as in principle capable of determining its own future and, on the other, the actual practices and structures of state and economic systems at the global level." Held (1996: 408–12) identifies four disjunctures that are particularly important. First, there is a gap between "the formal authority of the state and the actual system of production, distribution and exchange." That is, there is a misfit between the scale of the nation-state as a political entity and the scale of capitalism as a social and productive relation. Second, there is a disjuncture "between the idea of the state as an autonomous strategic, military actor and the development of a global system of states, characterized by the existence of hegemonic powers and power blocs." In other words, even in an era of "globalization," *imperialism* remains a potent force. Third, and related, there is a disjuncture in the nature of regulatory power usually assumed by states and that is now assumed by transnational and international governing bodies. Finally, there has developed a "gap between the idea of membership in a national political community, i.e., citizenship... and the development of international law which subjects individuals, governments and non-governmental organizations to new systems of regulation."[16] Space, and the way people, goods, and capital move through it, is being radically restructured. The role of the nation, and the nation-state is clearly up for grabs (though in no way can it be said that the nation-state is now impotent). Rather, there is, in Doreen Massey's (1994: 149) terms, a new "power geometry" that governs both geopolitics and everyday life.

This power geometry is marked most simply by the fact that "different social groups have distinct relationships to...differentiated mobility [of capital, goods, and people themselves]: some people are more in charge of it than others; some initiate flows and movement, others don't; some are more on the receiving-end of it than others; some are effectively imprisoned by it" (1994: 149). In other words, it is simply not enough to understand the world as an amorphous "network society" in which deterritorialization is the ruling process of the day. Indeed, the important point is that every *de*territorialization is simultaneously a *re*territorialization. New borders and boundaries are constructed even as old ones are torn down. With the destruction of the Berlin Wall came increased efforts to rid Germany of Turks and other foreigners; with the demise of the Iron Curtain came any number of demands for the construction of new states, new nation-spaces.

15   I hope that it is quite clear that I mean to implicate myself, and others like me – clearly members of the global elite – in the reproduction of globally unjust space. Academics are obvious beneficiaries of "deterritorialized reproduction" no matter how much some of us may want to question and contest it.

16   The 1998 arrest in London on Spanish charges of former Chilean dictator Augusto Pinochet is the most prominent example of the last of these disjunctures – and of the intense political conflict it engenders.

Figure 10.5 In the post-NAFTA period, the United States government has found it necessary to "harden" the border between the United States and Mexico, in hopes of at least slowing the flow of undocumented migrants. Built in 1997, this part of the fence divides Colonia Puerto de Anapra, Ciudad Juárez, from Sunland Park, New Mexico. Photography by Javier Aguilar; used by permission. Photo: Aperture.

The case of the implementation of the North American Free Trade Agreement (NAFTA) is particularly instructive. Designed to open the economic borders between the United States, Mexico, and Canada, it has also led to a hardening of the political borders between them. "The Mexican-American border has certainly been made easier to cross," *The Economist* (1998: 22) writes, "as long as you are inanimate or heading south. Mexicans still have a problem." Indeed, the very success of NAFTA – since success is defined as a more rapid circulation of capital between the countries – *requires* the maintenance of an only partially permeable border between Mexico and the United States: unevenness in wages, in life-chances, and in ecological and labor laws, is a precondition for the development of the maquiladora assembly plants that are the greatest legacy of NAFTA (figure 10.5). Social reproduction in an era of global flows demands the continual, geographical, reproduction of difference.

Deterritorialized identities

What then of identity – and particularly national identity? What sorts of "geographies of belonging" are now being constructed? For those most in control of mobility, the answer is a new form of elite cosmopolitanism, in which the pivotal spaces of power are the airport lounge, the swank restaurant, and floors of global stock exchanges (all linked by cellular phone). These are spaces open, to a larger degree than ever, to people regardless of nationality or race, and even to some extent gender. There is a globalized *class* in the making, a class defined by hyper-mobility, privilege, and unparalleled luxury. It is a class not tightly tied to any locale, but at home in many. It can escape the ravages of plummeting markets and incendiary terrorism, by retreating to the luxurious bunkers in or on the outskirts of New Delhi, London, Rio, Hong Kong, or Los Angeles, or flying off to more clement locations. Its members are, in the phrase of the 1980s, "masters of the universe." Loyalty is not to the nation but to the class, the class of investors, perhaps the first truly *global* cosmopolitan class in the history of the world.

Of course it is not only elite people that move at will, but capital too. Governed by new, draconian multinational agreements overseen by the World Trade Organization, capital is ever more free to move at the first indication of trouble, stranding those drawn into its orbit yet still tied to particular places. For much of the middle class in the industrialized world, this has led to a new precariousness, and in turn a virulent new localist politics, a politics that Neil Smith (1996: chapter 10) has termed "revanchist" – that is, a politics bent on revenge against those they see as the primary diagnostic indicators of their own weakness in the global economy: the homeless, the poor, and the *Ausländer*.

In fact, for countless numbers of the world's population, life is defined by something like a permanent *Ausländer* status and the development of something like a migrant identity. Now, however, this identity is defined less in terms of "mastering" the universe – or even the smallest portion of it – and more by the struggle to make a life as part of what Henry Mayhew back in the nineteenth century called "the wandering tribes" (see Cresswell 1997). Forever the objects of suspicion, forever able to avail themselves of fewer rights than citizens of host countries (a fact much to the advantage of employers of migrant and migratory labor, such as American agribusiness), and seemingly never quite "at home," more and more ordinary working people have found in "globalization" not a new and attractive "cosmopolitanism," but a permanent state of dislocation. "Deterritorialized identities" are certainly continually forming, but what they mean might be far more a function of *who* you are (in terms of class status) than *where* you are (Nogales, Nottingham, or Nairobi).

For those still rooted to place, globalization often means abandonment, as with Pitcairn Island, and Johnstown (chapter 4 above). Or it means learning to struggle for identity against the forces of capital and its enforcer-states. Perhaps the best example in this case is the peasants of Chiapas, who have found ways to use global communications media precisely to solidify their own (nationalist) identity, *and* to link it to other oppressed peoples in the world. The Zapatistas in Chiapas are fiercely regional, fiercely nationalist, but they aren't only that. Or, more accurately, the rebellious Mayans are constructing a new form of national identity, one clearly suited to the age of global communication, global political power, and deep, unforgiving spatial unevenness, an identity marked by a strong bid towards solidarity with other oppressed peoples. This new identity is perhaps best summarized by Zapatista leader Subcommandante Marcos when asked just *who* he is: "Marcos is gay in San Francisco, black in South Africa, Palestinian in

Israel, Jew in Germany, pacifist in Bosnia, a woman alone in the Metro at 10 pm, campesino without land, unemployed worker.... Marcos is all the minorities saying, 'enough!' "

Conclusion: Geometries of Power

It should be clear that the globalization of everything, from capital to everyday life, does not portend, as many argue, the end of the territorial state.[17] It does mean, however, that there has been a reconfiguration of power, in which the nature of state sovereignty has been radically transformed. As John Agnew (1995: 88), puts the point, the question faced by states in an era of intensive globalization, is "whether they represent the interests of territorially circumscribed populations or the interests of businesses that operate globally but which originated within their confines."[18] Is it the case, as John Berger (1998–9: 3, paraphrasing Subcommandante Marcos) says, that "the new task of the nation states is to manage what is allotted to them, to protect the interests of the market's mega-enterprises and, above all, to control and police the redundant"? That is, has the nation-state become subservient to structures of power and influence, to say nothing of key institutions, operating at a scale larger than the nation-state itself? Is nationalism thus only an anachronism, only the dying breath of an old and surpassed world?

To some degree the state has *always* been subservient to – or at least a construction of – processes larger than its own territories. Return to Ingrid Pollard's photographs. One of her "pastoral interludes" shows a man fishing with a net in a small ditch (figure 10.6). Beneath reads the caption "... a lot of what made ENGLAND GREAT is founded on the blood of slavery, the sweat of working people...an Industrial REVOLUTION without the Atlantic Triangle.... " The end of the sentence is easy to fill in: "impossible!"

Compound the fact that nations and states are always creatures of processes larger than themselves with the fact that populations *within* states are themselves highly fragmented, and responsive to processes operating at scales both larger and smaller than the nation-state, and it is clear that questions of deterritorialization are hardly simple. As Appadurai (1990: 304) puts it:

> One important feature of global cultural politics, tied to the disjunctive relationships between [the five "scapes" discussed above], is that the state and nation are at each other's throats, and the hyphen that links them is now less an icon of conjuncture than an index of disjuncture. This disjunctive relationship between nation and state has two levels: at the level of any given nation-state, it means that there is a battle of the imagination, with state and nation seeking to cannibalize one another. Here is the seedbed of brutal separatisms, majoritarianisms that seem to have appeared from nowhere, and micro-identities that have become political projects within the

17   A good analysis of the current "threat of globalization" and the ideological debates surrounding it, can be found in *Race and Class* 40 (2 and 3) (1998–9).

18   This is especially the case now that cross-border mergers (such as Daimler-Benz and Chrysler) have become an increasing means of survival for crisis-ridden capitalist firms.

. . . a lot of what made ENGLAND GREAT is founded on the blood of slavery, the sweat of working people . . . an Industrial REVOLUTION without the Atlantic Triangle . . .

Figure 10.6 Ingrid Pollard, from *Pastoral Interludes* (1984). Reproduced by permission of the artist.

nation-state. At another level . . . ideas of nationhood seem to be increasing in scale and regularly crossing existing state boundaries: sometimes, as with the Kurds, because of previous identities stretched across vast national space, or, as with the Tamils in Sri Lanka, the dormant threads of a transnational diaspora have been activated to ignite the micro-politics of a nation-state.

Here, then, we do meet Barber's "jihads," but they are anything but "parochial." Rather, they are the very culture wars that construct the worlds that govern our lives. They are culture wars marked by simultaneous de- and re-territorialization; culture wars in which "state" and "nation" are simultaneously transcended *and* reproduced. Where Marx and Engels saw processes of deterritorialization sweeping away national and local interests, in fact such interests have become both the fulcrum for deterritorialization itself and the object of political and social struggle – a social struggle marked by 2,300 racist crimes in Germany in 1996 alone. Culture wars are real wars.

Part IV

Conclusion

11

Cultural Rights, Cultural Justice, Cultural Geography

Culture wars are real wars. A critical cultural geography must therefore be focused on intervening in struggles over just what "culture" is – or could be. It cannot be content simply to describe or celebrate the sheer variety of cultural artifacts, movements, or "ways of life," as important as those tasks may be. *Cultural Geography: A Critical Introduction* has been written as a means to understand *where* to intervene. That is not at all a simple issue, and the sheer breadth of topics covered in this book suggests that "culture" is a site of struggle on many fronts. Yet to say that culture is in some simple sense a "site" is itself inaccurate, as we have seen in the preceding pages. Rather, the question of just what culture *is* is itself a source of endless contestation. "Culture" is thus best understood as a process, a set of relationships that gain efficacy as they are reified.

That is why chapter 10 ended with an invocation of Doreen Massey's ideas about "power geometries." I wanted to highlight the point that *any* cultural geography (that is, the actual, material geography of culture) is a geography of power. How and under what conditions that power is exercised, and how and under what conditions that power is made real on the ground and given causative effect (reified), are the true questions underlying any decent, *critical* cultural geography (that is, the analysis of the relationship between "culture" and geography). In chapters 2 and 3 we found that "culture" is a system of differentiation and a system of social reproduction; and we also found that it is not innocent of the powerful intentions of specific industries, social formations, and even certain people whose very job it is to differentiate, control, sort, and order, to construct meaning, and to produce the very artifacts that we call "culture." Such work – the work of culture in both senses of that phrase – is not at all a straightforward process. It is continually contested, often subverted, and frequently resisted (sometimes effectively, sometimes not), as we saw in Parts II and III. My own telling of the geography of "culture" in this book was itself purposely designed as an explicit act of cultural production, an act which I hope frequently stands in opposition to the dominant processes of social reproduction, social control, and *cultural* domination. This book is thus an intervention, no matter how slight, in the ongoing culture wars of our times. It is underlain, in other words, by a particular vision of cultural *justice*.

By way of conclusion, I would like to turn to this issue of cultural justice, since it is what the book has been pointing to all along. Given the powerful forces constantly reshuffling the spaces of our lives – the simultaneous processes of de- and re-territor-ialization examined in the previous chapter – what can "justice" possibly be anyway? What does it look like? How is it made to stick and under what conditions is it or isn't it reproduced? And whatever the answers to those question, what then is *cultural* justice?

Cultural Justice, Cultural Rights

Marx was famously skeptical of achieving a just society under capitalism. He saw capitalist social relations as inherently unjust, and hence any universal notions of justice were idealist to the core. Indeed, under the social relations of capitalism, the exploitation of workers and the expropriation of the value they produce *is* just. "Justice," for Marx, is always explicitly related to actual material social conditions; as such, it is a result, and perhaps a stabilization, of social struggle. In partial contrast, Engels was much more open to the power of a normative vision of justice. "Justice," he wrote,

> which is the organic, regulating, sovereign basic principle of societies, which has nevertheless been nothing up to the present, but which ought to be everything – what is that if not the stick with which to measure all human affairs, if not the final arbiter to be appealed to in all conflicts?   (Quoted in Merrifield and Swyngedouw 1995: 1)

"Justice" thus emerges as an ideal against which to measure the accomplishments, the practices, and the aims of any society. Engels's question is actually a plaintive call, more than it is a statement of existing relations. For as he further argues, "always . . . justice is but the ideologized expression of the existing economic relations, now from the conservative, and now from the revolutionary angle. The justice of the Greeks and Romans held slavery to be just; the justice of the bourgeois of 1789 demanded the abolition of feudalism on the grounds that it was unjust" (quoted in Merrifield and Swyngedouw 1995: 8). "Justice" is thus at once an idealized, normative vision, *and* an ideological tool for justifying forms of exploitation.[1] The key question, then, and the reason I put so much stock in what I have insisted throughout this book on calling "culture wars," is how normative visions and actual social relations are worked out and contested in particular places and at particular times.

In liberal capitalist society, justice is usually defined in terms of the individual and in terms of *rights* pertaining to the individual. Yet, "in a world increasingly beset by ethnocultural conflicts," or by culture wars more generally, according to Andrew Ross (1998: 190), "it has become clear that the liberal focus on individual rights,

---

1   The literature on social justice is vast, and I will not attempt to survey it here. Behind my own ideas lie the debates within the leftist literature on social justice, particularly as it has been expressed by Iris Marion Young (1990) and David Harvey (1996).

generalized by international conventions after World War II through the concept of human rights, cannot do justice to the claims now being raised on the basis of cultural differences and minority rights." The pre-eminent social justice struggle to be engaged at the outset of the twenty-first century will thus be the struggle over "cultural justice," over cultural *rights*. But this is not exactly a new development. As we have seen throughout this book, struggles over economy, over political representation, over the processes of social reproduction that govern our lives, have always been linked to processes, practices, and productions that we call "cultural." The very notion of the autonomous individual as the key actor in modern society is a question of "culture," at least if we see culture as a process of division and differentiation and hence part of a system of social integration (as I argued we should in chapter 3). "Cultural" rights have, in that sense, long been on the agenda. What is different, what is always different, is the *context* within which struggles over "culture" are engaged, contexts that have everything to do with who has the power to determine what is just, what is of value, what is right.

But why bother talking about "rights" at the end of a book on cultural geography? One part of the answer should be apparent from the preceding four chapters, which each in varying ways raised questions about the relationship between individual and group rights as they intersect with struggles over public and private spaces, and the role of the state, capital, and powerful others in constructing and controlling lives. Geography, as we have seen, is structured in fights – culture wars – over inclusion and exclusion, over the making or shaping of boundaries around race, gender, ethnicity, and sexuality, and over defining who constitutes part of the group, whether that group be a cosmopolitan elite, an imagined nation, or proper and well-heeled consumers. Geography is structured precisely by the question: Who has the *right* to space?

At the most basic level, "rights" means an institutional, societally sanctioned promise that you can *be*.[2] The modern, bourgeois, nation-state, however, has typically *not* enshrined the "right to be." It has instead been structured around the distribution of *negative rights*. Negative rights allow citizens to remain free *from* state interference in some aspect of life (such as speech and thought, religion, police brutality, etc.). The "right to be" has been at most a byproduct of these "negative" guarantees.

Yet! *positive rights* (the right *to* some good; the right to *be*) have now become the pre-eminent battleground in the struggle for social justice. The goal of many social justice struggles is to continually expand the realm of the positive, enshrining the right *to* particular social goods, such as housing, land, a living wage, and, significantly for the arguments put forth in this book, cultural autonomy. As is clear from these examples, contemporary states are more comfortable with negative rights, rights that spell out specific restrictions of state power (especially as they relate to state involvement in economic activity), than they are with positive rights, rights that mandate some level of equity and some degree of social justice within the polity. Current struggles to mandate a living wage in American cities, combined with what is now a global anti-sweatshop campaign, indicate just how strongly contemporary states are structured around negative rights, and just how much such a structuring

2   An excellent discussion of the geography of rights can be found in Blomley (1994).

works to the benefit of particular social actors. These campaigns are quite forcefully met, I know from my own experience, by arguments that the state should not unduly interfere in the business practices of particular firms.[3] That such arguments run smack up against populist arguments promoting the rights of people to safe, demo-cratic workplaces and access to decent wages suggests why positive rights have become such a fertile ground for the continual struggle to transform the state after images of economic, political, social, and cultural justice.

Indeed, struggles for positive rights govern cultural struggles throughout the world. Gays making space in the city are fighting explicitly for their right to *be*; so too are the Mayan peasants in Chiapas represented by Marcos and the Zapatistas; women seeking to "take back the night;" students in Strasbourg and Paris fighting to make "new situations;" and anti-racist movements in Europe fighting against the increased nationalism that has marked the post-Cold War era. In each case groups of people bound together by some commonality of identity seek to reconstruct the world in such a way that they may live on their own terms, not on the terms of those who seek to control them.[4] These are struggles also for *inclusion* within structures of power; but again, inclusion on the terms that each group establishes. The fact that these are struggles for certain "ways of life" is important. The struggle for rights – for inclusion – is more and more fought not at the level of the liberal individual (as was the case in the French and American revolutions), but at the level of the social (or cultural) group. That is precisely what debates over, for example, affirmative action and *The Bell Curve*, the maintenance of gay spaces such as bars and bathhouses, or simply Theresa Seamster's right to go about her shopping unmolested by security guards (see chapter 9 above), are all about.

A second reason to talk about rights at the end of a book about cultural geography, picks up on the themes of chapter 10 and has to do with the cultural nature of political space. What sort of territory, at what scale, circumscribes what sort of groups? How are rights within that territory parceled out, and to whom? To answer these questions entails an examination of the historical and contemporary relation-ship between "nation" and "state," between identity and social, institutionalized power, and it entails a close focus on the products and actions of the "critical infrastructure" who develop the languages through which meaning is given effective force. That is, it entails focusing not only on the actions of nation-states, but on the culture wars raging inside and across them. There is no doubt that the protection of rights by the nation-state has been limited and grudging; indeed the very notion of the nation-state is in part predicated on the institutionalization of *injustice*. Enunciated rights have never covered all residents of nation-states, rights-enforcement has been highly uneven, and often geared towards the advantage of the already-powerful, and

---

3   In USA history, such a sentiment was famously institutionalized in the Supreme Court's 1905 *Lochner* decision which declared that maximum workday length legislation interfered with firms' "right of contract." That decision has been chipped away at over the subsequent years, but the general tenor of the court, that the state should at most be minimally involved in contracts between private parties, remains. What is absent from such a stance, of course, is any realistic sense of the distribution of power.

4   And for just these reasons, the line that separates a progressive from a regressive social movement is a thin one and must be determined in terms of Engels's normative *ideal* of justice, not so much on the practices of the movements in question.

as Marx and Engels rightly noted, formal justice and formal rights have been predicated on a *particular* vision of what is just (slavery in Rome, bourgeois labor contracts in capitalism, etc.). It is also the case, of course, that rights themselves have often been exclusionary, serving to *limit* rather than expand the privileges of citizenship: first, rights have been reserved for *national* citizens; and second, they have often been restricted to a small subset of the population, typically men of a certain class. And, finally, the rise of the "rights-state" in Europe and America was itself predicated on the subjugation of other lands and peoples, on the construction of a national identity "at home" by controlling peoples and resources elsewhere (as Ingrid Pollard's photographs so eloquently attest). Yet, given all that, the nation-state has been the primary target of struggles for rights, and as independence has been won in colonial regions, new nation-states have been the site of severe battles over the nature and extent of rights within their borders. This contradiction, between the nation-state as the guarantor of rights and the nation-state as the denier of rights, is itself a key focus for cultural struggle, as for example in the numerous battles over the distribution of power between and among women, people of color, and sexual and national minorities examined in Part III of this book. Rights, in other words, are closely linked to identity.

In turn, identity, as it has been structured through the nation-state, has been closely linked to the land, to particular areas or regions. This raises a key issue for cultural geography, an issue that brings us back to the issues of landscape we discussed in chapters 4 and 5. To what degree is the landscape of a nation or region a reflection, or an incorporation or embodiment, of the people who live in it? To what degree is "landscape" exclusionary, little more than a means to establish the nation as "purely" English, American, German, Australian, or white? To what degree does the landscape reflect the *rights* of people to the land – and which people? Barbara Revelle's mural on the wall of the Denver Convention Center (chapter 1 above) gives one answer to that question; the racist right in Germany (chapter 10) quite another. The issue, then, is one of just *which* vision of the landscape will win out. And that is an issue that simply cannot be decided in these pages. It will be decided in the course of the struggles (on the ground, in the media, and even in the classroom) fought over just this question of what is *just*, what is *right* – and for whom. Beyond that, all the struggles by subjugated groups – women, gays, people of color – to represent themselves in the space of the countryside, the city, the nation, and on the global stage, all the struggles and culture wars we have examined in this book are struggles over how and in what spaces representation can be possible. The general notion of "resistance" explored in chapter 6 requires us always to ask what is being resisted, what sorts of space and "situations" are worthy of being resisted. And it asks us to think about precisely what sorts of tactics and strategies, what actions in the realm of "cultural production," are best for creating more effective representation.

That leads us to a third reason to talk about rights at the end of a book on cultural geography. In Part I of the book, I made much of the fact that the production of "culture" is a highly structured affair, that certain groups, certain divisions of labor, were charged with naming and locating culture, with pinning it down as something real and of value. The corollary of that fact is that any ideas about the development or maintenance of "cultural autonomy," for no matter what group and at no matter what scale, must be thoroughly grounded in a critical analysis of the actual social processes, working at all scales, that *make* "culture" in the first place. If culture is a production, then the important issue is the *conditions* and *relations* under which it is produced. The president of the Nabisco Company, quoted in the introduction to this book, was not joking when he said he dreamed of a world of culturally homogeneous consumption. He, working with and through the expanding relations of capital that now go under the name "globalization," has the power to go quite a long way in assuring just that. But with the expansion of the relations of production and consumption that Nabisco (now a part of the RJ Reynolds tobacco conglomerate) dreams of, comes a thorough reconfiguration of the "ways of life" upon which production and consumption around the globe are based. Nabisco's dream is strongly contested, of course, and it certainly is the fact that the relations of production and consumption within capitalism itself demand a certain kind of differentiation of the space of the globe (as we saw in chapter 3), but that differentiation develops within and as part of a larger process that sets social relations on largely homogeneous grounds: the grounds staked out by the necessity of selling one's labor so as to buy what is necessary to survive (or to live well).

"Cultural autonomy" within an era of rapid "globalization," then, must be seen as a particularly curious affair – or as something to be keenly struggled for. The structuring power of the culture industries – which surely must now include the industries that produce the durable goods and consumer products that structure our lives as well as the makers of films, music, or books – is both strong enough, and universal enough, that it must be reckoned with in *any* accounting of cultural geography. If a fundamental basis of cultural justice is the "right to be," then the primary question for cultural geography must always be: What are the material conditions under which it is *possible* to be?

Finally, and following on from the questions of what makes it possible to *be* and what is meant by "cultural autonomy," there is a fourth reason to conclude this book with a discussion of justice. Discussions of cultural autonomy are often based on a keenly felt sense that local cultures, particular ways of life, deserve to be preserved and protected against the universalizing onslaught of modernism and capitalist relations. Therefore, the argument usually goes, any progressive sense of cultural justice must be alive to the radical *relativity* of different ways of life. There can be no single or universal yardstick against which to judge acts within particular locales; rather we must be attuned, as Herder so long ago urged (see chapter 1 above) to how differences across cultures do not necessarily imply that any culture is necessarily any better than any other. In terms of justice, Michael Walzer (1983, quoted in Harvey 1996: 350–1) urges us to be "radically particularist" in our theories. He says that "all of us" are

> culture-producing creatures; we make and inhabit meaningful worlds. Since there is no way to rank order these worlds with regard to their understanding of social goods, we do justice to actual men and women by respecting their particular creations. And they claim justice, and resist tyranny, by insisting on the meaning of social goods among themselves. Justice is rooted in the distinct understanding of places, honors, jobs, things of all sorts, that constitute a shared way of life. To override that understanding is (always) to act unjustly.

That's an attractive vision and one that has much to commend it. But it is ignorant of both power and the long history of "globalization" itself that has simply made it impossible to talk of local cultures as if they exist as an identifiable and autonomous thing. As David Harvey (1996: 351) remarks: "if we take Walzer at his word, it would be as unjust to try to override the cultural achievements of slavery, apartheid, fascism, or a caste society as it would be to deny the self-determination of native-Americans or Vietnamese peasants." Any negotiation of "justice," therefore, must be fully situated within a politics of scale, in a thorough understanding of how the global and local are fully implicated in each other, as Harvey among others argues.

One of the goals of this book has been to situate the production of places, and the production of "culture," within such a politics of scale. Whether considering the fate of Johnstown and its landscape, the "spatial entrapment" of women in suburbia, or the status of identity within a "deterritorializing" world, explanations have been firmly rooted in a consideration of scale. I have tried to make this book a model of what a non-localist cultural geography might look like. If one of the frustrations geographers had with "old" cultural geography (see chapters 1 and 2) was its localist and exceptionalist sensibility, then my goal, like that of other "new cultural geo-graphers," has been to explode the boundaries of the local to show just how the local itself is the product of processes working at *all* scales. My reason for doing so, however, has been rooted in exactly the critique of localist relativism that Harvey makes. Such a localism makes for a dangerous politics. Instead, I have written this account to explore what it means to live in a world where people (and peoples) are radically differentially situated in relation to the processes of cultural production. We are *not* "all of us" "culture-producing creatures," at least not equally. Any struggle for cultural justice *has* to take that fact into account, and I have meant *Cultural Geography: A Critical Introduction* as the beginnings of an analysis of just what those differences in culture-producing ability are, and what they might mean.

Taken together, these four points suggest that like "culture," justice is always to be fought over, always to be negotiated, always an *outcome* rather than an *input* to culture wars. Yet ideals of cultural justice are strong motivating forces, if for no other reason than that the current systems through which "culture" is produced are patently *un*just. The key point, therefore, is that any ideal of justice must be situated within an analysis of the material social relations that govern life, an analysis that starts from the question of *who* benefits from the current arrangement, and why. My hope is that this book has exposed at least some of those processes, revealed if only in outline, who they stand to benefit, and shown just how complex the cultural relations within which the world is structured really are. For without such an understanding, cultural justice can only ever be an abstract, unattainable ideal, and never a pivot for political action and social transformation.

What Is Culture? What Is Cultural Geography?

Culture consists in relationships. It is not a "thing" until very powerful forces make it so. These forces, as we have seen time and time again in this book, are always open to contestation and resistance. But so too does reified "culture" – always in conjunction with the economic, social, and political forces that have made it – have real power. Culture, like landscape, has work to do. That work is sometimes beautiful, sometime liberatory, but often brutal and ugly. "Culture" is both a source of power and a source of domination. And when it is linked with geography – with the spaces, places, and landscapes that make it possible – it is a source of power and domination that must always be reckoned with. "Culture," then, is *both* flux and stability, *both* a set of constantly changing relationships and a (socially produced) thing.

The key trick for cultural geography, therefore, is to begin to understand the dialectic between constant change, the ever-present flux of social relationships, and the relative permanence of reified ways of knowing, standardized "maps of meaning," and solidified cultural productions (from lyrics to landscapes, movies to monuments). The forces and processes that reify – and that resist – are themselves part of a dialectic between "universal" social processes (the expanding relations of capitalist production, or the historical structures of patriarchy, for example) and the particular events, places, and incidents within which those universal processes are given shape and meaning. As Harvey (1996: 362) puts it, "universality must be constructed in dialectic relation with particularity. Each defines the other in such a way as to make the universality criterion always open to negotiation through the particularities of difference." No better remit for cultural geography could be given. Cultural geography is precisely the study of how particular social relations intersect with more general processes, a study grounded in the production and reproduction of actual places, spaces, and scales *and* the social structures that give those places, spaces, and scales meaning. But cultural geography must be more than study and analysis. Since "culture is politics by another name," cultural geography must become an intervention in cultural politics. No other cultural geography is sufficient to the work of cultural justice that everywhere remains to be done.

Bibliography

Abu-Loghod, Janet (1974), "Planning a City for All," in L. Hapgood and J. Getzels (eds.), *Planning, Women and Change* (Chicago: American Society of Planning Officials).

Adorno, Theodor, and Horkheimer, Max (1993), "The Culture Industry: Enlightenment as Mass Deception," reprinted in Simon During (ed.), *The Cultural Studies Reader* (London: Routledge), 29–43.

Aglietta, M. (1976), *A Theory of Capitalist Regulation* (London: New Left Books).

Agnew, John (1995), "Democracy and Human Rights after the Cold War," in R.J. Johnston, Peter Taylor, and Michael Watts (eds.), *Geographies of Global Change* (Oxford: Blackwell), 82–96.

Aitken, Stuart (1998), *Family Fantasies and Community Space* (New Brunswick: Rutgers University Press).

Anderson, Benedict (1991), *Imagined Communities: Reflections on the Origin and Spread of Nationalism* (London: Verso, revised edition).

Anderson, Kay (1987), "The Idea of Chinatown: The Power of Place and Institutional Practice in the Making of a Racial Category," *Annals of the Association of American Geographers* 77, 580–98.

Anderson, Kay (1988), "Cultural Hegemony and the Race-Definition Process in Chinatown, Vancouver: 1880–1980," *Environment and Planning D: Society and Space* 6, 127–49.

Anderson, Kay (1991), *Vancouver's Chinatown: Racial Discourse in Canada, 1875–1980* (Montreal and Kingston: McGill-Queens University Press).

Ang, Ien (1993), "*Dallas* and the Ideology of Mass Culture," in Simon During (ed.), *The Cultural Studies Reader* (London: Routledge), 403–20.

Appadurai, Arjun (1990), "Disjuncture and Difference in the Global Cultural Economy," *Theory, Culture and Society* 7, 295–310.

Baker, Alan (1992), "Introduction: On Ideology and Landscape," in A. Baker and G. Biger (eds.), *Ideology and Landscape in Historical Perspective* (Cambridge: Cambridge University Press).

Bakhtin, M. (1984), *Rabelais and His World* (Bloomington: Indiana University Press).

Balibar, Etienne (1996), "The Nation Form: History and Ideology," in Geoff Eley and Grigor Suny (eds.), *Becoming National: A Reader* (Oxford: Oxford University Press), 132–49.

Barber, Benjamin (1992), "Jihad vs. McWorld," *Atlantic Monthly*, March, 53–63.

Barnes, Trevor, and Duncan, James (1992), "Introduction: Writing Worlds," in Trevor Barnes and James Duncan (eds.), *Writing Worlds: Discourse, Text and Metaphor in the Representation of Landscapes* (London: Routledge), 1–17.

Barnett, Clive (1998), "Cultural Twists and Turns," *Environment and Planning D: Society and Space* 16, 631–4.

Barrell, John (1980), *The Dark Side of Landscape: The Rural Poor in English Painting: 1730–1840* (Cambridge: Cambridge University Press).

Bassin, Mark (1987a), "Imperialism and the Nation State in Friedrich Ratzel's Political Geography," *Progress in Human Geography* 11, 473–95.

Bassin, Mark (1987b), "Race Contra Space: The Conflict Between German *Geopolitik* and National Socialism," *Political Geography Quarterly* 6, 473–95.

Bell, David (1995), "Perverse Dynamics, Sexual Citizenship, and the Transformation of Intimacy," in David Bell and Gill Valentine (eds.), *Mapping Desire: Geographies of Sexualities* (London: Routledge), 304–17.

Bell, David, Binnie, Jon, Cream, Julia, and Valentine, Gill (1994), "All Hyped Up and No Place to Go," *Gender, Place and Culture* 1, 31–47.

Bell, David, and Valentine, Gill (1995a), "Introduction: Orientations," in D. Bell and G. Valentine (eds.), *Mapping Desire: Geographies of Sexualities* (London: Routledge), 1–27.

Bell, David, and Valentine, Gill (eds.) (1995b), *Mapping Desire: Geographies of Sexualities* (London: Routledge).

Bell, Morag, Butlin, Robin, and Heffernan, Michael (eds.) (1995), *Geography and Imperialism, 1820–1940* (Manchester: Manchester University Press).

Bello, Walden (1994), *Dark Victory: The United States, Structural Adjustment, and Global Poverty* (London: Pluto Press, and Oakland: Food First).

Bender, Barbara (ed.) (1993), *Landscape: Politics and Perspectives* (Oxford: Berg).

Benhabib, Seyla (1999), "Germany Opens Up," *The Nation*, 21 June, 6–7.

Benjamin, Walter (1968), "The Work of Art in the Age of Mechanical Reproduction," in *Illuminations: Essays and Reflections* (New York: Schocken Books, 1968, originally published 1936).

Benko, George, and Strohmeyer, Ulf (eds.) (1997), *Space and Social Theory: Interpreting Modernity and Postmodernity* (Oxford: Blackwell).

Berger, John (1972), *Ways of Seeing* (London: Penguin).

Berger, John (1998/9), "Against the Great Defeat of the World," *Race and Class* 40 (2/3), 1–4.

Berger, Karl (ed.) (1985), *Johnstown: The Story of a Unique Valley* (Johnstown: Johnstown Flood Museum).

Berger, P., and Pullberg, S. (1964–5), "Reification and the Sociological Critique of Consciousness," *History and Theory* 4, 196–211.

Berman, Marshall (1982), *All That Is Solid Melts Into Air: The Experience of Modernity* (New York: Simon and Schuster).

Bermingham, Ann (1987), *Landscape and Ideology: The English Rustic Tradition, 1740–1840* (London: Thames and Hudson).

Bérubé, Michael (1994), *Public Access: Literary Theory and American Cultural Politics* (New York: Verso).

Binnie, Jon (1995), "Trading Places: Consumption, Sexuality, and the Production of Queer Space," in D. Bell and G. Valentine (eds.), *Mapping Desire: Geographies of Sexualities* (London: Routledge), 183–99.

Birnbaum, Norman (1993), "What Rough Beast is Reborn," *The Nation*, April 3, 441–4.

Blomley, Nicholas (1994), "Mobility, Empowerment, and the Rights Revolution." *Political Geography*, 13, 407–22.

Bluestone, Barry, and Harrison, Bennett (1982), *The Deindustrialization of America* (New York: Basic Books).

Bodmer, W.F. (1972), "Race and IQ: The Genetic Background," in K. Richardson, D. Spears, and M. Richards (eds.), *Race, Culture and Intelligence* (Harmondsworth: Penguin).

Bondi, Liz, and Peake, Linda (1988), "Gender and the City: Urban Politics Revisited," in Jo Little, Linda Peake, and Pat Richardson (eds.), *Women in Cities: Gender and the Urban Environment* (New York: New York University Press), 21–40.

Borneman, John (1998), *Subversions of International Order: Studies in the Political Anthropology of Culture* (Albany: SUNY Press).

Bourdieu, Pierre (1984), *Distinctions: A Social Critique of the Judgement of Taste* (Cambridge, MA: Harvard University Press, trans. Richard Nice).

Boyer, B. (1990), *The Regulation School: A Critical Introduction* (New York: Columbia University Press).

Boyle, Mark, and Hughes, George (1991), "The Politics of the Representation of 'The Real': Discourses from the Left on Glasgow's Role as European City of Culture, 1990," *Area* 23, 217–28.

Brant, John (1996), "Unemployment: The Theme Park," *New York Times*, January 28, Section 6: 46.

Brewer, John, and Porter, Roy (eds.) (1993), *Consumption and the World of Goods* (New York: Routledge).

Broek, Jan, and Webb, John (1973), *A Geography of Mankind* (New York: McGraw-Hill, 2nd edition).

Brown, Michael (1996), "Closet Geography," *Environment and Planning D: Society and Space* 14, 762–70.

Brown, Michael (1997), *RePlacing Citizenship: AIDS Activism and Radical Democracy* (New York: Guilford Press).

Brownill, Sue (1984), "From Critique to Intervention: Socialist Feminist Perspectives on Urbanization," *Antipode* 16, 21–34.

Boyle, T. Coraghessan (1995), *The Tortilla Curtain* (New York: Viking).

Brumburg, Joan Jacobs (1997), *The Body Project: An Intimate History of American Girls* (New York: Random House).

Bunge, William (1971), *Fitzgerald: Geography of a Revolution* (Cambridge, MA: Schenkman Publishing).

Bunske, Edmunds (1996), "Humanism: Wisdom of the Heart and Mind," in C. Earle, K. Mathewson, and M. Kenzer (eds.), *Concepts in Human Geography* (Lanham, MD: Rowman and Littlefield), 355–81.

Burke, P. (1978), *Popular Culture in Early Modern Europe* (New York: New York University Press).

Buss, Terry (1983), *Shutdown at Youngstown: Public Policy for Mass Unemployment* (Albany: State University of New York Press).

Butler, Judith (1990), *Gender Trouble: Feminism and the Subversion of Identity* (London: Routledge).

Butler, Judith (1993), *Bodies that Matter: On the Discursive Limits of "Sex"* (London: Routledge).

Butler, Judith (1994), "Gender as Performance," *Radical Philosophy* 67, 32–9.

Buttimer, Anne (1993), *Geography and the Human Spirit* (Baltimore: Johns Hopkins University Press).

Calhoun, Craig (1989), "Tiananmen, Television and the Public Sphere: Internationalization of Culture and the Beijing Spring of 1989," *Public Culture* 2, 54–71.

Calhoun, Craig (1992), "Introduction: Habermas and the Public Sphere," in Craig Calhoun (ed.), *Habermas and the Public Sphere* (Cambridge, MA: MIT Press), 1–48.

Callahan, Bob (1981), "Introduction," in Carl Sauer, *Selected Essays, 1963–1975*, ed. Bob Callahan (Berkeley: Turtle Island Foundation).

Callard, Felicity (1998), "The Body in Theory," *Environment and Planning D: Society and Space* 16, 387–400.

Castells, Manuel (1983), *The City and the Grassroots* (Berkeley: University of California Press).

Castells, Manuel (1989), *The Informational City: Information Technology, Economic Restructuring, and the Urban-Regional Process* (Oxford: Blackwell).

Castells, Manuel (1996), *The Network Society* (Oxford: Blackwell).

Castles, S., with Booth, H., and Wallace, T. (1984), *Here for Good: Western Europe's New Ethnic Minorities* (London: Pluto Press).

Centre for Contemporary Cultural Studies (1982), *The Empire Strikes Back: Race and Racism in 70s Britain* (London: Hutchinson).

Chambers, Iain (1993), *Migrancy, Culture, Identity* (London: Routledge).

Chauncy, George (1994), *Gay New York: Gender, Urban Culture, and the Making of the Gay Male World, 1890–1940* (New York: Basic Books).

Chen, Kuan-Hsing (1996), "The Formation of a Diasporic Intellectual: An Interview with Stuart Hall," in David Morley and Kuan-Hsing Chen (eds.), *Stuart Hall: Critical Dialogues in Cultural Studies* (London: Routledge), 484–503.

Cheney, Lynne (1994), "The End of History," *Wall Street Journal*, October 20.

Chouinard, Vera, and Grant, Ali (1996), "On Being Not Even Anywhere Near 'The Project': Ways of Putting Ourselves in the Picture," in Nancy Duncan (ed.), *BodySpace: Destabilizing Geographies of Gender and Sexuality* (New York: Routledge), 170–93.

Chow, Rey (1993), "Listening Otherwise, Music Miniaturized: A Different Type of Question About Revolution," in Simon During (ed.), *The Cultural Studies Reader* (New York: Routledge), 382–99.

Clarke, J., Hall, S., Jefferson, T., and Roberts, B. (1976), "Subcultures, Cultures and Class: A Theoretical Overview," in S. Hall and J. Henderson (eds.), *Resistance Through Rituals* (London: Hutchinson/Centre for Contemporary Cultural Studies), 9–74.

Clifford, James (1986), "Introduction: Partial Truths," in J. Clifford and G. Marcus (eds.), *Writing Culture* (Berkeley: University of California Press).

Clifford, James (1988), *The Predicament of Culture: Twentieth Century Ethnography, Literature and Art* (Cambridge, MA: Harvard University Press).

Clifford, James (1992), "Traveling Cultures," in L. Grossberg, C. Nelson, and P. Treichler (eds.), *Cultural Studies* (New York: Routledge), 96–112.

Connelly, Frank, and Jenks, George (1889), *Official History of the Johnstown Flood* (Pittsburgh: Journalist Publishing Co.).

Coon, Carleton (1962), *The Origin of Races* (New York, Alfred A. Knopf).

Cosgrove, Denis (1983), "Towards a Radical Cultural Geography," *Antipode* 15, 1–11.

Cosgrove, Denis (1984), *Social Formation and Symbolic Landscape* (London: Croom Helm).

Cosgrove, Denis (1985), "Prospect, Perspective and the Evolution of the Landscape Idea," *Transactions of the Institute of British Geographers* 10, 45–62.

Cosgrove, Denis (1993a), "Commentary on 'The Reinvention of Cultural Geography,' by Price and Lewis," *Annals of the Association of American Geographers* 83, 515–17.

Cosgrove, Denis (1993b), *The Palladian Landscape: Geographical Change and Its Cultural Representations in Sixteenth-Century Italy* (University Park: Pennsylvania State University Press).

Cosgrove, Denis, and Daniels, Stephen (eds.) (1988), *The Iconography of Landscape: Essays on the Symbolic Representation, Design, and Use of Past Landscapes* (Cambridge: Cambridge University Press).

Cosgrove, Denis, and Jackson, Peter (1987), "New Directions in Cultural Geography," *Area* 19, 95–101.

Crang, Mike (1998), *Cultural Geography* (London: Routledge).

Crawford, Margaret (1992), "The World in a Shopping Mall," in M. Sorkin (ed.), *Variations on a Theme Park: The New American City and the End of Public Space* (New York: Hill and Wang), 3–30.

Cream, Julia (1995), "Re-Solving Riddles: The Sexed Body," in David Bell and Gill Valentine (eds.), *Mapping Desire: Geographies of Sexualities* (London: Routledge), 31–40.

Cresswell, Tim (1996), *In Place/Out of Place: Geography, Ideology and Transgression* (Minneapolis: University of Minnesota Press).

Cresswell, Tim (1997), "Imagining the Nomad: Mobility and the Postmodern Primitive," in George Benko and Ulf Strohmeyer (eds.), *Space and Social Theory: Interpreting Modernity and Postmodernity* (Oxford: Blackwell), 360–79.

Crilley, Darrell (1993), "Megastructures and Urban Change: Aesthetics, Ideology and Design," in Paul Knox (ed.), *The Restless Urban Landscape* (Englewood Cliffs, NJ: Prentice-Hall), 127–64.

Damer, Seán (1990), *Glasgow: Going for a Song* (London: Lawrence and Wishart).

Daniels, Roger (1962), *The Politics of Prejudice: The Anti-Japanese Movement in California and the Struggle for Japanese Exclusion* (Berkeley: University of California Press).

Daniels, Stephen (1989), "Marxism, Culture, and the Duplicity of Landscape," in Richard Peet and Nigel Thrift (eds.), *New Models in Geography*, volume 2 (London: Unwin Hyman), 196–220.

Daniels, Stephen (1993), *Fields of Vision: Landscape Imagery and National Identity in England and the United States* (Princeton: Princeton University Press).

Daniels, Stephen, and Cosgrove, Denis (1988), "Introduction: The Iconography of Landscape," in D. Cosgrove and S. Daniels (eds.), *The Iconography of Landscape: Essays of the Symbolic Representation, Design, and Use of Past Environments* (Cambridge: Cambridge University Press), 1–10.

Daniels, Stephen, and Cosgrove, Denis (1993), "Spectacle and Text: Landscape Metaphors in Cultural Geography," in James Duncan and David Ley (eds.), *Place/Culture/Representation* (London: Routledge), 57–77.

Davis, Mike (1990), *City of Quartz: Excavating the Future in Los Angeles* (London: Verso).

Davis, Mike (1998), *The Ecology of Fear: Los Angeles and the Ecology of Disaster* (New York: Metropolitan Books).

Davis, Tim (1995), "The Diversity of Queer Politics and the Redefinition of Sexual Identity and Community in Urban Space," in David Bell and Gill Valentine (eds.), *Mapping Desire: Geographies of Sexualities* (London: Routledge), 284–303.

Dear, Michael (1986), "Postmodernism and Planning," *Environment and Planning D: Society and Space* 4, 367–84.

Dear, Michael (1988), "The Postmodern Challenge: Reconstructing Human Geography," *Transactions of the Institute of British Geographers* 13, 262–74.

Dear, Michael (1991), "The Premature Demise of Postmodern Urbanism," *Cultural Anthropology* 6, 535–48.

Debord, Guy (1994), *The Society of the Spectacle* (New York: Zone Books, trans. Donald Nicholson-Smith).

de Certeau, Michel (1984), *The Practice of Everyday Life* (Berkeley: University of California Press, trans. Steven Rendall).

Denning, Michael (1996), *The Cultural Front: The Laboring of American Culture in the Twentieth Century* (London: Verso).

Diamond, Jared (1994), "Race Without Color," *Discover* (November), 83–9.

Diamond, Jared (1997), *Guns, Germs, and Steel: The Fates of Human Society* (New York: W.W. Norton).

Dieck, Herman (1889), *The Johnstown Flood* (Philadelphia: Publisher Unknown).

Domosh, Mona (1996a), "Feminism and Human Geography," in Carville Earle, Kent Mathewson, and Martin Kenzer (eds.), *Concepts in Human Geography* (Lanham, MD: Rowman and Littlefield), 411–27.

Domosh, Mona (1996b), *Invented Cities* (New Haven: Yale University Press).

Domosh, Mona (1998), "Those 'Gorgeous Incongruities': Polite Politics and Public Space on the Streets of Nineteenth-Century New York City," *Annals of the Association of American Geographers* 88, 209–26.

Driver, Harold (1972), "Lowie, Robert H.," *International Encyclopedia of the Social Sciences* (New York: Macmillan and The Free Press), 480–3.

Dubofsky, Melvyn (1988), *We Shall Be All: A History of the Industrial Workers of the World* (Urbana: University of Illinois Press, second edition).

Duby, Georges (1985), "Ideologies in History," in J. Le Goff and P. Nora (eds.), *Constructing the Past: Essays in Historical Methodology* (Cambridge: Cambridge University Press).

Duncan, James (1980), "The Superorganic in American Cultural Geography," *Annals of the Association of American Geographers* 70, 181–98.

Duncan, James (1990), *The City as Text: The Politics of Landscape Interpretation in the Kandyan Kingdom* (Cambridge: Cambridge University Press).

Duncan, James (1993a), "Commentary on 'The Reinvention of Cultural Geography,' by Price and Lewis," *Annals of the Association of American Geographers* 83, 517–19.

Duncan, James (1993b), "Landscapes of Self/Landscapes of the Other(s): Cultural Geography, 1991–92," *Progress in Human Geography* 17, 367–77.

Duncan, James (1994), "After the Civil War: Reconstructing Cultural Geography as Heterotopia," in Kenneth Foote, Peter Hugill, Kent Mathewson, and Jonathan Smith (eds.), *Re-Reading Cultural Geography* (Austin: University of Texas Press), 401–8.

Duncan, James, and Duncan, Nancy (1988), "(Re)Reading the Landscape," *Environment and Planning D: Society and Space* 6, 117–26.

Duncan, James, and Ley, David (eds.) (1993), *Place/Culture/Representation* (London: Routledge).

Duncan, Nancy (ed.) (1996a), *BodySpace: Destabilizing Geographies of Gender and Sexuality* (London: Routledge).

Duncan, Nancy (1996b), "Negotiating Gender and Sexuality in Public and Private Spaces," in Nancy Duncan (ed.), *BodySpace: Destabilizing Geographies of Gender and Sexuality* (New York: Routledge), 126–45.

During, Simon (ed.) (1993a), *The Cultural Studies Reader* (London and New York: Routledge).

During, Simon (1993b), "Introduction," in Simon During (ed.), *The Cultural Studies Reader* (London: Routledge), 1–25.

Eagleton, Terry (1987), "Awaking from Modernity," *Times Literary Supplement*, February 20.

The Economist (1998), "Good Fences," December 19, 19–22.

Elder, Glen (1996), "Reading the Spaces in George Chauncy's *Gay New York*," *Environment and Planning D: Society and Space* 14, 755–8.

Ellickson, Robert (1996), "Controlling Chronic Misconduct in City Spaces: Of Panhandlers, Skid Rows, and Public-Space Zoning," *Yale Law Journal* 105, 1165–1248.

England, Kim (1993), "Suburban Pink Collar Ghettos: The Spatial Entrapment of Women?" *Annals of the Association of American Geographers* 83, 225–42.

Enloe, Cynthia (1990), *Bananas, Beaches, and Bases: Making Feminist Sense of International Politics* (Berkeley: University of California Press).

Entrikin, J. Nicholas (1984), "Carl Sauer, Philosopher in Spite of Himself," *Geographical Review* 74, 387–407.

Ewan, Stuart (1988), *All Consuming Images: The Politics of Style in Contemporary Culture* (New York: Basic Books).

Fagen, Donald (1982), "I.G.Y.," *Nightfly* (Burbank: Warner Brothers, 23696–2).

Faludi, Susan (1992), *Backlash: The Undeclared War Against American Women* (New York: Doubleday).

Fanon, Frantz (1986), *Black Skin, White Masks* (London, Pluto, trans. Charles Lamm Markmann).

Fein, Leonard (1997), "Israel's Un-Orthodox Battle," *The Nation*, July 7, 21–4.

Ferris, George (1889), *The Complete History of the Johnstown and Connemaugh Valley Flood* (New York: H.S. Goodspeed and Co.).

Fishman, Robert (1987), *Bourgeois Utopias: The Rise and Fall of Suburbia* (New York: Basic Books).

Fiske, John (1989), *Reading the Popular* (Boston: Unwin Hyman).

Fiske, John (1992), "British Cultural Studies and Television," in R.C. Allen (ed.), *Channels of Discourse, Reassembled* (Chapel Hill: University of North Carolina Press).

FitzGerald, Frances (1986), *Cities on a Hill: A Journey Through Contemporary American Cultures* (New York: Simon and Schuster).

Foner, Philip (1965), *History of the Labor Movement in the United States, Volume IV: The Industrial Workers of the World, 1905–1917* (New York: International Publishers).

Foner, Philip (1981), *Fellow Workers and Friends: Free Speech Fights as Told by Participants* (Westport, CT: Greenwood Press).

"Food Courts: Tasty!" (1990), *Stores* (August), 52–4.

Forsyth, Ann (1997), "'Out' in the Valley," *International Journal of Urban and Regional Restructuring* 21, 38–62.

Foster, Susan (1992), "Dancing Bodies," in J. Crary and S. Kwinter (eds.), *Incorporations* (New York: Zone Books).

Foucault, Michel (1972), *The Archeology of Knowledge* (New York: Harper).

Foucault, Michel (1978), *The History of Sexuality. Volume One: An Introduction* (New York: Pantheon, trans. R. Hurley).

Foucault, Michel (1986), "Of Other Spaces," *Diacritics* 16, 22–7, trans. Jay Miskowiec.

Fox, Richard (1889), *The Johnstown Flood, Illustrated* (New York: Richard K. Fox).

Frank, Thomas (1997a), *The Conquest of Cool* (Chicago: University of Chicago Press).

Frank, Thomas (1997b), "Why Johnny Can't Dissent," in Thomas Frank and Matt Weiland (eds.), *Commodify Your Dissent: Salvos from* The Baffler (New York: W.W. Norton), 31–45.

Frank, Thomas, and Weiland, Matt (eds.) (1997), *Commodify Your Dissent: Salvos from* The Baffler (New York: W.W. Norton).

Fraser, Nancy (1992), "Rethinking the Public Sphere: A Contribution to the Critique of Actually Existing Democracy," in Craig Calhoun (ed.), *Habermas and the Public Sphere* (Cambridge: MIT Press), 109–42.

Fraser, Steven (ed.) (1995), *The Bell Curve Wars: Race, Intelligence, and the Future of America* (New York: Basic).

Friedan, Betty (1963), *The Feminine Mystique* (New York: W.W. Norton).

Fulbrook, Mary (1994), "Aspects of Society and Identity in the New Germany," *Daedalus* 123, 211–34.

Fusco, Margie (1988), "Johnstown Flood Centennial Project is Unique," *Centennial Reports*, 2, 3.

Fyfe, Nicholas, and Bannister, Jon (1996), "City Watching: Closed Circuit Television Surveillance in Public Spaces," *Area* 29, 37–46.

Fyfe, Nicholas, and Bannister, Jon (1998), "'The Eyes Upon the Street': Closed-Circuit Television Surveillance and the City," in N. Fyfe (ed.), *Images of the Street: Planning, Identity and Control in Public Space* (London: Routledge), 254–67.

Garreau, Joel (1991), *Edge City: Life on the New Frontier* (New York: Doubleday).

Gates, Jr., Henry Louis (1995), "Why Now?" in Steven Fraser (ed.), *The Bell Curve Wars: Race, Intelligence, and the Future of America* (New York: Basic), 94–6.

Geltmaker, T. (1992), "The Queer Nation Acts Up: Health Care, Politics, and Sexual Diversity in the County of Angels, *Environment and Planning D: Society and Space* 10, 609–50.

Genocchio, Benjamin (1995), "Discourse, Discontinuity, Difference: The Question of 'Other' Spaces," in Sophie Watson and Katherine Gibson (eds.), *Postmodern Cities and Spaces* (Oxford: Blackwell), 35–46.

Gilroy, Paul (1987), *There Ain't No Black in the Union Jack: The Cultural Politics of Race and Nation* (London: Hutchinson).

Gilroy, Paul (1992), "Cultural Studies and Ethnic Absolutism," in L. Grossberg, C. Nelson, and P. Treichler (eds.), *Cultural Studies* (New York: Routledge), 187–98.

Gilroy, Paul (1993), *The Black Atlantic: Modernity and Double Consciousness* (Cambridge, MA: Harvard University Press).

Gitlin, Todd (1995), *The Twilight of Common Dreams: Why America Is Wracked by Culture Wars* (New York: Metropolitan Books).

Gluck, Carol (1994), "History According to Whom?" *New York Times*, November 19.

Godlewska, Anne, and Smith, Neil (eds.) (1994), *Geography and Empire* (Oxford: Blackwell).

Gold, M. (1984), "A History of Nature," in Doreen Massey and John Allen (eds.), *Geography Matters! A Reader* (Cambridge: Cambridge University Press), 12–33.

Goldberg, Vicky (1997), "It Once Was S–x, Truly Shocking; Now It's a Bore," *New York Times*, April 20, H33.

Goodman, Walter (1997), "Critics Notebook: Day of Prayerful Messages for the Crowd on the Mall," *New York Times*, October 6, E3.

Goodstein, Laura (1997a), "Putting Politics Aside," *New York Times*, October 6, A1.

Goodstein, Laura (1997b), "Women and the Promise Keepers: Good for the Gander, but the Goose Isn't So Sure," *New York Times*, October 5, Section 4, 4.

Goodwin, June (1984), *Cry Amandla: South African Women and the Question of Power* (New York: Africana Publishing Company).

Goss, Jon (1992), "Modernity and Postmodernity in the Retail Built Environment," in K. Anderson and F. Gale (eds.), *Inventing Places* (Melbourne: Longman Scientific), 159–77.

Goss, Jon (1993), "The 'Magic of the Mall': An Analysis of Form, Function, and Meaning in the Contemporary Retail Built Environment," *Annals of the Association of American Geographers* 83, 18–47.

Goss, Jon (1996), "Disquiet on the Waterfront: Reflections on Nostalgia and Utopia in the Urban Archetypes of Festival Marketplaces," *Urban Geography* 17, 221–47.

Gould, Stephen Jay (1981), *The Mismeasure of Man* (New York: W.W. Norton).

Gould, Stephen Jay (1985a), "Bound by the Great Chain," in *The Flamingo's Smile: Reflections in Natural History* (New York: W.W. Norton), 281–90.

Gould, Stephen Jay (1985b), "Human Equality as a Contingent Fact of History," in *The Flamingo's Smile: Reflections in Natural History* (New York: W.W. Norton), 185–98.

Gould, Stephen Jay (1995), "Curveball," in Steven Fraser (ed.), *The Bell Curve Wars: Race, Intelligence, and the Future of America* (New York: Basic), 11–22.

Gramsci, Antonio (1971), *Selections from the Prison Notebooks* (London: Lawrence and Wishart, ed. and trans. Quentin Hoare and Geoffrey Nowell-Smith).

Gregory, Derek (1994), *Geographical Imaginations* (Oxford: Blackwell).

Gregory, Derek (1997), "Lacan and Geography: The Production of Space Revisited," in Georges Benko and Ulf Strohmeyer (eds.), *Space and Social Theory: Interpreting Modernity and Postmodernity* (Oxford: Blackwell), 203–31.

Gross, S.H., and Rojas, M.H. (1986), *But Women Have No History! Images of Women in the Public History of Washington, DC* (St. Louis Park, MN: Glenhurst Publications).

Grosz, Elizabeth (1990), *Jacques Lacan: A Feminist Introduction* (London: Routledge).

Grosz, Elizabeth (1995), "Women, *Chora*, Dwelling," in Sophie Watson and Katherine Gibson (eds.), *Postmodern Cities and Spaces* (Oxford: Blackwell), 47–58.

Guelke, Leonard (1974), "An Idealist Alternative in Human Geography," *Annals of the Association of American Geography* 64, 193–202.

Gulick, John (1998), "The 'Disappearance of Public Space': An Ecological Marxist and Lefebvrian Approach," in Andrew Light and Jonathan Smith (eds.), *The Production of Public Space* (Lanham, MD: Rowman and Littlefield), 135–55.

Habermas, Jürgen (1989), *The Structural Transformation of the Public Sphere* (Cambridge, MA: MIT Press).

Hacker, Andrew (1995), "Caste, Crime, and Precocity," in Steven Fraser (ed.), *The Bell Curve Wars: Race, Intelligence, and the Future of America* (New York: Basic), 97–108.

Hall, Stuart (1979), "Cultural Studies and the Centre: Some Problematics and Problems," in Stuart Hall, Dorothy Hobson, Andrew Lowe, and Paul Willis (eds.), *Culture, Media, Language: Working Papers in Cultural Studies, 1972–1979* (London: Hutchinson), 15–47.

Hall, Stuart (1988), *The Hard Road to Renewal: Thatcherism and the Crisis of the Left* (London: Verso).

Hall, Stuart (1991), "Old and New Identities, Old and New Ethnicities," in Anthony King (ed.), *Culture, Globalization, and the World System* (Basingstoke: Macmillan), 41–68.

Hall, Stuart (1992), "Cultural Studies and its Theoretical Legacies," in Lawrence Grossberg, Cary Nelson, and Paula Treichler (eds.), *Cultural Studies* (New York: Routledge), 277–94.

Hall, Stuart (1996), "Introduction: Who Needs Identity," in Stuart Hall and Paul du Gay (eds.), *Questions of Cultural Identity* (Thousand Oaks: Sage), 1–17.

Hall, S., Critcher, C., Jefferson, T., Clarke, J., and Roberts, B. (1978), *Policing the Crisis: Mugging, the State, and Law and Order* (London: Hutchinson).

Hall, Stuart, and du Gay, Paul (eds.) (1996), *Questions of Cultural Identity* (Thousand Oaks: Sage).

Hall, Stuart, and Jacques, Martin (eds.) (1983), *The Politics of Thatcherism* (London: Lawrence and Wishart).

Hall, Stuart, and Jefferson, Tim (1976), *Resistance Through Rituals: Youth Subcultures in Post-War Britain* (London: Hutchinson).

Hammer, Joshua (1996), "Nigeria Crude: A Hanged Man and an Oil-fouled Landscape," *Harper's Magazine*, June, 58–69.

Hanson, Susan, and Pratt, Geraldine (1994), "On *Suburban Pink Collar Ghettos: The Spatial Entrapment of Women?* by Kim England," *Annals of the Association of American Geographers* 84, 500–2.

Hanson, Susan, and Pratt, Geraldine (1995), *Gender, Work and Space* (New York: Routledge).

Haraway, Donna (1989), *Primate Visions: Gender, Race and Nature in the World of Modern Science* (New York: Routledge).

Hart, John Fraser (1982), "The Highest Form of the Geographer's Art," *Annals of the Association of American Geographers* 72, 1–29.

Hartshorne, Richard (1939), *The Nature of Geography: A Critical Survey of Current Thought in Light of the Past* (Lancaster, PA: Association of American Geographers).

Harvey, David (1969), *Explanation in Geography* (London: Edward Arnold).

Harvey, David (1973), *Social Justice and the City* (Baltimore: Johns Hopkins University Press).

Harvey, David (1979), "Monument and Myth," *Annals of the Association of American Geographers* 69, 362–81.

Harvey, David (1982), *The Limits to Capital* (Chicago: University of Chicago Press).

Harvey, David (1989a), *The Condition of Postmodernity: An Enquiry into the Origins of Cultural Change* (Oxford: Blackwell).

Harvey, David (1989b), *The Urban Experience* (Oxford: Blackwell).

Harvey, David (1996), *Justice, Nature, and the Geography of Difference* (Oxford: Blackwell).

Harvey, David (1998), "The Body as Accumulation Strategy," *Environment and Planning D: Society and Space* 16, 401–21.

Harwit, Martin (1996), *An Exhibit Denied: Lobbying the History of Enola Gay* (New York: Copernicus).

Haug, W.F. (1986), *Critique of Commodity Aesthetics* (Minneapolis: University of Minnesota Press).

Hayden, Delores (1980), "Redesigning the Domestic Workplace," in G. Werkele, R. Peterson, and D. Morley (eds.), *New Space for Women* (Boulder, CO: Westview Press), 101–27.

Hayden, Delores (1981), *The Grand Domestic Revolution: A History of Feminist Designs for American Homes, Neighborhoods and Cities* (Cambridge, MA: MIT Press).

Hayden, Delores (1984), *Redesigning the American Dream: The Future of Housing, Work, and Family Life* (New York: W.W. Norton).

Held, David (1996), "The Decline of the Nation State," in Geoff Eley and Grigor Suny (eds.), *Becoming National: A Reader* (Oxford: Oxford University Press), 407–16.

Helsinger, Elizabeth (1994), "Turner and the Representation of England," in W.J.T. Mitchell (ed.), *Power and Landscape* (Chicago: University of Chicago Press), 103–25.

Henley, D.L., and Kerr, A.P. (eds.), (1989), *May '68: Coming of Age* (London: MacMillan).

Herbert, Steven (1996), *Policing Space: Territoriality and the Los Angeles Police Department* (Minneapolis: University of Minnesota Press).

Hernandez, Roger (1995), "On Not Getting It," in Russell Jacoby and Naomi Glauberman (eds.), *The Bell Curve Debate: History, Documents, Opinions* (New York: Times Books), 314–15.

Herrnstein Richard, and Murray, Charles (1994), *The Bell Curve: Intelligence and Class Structure in American Life* (New York: Free Press).

Hershkovitz, Linda (1993), "Tiananmen Square and the Politics of Place," *Political Geography* 12, 395–420.

Hilburn, Robert, and Crowe, Jerry (1996), "Sex Pistols Prove that Bands are Never Too Old to Get High Off Fame," *Detroit News*, July 18.

Hoare, Quentin, and Nowell-Smith, Geoffrey (1971), "General Introduction," in Antonio Gramsci, *Selections from the Prison Notebooks* (London: Lawrence and Wishart, ed. and trans. Quentin Hoare and Geoffrey Nowell-Smith), xvii–xcvi.

Hobsbawm, Eric, and Ranger, Terence (eds.) (1983), *The Invention of Tradition* (Cambridge: Cambridge University Press).

Hoggart, Richard (1957), *The Uses of Literacy* (London: Chatto and Windus).

Holdsworth, Deryck (1990), "The Landscape and the Archives: Texts for the Analysis of the Built Environment," in Paul Groth (ed.), *Vision, Culture, and Landscape*, Working Papers from the Berkeley Symposium on Cultural Landscape Interpretation, Department of Landscape Architecture, University of California, Berkeley, 187–204.

Holdsworth, Deryck (1993), "Revaluing the House," in James Duncan and David Ley (eds.), *Place/Culture/Representation* (New York: Routledge), 95–109.

hooks, bell (1992), "Representing Whiteness in the Black Imagination," in L. Grossberg, C. Nelson, and P. Treichler (eds.), *Cultural Studies* (New York: Routledge), 338–46.

Hooson, David (ed.) (1994), *Geography and National Identity* (Oxford: Blackwell).

Hopkins, Jeffrey (1990), "West Edmonton Mall: Landscapes of Myth and Elsewhereness," *Canadian Geographer* 30, 2–17.

Huntington, Ellsworth (1915), *Climate and Civilization* (New Haven: Yale University Press).

Inglis, Fred (1993), *Cultural Studies* (Oxford: Blackwell).

Inglis, Fred (1995), *Raymond Williams* (London: Routledge).

Irigaray, Luce (1985a), *Speculum of the Other Woman* (Ithaca: Cornell University Press).

Irigaray, Luce (1985b), *The Sex Which Is Not One* (Ithaca: Cornell University Press).

Irigaray, Luce (1992), *Sexes and Genealogies* (New York: Columbia University Press).

Jackson, Peter (1980), "A Plea for Cultural Geography," *Area* 12, 110–13.

Jackson, Peter (1987a), "The Idea of 'Race' and the Geography of Racism," in Peter Jackson (ed.), *Race and Racism: Essays in Social Geography* (London: Allen and Unwin), 3–21.

Jackson Peter (ed.) (1987b), *Race and Racism: Essays in Social Geography* (London: Allen and Unwin).

Jackson, Peter (1988), "Street Life: The Politics of Carnival," *Environment and Planning D: Society and Space* 6, 213–27.

Jackson, Peter (1989), *Maps of Meaning: An Introduction to Cultural Geography* (London: Unwin Hyman).

Jackson, Peter (1991a), "Mapping Meanings: A Cultural Critique of Locality Studies," *Environment and Planning A* 23, 216–28.

Jackson, Peter (1991b), "The Cultural Politics of Masculinity: Towards a Social Geography," *Transactions of the Institute of British Geographers* 16, 199–213.

Jackson, Peter (1992a), "The Politics of the Streets: A Geography of Caribana," *Political Geography* 11, 130–51.

Jackson, Peter (1992b), "The Racialization of Labour in Post-War Bradford," *Journal of Historical Geography* 18, 190–209.

Jackson, Peter (1993a), "Berkeley and Beyond: Broadening the Horizon of Cultural Geography," *Annals of the Association of American Geographers* 83, 519–20.

Jackson, Peter (1993b), "Towards a Cultural Politics of Consumption," in J. Bird, B. Curtis, T. Putnam, G. Robertson, and L. Tickner (eds.), *Mapping the Futures: Local Cultures, Global Change* (London: Routledge), 207–28.

Jackson, Peter (1994), "Black Male: Advertising and the Cultural Politics of Masculinity," *Gender, Place and Culture* 1, 49–59.

Jackson, Peter (1995), "Gender Trouble – Or Just Shopping?" *Gender, Place and Culture* 2, 107–8.

Jackson, S. (1992), "The Amazing Deconstructing Woman," *Trouble and Strife* 25, 25–36.

Jacoby, Russell, and Glauberman, Naomi (eds.) (1995), *The Bell Curve Debate: History, Documents, Opinions* (New York: Times Books).

Jay, Martin (1992), "Scopic Regimes of Modernity," in Scott Lash and Jonathan Friedman (eds.), *Modernity and Identity* (Oxford: Blackwell), 178–95.

Johnson, Nuala (1995), "The Renaissance of Nationalism," in R.J. Johnston, Peter Taylor, and Michael Watts (eds.), *Geographies of Global Change* (Oxford: Blackwell), 99–110.

Johnson, Willis (1889), *History of the Johnstown Flood* (Philadelphia: Edgewood Publishing Co.).

Johnston, R.J., Gregory, Derek, and Smith, David (eds.) (1994), *The Dictionary of Human Geography* (Oxford: Blackwell, third edition).

Jones, Jacqueline (1995), "Back to the Future with *The Bell Curve*: Jim Crow, Slavery, and G," in Steven Fraser (ed.), *The Bell Curve Wars: Race, Intelligence, and the Future of America* (New York: Basic), 80–93.

Kahn, Joel (1995), *Culture, Multiculture, Postculture* (Thousand Oaks: Sage).

Kantrowitz, B., and Senna, D. (1993), "A Town Like No Other," *Newsweek*, June 21, 56–7.

Karacs, Imre (1998), "Race Rears Shaven Head at the Polls; 'Criminal Foreigners Out' is the Call in Saxony-Anhalt," *Independent*, April 26, 19.

Katz, Jennifer (1997), "Take Back the Night: Occupying Urban Space as Political Activism, Female Empowerment, and Personal Healing," Department of Geography, McGill University.

Kay, Jeanne (1997), "Sweet Surrender, but What's the Gender: Nature and the Body in the Writings of Nineteenth-century Mormon Women," in John Paul Jones III, Heidi Nast, and Susan Roberts (eds.), *Thresholds in Feminist Geography* (Lanham, MD: Rowman and Littlefield), 361–82.

Kearns, Gerry, and Philo, Chris (eds.) (1994), *Selling Places: Culture and Capital in the Contemporary City* (Oxford: Pergamon).

Keith, Michael, and Cross, Michael (1993), "Postmodernism and Utopia: An Unholy Alliance," in M. Cross and M. Keith (eds.), *Racism, the City, and the State* (London: Routledge).

Keith, Michael, and Pile, Steve (eds.) (1993), *Place and the Politics of Identity* (London: Routledge).

Kelley, Robin (1998), *Yo' Mama's Disfunktional! Fighting the Culture Wars in Urban America* (Boston: Beacon Press).

Kelman, James (1992), *Some Recent Attacks: Essays Cultural and Political* (Stirling: AK Press).

Kenzer, Martin (1987), "Tracking Sauer Across Sour Terrain," *Annals of the Association of American Geographers* 77, 469–74.

Kerr, Clark (1963), *The Uses of the University* (Cambridge, MA: Harvard University Press).

King, Anthony (ed.) (1996), *Re-Presenting the City: Ethnicity, Capital and Culture in the 21st Century Metropolis* (New York: New York University Press).

Kinsman, Phil (1995), "Landscape, Race and National Identity: The Photography of Ingrid Pollard," *Area* 27, 300–10.

Kinzer, Stephen (1994), "A Climate for Demagogues," *Atlantic Monthly*, February, 21–34.

Kirby, Andrew (1993), *Power/Resistance: Local Politics and the Chaotic State* (Bloomington: Indiana University Press).

Kirsch, Scott (1997), "Watching the Bombs Go Off: Photography, Nuclear Landscapes, and Spectator Democracy," *Antipode* 29, 227–55.

Kirsch, Scott, and Mitchell, Don (1998), "Earth Moving as the 'Measure of Man': Edward Teller, Geographical Engineering, and the Matter of Progress," *Social Text* 54, 101–34.

Klages, Gregory (n.d.), "Kill Your Idol: the Sex Pistols Question Their Own Integrity," *http:// www.idmagazine.com/music/4article/sex.htm*.

Klimt, Andrea (1989), " 'Returning Home': Portuguese Migrant Notions of Temporariness, Permanence, and Commitment," *New German Critique* 46 (Winter).

Knopp, Lawrence (1990a), "Exploiting the Rent-Gap: The Theoretical Significance of Using Illegal Appraisal Schemes to Encourage Gentrification in New Orleans," *Urban Geography* 11, 48–64.

Knopp, Lawrence (1990b), "Some Theoretical Implications of Gay Involvement in an Urban Land Market," *Political Geography Quarterly* 9, 337–52.

Knopp, Lawrence (1992), "Sexuality and the Spatial Dynamics of Capitalism," *Environment and Planning D: Society and Space* 10, 651–69.

Knopp, Lawrence (1995), "Sexuality and Space: A Framework for Analysis," in David Bell and Gill Valentine (eds.), *Mapping Desire: Geographies of Sexualities* (London: Routledge), 149–61.

Knox, Paul (1993a), "Capital, Material Culture and Socio-Spatial Differentiation," in Paul Knox (ed.), *The Restless Urban Landscape* (Englewood Cliffs, NJ: Prentice Hall) 1–34.

Knox, Paul (ed.) (1993b), *The Restless Urban Landscape* (Englewood Cliffs, NJ: Prentice-Hall).

Kobayashi, Audrey (ed.) (1994), *Women, Work, and Place* (Montreal and Kingston: McGill-Queens University Press).

Kroeber, Alfred L. (1904), "Types of Indian Culture in California," University of California, *Publications in American Archaeology and Ethnology* 2, 81–103.

Kroeber, Alfred (1917), *The Nature of Culture* (Chicago: University of Chicago Press).

Kroeber, Alfred L. (1936), *Cultural and Natural Areas of Native North America* (Berkeley: Publications in American Archaeology and Ethnology, Volume 38).

Kruger, Darrell (1992), "District Six, Cape Town: An Apartheid Landscape," *Landscape* 31(2), 9–15.

Latour, Bruno (1987), *Science in Action: How to Follow Scientists and Engineers Through Society* (Cambridge, MA: Harvard University Press).

Lauria, Mickey, and Knopp, Lawrence (1985), "Toward an Analysis of the Role of Gay Communities in the Urban Renaissance," *Urban Geography* 6, 152–69.

Lears, T.J. Jackson (1985), "The Concept of Cultural Hegemony: Problems and Possibilities," *American Historical Review* 90, 567–93.

Lefebvre, Henri (1974), *The Survival of Capitalism* (London: Allison and Busby).

Lefebvre, Henri (1991), *The Production of Space* (Oxford: Blackwell, trans. Donald Nicholson-Smith).

Leighly, John (ed.) (1963), *Land and Life: A Selection of the Writings of Carl Ortwin Sauer* (Berkeley: University of California Press).

Leighly, John (1976), "Carl Ortwin Sauer, 1889–1975," *Annals of the Association of American Geographers* 66, 337–48.

Leighly, John (1978), "Scholar and Colleague: Homage to Carl Sauer," *Yearbook of the Association of Pacific Geographers* 40, 117–33.

Lerner, G. (1980), "The Lady and the Mill Girl: Changes in the Status of Women in the Age of Jackson," in E. Katz and A. Rapone (eds.), *Women's Experiences in America: A Historical Anthology* (New Brunswick, NJ: Transaction Books).

Levine, Bruce, et al. (1989), *Who Built America?* Volume 1: *From Conquest and Colonization through Reconstruction and the Great Uprising of 1877* (New York: Pantheon).

Lewis, Martin (1991), "Elusive Societies: A Regional-Cartographical Approach to the Study of Human Relatedness," *Annals of the Association of American Geographers* 81, 605–26.

Lewis, Peirce (1976), *New Orleans: The Making of an Urban Landscape* (Cambridge, MA: Ballinger Publishing).

Lewis, Peirce (1979), "Axioms for Reading the Landscape: Some Guides to the American Scene," in Donald Meinig (ed.), *The Interpretation of Ordinary Landscape: Geographical Essays* (New York: Oxford University Press), 11–32.

Lewis, Peirce (1983), "Learning from Looking: Geographical and Other Writing About the American Cultural Landscape," *American Quarterly* 35, 242–61.

Ley, David (1996), *The New Middle Class and the Remaking of the Central City* (Oxford: Oxford University Press).

Ley, David, and Samuels, Marwyn (eds.) (1978), *Humanistic Geography: Prospects and Problems* (London: Croom Helm).

Light, Andrew, and Smith, Jonathan (eds.) (1998), *The Production of Public Space* (Lanham, MD: Rowman and Littlefield).

Limerick, Patricia Nelson (1991), "The Trail to Santa Fe: The Unleashing of the Western Public Intellectual," in Patricia Nelson Limerick, Clyde A. Milner II, and Charles E. Rankin (eds.), *Trails: Toward a New Western History* (Lawrence: University Press of Kansas), 59–77.

Lind, Michael (1995), "Brave New Right," in Steven Fraser (ed.), *The Bell Curve Wars: Race, Intelligence, and the Future of America* (New York: Basic), 172–7.

Lind, Michael (1998), "The Beige and the Black," *New York Times Magazine*, August 16, 38–9.

Lipietz, Alain (1986), "New Tendencies in the International Division of Labor: Regimes of Accumulation and Modes of Regulation," in Alan Scott and Michael Storper (eds.), *Production, Work, Territory* (Boston: Allen and Unwin), 16–40.

Livingstone, David (1992), *The Geographical Tradition* (Oxford: Blackwell).

Loukaki, Argyro (1997), "Whose *Genius Loci?* Contrasting Interpretations of the 'Sacred Rock of the Athenian Acropolis,'" *Annals of the Association of American Geographers* 87, 306–29.

Lowenthal, David, and Prince, Hugh (1965), "English Landscape Tastes," *Geographical Review* 55, 186–222.

Lowie, Robert (1947), *Primitive Society* (New York: Liveright; originally published 1920).

Lukács, Georg (1971), "Reification and the Consciousness of the Proletariat," in *History and Class Consciousness: Studies in Marxist Dialectics* (Cambridge, MA: MIT Press), 83–222.

Lynd, Staughton (1982), *The Fight Against Shutdowns: Youngstown's Steel Mill Closings* (San Pedro, CA: Single Jack Books).

McClintock, Anne (1996), "'No Longer a Future in Heaven': Nationalism, Gender, and Race," in Geoff Eley and Grigor Suny (eds.), *Becoming National: A Reader* (Oxford: Oxford University Press), 260–84.

McCullogh, David (1968), *The Johnstown Flood* (New York: Simon and Schuster).

McDowell, Linda (1983), "Towards an Understanding of the Gender Division of Urban Space," *Environment and Planning D: Society and Space* 1, 59–72.

McDowell, Linda (1994), "The Transformation of Cultural Geography," in Derek Gregory, Ron Martin, and Graham Smith (eds.), *Human Geography: Society, Space and Social Science* (Minneapolis: University of Minnesota Press), 146–73.

McDowell, Linda (1995), "Body Work: Heterosexual Gender Performances in City Workplaces," in David Bell and Gill Valentine (eds.), *Mapping Desire: Geographies of Sexuality* (London: Routledge), 75–95.

MacKenzie, Evan (1994), *Privatopia: Homeowners Associations and the Rise of Residential Private Government* (New Haven: Yale University Press).

MacKenzie, Suzanne, and Rose, Dameris (1983), "Industrial Change, the Domestic Economy, and Home Life," in J. Anderson, S. Duncan, and R. Hudson (eds.), *Redundant Spaces in Cities and Regions* (New York: Academic Press), 155–200.

McLaurin, J.J. (1890), *The Story of Johnstown* (Harrisburg: James M. Place).

McLay, Farquhar (1988), "Introduction," in Farquhar McLay (ed.), *Workers City* (Glasgow: Clydeside Press).

Macpherson, Anne (1987), "Preparing for the National Stage: Carl Sauer's First Ten Years at Berkeley," in Martin S. Kenzer (ed.), *Carl O. Sauer: A Tribute* (Corvalis, OR: Oregon State University Press), 69–89.

Maharidge, Dale, and Williamson, Michael (1996), *Journey to Nowhere: The Saga of the New Underclass* (New York, Hyperion, second edition).

Mair, Andrew (1986), "The Homeless and the Post-industrial City," *Political Geography Quarterly* 5, 351–68.

Mairowitz, David Zane (1997), "Fascism à la Mode: In France, the Far Right Presses for National Purity," *Harper's Magazine*, October.

Marcus, Greil (1989), *Lipstick Traces: A Secret History of the Twentieth Century* (Cambridge, MA: Harvard University Press).

Marston, Sallie (1990), "Who are 'the People'? Gender, Citizenship and the Making of the American Nation," *Environment and Planning D: Society and Space* 8, 449–58.

Martin, Geoffrey (1987), "Foreword," in Martin S. Kenzer (ed.), *Carl O. Sauer: A Tribute* (Corvalis, OR: Oregon State University Press), ix–xvi.

Marx, Karl (1970a), Preface to *A Contribution to the Critique of Political Economy* (Moscow: Progress Publishers).

Marx, Karl (1970b), *The German Ideology* (New York: International Publishers).

Marx, Karl (1987), *Capital* (Volume I) (New York: International Publishers).

Marx, Karl, and Engels, Friedrich. (1998), *The Communist Manifesto: A Modern Edition* (London: Verso, originally published 1848).

Massey, Doreen (1984), *Spatial Divisions of Labor* (London: Macmillan).

Massey, Doreen (1994), *Space, Place, and Gender* (Minneapolis: University of Minnesota Press).

Massey, Doreen (1996), "Masculinity, Dualisms, and High Technology," in Nancy Duncan (ed.), *BodySpace: Destabilizing Geographies of Gender and Sexuality* (New York: Routledge), 109–26.

Massey, Douglas, and Denton, Nancy (1993), *American Apartheid: Segregation and the Making of the American Underclass* (Cambridge, MA: Harvard University Press).

Mathewson, Kent (1996), "High/Low, Back/Center: Culture's Stages in Human Geography," in C. Earle, K. Mathewson, and M. Kenzer (eds.), *Concepts in Human Geography* (Lanham, MD: Rowman and Littlefield), 97–125.

Matless, David (1995), "Culture Run Riot? Work in Social and Cultural Geography, 1994," *Progress in Human Geography* 19, 395–403.

Matless, David (1996), "New Material? Work in Cultural and Social Geography, 1995," *Progress in Human Geography* 20, 379–91.

Matless, David (1998), *Landscape and Englishness* (London: Reaktion Books).

Meinig, Donald (ed.) (1979), *Interpretations of Ordinary Landscapes: Geographic Essays* (New York: Oxford University Press).

Merchant, Carolyn (1980), *The Death of Nature: Women, Ecology, and the Scientific Revolution* (San Francisco: Harper and Row).

Merrifield, Andrew, and Swyngedouw, Eric (1995), "Social Justice and the Urban Experience," in A. Merrifield and E. Swyngedouw (eds.), *The Urbanization of Injustice* (London: Lawrence and Wishart), 1–17.

Metzger, Jack (1980), "Plant Shutdowns and Worker Response: The Case of Johnstown, Pa," *Socialist Review* 10, 9–49.

Metzger, Jack (1985), "Johnstown, Pa: Ordeal of a Union Town," *Dissent* 32, 160–3.

Mikesell, Marvin (1987), "Sauer and 'Sauerology': A Student's Perspective," in Martin S. Kenzer (ed.), *Carl O. Sauer: A Tribute* (Corvalis, OR: Oregon State University Press), 144–50.

Miles, Robert (1982), *Racism and Migrant Labour* (London: Routledge and Kegan Paul).

Mill, Hugh Robert (1901), "On Research in Geographical Science," *Geographical Journal* 18.

Miller, Adam (1995), "Professors of Hate," in Russell Jacoby and Naomi Glauberman (eds.), *The Bell Curve Debate: History, Documents, Opinions* (New York: Times Books), 162–78.

Miner, Curtis, and Burkert, Richard (1992), "The Myth of Demythification: A Response to Don Mitchell's 'Heritage, Landscape, and the Production of Cummunity,'" *Pennsylvania History* 59, 227–32.

Mintz, Sidney (1974), *Caribbean Transformation* (Chicago: Aldine).

Mintz, Sidney (1985), *Sweetness and Power: The Place of Sugar in Modern History* (New York: Viking Penguin).

Mitchell, Don (1989), *A History of Homelessness – A Geography of Control: The Production of the Spaces of Order and Marginality in Johnstown, Pennsylvania*, Unpublished Master's Thesis, Department of Geography, Pennsylvania State University.

Mitchell, Don (1992a), "Heritage, Landscape and the Production of Community: Consensus History and its Alternatives in Johnstown, Pennsylvania," *Pennsylvania History* 59, 198–226.

Mitchell, Don (1992b), "Iconography and Locational Conflict from the Underside: Free Speech, People's Park, and the Politics of Homelessness in Berkeley, California," *Political Geography* 11, 152–69.

Mitchell, Don (1992c), "Whose History and History for Whom? Questions About the Politics of Heritage: A Reply to Miner and Burkert," *Pennsylvania History* 59, 233–5.

Mitchell, Don (1993), "Public Housing in Single-industry Towns: Changing Landscapes of Paternalism," in James Duncan and David Ley (eds.), *Place/Culture/Representation* (London: Routledge), 110–27.

Mitchell, Don (1994), "Landscape and Surplus Value: The Making of the Ordinary in Brentwood, California," *Environment and Planning D: Society and Space* 12, 7–30.

Mitchell, Don (1995a), "The End of Public Space? People's Park, Definitions of the Public, and Democracy," *Annals of the Association of American Geographers* 85, 108–33.

Mitchell, Don (1995b), "There's No Such Thing as Culture: Towards a Reconceptualization of the Idea of Culture in Geography," *Transactions of the Institute of British Geographers* 20, 102–16.

Mitchell, Don (1996a), *The Lie of the Land: Migrant Workers and the California Landscape* (Minneapolis: University of Minnesota Press).

Mitchell, Don (1996b), "Political Violence, Order, and the Legal Construction of Public Space: Power and the Public Forum Doctrine," *Urban Geography* 17, 158–78.

Mitchell, Don (1997), "The Annihilation of Space By Law: The Roots and Implications of Anti-homeless Laws in the United States," *Antipode* 29, 303–35.

Mitchell, Timothy (1990), "Everyday Metaphors of Power," *Theory and Society* 19, 545–77.

Mitchell, W.J.T. (1994), "Introduction," in W.J.T. Mitchell (ed.), *Power and Landscape* (Chicago: University of Chicago Press), 1–4.

Molotch, Harvey (1996), "L.A. as Design Product: How Art Works in a Regional Economy," in Allen Scott and Edward Soja (eds.), *The City: Los Angeles and Urban Theory at the End of the Twentieth Century* (Berkeley: University of California Press), 225–75.

Monk, Janice (1992), "Gender in the Landscape: Expressions of Power and Meaning," in K. Anderson and F. Gale (eds.), *Inventing Places: Studies in Cultural Geography* (Melbourne: Longman Cheshire), 123–38.

Morawska, Ewa (1985), *For Bread with Butter: Life-Worlds of East Central Europeans in Johnstown, Pennyslvania, 1890–1940* (Cambridge: Cambridge University Press).

Morley, David, and Robins, Kevin (1995), *Spaces of Identity: Global Media, Electronic Landscapes, and Cultural Boundaries* (London: Routledge).

Morley, David, and Robins, Kevin (1996), "No Place like *Heimat*: Images of Home(land) in European Culture," in Geoff Eley and Grigor Suny (eds.), *Becoming National: A Reader* (Oxford: Oxford University Press), 456–78.

Morris, Meaghan (1993), "Things to Do with Shopping Centres," in Simon During (ed.), *The Cultural Studies Reader* (London: Routledge), 295–319.

MTV (1996), "Sex Pistols to Do It All Again," *News Archive, http://www.mtv.com/mtv/news/gallery/s/sex960422.html*, March 22.

Mulvey, Laura (1989), *Visual and Other Pleasures* (London: Macmillan).

Muschamp, Herbert (1997), "Becoming Unstuck in the Suburbs," *New York Times*, October 19, WK-4.

Muwakkil, Salim (1995), "Timing is Everything," in Russell Jacoby and Naomi Glauberman (eds.), *The Bell Curve Debate: History, Documents, Opinions* (New York: Times Books), 258–62.

Myslik, Wayne (1996), "Renegotiating the Social/Sexual Identities of Places: Gay Communities as Safe Havens or Sites of Resistance?" in Nancy Duncan (ed.), *Body Space: Destabilizing Geographies of Gender and Sexuality* (New York: Routledge), 156–69.

Nairn, Tom (1996), "Scotland and Europe," in Geoff Eley and Grigor Suny (eds.), *Becoming National: A Reader* (Oxford: Oxford University Press), 79–104.

Namaste, Ki (1992), "If You're in Clothes, You're in Drag," *Fuse* (Fall), 7–9.

Nash, Catherine (1996), "Reclaiming Vision: Looking at Landscape and the Body," *Gender, Place and Culture* 3, 149–69.

Nash, Gary, and Crabtree, Charlotte (1994), Letter to the Editor, "A History of All People Isn't PC," *Wall Street Journal*, November 21.

Nast, Heidi, and Kobayashi, Audrey (1996), "Re-corporealizing Vision," in Nancy Duncan (ed.), *BodySpace: Destabilizing Geographies of Gender and Sexuality* (New York: Routledge), 75–93.

Nelson, Cary, Treichler, Paula, and Grossberg, Lawrence (1992), "Cultural Studies: An Introduction," in L. Grossberg, C. Nelson, and P. Treichler (eds.), *Cultural Studies* (New York: Routledge), 1–16.

Nelson, K. (1986), "Labor Demand, Labor Supply, and the Suburbanization of Low-wage Office Work," in Allen J. Scott and Michael Storper (eds.), *Production, Work, Territory: The Geographical Anatomy of Industrial Capitalism* (Boston: Allen and Unwin), 149–71.

New Statesman and Society (1996), "Influences: Stuart Hall," February 9.

New York Times (1994), "Plan to Teach U.S. History Said to Slight White Males," October 26.

New York Times (1996), "AIDS Quilt of Grief on Capital Mall," October 13.

New York Times, (1998), "Germany's Racist Resurgence," February 11, 28.

Norberg-Hodge, Helena (1996), "Break Up the Monoculture," *The Nation*, July 15/22, 20–3.

"Off Limits" (1996), *Westword*, September 12–18.

Olwig, Kenneth (1984), *Nature's Ideological Landscape* (London: Allen and Unwin).

Olwig, Kenneth (1993), "Sexual Cosmology: Nation and Landscape at the Conceptual Interstices of Nature and Culture, or: What does Landscape Really Mean?" in Barbara Bender (ed.), *Landscape: Politics and Perspectives* (Oxford: Berg), 307–43.

Olwig, Kenneth (1996a), "Nature – Mapping the Ghostly Traces of a Concept," in C. Earle, K. Mathewson, and M. Kenzer (eds.), *Concepts in Human Geography* (Lanham, MD: Rowman and Littlefield), 63–96.

Olwig, Kenneth (1996b), "Recovering the Substantive Nature of Landscape," *Annals of the Association of American Geographers* 86, 630–53.

Pain, Rachel (1991), "Space, Sexual Violence, and Social Control: Integrating Geographical and Feminist Analyses of Women's Fear of Crime," *Progress in Human Geography* 15, 379–94.

Peake, Linda (1993), " 'Race' and Sexuality: Challenging the Patriarchal Structuring of Urban Social Space," *Environment and Planning D: Society and Space* 11, 415–32.

Peck, Jeffrey (1996), "Rac(e)ing the Nation: Is There a German 'Home,' " in Geoff Eley and Grigor Suny (eds.), *Becoming National: A Reader* (Oxford: Oxford University Press), 481–94.

Peet, Richard (1985), "The Social Origins of Environmental Determinism," *Annals of the Association of American Geographers* 75, 309–33.

Peet, Richard (1996), "A Sign Taken for History: Daniels Shays' Memorial in Petersham, Massachusetts," *Annals of the Association of American Geographers* 86, 21–43.

Peet, Richard (1998), *Modern Geographic Thought* (Oxford, Blackwell).

Pile, Steve, and Keith, Michael (eds.) (1997), *Geographies of Resistance* (London: Routledge).

Price, Jennifer (1996), "Looking for Nature at the Mall: A Field Guide to the Nature Company," in William Cronon (ed.), *Uncommon Ground: Rethinking the Human Place in Nature* (New York: Norton), 186–203.

Price, Marie, and Lewis, Martin (1993a), "Reinventing Cultural Geography," *Annals of the Association of American Geographers* 83, 1–17.

Price, Marie, and Lewis, Martin (1993b), "Reply: On Reading Cultural Geography," *Annals of the Association of American Geographers* 83, 520–2.

Pugh, Simon (ed.) (1990), *Reading Landscape: Country-City-Capital* (Manchester: Manchester University Press).

Ratzel, Friedrich (1896), *Anthropogeographie*, Volume 2: *The History of Mankind* (London: Macmillan), originally published as *Die Geographische Verbreitung des Menschen* (Stuttgart: J. Engelhorn, 1891).

Rauber, Paul (1998), "All Hail the Multinationals! The Secret Deal that Corporations Hope You Never Hear About," *Sierra* July/August, 16–17.

Reader, Keith, with Wadia, Kursheed (1993), *The May 1968 Events in France: Reproductions and Interpretations* (New York: St. Martin's).

Richardson, Miles (1981), "On the Superorganic in American Cultural Geography," *Annals of the Association of American Geographers* 71, 284–7.

Robertson, Roland (1992), *Globalization: Social Theory and Global Culture* (London: Sage).

Robinson, Jennifer (1990), "A Perfect System of Control? State Power and 'Native Locations' in South Africa," *Environment and Planning D: Society and Space* 8, 135–62.

Rock, Cynthia, Torre, Susan, and Wright, Gwendolyn (1980), "The Appropriation of the House: Changes in House Design and Concepts of Domesticity," in G. Werkele, R. Peterson, and D. Morley (eds.), *New Space for Women* (Boulder, CO: Westview Press), 83–100.

Roediger, David (1991), *The Wages of Whiteness: Race and the Making of the American Working Class* (London: Verso).

Roiphe, Katie (1993), *The Morning After: Sex, Fear, and Feminism on Campus* (Boston: Little, Brown).

Rollins, W.H. (1995), "Whose Landscape? Technology, Fascism and Environmentalism on the National Socialist Autobahn," *Annals of the Association of American Geographers* 85, 494–520.

Rose, Gillian (1993), *Feminism and Geography: The Limits of Geographical Knowledge* (Minneapolis: University of Minnesota Press).

Rose, Gillian (1996), "As If the Mirrors Had Bled: Masculine Dwelling, Masculinist Theory and Feminist Masquerade," in Nancy Duncan (ed.), *Body Space: Destabilizing Geographies of Gender and Sexuality* (New York: Routledge), 56–74.

Rose, Gillian (1997), "Performing Inoperative Community: The Space and the Resistance of Some Community Arts Projects," in Steve Pile and Michael Keith (eds.), *Geographies of Resistance* (London: Routledge), 184–202.

Rose, Jacqueline (1986), *Sexuality in the Field of Vision* (London: Verso).

Ross, Andrew (1998), *Real Love: In Pursuit of Cultural Justice* (New York: New York University Press).

Rothenberg, Tamar (1995), " 'And She Told Two Friends': Lesbians Creating Urban Social Space," in David Bell and Gill Valentine (eds.), *Mapping Desire: Geographies of Sexualities* (London: Routledge), 165–81.

Rowntree, Lester, Foote, Kenneth, and Domosh, Mona (1989), "Cultural Geography," in Gary Gaile and Cort Wilmott (eds.), *Geography in America* (Columbus: Merrill), 209–17.

Roy, Arundhati (1998), "The End of Imagination," *The Nation*, September 28, 11–19.

Rubin, Gayle (1975), "The Traffic in Women: Notes on the 'Political Economy' of Sex," in R. Reiter (ed.), *Toward an Anthropology of Women* (New York: Monthly Review Press), 157–210.

Sack, Robert (1988), "The Consumer's World: Place as Context," *Annals of the Association of American Geographers* 78, 642–64.

Sack, Robert (1992), *Place, Modernity, and the Consumer's World: A Relational Framework for Geographical Analysis* (Baltimore: Johns Hopkins University Press).

Saff, Grant (1994), "The Changing Face of the South African City: From Urban Apartheid to the Deracialization of Space," *International Journal of Urban and Regional Restructuring* 18, 377–91.

Said, Edward (1993), *Culture and Imperialism* (New York: Alfred A. Knopf).

Sanders, Claire (1994), "A Leading Indicator," *The Higher*, May 13, 17–18.

Sandner, Gerhard (1994), "In Search of Identity: German Nationalism and Geography, 1871–1910," in D. Hooson (ed.), *Geography and National Identity* (Oxford: Blackwell), 71–91.

Sauer, Carl (1925), "The Morphology of Landscape," *University of California Publications in Geography* 2, 19–54, reprinted in Leighly (1963), 315–50.

Sauer, Carl (1941), "Foreword to Historical Geography," *Annals of the Association of American Geographers* 31, 1–24, reprinted in Leighly (1963), 351–79.

Sauer, Carl (1952), *Agricultural Origins and Dispersals* (New York: American Geographical Society).

Sauer, Carl (1956), "The Agency of Man on Earth," in William L. Thomas, Jr. (ed.), *Man's Role in Changing the Face of the Earth* (Chicago: University of Chicago Press), 49–69.

Sauer, Carl (1974), "The Fourth Dimension in Geography," *Annals of the Association of American Geographers* 64, 189–92; republished in Sauer (1981), 279–86.

Sauer, Carl (1975), *Man in Nature* (Berkeley: Turtle Island Foundation, originally published 1939).

Sauer, Carl (1976), *Northern Mists* (Berkeley: Turtle Island Foundation, originally published 1968).

Sauer, Carl (1980), *Seventeenth Century America* (Berkeley: Turtle Island Foundation, originally published 1971).

Sauer, Carl (1981), *Selected Essays, 1963–1975* (Berkeley: Turtle Island Foundation, ed. Bob Callahan).

Saxton, Alexander (1971), *The Indispensable Enemy: Labor and the Anti-Chinese Movement in California* (Berkeley: University of California Press).

Sayer, Andrew (1994), "Cultural Studies and 'the Economy, Stupid,'" *Environment and Planning D: Society and Space* 12, 635–7.

Schama, Simon (1995), *Landscape and Memory* (New York: Alfred Knopf).

Scott, Alan (1988), *New Industrial Spaces* (London: Pion).

Scott, James (1985), *Weapons of the Weak: Everyday Forms of Peasant Resistance* (New Haven: Yale University Press).

Sedgwick, Eve Kosofsky (1990), *Epistemology of the Closet* (Berkeley: University of California Press).

Sedgwick, Eve Kosofsky (1993), "Axiomatic," in Simon During (ed.), *The Cultural Studies Reader* (London: Routledge), 243–68.

Semple, Ellen Churchill (1903), *American History and its Geographical Conditions* (Boston: Houghton Mifflin).

Semple, Ellen Churchill (1911), *Influences of Geographic Environment on the Basis of Ratzel's System of Anthropo-geography* (New York: Russell and Russell).

Sennett, Richard (1994), *Flesh and Stone: The Body and the City in Western Civilization* (New York: W.W. Norton).

Sex Pistols (1977), "God Save the Queen," *Never Mind the Bollocks: Here's the Sex Pistols* (Burbank: Warner Brothers BSK 3147).

Shanti Jefferson, Elana (1996), "Up Against the Wall," *Westword*, February 7–13.

Shields, Rob (1991), *Places on the Margin: Alternative Geographies of Modernity* (London: Routledge).

Shilts, Randy (1982), *The Mayor of Castro Street: The Life and Times of Harvey Milk* (New York: St. Martin's).

Short, John R. (1991), *Imagined Country: Society, Culture and Environment* (London: Routledge).

Shreeve, James (1994), "Terms of Estrangement: Race is a Small but Volatile World . . .," *Discover* (November), 57–63.

Shurmer-Smith, Pamela (ed.) (1996), *All Over the Place: Postgraduate Work in Social and Cultural Geography*, University of Portsmouth Working Papers in Geography #36 (Portsmouth: University of Portsmouth).

Shurmer-Smith, Pamela, and Hannam, Kevin (1994), *Worlds of Desire, Realms of Power: A Cultural Geography* (London: Edward Arnold).

Sibley, David (1995), *Geographies of Exclusion* (London: Routledge).

Singer, Daniel (1996), "Liberté, Egalité, Racisme?" *The Nation*, October 21.

Smith, Anthony (1991), *National Identity* (London: Penguin).

Smith, Anthony (1996), "The Origin of Nations," in Geoff Eley and Grigor Suny (eds.), *Becoming National: A Reader* (Oxford: Oxford University Press), 106–30.

Smith, Neil (1989), "Geography as Museum: Private History and Conservative Idealism in *The Nature of Geography*," in J. Nicholas Entrikin and Stanley D. Brunn (eds.), *Reflections on Richard Hartshorne's* The Nature of Geography (Washington DC: Occasional Publications of the Association of American Geographers), 91–120.

Smith, Neil (1990), *Uneven Development: Nature, Capital and the Production of Space* (Oxford: Blackwell, second edition).

Smith, Neil (1993), "Homeless/Global," in J. Bird, B. Curtis, G. Robertson, and L. Tickner (eds.), *Mapping the Futures: Local Culture and Global Change* (London: Routledge), 67–83.

Smith, Neil (1996), *The New Urban Frontier: Gentrification and the Revanchist City* (New York: Routledge).

Smith, Neil (1999), "What Happened to Class?" Unpublished paper, Department of Geography, Rutgers University.

Smith, Susan (1989), *The Politics of "Race" and Residence: Citizenship, Segregation and White Supremacy in Britain* (Cambridge: Polity Press).

Smith, Susan, and Mercer, John (eds.) (1987), *New Perspectives on Race and Housing in Britain* (Glasgow: Centre for Housing Research).

Soja, Edward (1989), *Postmodern Geographies: The Reassertion of Space in Critical Social Theory* (Oxford: Blackwell).

Soja, Edward (1996), *ThirdSpace: Journeys to Los Angeles and Other Real-and-Imagined Places* (Oxford: Blackwell).

Solimene, Peggy (1997), Letter to the Editor, *Hartford Courant*, October 18, A10.

Sparke, Matthew (1996), "Displacing the Field in Fieldwork: Masculinity, Metaphor and Space," in Nancy Duncan (ed.), *Body Space: Destabilizing Geographies of Gender and Sexuality* (New York: Routledge), 212–33.

Speth, William (1987), "Historicism, The Disciplinary World View of Carl O. Sauer," in Martin S. Kenzer (ed.), *Carl O. Sauer: A Tribute* (Corvalis, OR: Oregon State University Press), 11–39.

Spring, Ian (1990), *Phantom Village: The Myth of the New Glasgow* (Edinburgh: Polygon).

Staeheli, Lynn (1994), "Restructuring Citizenship in Pueblo, Colorado," *Environment and Planning A* 26, 849–71.

Staeheli, Lynn (1996), "Publicity, Privacy and Women's Political Action," *Environment and Planning D: Society and Space* 14, 601–19.

Stallybrass, Peter, and White, Allon (1986), *The Politics and Poetics of Transgression* (Ithaca, NY: Cornell University Press).

Stallybrass, Peter, and White, Allon (1993), "Bourgeois Hysteria and the Carnivalesque," in Simon During (ed.), *The Cultural Studies Reader* (London: Routledge), 284–92.

Staunton, Denis (1998), "Young Right in Germany: Learning to Love Hate in the Kindergarten for Young Hitlers," *Observer*, April 12, 23.

Stoddart, David (1986), *On Geography and Its History* (Oxford: Blackwell).

Storey, John (1996), "Cultural Studies," in Adam Kuper and Jessica Kuper (eds.), *The Social Science Encyclopedia* (London: Routledge, second edition), 159–61.

Storper, Michael, and Walker, Richard (1989), *The Capitalist Imperative: Territory, Technology and Industrial Growth* (Oxford: Blackwell).

Strathern, Marilyn (1987), "Out of Context: The Persuasive Fictions of Anthropology," *Current Anthropology*, 28, 251–81.

Strohmeyer, Ulf, and Hannah, Matthew (1992), "Domesticating Postmodernism," *Antipode* 24, 29–55.

Sturken, M. (1992), "Conversations with the Dead: Bearing Witness in the AIDS Memorial Quilt," *Socialist Review* 77.

Suhr, Heidrun (1989), "*Ausländerliterature*: Minority Literature in the Federal Republic of Germany," *New German Critique* 46 (Winter).

Symanski, Richard (1981), "A Critique of the Superorganic in American Cultural Geography," *Annals of the Association of American Geographers* 71, 287–9.

Talbot, Margaret (1994), "Back to the Future: Pining for the Old Days in Germany," *New Republic*, 18 and 25 July, 11–14.

Taylor, Charles (1975), *Hegel* (Cambridge: Cambridge University Press).

Tempest, Rone (1996), "China Launches Cultural Cleanup," *Boulder Daily Camera*, October 16.

"The New Johnstown Flood Museum to Play a New Role in the Community" (1989), *Centennial Reports* 3, 6.

Thomas, Jr., William L. (ed.) (1956), *Man's Role in Changing the Face of the Earth* (Chicago: University of Chicago Press).

Thomas-Emeagwali, Gloria (1995), *Women Pay the Price: Structural Adjustment in Africa and the Caribbean* (Trenton, NJ: Africa World Press).

Thompson, E.P. (1963), *The Making of the English Working Class* (Harmondsworth: Penguin).

Thompson, E.P. (1975), *Whigs and Hunters: The Origin of the Black Act* (London: Allen Lane).

Thompson, E.P. (1980), *Writing by Candlelight* (London: Merlin Press).

Thompson, E.P. (1988), "Last Dispatch from the Border Country: Raymond Williams, 1921–1988," *The Nation*, March 5.

Thompson, J.B. (1984), *Studies in the Theory of Ideology* (Cambridge: Cambridge University Press).

Thrift, Nigel (1991), "Over Wordy Worlds? Thoughts and Worries," in Chris Philo (compiler), *New Words, New Worlds: Reconceptualizing Social and Cultural Geography* (Aberystwyth: Cambrian Printers), 144–8.

Thrift, Nigel (1995), "A Hyperactive World," in R.J. Johnston, Peter Taylor, and Michael Watts (eds.), *Geographies of Global Change* (Oxford: Blackwell), 18–35.

The Times (London) (1988), "Prof Raymond Williams: Culture and Society," January 27.

Tomasky, Michael (1996), *Left for Dead: The Life, Death and Possible Resurrection of Progressive Politics in America* (New York: Free Press).

Trap, J.P. (1864), *Statistik-Topographisk Berskrivelse af Hertugdømmet Slesvig* (Copenhagen: Gad).

Traynor, Ian (1996), " 'Nazi' Attack Kills 10 in Germany," *Guardian*, January 19, 2.

Traynor, Ian (1997), "Neo-Nazis Set Up No-Go Zones," *Guardian*, December 11, 13.

Trewartha, Glenn (1926), "Recent Thoughts on the Problem of White Acclimatization in the Wet Tropics," *Geographical Review* 16, 467–78.

Turner, Frederick Jackson (1920), *The Frontier in American History* (New York: Henry Holt).

Valentine, Gill (1989), "The Geography of Women's Fear," *Area* 21, 385–90.

Valentine, Gill (1993), "(Hetero)sexing Space: Lesbian Perceptions and Experiences of Everyday Spaces," *Environment and Planning D: Society and Space* 11, 396–413.

Valentine, Gill (1995), "Out and About: Geographies of Lesbian Landscapes," *International Journal of Urban and Regional Restructuring* 19, 96–111.

Valentine, Gill (1996), "Creating Transgressive Space: The Music of k.d. lang," *Transactions of the Institute of British Geographers* 20, 474–85.

Valentine, Gill (1997), "Making Space: Separatism and Difference," in John Paul Jones III, Heidi Nast, and Susan Roberts (eds.), *Thresholds in Feminist Geography* (Lanham, MD: Rowman and Littlefield), 65–76.

Van den Berghe, Pierre (1994), *The Quest for the Other: Ethnic Tourism in San Cristóbal, Mexico* (Seattle: University of Washington Press).

Wagner, Philip, and Mikesell, Marvin (1962), "General Introduction: The Themes of Cultural Geography," in Philip Wagner and Marvin Mikesell, *Readings in Cultural Geography* (Chicago: University of Chicago Press), 1–24.

Walker, James (1889), *The Johnstown Horror* (Chicago: L.P. Miller and Co.).

Walker, Richard (1981), "A Theory of Suburbanization: Capitalism and the Construction of Urban Space in the United States," in M. Dear and A. Scott (eds.), *Urbanization and Urban Planning in Capitalist Society* (London: Methuen), 383–429.

Wallace, Kim E. (ed.) (1985), *The Character of a Steel Mill City: Four Historic American Neighborhoods of Johnstown, Pennsylvania*, Draft Report, Historic American Building Survey/Historic American Engineering Record (Washington, DC: National Park Service).

Walzer, Michael (1983), *Spheres of Justice: A Defense of Particularism and Equality* (New York: Basic Books).

Warner, Marina (1985), *Monuments and Maidens: The Allegory of the Female Form* (London: Weidenfeld and Nicolson).

Warner, Michael (1991), "Introduction: Fear of a Queer Planet," *Social Text* 29, 3–17.

Warner, Michael (ed.) (1993), *Fear of a Queer Planet: Queer Politics and Social Theory* (Minneapolis: University of Minnesota Press).

Watts, Michael (1997), "Black Gold, White Heat: State Violence, Local Resistance and the National Question in Nigeria," in Steve Pile and Michael Keith (eds.), *Geographies of Resistance* (London: Routledge), 33–67.

Welter, B. (1966), "The Cult of True Womanhood, 1820–1860," *American Quarterly* 18, 151–74.

Werkele, Gerda, Peterson, Rebecca, and Morley, David (eds.) (1980), *New Space for Women* (Boulder, CO: Westview Press).

Westermarch, Edward A. (1889), *The History of Human Marriage*, 3 volumes (New York: Macmillan).

Western, John (1996), *Outcast Cape Town* (Berkeley: University of California Press, second edition).

White, Gayle (1997), "The Promise Keepers: A Word from the Wives," *Atlanta Journal and Constitution*, October 8, 1D.

Whitehand, J.W.R. (1992), *The Making of the Urban Landscape* (Cambridge, MA: Blackwell).

Wickham, De Wayne (1995), "Born to Lose," in Russell Jacoby and Naomi Glauberman (eds.), *The Bell Curve Debate: History, Documents, Opinions* (New York: Times Books), 252–4.

Williams, Juan (1994), "Violence, Genes, and Prejudice: Can Genes Make One Person More Likely to Act Violently than Another?" *Discover* (November), 93–102.

Williams, Raymond (1958), *Culture and Society* (London: Chatto and Windus).

Williams, Raymond (1961), *The Long Revolution* (London: Chatto and Windus).

Williams, Raymond (1973), *The Country and the City* (New York: Oxford University Press).

Williams, Raymond (1976), *Keywords: A Vocabulary of Culture and Society* (London: Fontana).

Williams, Raymond (1977), *Marxism and Literature* (Oxford: Oxford University Press).

Williams, Raymond (1980), *Problems in Materialism and Culture* (London: Verso).

Williams, Raymond (1982), *The Sociology of Culture* (New York: Schocken Books).

Williams, Raymond (1993), "Culture is Ordinary," in Ann Gray and Jim McGuigan, (eds.), *Studying Culture: An Introductory Reader* (London: Edward Arnold, originally published 1958), 1–14.

Willis, Paul (1977), *Learning to Labour: How Working Class Kids Get Working Class Jobs* (London: Gower).

Wilson, Alexander (1991), *The Culture of Nature: From Disney to the Exxon Valdez* (Oxford: Blackwell).

Wilson, Elizabeth (1991), *The Sphinx in the City: Urban Life, the Control of Disorder, and Women* (Berkeley: University of California Press).

Wilson, James Q., and Kelling, George (1982), "Broken Windows: The Police and Neighborhood Safety," *Atlantic Monthly* (March), 29–38.

Witcher, T.R. (1995), "Cover Your Head in Shame: A Middle-aged Black Woman is Rousted from the Greeley Mall for Wearing a Blue Bandana," *Westword*, December 20, 10.

Women's Studies Group, Centre for Contemporary Cultural Studies (1978), *Women Take Issue: Aspects of Women's Subordination* (London: Hutchinson).

Wright, J.K. (1947), "*Terrae Incognitae*: The Place of the Imagination in Geography," *Annals of the Association of American Geographers* 37, 1–15.

Wyatt, David (1986), *Fall into Eden: Landscape and Imagination in California* (Cambridge: Cambridge University Press).

Yeoman, Barry (1998), "Art and States' Rights," *The Nation*, June 29, 31–3.

Young, Iris Marion (1990), *Justice and the Politics of Difference* (Pittsburgh: Pittsburgh University Press).

Zelinsky, Wilbur (1973), *The Cultural Geography of the United States* (Englewood Cliffs, NJ: Prentice-Hall).

Zelinsky, Wilbur (1975), "The Demigod's Dilemma," *Annals of the Association of American Geographers* 65, 123–43.

Zelinsky, Wilbur (1987), "Commentary on 'Housing Tenure and Social Cleavages in Urban Canada,'" *Annals of the Association of American Geographers* 77, 651–2.

Zha, Jianying (1995), *China Pop: How Soap Operas, Tabloids, and Bestsellers are Transforming a Culture* (New York: New Press).

Zukin, Sharon (1991), *Landscapes of Power: From Detroit to Disney World* (Berkeley: University of California Press).

Zukin, Sharon (1995), *The Cultures of Cities* (Oxford: Blackwell).

Index